KU-441-178

SEARCHING FOR SHAKESPEARE

SEARCHING FOR SHAKESPEARE

Tarnya Cooper

With essays by
Marcia Pointon, James Shapiro and Stanley Wells

National Portrait Gallery
LONDON

Published in Great Britain by
National Portrait Gallery Publications,
National Portrait Gallery,
St Martin's Place, London WC2H OHE

Published to accompany the exhibition
Searching for Shakespeare,
held at the National Portrait Gallery, London,
from 2 March to 29 May 2006, and the
Yale Center for British Art, New Haven,
from 24 June to 27 September 2006.

London exhibition sponsor

For a complete catalogue
of current publications
please write to the address above,
or visit our website at
www.npg.org.uk/publications

2006 marks the 150th Anniversary
of the National Portrait Gallery, supported
by the Anniversary Partner, Herbert Smith.

ISBN 1-85514-361-5 Hardback
978-1-85514-361-6 Hardback
ISBN 1-85514-369-0 Paperback
978-1-85514-369-2 Paperback

A catalogue record for this book
is available from the British Library.

Publishing Manager: Celia Joicey
Editor: Caroline Brooke Johnson
Design: Philip Lewis
Production Manager: Ruth Müller-Wirth
Printed and bound by
Butler and Tanner, England

FRONTISPIECE William Shakespeare?, known as
the Chandos portrait (cat.3)

THIS PAGE Title page of *Romeo and Juliet* (cat.105)

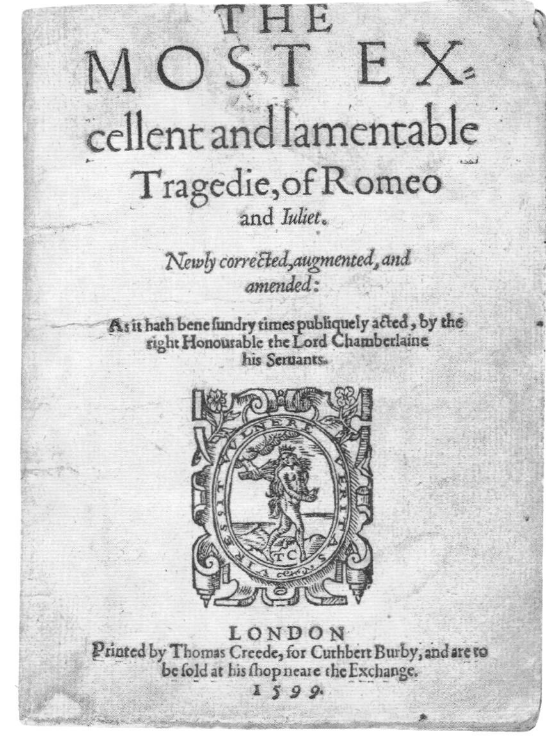

THE
MOST EX-
cellent and lamentable
Tragedie, of Romeo
and *Iuliet*.

*Newly corrected, augmented, and
amended:*

As it hath bene sundry times publiquely acted, by the
right Honourable the Lord Chamberlaine
his Seruants.

LONDON
Printed by Thomas Creede, for Cuthbert Burby, and are to
be sold at his shop neare the Exchange.
1599.

Contents

DIRECTOR'S FOREWORD

> I have heard of your paintings too, well enough. God hath given you one face, and you make yourselves another: you jig, you amble, and you lisp, and nickname God's creatures, and make your wantonness your ignorance.
> *Hamlet* (Act III, Scene i, line 45–9)

Hamlet's accusation of Ophelia and her 'paintings' (make-up), in the heat of his madness, offers an insight into Shakespeare himself: that he understood every aspect of disguise and the processes by which a person's character may be mapped across their face. A portrait is generally a record of a person's looks, but it may be only a partial account. Similarly a person may only deliberately give themselves up in part to being captured within a portrait.

Shakespeare lived in difficult times and he knew much about invisibility. He has come to us with some basic biography – there are the papers relating to his birth, death and property ownership, but almost no letters or diary entries, and only a small number of key documents. Yet in the case of such an extraordinary chronicler of human intent and behaviour, a playwright and poet of such immense stature, the search for the man holds an endless allure. We want to know what he looked like, and we also want to understand him: to meet him as if on our own terms.

William Shakespeare is famously under-served by the two images most likely to have been created by those who knew him in person. The Droeshout engraving for the First Folio editions (cat.1) has the merit of clarity of line and it is the origin of the defining characteristics of Shakespeare's high forehead, arched eyebrows and receding hairline. Whereas the memorial statue in Holy Trinity Church, Stratford-upon-Avon, depicts a rather plump Warwickshire citizen. This caricature may be near the mark, but it appeared insufficiently grand for what would be required of its dead subject.

The starting point of this exhibition is a third image that goes back to Shakespeare's period. If the Chandos portrait (cat.3) does represent Shakespeare, it offers a dark and faintly piratical vision of the man. We may never know for certain whether this is the writer – especially now that there is relatively little paint on the canvas from which to learn more – but the association with Shakespeare goes all the way back to his own time, the work having belonged to his godson. As a portrait, it has a considerable history of its own, through its owners and its role in the veneration paid to Shakespeare.

This is where the exhibition starts, but not where it finishes. Tarnya Cooper, Curator of the exhibition, has assembled most of the key portraits previously thought to derive from the seventeenth century. These portraits – all regarded at different points as being a 'contender', as a definitive image of the writer – have widely differing virtues. For some we have a date and no certainty of the subject, for others we have a construction of the subject but a date that does not match the period of his life. The history of each painting plays a fascinating and vital part in the holy grail question of whether a painted portrait can ever be authenticated. They are brought together now with a range of the material from his surrounding world, relating to his life in London and Stratford-upon-Avon as well as the Elizabethan theatre and to his contemporaries.

My first thanks go to the owners of the portraits, who have been extraordinarily generous in lending to the exhibition, in some cases allowing a technical team to carry out further investigation. In this respect, I should particularly like to thank David Howells (Royal Shakespeare Company) and Stella Butler (John Rylands University Library, Manchester). We are indebted to the many other lenders, both private and institutional, who have been supportive of the exhibition from early on in our investigations.

The advisory committee for the exhibition have given generously of their time and expertise and I am very grateful for that help. Professor Stanley Wells graciously agreed to act as our key adviser at the outset of the project and his unstinting efforts on our behalf and the depth of his scholarship have provided our team with a constant source of invaluable advice. We have also been particularly fortunate with our many distinguished contributors, who have produced fascinating and authoritative texts that illuminate different aspects of Shakespeare's time.

We have had a very productive relationship with the BBC Culture Show, resulting in three short films relating to the investigation of three 'contender' portraits. We are delighted that the exhibition will travel to the Yale Center for British Art in New Haven, and my thanks go to Director Amy Meyers and her team for making this possible. We are extremely grateful to Credit Suisse for sponsoring the exhibition.

Finally I should like to thank warmly Dr Tarnya Cooper, Sixteenth Century Curator at the Gallery, for all her hard work and determination in developing and realizing such an ambitious exhibition, made for the Gallery's 150th Anniversary year.

Sandy Nairne

DIRECTOR, NATIONAL PORTRAIT GALLERY

Exhibition advisers

PRINCIPAL EXHIBITION ADVISER

Stanley Wells, Chairman, Shakespeare Birthplace Trust, Stratford-upon-Avon

ASSOCIATES ADVISERS

Robert Bearman, Head of Archives, Shakespeare Birthplace Trust, Stratford-upon-Avon
Erin Blake, Curator of Art, Folger Shakespeare Library, Washington, DC
Paul Edmondson, Head of Education, Shakespeare Birthplace Trust, Stratford-upon-Avon
Andrew Gurr, Professor of English, University of Reading
Sally-Beth MacLean, Executive Editor, Records of Early English Drama, Toronto
Lena Orlin, Executive Director of the Shakespeare Association of America, University of Maryland
Mark Rylance, Actor and Chairman, The Shakespearean Authorship Trust
Patrick Spottiswoode, Director of Education, Shakespeare's Globe Theatre, London
Jenny Tiramani, Costume Designer

SPONSOR'S FOREWORD

Credit Suisse is delighted to have the opportunity of sponsoring the exhibition *Searching for Shakespeare* at the National Portrait Gallery in a year when both institutions are celebrating their 150th anniversaries.

Credit Suisse has a long tradition of supporting the arts, but this sponsorship is particularly meaningful to us as a symbol of our commitment to the UK. We are therefore proud to support something as quintessentially English as an exhibition on Shakespeare. At the same time, he is an author whose appeal transcends borders and has stood the test of time like no other.

The exhibition is designed to be provocative – whatever happened to our assumption that Shakespeare looked just like the portrait we have seen in textbooks? It is a bold and thought-provoking venture to investigate not just the history of portraits of the man, but also to present a meticulously researched overview of Shakepeare's many images. In addition it brings together a remarkable range of objects from the period.

With its spirit of curiosity and innovative approach to values that have endured down the generations, *Searching for Shakespeare* reflects our values – there can be nothing more appropriate for Credit Suisse to support.

Credit Suisse is very grateful to the National Portrait Gallery, the Director, Sandy Nairne, and the Curator, Tarnya Cooper, for putting together one of the most intellectually invigorating exhibitions of our time.

We wish you, the reader and viewer, an enjoyable experience.

Jeremy Marshall
CHIEF EXECUTIVE OFFICER, CREDIT SUISSE (UK) LIMITED

CURATOR'S PREFACE

Surprisingly, the founding portrait of the National Portrait Gallery, known as NPG number 1, was not that of a monarch or a member of the nobility but a painting long considered to represent England's greatest poet and playwright, William Shakespeare. It was offered to the nation in 1856 by Lord Ellesmere in an exemplary act of benefaction. As the most probable contender to be a portrait of Shakespeare made in his lifetime, the Chandos portrait (NPG 1) has graced the covers of several shelves of books on the playwright. As a result it has effectively become a visual emblem of English literary achievement. This book, and the exhibition that accompanies it, investigates the history of this portrait and explores the existing material evidence about Shakespeare's life.

Both the quest for a lifetime portrait of Shakespeare and interest in his biography began within fifty years of his death and continue apace today. Rediscovering the identity of portraits centuries after they were painted is a complex task at the centre of our day-to-day research at the National Portrait Gallery. Research on portraits of Shakespeare is a particularly contentious field and since the nineteenth century numerous scholars have sought to interpret the many contender portraits. *The Life Portraits of William Shakespeare* by J. Hain Friswell appeared in 1864 and in 1909 M.H. Spielmann published his long essay *The Portraits of William Shakespeare*. In 1964 the National Portrait Gallery staged an exhibition entitled *O Sweet Mr Shakespeare*, with a catalogue by David Piper that explored the many posthumous images of Shakespeare. This was followed in 1975 and 1981 by two groundbreaking books by S. Schoenbaum on the surviving documentary evidence of Shakespeare's life, which included information about the various disputed portraits.

Searching for Shakespeare presents new research to provide an account of our current knowledge on the complex subject of Shakespeare's likeness. The National Portrait Gallery holds the largest public collection of sixteenth- and seventeenth-century British portraits and is particularly well placed to explore the surviving material evidence from Shakespeare's own time. Consequently, only the key contender portraits of Shakespeare considered at one time to date from the sixteenth and seventeenth centuries are included here. Many of the details of Shakespeare's life have been lost: there are few original objects connected to him and no surviving letters in his hand. Yet the material evidence that does exist is compelling and tells us much about his life in Stratford-upon-Avon and London. This book examines the material culture of his time in the search for the Shakespeare who was known and admired by his fellow actors and writers, as well as by the courtiers who became the patrons of his plays and poems.

Tarnya Cooper

SIXTEENTH CENTURY CURATOR, NATIONAL PORTRAIT GALLERY

CHRONOLOGY

1564 William Shakespeare is born in Stratford-upon-Avon, Warwickshire, the third child of John Shakespeare, a glover, and Mary Arden, a prosperous farmer's daughter.
He is baptized on 26 April at Holy Trinity Church in Stratford-upon-Avon.
Plague strikes Stratford in July, claiming 200 victims out of a population of around 1800.

1565 John Shakespeare becomes an alderman of Stratford.

1568 John Shakespeare is elected bailiff of Stratford, the town's highest office (cat.10).
Travelling theatre companies visit Stratford for the first time.

1569 Probable date that Shakespeare begins to attend 'petty school', where he learns to read and write.

1570 John Shakespeare is charged with usury and illegal wool-dealing.
Pope Pius V excommunicates Elizabeth I from the Catholic Church.

1572 Likely date that Shakespeare begins at the local grammar school, the King's New School, Stratford-upon-Avon, where he receives a thorough grounding in classical literature and rhetoric.
An 'Acte for the punishement of Vacabondes' ensures that companies of actors require the patronage of the nobility.

1576 First permanent playhouse, the Theatre, is built in Shoreditch, London, by James Burbage.

1577 The Curtain Theatre opens, also in Shoreditch.
Theatres suffer frequent closures until 1581 due to the plague.

1579 Probable date that Shakespeare leaves school.
Heavily in debt, John Shakespeare is forced to sell part of his wife's inheritance.

1580 Shakespeare may have been employed as a tutor and 'player' by the De Hoghton family in Lancashire.

1581 Master of the Revels, Edmund Tilney, is granted powers to censor plays and license theatrical venues.

1582 Shakespeare marries Anne Hathaway, a local farmer's daughter, who is already pregnant with their first child (cat.17).

1583 Shakespeare's daughter Susanna is born and baptized on 26 May (cat.11).

1585 Shakespeare becomes the father of twins, Hamnet and Judith, baptized on 2 February.

1586 John Shakespeare is replaced as alderman of Stratford after a decade of financial difficulties.

1587 The Queen's Men visit Stratford. Shakespeare may have joined the company and left Stratford shortly afterwards.
The Rose Theatre opens in Southwark, London.
Christopher Marlowe's *Tamburlaine* is performed for the first time (cat.23).
Execution of Mary, Queen of Scots.

1588 England comes under attack from Spain. The Spanish Armada is defeated in the English Channel.
Thomas Kyd's *The Spanish Tragedy* is performed for the first time (cat.24).

1590 Shakespeare writes *The Two Gentlemen of Verona.*

1591 Shakespeare completes *The Taming of the Shrew* and *The First Part of the Contention of the Two Famous Houses of York and Lancaster* (later known as *Henry VI, Part 2*) and writes *The True Tragedie of Richard Duke of York* (later known as *Henry VI, Part 3*).
Christopher Marlowe's *Dr Faustus* is performed for the first time.

1592 First reference to Shakespeare in print, by Robert Greene (see p.15), shows that he is already established on the theatrical scene.
Shakespeare writes *Titus Andronicus, Henry VI, Part 1* and *Richard III* around this time.
John Shakespeare is listed as a recusant for non-attendance at his parish church (cat.12).
Theatres closed until 1594 due to the plague.

1593 Shakespeare writes the poem *Venus and Adonis* (cat.48), the first of his works to be published. Around 1593, many of the sonnets are probably written and privately circulated.
Anthony Munday and others may have written the first version of *Sir Thomas More*, which Shakespeare was later to help revise (cat.66).
Christopher Marlowe is killed in a tavern brawl.

1594 Shakespeare completes *The Comedy of Errors*, and the poem *Lucrece* is published.
The Lord Chamberlain's Men are founded under the patronage of Lord Hunsdon and become the greatest company of actors in the country (cat.45). Shakespeare joins them as house dramatist, actor and shareholder.
The theatrical patron Ferdinando Stanley, Earl of Derby, is fatally poisoned at his home in Lancashire (cat 44).
First of a four-year run of failed harvests.

1594–5 Shakespeare completes *Love's Labour's Lost* and writes *A Midsummer Night's Dream*, *Romeo and Juliet*, *Richard II* and part of *Edward III*.
John Donne writes his earliest surviving poems, the *Satires*, around this period (cat.80).
The Swan Theatre opens in Southwark, London (cat.27).

1596 Shakespeare completes *King John*. He is recorded living in Bishopsgate, London.
Hamnet Shakespeare dies at the age of eleven.
The Shakespeare family is granted a coat of arms (cat.54).

1597 Shakespeare completes *The Merchant of Venice* and writes *Henry IV, Part 1*, *The Merry Wives of Windsor* and *Henry IV, Part 2* around this date.
Shakespeare buys New Place, the second largest house in Stratford.

1598 Shakespeare writes *Much Ado about Nothing*.
Ben Jonson writes *Every Man in his Humour*, which is performed by the Lord Chamberlain's Men with Shakespeare in the cast.

1599 Shakespeare completes *Henry V* and writes *Julius Caesar* and *As You Like It*. Shakespeare is recorded living in Southwark, London.
The Globe Theatre is built on Bankside from the dismantled timbers of the Theatre. The Lord Chamberlain's Men begin to perform there regularly.

1600 Shakespeare writes *Hamlet*.
The Fortune Theatre opens in Clerkenwell, London, run by Philip Henslowe and Edward Alleyn.

1601 Shakespeare writes *Twelfth Night* and the poem *The Phoenix and the Turtle*.
John Shakespeare dies.
2nd Earl of Essex attempts a rebellion against Elizabeth I and is executed (cats 68, 70). Henry Wriothesley, 3rd Earl of Southampton, is imprisoned for his involvement in the uprising (cats 46, 47).

1603 Shakespeare writes *Troilus and Cressida*, *Measure for Measure*, *Othello* and the poem *A Lover's Complaint* around this time.
Death of Elizabeth I and accession of James I.
James I (cat.71) becomes patron of the Lord Chamberlain's Men who are henceforth known as the King's Men and frequently perform at court. Theatres closed for almost a year due to further outbreaks of the plague in which a sixth of London's population dies.

1604 Shakespeare completes *All's Well that Ends Well* and (with Thomas Middleton) *Timon of Athens* around this time. Shakespeare is recorded living in Cripplegate, near St Paul's, London.
James I ends war with Spain.

1605 Shakespeare buys a one-fifth share in the tithes for Stratford.
The Gunpowder Plot: Guy Fawkes and his fellow conspirators attempt to blow up the Royal Family in the Houses of Parliament.
Ben Jonson writes *Volpone*. His controversial *Masque of Blackness* is also performed at court for the first time with Queen Anne in a central role.

1606 Shakespeare completes *King Lear* and writes *Macbeth*.

1607 Shakespeare completes *Antony and Cleopatra* and writes *Pericles*.
Susanna, Shakespeare's elder daughter, marries the physician John Hall.

1608 Shakespeare writes *Coriolanus*.
The King's Men acquire the lease of the prestigious Blackfriars Theatre as a year-round venue.
Mary Arden, Shakespeare's mother, dies.

1609 Shakespeare writes *The Winter's Tale* and *Cymbeline* around this date.

1610 Ben Jonson writes *The Alchemist*.
John Donne writes the *Holy Sonnets*.

1611 Shakespeare writes *The Tempest*.
King James Bible is published.

1613 Shakespeare writes *Henry VIII (All is True)*.
Marriage of James I's daughter Elizabeth to Frederick, Elector Palatine; during the festivities the King's Men perform fourteen plays (cat.75).
Shakespeare buys the gatehouse of the old Dominican priory in Blackfriars.
The Globe Theatre burns down during a performance of *Henry VIII (All is True)*. It is rebuilt soon after.

1614 Shakespeare completes *The Two Noble Kinsmen* with John Fletcher.
The Hope Theatre opens on Bankside, London, run by Philip Henslowe and Edward Alleyn in competition with the neighbouring Globe.

1615 William Herbert, 3rd Earl of Pembroke, is appointed Lord Chamberlain (cat.87).

1616 Judith, Shakespeare's younger daughter, marries Thomas Quiney.
Shakespeare returns to Stratford and dictates his will, leaving most of his property and possessions to his elder daughter, Susanna (cat.92).
Shakespeare dies in Stratford-upon-Avon and is buried in Holy Trinity Church in the town.
Execution of Sir Walter Ralegh (cat.89).

1623 In or before 1623, a monument to Shakespeare is erected in Holy Trinity Church, Stratford-upon-Avon.
Anne Hathaway dies.
The first collected edition of Shakespeare's plays, the First Folio, is published under the auspices of his friends and colleagues John Heminges and Henry Condell.

Non, Sanz Droict
non sanz droict

NON SANZ DROICT

Shakespere 1596

N° 23

To all & singuler Noble & Gentillmen of what estate or degree bearing Arms to whom these presentes shall come. William Dethick als Garter. principall king of Arms sendeth greetinges. Knowe yee that whereas by the authorite & auncyent [illegible] my office [illegible] from the Quenes most [illegible] and her highnes most noble & victorious progenitors I am to take generall notice & record & to make publique demonstracon & testemonie for all ~~matters~~ causes of Arms and matters of Gentrie thorough all her Maties kingdoms & dominions, principalites, Isles & provinces. To the end that as some by theyre auncyent names families kyndredes & descentes have & enioye sondry enseignes & cotes of Arms. So other for theyr valiant factes magnanimite vertu dignites & desertes may [illegible] suche tokens of honour & worthinesse whereby theyr name & good fame [illegible] divulged & theyr children & posterite [illegible] Beinge solicited [illegible]

In consideration [illegible] John Shakespeare of Stratford uppon Avon in the Counte of Warwike credible report informed [illegible] whose parentes & late antecessors were for theyr valeant & faithfull service advanced & rewarded by the most prudent prince king Henry the seventh of famous memorie [illegible] reputacon & credit [illegible] In consideration whereof & for encouragement of his posterite I have assigned [illegible] graunted [illegible] this shield or cote of Arms. Viz. Gould on a bend sable a speare of the first steeled argent proper

And for his creast or cognizaunce a falcon his winges displayed Argent standing on a wrethe of his coullers supporting a speare Gould steeled [illegible] sett uppon a helmett with mantelles and tasselles as more playnely appeareth depicted on this margent. Signefieing hereby that it shalbe lawfull for the said John Shakespeare gent. and for his children yssue & posterite [illegible] to beare [illegible] the same [illegible] or otherwise [illegible] in all lawfull warlike factes or civile [illegible] without let or interruption of any [illegible] In wittnesse whereof I have hereunto subscribed my name & fastened the Seale of my office endorzed with the signett of my Arms. At the office of Arms London the [illegible] daye of october the [illegible] yeare of the reigne of our Soveraigne Lady Elizabeth by the grace of God Quene of England France & Ireland defender of the faith &c. 1596.

[illegible] achivment maye descend by the auncient custom and lawes of Armes.

'SWEET MASTER SHAKESPEARE' 1564–1616

STANLEY WELLS

The career of William Shakespeare, a glover's son baptized in Holy Trinity Church, Stratford-upon-Avon, Warwickshire, on 26 April 1564 is a remarkable example of the upward mobility that was possible in the period.[1] In spite of the legend that all we know about him could be written on the back of an envelope, in fact much information about his life and family survives in legal and other records. His father, John Shakespeare (d.1601), appears not to have been able to write but took a prominent part in the town's affairs, becoming an alderman and, in 1568, bailiff, or mayor. He figures frequently in the town council's minute books (cat.10) during the 1560s and 1570s. William's mother, born Mary Arden (d.1608), lived originally in the nearby village of Wilmcote, in the farmhouse that can be visited to the present day. Like Shakespeare's birthplace and other houses associated with the poet, it is maintained by the Shakespeare Birthplace Trust.

Shakespeare would have taken his first steps in education at a 'petty' (junior) school, where he would have learned his letters from a hornbook – a simple board mounted on a handle and bearing a sheet of paper printed with teaching tools such as the alphabet, the vowels, the doxology ('In the name of the Father, the Son and the Holy Ghost') and the Lord's Prayer, like the one illustrated on p.84. Yet the real foundations of his success were most probably laid at the local grammar school, the King's New School (fig.1), where he received a thorough training in classical literature and rhetoric and developed a love of reading that was to sustain him in all he did and wrote.

His education in Latin would perforce have originated in study from an early age of the frequently reprinted *Short Introduction of Grammar* by William Lily (1468?–1522/3), first published in 1540 and prescribed by royal proclamation for use in all the grammar schools of the realm (cat.16). Shakespeare later portrayed a boy with his own name – William – being put through his paces in phrases derived from this book in his comedy *The Merry Wives of Windsor* (Act IV, Scene i), probably written in 1597.

Among Shakespeare's favourite books that he would have studied at school was Ovid's *Metamorphoses*, on which he drew from early in his career, in *Titus Andronicus* – where he actually brings the book on the stage – to *The Tempest*, where one of Prospero's greatest speeches – the one beginning 'Ye elves of hills, brooks, standing lakes and groves' (Act V, Scene i, line 33) – virtually paraphrases Ovid. Shakespeare

Grant of arms to John Shakespeare (draft), 1595 (cat.54)

fig.1 **Schoolroom at King's New School, Stratford-upon-Avon, as it is today**

knew the poem from Arthur Golding's English translation of 1567, as well as from the original Latin (cat.65).

Like some other great writers of his time, such as the immensely learned Ben Jonson (1572–1637) – who was well taught at Westminster School and continued to educate himself throughout his life – Shakespeare did not proceed from grammar school to university. He married young and in a hurry. On 27 November 1582, when he was eighteen, the Consistory Court of the Bishopric of Worcester issued a licence permitting William Shakespeare of Stratford-upon-Avon to marry Anne Whateley – apparently a scribe's mistake for the bride he married, Anne Hathaway (1555/6–1623) – after only one calling of the banns, and on the next day two Stratford townsmen entered into a bond in the large sum of £40 guaranteeing that there were no legal obstacles to the marriage of William Shakespeare and Anne Hathaway (cat.17).[2] Anne, eight years his senior, was the daughter of a yeoman farmer from Shottery, a village less than a mile away from Stratford. At the time of the marriage she was pregnant. Their first daughter, Susanna, was born six months after the marriage, and twins, Judith and Hamnet, followed in 1585.[3] We do not know how Shakespeare supported his family in their early years – his so-called 'lost years' from 1585 to 1592. Speculation about what he did during them has been rife. Was he a butcher's apprentice or a scrivener, a schoolteacher or a lawyer, a soldier or a sailor? Or none of them? A popular current theory is that he is to be identified with the William Shakeshaft named in the will of a Catholic landowner in 1581, and that Shakespeare himself was a secret Catholic, but the evidence is slim.[4] The most we can say with reasonable certainty is that at some point during the later 1580s he joined a company of actors – possibly the Queen's Men – and embarked on a lifelong career that was to embrace acting, playwriting, the composition of non-dramatic poetry and theatre administration. Although players toured the provinces, and although Shakespeare's family remained in Stratford, the theatrical profession centred on London and Shakespeare must have spent much of his time there throughout his working life.

In Shakespeare's time, as at many others, the London literary scene was rife with malice. The first reference to Shakespeare in print, in the book published as *Greene's Groatsworth of Wit Bought with a Million of Repentance* of 1592, exemplifies this desire to make mischief. The dying playwright Robert Greene (1558–92), whose authorship of this work has been questioned, attacks Shakespeare as an 'upstart crow, beautified with our feathers' who thinks himself 'the only Shake-scene in a country'.[5] The criticism, clearly motivated by envy, is cryptic; it may imply an accusation of plagiarism. Another writer, Henry Chettle (d.1603–7), leapt to Shakespeare's defence, praising his 'uprightness of dealing', as well as his 'grace in writing'.[6] It is remarkable that Greene's is by far the least complimentary of all surviving references to Shakespeare, both professionally and personally, from his lifetime. Though one or two later writers, notably Ben Jonson, expressed mixed feelings about him as an artist, none of them wrote ill of him as a man: for many of his contemporaries, as well as for Gullio in *The Return from Parnassus* (see Tarnya Cooper's 'Silent "oratory"', p.42), he was 'sweet Master Shakespeare'.

As Greene's allusion shows, by 1592 Shakespeare was established as a writer of plays. The closure of London theatres in that year because of plague may have warned him of the need for an alternative career. In the following year he published the first of the two long poems by which he set forth his claim to be a non-dramatic poet. *Venus and Adonis*, erotically comic and based on a myth from the *Metamorphoses*, bears a dedication to Shakespeare's only known literary patron, Henry Wriothesley, 3rd Earl of Southampton (1573–1624), an androgynous, good-looking and highly intelligent man some ten years younger than himself (cats 46, 47). Only a single copy of the first printing survives. A tragic counterpart, *Lucrece*, appeared a year later with a second dedication to the Earl of Southampton that suggests the relationship had warmed into an intimacy that warranted the name of love: 'The love I dedicate to your lordship is without end .... What I have done is yours, what I have to do is yours, being part in all I have, devoted yours.'[7]

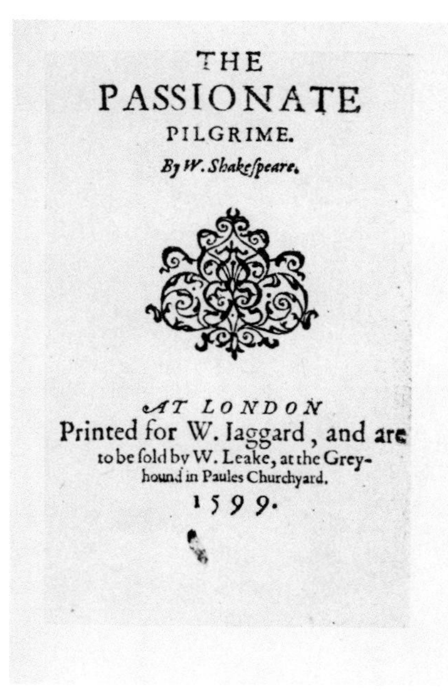
THE PASSIONATE PILGRIME.
By W. Shakespeare.
AT LONDON
Printed for W. Iaggard, and are to be sold by W. Leake, at the Grey-hound in Paules Churchyard.
1599.

fig.2 **Title page for *The Passionate Pilgrime***, 1599
William Shakespeare
The Huntington Library, San Marino, California

It was probably during the 1590s that Shakespeare wrote most of the 154 sonnets that, however, were not published as a collection until 1609. In 1598 Francis Meres (1565/6–1647), in his critically naïve but historically invaluable treatise *Palladis Tamia, or Wit's Treasury*, wrote that 'the sweet witty soul of Ovid lives in mellifluous and honey-tongued Shakespeare, witness his *Venus and Adonis*, his *Lucrece*, his sugared sonnets among his private friends, etc.'[8] Two of the poems eventually printed in the 1609 volume were included in an unauthorized collection, *The Passionate Pilgrim*, in 1599 (fig.2). The delay in publication is significant. The sonnets, it seems, were written not, like the narrative poems, for Shakespeare's immediate professional advancement but rather for his personal satisfaction, and for his close friends. Who these friends were has been the subject of endless, and probably fruitless, speculation. Some of the sonnets are 'public' poems in the sense that they could have appeared without seeming out of place in poetical miscellanies of the time, but others, rebelling totally against the conventions associated with the sonnet form, are deeply, even embarrassingly private, speaking of self-loathing, sexual revulsion, betrayal and contempt.

One of their most conspicuous departures from convention lies in the fact that many of the first 126 poems in the collection express love for a young man, not for a woman. Whether all of these poems address the same young man is one of the many questions that they provoke. It is natural to ask whether they may represent an intimate extension of the formal expression of love for Southampton declared in the dedication to *Lucrece*. The problems associated with the poems are compounded by the dedication, composed not by the author, but by the publisher, Thomas Thorpe:

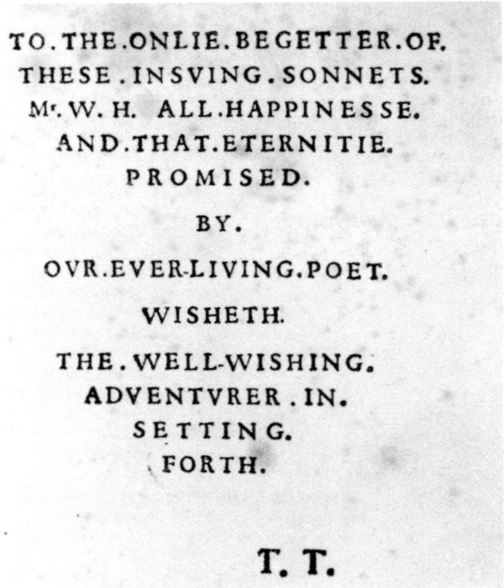

TO.THE.ONLIE.BEGETTER.OF.
THESE.INSVING.SONNETS.
Mr.W.H. ALL.HAPPINESSE.
AND.THAT.ETERNITIE.
PROMISED.
BY.
OVR.EVER-LIVING.POET.
WISHETH.
THE.WELL-WISHING.
ADVENTVRER.IN.
SETTING.
FORTH.

T. T.

fig.3 **Dedication of *Shake-speares Sonnets***, 1609
Shakespeare's Birthplace Trust

What is the meaning of 'begetter'? Does it mean inspirer, or procurer (of the manuscript), or even author? Who is 'Mr W.H.'? Why is his identity only half-revealed? Is 'W.H.' a deliberate inversion of Henry Wriothesley's initials? If so, why is an earl described as 'Mr'?

The sonnets themselves hint at an underlying narrative that never comes to the surface. Is the poet Shakespeare himself, or Shakespeare adopting a fictional persona, or sometimes one, sometimes the other? Who is the rival poet who vies with the author for a young man's favours? And, biggest mystery of all, who is the 'black' woman (if there is only one woman) for whom the poet expresses simultaneous adoration and contempt:

> In faith, I do not love thee with mine eyes,
> For they in thee a thousand errors note;
> But 'tis my heart that loves what they despise,
>   Who in despite of view is pleased to dote. (Sonnet 141, lines 1–4)

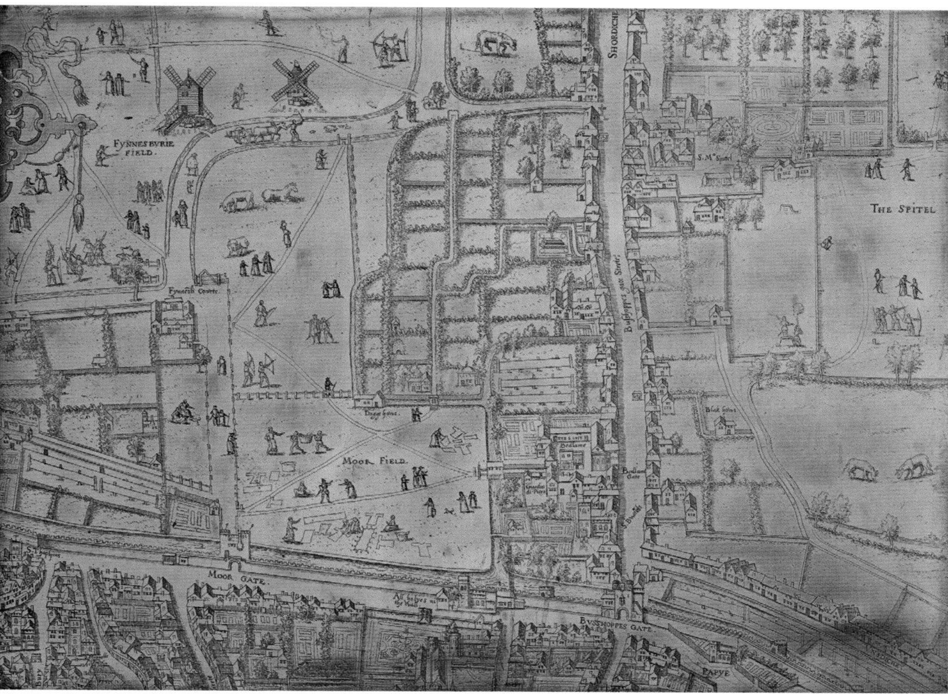

fig.4 **Copperplate map showing Bishopsgate**, 1559 (detail)
377 × 505mm (14⅞ × 19⅞ in)
Museum of London

The sonnets are at once the most revealing and the most enigmatic of Shakespeare's compositions (cat.50).[9]

It is possible that Shakespeare lived for a while in the Earl of Southampton's household. Henry Wriothesley had houses in both London and Titchfield, Hampshire. It is known that Shakespeare lived in lodgings in London from time to time during the 1590s; he is listed as a tax defaulter in Bishopsgate ward (fig.4) in November 1597 and in October 1598.[10] He must sometimes have been on tour with his fellow actors. However, he maintained close links with his home town, where his son Hamnet died and was buried in August 1596.[11] Shakespeare's father's fortunes had declined; in 1592 he was listed among a number of Stratford residents who did not attend church regularly, some because they were secret Catholics, others, including John Shakespeare, because they feared being arrested for debt (cat.12).[12] Nevertheless, in 1596 John – or perhaps William on his behalf – applied to the College of Arms for, and was granted, a coat of arms, conferring upon him and his descendants the much-coveted formal status of gentleman (cat.54).

A note preserved in the records held at the College of Arms, London, and setting out the grounds of the application shows that John had initiated a similar application some twenty years before, that he was a Justice of the Peace in Stratford, that he had 'lands and tenements of good wealth and substance', £500, and that he had married 'a daughter and heir of Arden, a gentleman of worship'. Now he was granted the right to a heraldic shield depicting a spear and, as his 'crest or cognizance', a falcon, 'his wings displayed', standing on a wreath and supporting a spear set upon a helmet.

The spear alludes to the family name. The Shakespeares were now officially gentlemen, with NON SANS DROIT ('not without right') as their family motto. The shield and crest are displayed on William Shakespeare's monument and his daughter Susanna's seal combines the arms with those of her husband.[13] In 1597 William consolidated his local status by buying the second largest house in Stratford, New Place, a grand establishment that was pulled down in the eighteenth century.[14]

William Shakespeare was now a man of means, dividing his time between Stratford and London. On 25 October 1598 Richard Quiney, who had been both alderman and bailiff of Stratford, wrote to him from the Bell Inn, near St Paul's Cathedral in London, requesting a loan of £30, probably on behalf of the townspeople (cat.58). As the letter was found among Quiney's papers, it seems never to have been delivered; he may have been able to speak to Shakespeare in person.[15] No other letter – either to or from Shakespeare – survives. His father died in Stratford in 1601, and in the following year Shakespeare paid £320 for land in Old Stratford.[16] The glover's son was now both a member of the gentry and a wealthy property owner.

The narrative poems were to be among Shakespeare's most popular works for half a century and more; *Venus and Adonis* was more frequently reprinted than any of his plays. They established a reputation to which an increasing number of references in both manuscript and print testify. The Muses themselves, Francis Meres wrote in 1598, 'would speak with Shakespeare's fine-filed phrase if they could speak English'. In the same year Richard Barnfield (1574–1627) published the first verse tribute to Shakespeare, again centring on his poems:

And Shakespeare, thou whose honey-flowing vein,
Pleasing the world, thy praises doth obtain;
Whose *Venus* and whose *Lucrece* – sweet, and chaste –
Thy name in fame's immortal book have placed;
Live ever you, at least in fame live ever.
Well may the body die, but fame dies never.[17]

And 'honey' supplied a metaphor for Shakespeare's style yet again in a rather clumsily written epigram by John Weever of 1599, which describes him as 'honey-tongued Shakespeare' and which refers to both of the narrative poems as well as to 'Romeo, Richard, more whose names I know not' and to their 'sugared tongues and power-attractive beauty'.[18] A manuscript treatise on poetry of around 1599, written by a young student named William Scott, which came to light only in 2003 and is still unpublished, refers admiringly to both *Lucrece* and *The Tragedy of King Richard II*, and quotes from both works, though without naming their author.[19]

Shakespeare's reputation as both poet and playwright was growing. Plays were written primarily to be performed; many never got into print. Only half of Shakespeare's were published during his lifetime, and there is reason to believe that he wrote two – *Love's Labour's Won* and *Cardenio*, the latter co-written with John Fletcher (1579–1625) – which have disappeared altogether. Yet plays by him began to appear in print in 1594, at first anonymously, but then in 1598, in the second editions of *Richard II* and *Richard III* and the first edition of *Love's Labour's Lost*, with his name on the title page.

Increasingly a public figure, he nevertheless appears to have been able to sustain an enjoyable private life, if we are to believe an anecdote preserved in the diaries of John Manningham (*c*.1575–1622), a law student of the Middle Temple, writing on 13 March 1602. He records that once, when Richard Burbage (1568–1619), the leading actor of Shakespeare's company, was playing the part of Richard III a citizen's wife 'grew so far in liking with him' – that is, fancied him so much – that before leaving the theatre she made an assignation with him, telling him to come to her that night under the name of Richard III. However, says Manningham, Shakespeare, 'overhearing their conclusion, went before, was entertained, and at his game ere Burbage came. Then message being brought that Richard III was at the door, Shakespeare caused return to be made that William the Conqueror was before Richard III.'[20]

We certainly catch a more authentic glimpse of Shakespeare the private man in papers relating to a lawsuit of 1612, which refer to events that took place eight years earlier.[21] The suit was brought by Stephen Belott against Christopher Mountjoy, a maker of tires, or tiaras, who lived in Silver Street, in the north of the City. Belott, his former apprentice, had married Mountjoy's daughter Mary on 19 November 1604. Some years later Belott quarrelled with his father-in-law, accusing him of having broken promises to pay a dowry of £60 and to leave his daughter £200 in his will. It emerges from testimony given in court that Shakespeare had been living in the house as a lodger for some two years before the marriage. Mountjoy had asked him to act as a go-between in the marriage negotiations. Shakespeare spoke well of the young man, whom he had regarded as 'a very good and industrious servant' and to whom Mountjoy had shown 'great good will and affection'. Mrs Mountjoy had begged Shakespeare to speak to Belott on her daughter's behalf, and Shakespeare had done this kind office. He claimed not to know, or to remember, many details about the case, but agreed that they had had many 'conferences [conversations] about their marriage which afterwards was consummated and solemnized'. Belott was awarded damages against his father-in-law, but had difficulty in recovering the money from him. It is regrettable that the testimony Shakespeare gave in court does little to illuminate his share in the proceedings. He seems to have been well disposed towards his landlord's family and the young lovers, but not to have wished to take sides when the dispute came to court.

During the early years of the seventeenth century Shakespeare continued to add to his Stratford estates, most notably by paying the very large sum of £440 for an interest in a lease of tithes in the Stratford area in 1605.[22] (This amount represents several hundreds of thousands of pounds in modern terms.) Two years later his daughter Susanna married Dr John Hall, a distinguished physician, in the town.[23] They had one child, Elizabeth, baptized eight months later. Shakespeare's mother was also buried there on 9 September 1608.[24] His only major purchase of property in London came in March 1613, when he bought a gatehouse in Blackfriars,[25] close to his company's indoor theatre; by this time he had written his last play. There is no evidence that he ever lived in the Blackfriars house, but he became engaged in litigation concerning it in April 1615.

Back in Stratford, he had been involved in disputes concerning the enclosure of land. A disastrous fire had ravaged the town in July 1614, increasing the already severe poverty, and soon afterwards proposals were made to convert large areas of public arable land in the nearby village of Welcombe into sheep pasturage. Residents, believing that this measure would reduce both income and employment and increase the price of grain, were up in arms. Town records show that Shakespeare, who owned much of the land, was implicated, and he has been suspected of acting against the best interests of the poor; but his exact attitude is difficult to determine.[26]

In January 1616, Shakespeare had a lawyer draft his will (cat.92). A few weeks later his daughter Judith married a tavern keeper and wine merchant, Thomas Quiney, son of the letter-writing Richard.[27] They had failed to obtain the special licence required for marriage in Lent, and as a result Thomas was excommunicated. Like Shakespeare before them, they had reasons to marry quickly. It emerged that the husband had had a child with a Margaret Wheeler, who was buried with the baby on 15 March. Quiney was sentenced to perform public penance. Discovery of the affair appears to have caused Shakespeare to change his will.[28] The first sheet, which mostly concerns Judith, has been recopied, apparently because Shakespeare, mistrusting her husband, made changes to protect Judith's interests. In the final draft, dated 25 March, she received £100 as a marriage portion, and the interest on a further £150 for as long as she was married; but her husband could claim the interest only if he settled lands of equal value on her. She was also to inherit her father's 'broad silver-gilt bowl'. It is possible that this item still survives somewhere, but such objects were often melted down for the value of their precious metal. There were personal bequests, including his sword to his friend Thomas Combe, a member of a prominent Stratford family, and twenty shillings in gold to his seven-year-old godson William Walker, but the bulk of the estate went to his eldest daughter, Susanna. His granddaughter Elizabeth Hall received all his plate except for the silver-gilt bowl. When she died, childless, in 1670 Shakespeare's direct line ended. It is impossible to find precise modern equivalents for the value of Shakespeare's estate at the time of his death, but it is fair to say that in today's terms he was worth well over one million pounds. (He would not, however, have been by any means the richest man in the town.)

Shakespeare is notorious for leaving only the second-best bed to his wife, and even that was an afterthought. However, she may have been automatically entitled to a share of the estate, and she continued to live in New Place until she died, in 1623. Shakespeare himself died on 23 April 1616, and is buried in the chancel of Holy Trinity Church, Stratford-upon-Avon. His grave (not a tomb, as is often said) bears the epitaph:

fig.5 **Epitaph on Shakespeare's grave at Holy Trinity Church, Stratford-upon-Avon**

Essentially this is a plea that the sexton should not throw his bones into the charnel house neighbouring the church, common practice at the time. Close to the grave is the monument bearing the bust executed by the Dutch craftsman Gerrat Johnson the Younger (or Gheerart Janssen; active 1612–23) and adorned with inscriptions in both English and Latin comparing the former Stratford schoolboy with great figures of classical antiquity, and praising his genius (cat.2).[29]

Among Shakespeare's lesser bequests are sums of 26*s*. 8*d*. to buy mourning rings for his colleagues Richard Burbage, John Heminges (bap.1566, d.1630) and Henry Condell (1576–1627). These actors were his lifelong colleagues. Burbage died in 1619, but Heminges and Condell undertook responsibility for the assembling and publication of Shakespeare's collected plays in the First Folio, of 1623. In doing so they produced Shakespeare's greatest monument: without it we should have lacked half of Shakespeare's plays, including some of the greatest.

Notes

1 Facsimiles of Shakespeare's life records and other important biographical material are finely reproduced and discussed in Schoenbaum 1975. Supplementary documents are reproduced in Schoenbaum 1981, which includes detailed discussion of the portraits.
2 Schoenbaum 1975, pp.66–72.
3 Schoenbaum 1975, pp.75–6.
4 I discuss this point in Wells 2002, pp.21–6.
5 Sig. A3v; reproduced in Schoenbaum 1975, pp.115–16.
6 Henry Chettle, *Kind-Harts Dreame* (1592), sig. A4; reproduced in Schoenbaum 1975, p.117.
7 The dedications are reproduced in Schoenbaum 1975, pp.128, 132.
8 Schoenbaum 1975, p.140.
9 For discussion of the sonnets and their problems, see Edmondson and Wells 2004.
10 Schoenbaum 1975, p.162.
11 Schoenbaum 1975, p.164.
12 Schoenbaum 1975, p.39.
13 Schoenbaum 1975, pp.166–72.
14 Schoenbaum 1975, pp.173–8.
15 Schoenbaum 1975, p.180.
16 Schoenbaum 1975, p.188.
17 'A Remembrance of Some English Poets' from *Poems in Divers Humours* (1598), reprinted in *Richard Barnfield: The Complete Poems*, ed. George Klawitter (Associated University Presses, London and Toronto, 1990), p.182.
18 Wells and Taylor 2005, p.xli.
19 It is described by Stanley Wells in 'Shakespeare's First Serious Critic Revealed', *Times Literary Supplement*, 26 September 2003.
20 Schoenbaum 1975, p.152.
21 Schoenbaum 1975, pp.208–13.
22 Schoenbaum 1975, p.192.
23 Schoenbaum 1975, p.235.
24 Schoenbaum 1975, p.181.
25 Schoenbaum 1975, pp.220–5.
26 Schoenbaum 1975, pp.230–4.
27 Schoenbaum 1975, pp.238–40.
28 Schoenbaum 1975, pp.242–50.
29 Schoenbaum 1975, pp.252–3.

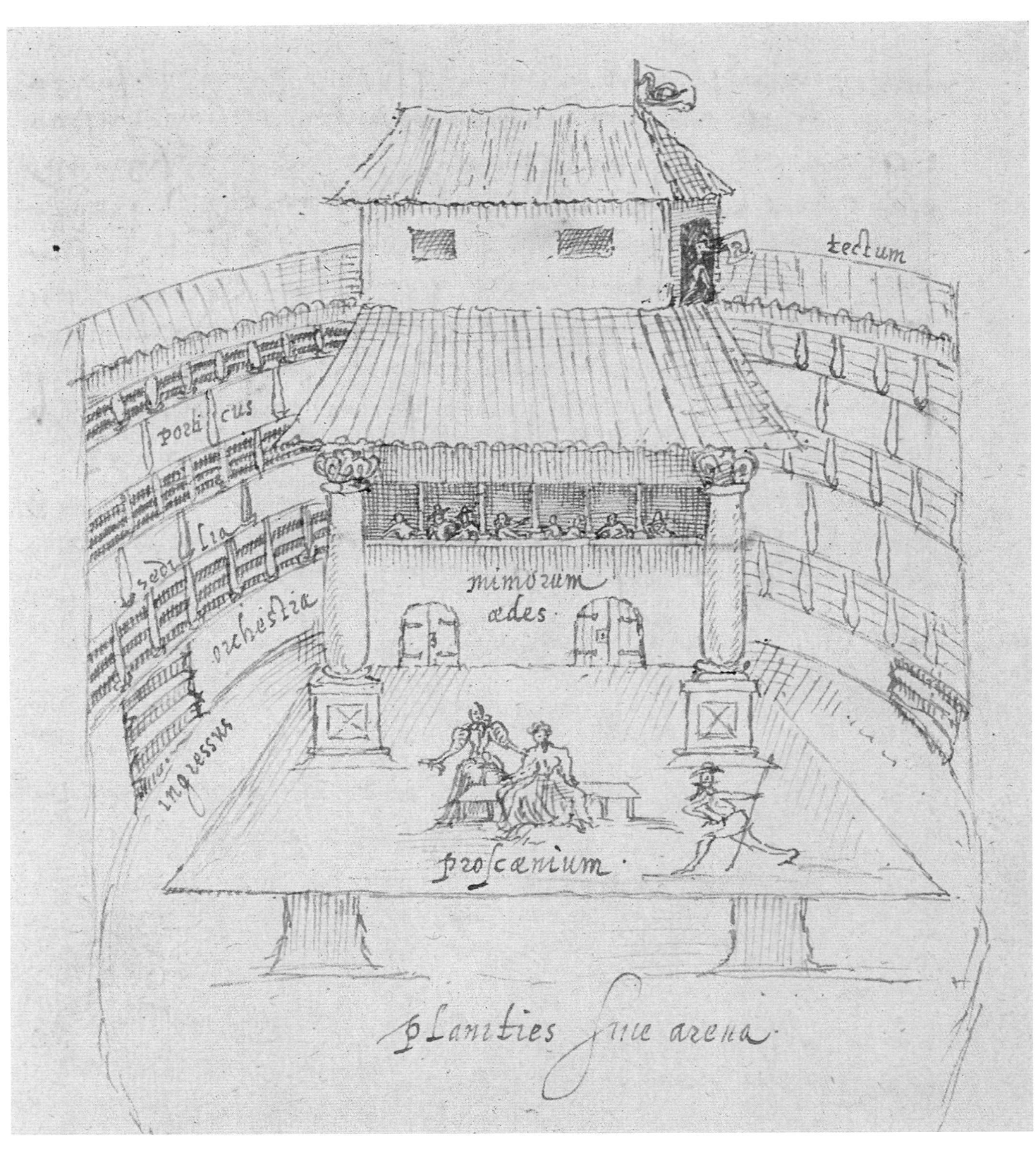
tectum
porticus
sedilia
orchestra
mimorum
ædes
ingressus
proscænium
planities siue arena

SHAKESPEARE'S PROFESSIONAL WORLD

JAMES SHAPIRO

At the centre of Shakespeare's professional life was his playing company, the Chamberlain's Men, formed under the patronage of the Lord Chamberlain, Henry Carey, Lord Hunsdon (1526–96). For two decades, from 1594 until he stopped writing and acting around 1613, Shakespeare was one of eight or so shareholders in this troupe (renamed the King's Men after the accession of James I in 1603).[1] The company was made up of veteran actors, most of whom had already worked with each other in companies that had broken up and reformed in the early 1590s – including Strange's Men and Pembroke's Men (the vulnerable actors, always viewed with suspicion by London's city fathers, needed the official patronage and protection of noblemen). We do not know to which company Shakespeare belonged before joining the Chamberlain's Men but if it had been Pembroke's Men, which staged Marlowe's work, it helps explain his deep familiarity with the drama of his formidable rival.[2] Plays as well as players passed from company to company in the early 1590s – including a few in which Shakespeare may have acted and which he would later rewrite: *Hamlet*, *King Lear*, *The Famous Victories of Henry V* and *The Troublesome Reign of King John*.[3]

Shakespeare and his fellow sharers spent their mornings rehearsing and their afternoons performing alongside hired men and boys who were needed to fill out the cast of approximately fifteen. Except for a break during Lent and the occasional closing of the theatres due to scandal or plague, performances went on all year round. As Elizabethan audiences expected a different play every day, actors had to master a score of new roles every year – as well as recall old favourites needed to flesh out the repertory.[4] Shakespeare had the added pressure of providing his company with, on average, two new plays a year, though he tended to write plays in inspired bunches. Other new plays were acquired from a score of freelance dramatists who were paid on average £6 a play (at a time when a schoolmaster might earn £20 a year).[5] What little free time Shakespeare had at the start and end of his working day must have been devoted to reading and writing. We know that Shakespeare was still acting alongside his fellow sharers as late as 1603 (in Ben Jonson's *Sejanus*) and there is little evidence that he took time off to write. The unrelenting schedule of rehearsing, performing, reading and writing was a punishing one and may explain why Shakespeare stopped writing plays at the age of forty-nine – at the height of his powers – and probably gave up full-time acting sometime before that.

Swan Theatre in London, *c*.1596–7 (detail; cat.27)

In the mid 1590s the Chamberlain's Men performed at the Theatre; when their landlord, Giles Allen, refused to renew their lease they relocated to the other Shoreditch playhouse, the Curtain. In 1599, following the dismantling of the Theatre (for Giles Allen owned the land but not the building) and its reconstruction as the Globe in Southwark, Shakespeare, Richard and Cuthbert Burbage, John Heminges, Will Kemp, Thomas Pope and Augustine Phillips became co-owners of their theatre – the first time that a group of actors had ever operated their own playhouse.[6] In 1608–9 the core of this group – the Burbages, Heminges and Shakespeare – also became joint owners of the indoor and more intimate Blackfriars Theatre (along with Will Sly, Henry Condell and Thomas Evans), where they catered to a more privileged audience during the winter months. From May to September Blackfriars remained unused, while the company performed at the Globe.[7]

Shakespeare and his fellow player-investors were fairly close in age and came from the same middle classes. They seem to have been creatively and temperamentally well matched too (and seem not to have suffered from the violent quarrels that plagued their main competitors, the Admiral's Men).[8] There were no producers or directors in the Elizabethan theatre: it was a collective effort that depended on mutual reliance and recognition of each other's strengths. Shakespeare wrote his plays with particular actors in mind: the parts of Richard III, Romeo and Hamlet were created for the company's leading man, Richard Burbage (1568–1619), while the broad clowning of Bottom, Peter and probably Falstaff as well were designed for their comic star, Will Kemp (active 1585–1602, fig.6). We know little about the roles Shakespeare wrote for himself, though anecdotal tradition records that he played 'kingly parts' as well as the Ghost in *Hamlet* and old Adam in *As You Like It*.[9]

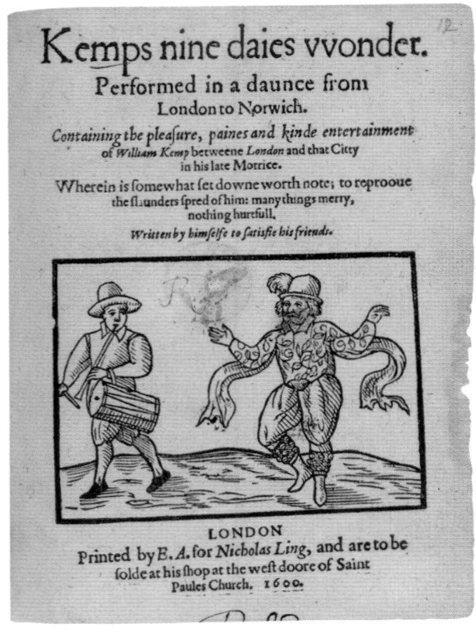

fig.6 **Title page for *Kemp's Nine Days Wonder*,** 1600
William Kemp
The Bodleian Library, University of Oxford

For the duration of Shakespeare's career the Chamberlain's/King's Men was a remarkably profitable and stable company. The only major falling out took place shortly before the move to the Globe, when Kemp quit. We do not know why he left, though his subsequent grumbling about 'Shakerags' points to a rift between the company's most popular performer and its talented playwright:[10] it may well have been a disagreement about the direction of the company and whether this was to be an actors' or playwrights' theatre. If so, it was a battle that Shakespeare won. Kemp tried a solo career for a while, joined up with other players, and died a few years later, impoverished. The Chamberlain's Men replaced him with Robert Armin (1563–1615), more of a witty fool than an improvisational clown like Kemp – and Shakespeare rewarded Armin (and posterity) with such roles as Feste in *Twelfth Night* and the Fool in *King Lear*.[11]

Shakespeare had the good fortune to have turned to playwriting at a time when London's theatre world was rapidly expanding. When he arrived in the metropolis in the late 1580s, there were, in addition to various inns where players performed, only three permanent outdoor playhouses: the Theatre, erected in 1576, the Curtain, which opened a year later, and the Rose, in Southwark, built in 1587. By the time that he left, London was ringed by the Swan and the Globe in Southwark; the Fortune and Red Bull in the northern suburbs; the Boar's Head in the east; and Blackfriars and St Paul's within the city walls.[12]

Even foreigners were struck by the popularity of playgoing: 'It was at the theatre,' noted Thomas Platter, a Swiss tourist who attended plays in London in 1599, that 'the English pass their time, learning at the play what is happening abroad.'[13] In 1600, in an England of 4,000,000, London and its immediate environs held a population of roughly 200,000. If, on any given day, just two plays were staged in playhouses that held as many as 2–3,000 spectators each, with theatres even half full, as many as 3,000 or so Londoners were attending a play. Over the course of a week – conservatively assuming five days of performances each week – 15,000 Londoners paid to see a play.[14] Some, including the very young and the very old, went rarely, if at all, while others – including law students at the Inns of Court – made up for that, seeing dozens of plays a year. But, on average, over a third of London's adult population would have seen a play every month. Shakespeare and his fellow dramatists were therefore writing for the most experienced and demanding playgoers in history.

While some of the success of the Chamberlain's Men can be attributed to luck, timing, organization and stability, much of it was a function of raw talent. No other company was nearly as successful. The Chamberlain's/King's Men were blessed with the best playwright in the land, the best clowns, the most charismatic male lead and the greatest depth. Though their names are lost to us, their boy actors, who played women's parts – for whom Shakespeare wrote such demanding roles as Juliet, Beatrice, Rosalind, Lady Macbeth and Cleopatra – must have been exceptionally talented. As a result, the company was able to attract some of the finest freelance work of Ben Jonson (1572–1637), Thomas Heywood (1573?–1641), Thomas Dekker (*c.*1572–1632) and other leading playwrights.[15] When Shakespeare retired, his place as resident playwright was quickly filled by the up-and-coming John Fletcher (1579–1625), who had already collaborated with him on *The Two Noble Kinsmen*, *The Famous History of the Life of King Henry VIII* and the lost *Cardenio*.[16]

Fletcher was not Shakespeare's only collaborator; at the beginning and end of his career as a playwright – in *Titus Andronicus* and *The First Part of King Henry VI* and later, in *Pericles* – Shakespeare had co-authored plays with other writers. In fact, Elizabethan plays were typically composed this way, with a group of two, three, four or more playwrights dividing the work – enabling them to draft a play in a few weeks' time, so that, for instance, a freelancer like Thomas Dekker was able to write or co-author ten plays in the course of an industrious year, and he was by no means exceptional.[17] It may well be that Shakespeare's unusual role as both playwright and actor precluded this kind of collaboration; he simply may not have had the time, except perhaps early and late in his career when not acting full time, to work closely with other writers (and, curiously, the work that he did manage to co-author is not his most distinguished).

No drafts of Shakespeare's plays survive, though his hand has been identified in the manuscript of a collaborative play that was never staged, *Sir Thomas More* (cat. 66). Much remains unclear about this play, but scholars have proposed that Shakespeare may have been brought in to revise the manuscript, on which the Master of the Revels, Edmund Tilney (1535/6–1610), had scribbled the warning: 'Leave out the insurrection wholly and the cause thereof.'[18]

All scripts had to be submitted to the Revels office for approval. Once Shakespeare had finished writing and revising a play he would turn it over to a professional scribe to prepare a clean copy to be vetted by the authorities (the Master of the Revels was responsible for ensuring that staged plays contained nothing seditious or otherwise offensive; censorship of printed works was under the supervision of the Archbishop of Canterbury and the Bishop of London).[19] After the text of the play was authorized, it remained in the possession of the company and may have served as the playhouse promptbook. A scribe would copy out on strips of paper the lines for each actor, which were then pasted together on a separate scroll or roll (which is why we speak of actors learning their roles, from the French *rôle*). Only one of these is extant, for the title role in Robert Greene's *Orlando Furioso* (fig.7), probably performed in 1592 by Edward Alleyn (1566–1626; fig.8), one of the leading tragedians of the day.[20] To enable actors to remember their entrances and exits, a 'platt' or plot summary hung on a peg in the tiring-house, such as the one that survives for the anonymous *The Second Part of the Seven Deadly Sins* (*c.*1591?, cat.28).[21]

At a time when he was still considering a career that depended on a patron's largesse, Shakespeare showed great care when publishing his first two poems, *Venus and Adonis* and *Lucrece*, relying on a schoolmate from Stratford-upon-Avon, Richard Field (1561–1624), who had become an established London printer. Yet he never showed the same concern for putting his plays into print (unlike, say, Ben Jonson, who carefully oversaw the printing of his plays in both quarto and folio editions). Shakespeare's name did not even appear on a title page of one of his plays until 1598, when publishers began to realize that his reputation had grown to the point where identifying him as the author could help sales. Not long after, one unscrupulous publisher, William Jaggard, successfully passed off a poetic miscellany containing a handful of Shakespeare's lyrics, but mostly works by others, as *The Passionate Pilgrime by W. Shakespeare* (1599; fig.2). Copyright at the time belonged to the publisher, not the author, so there was little incentive for Shakespeare or his company to make plays in their current repertory widely available (and there was always the risk that another group of players could get hold of and perform the work).

Yet Shakespeare did not seem to care that every word he wrote was recited on stage either. On more than one occasion – including *Hamlet* – he turned over to his fellow players a script far too long to enact in the 'two hours' traffic of our stage' (*Romeo and Juliet*, Prologue, line 12).[22] At nearly 3,800 lines, this *Hamlet* (a version of which survives in the 1623 First Folio) would have run close to four hours. With performances beginning at two in the afternoon, it would have been impossible to finish the play in late autumn or winter before darkness fell. The play, and others too, had to be trimmed to a manageable size, though whether Shakespeare or others did the cutting is unknown. Why Shakespeare wrote plays that ran longer than could be staged – yet made no effort to see the fuller versions published – remains hotly debated.

While writing and acting in plays for popular audiences in London were at the heart of Shakespeare's professional life, his creative life extended beyond the confines of the Globe and Blackfriars. Though the Chamberlain's/King's Men relied financially upon several thousand Londoners willing to pay a penny and more, day in, day

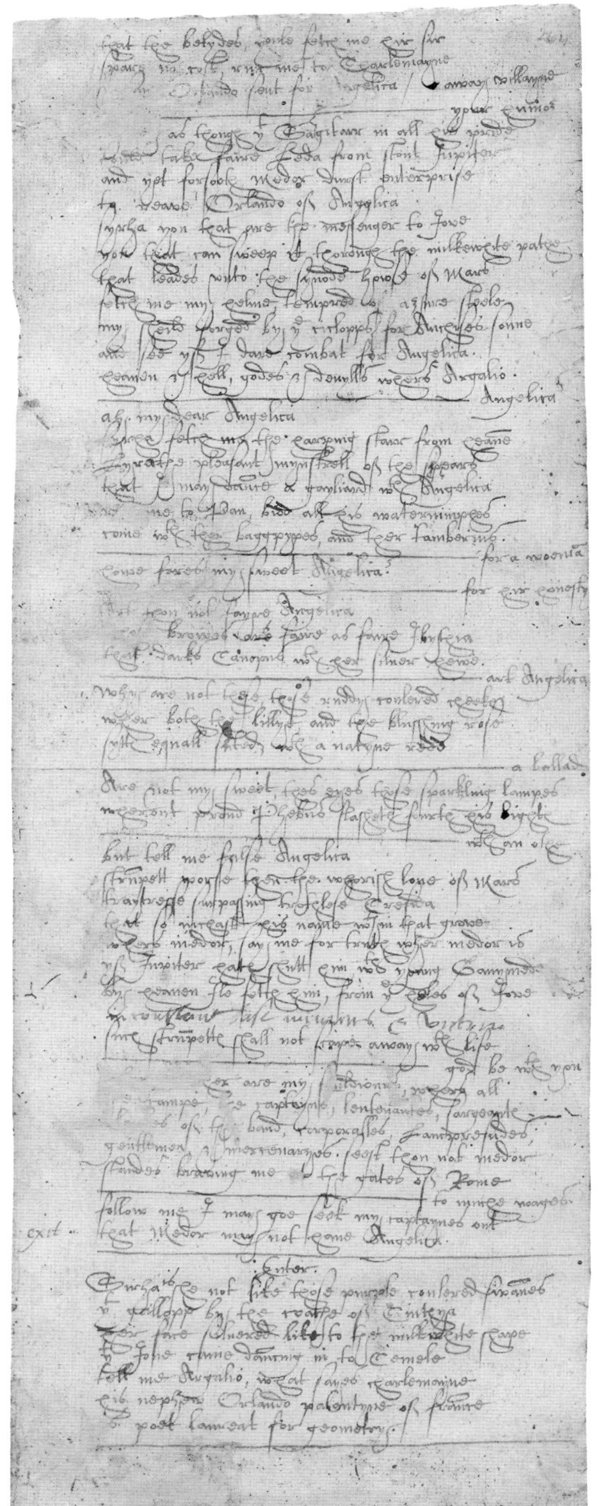

fig.8 **Edward Alleyn**, 1626
Unknown English artist
Oil on canvas, 2038 × 1140mm (80¼ × 44⅞in)
Dulwich Picture Gallery, London

fig.7 **Speaking part for Orlando in *Orlando Furioso***, 1592?
Robert Greene
416 × 150mm (16⅜ × 5⅞in)
Dulwich College, London

out, to see them perform, their long-term political security depended on patronage at court. It was fortunate for the London actors and playwrights that their monarchs enjoyed the theatre. However, neither Elizabeth I nor her successor James I wanted to pay to keep a retinue of actors for only a half-dozen or so command performances a year. They found it easier and much less expensive to reward the players with a payment each time they played at court.[23] Courtiers frequented the playhouses, but monarchs never set foot in the public theatres. The fiction – which also happened to be the official position of Elizabeth's Privy Council – was that public performances were essentially dress rehearsals whereby the leading companies 'might be the better enabled and prepared to show such plays before her Majesty as they shall be required at times meet and accustomed, to which end they have been chiefly licensed and tolerated'.[24] Shakespeare wrote primarily for popular audiences, who saw his plays before their monarch did.

Over the course of his career Shakespeare performed many times at royal residences – including Richmond, Wilton, Hampton Court (fig.9) and especially Whitehall.[25] These visits not only put him in the orbit of the court, with its gossip, faction and intrigue, but also brought him into contact with some of the great collections of art in the realm. Shakespeare was inspired both by what he read and by what he saw and heard, and much of what he experienced at court – from an ornate tapestry of the 'murder' of Julius Caesar[26] to sermons by leading preachers like Lancelot Andrewes[27] – had an impact on his work. We need only think of William Scrots's eye-catching painting of young Edward VI (1546; fig.16, p.41) that he would have passed when entering Whitehall Palace (and which now hangs in the National Portrait

Gallery, London). As one contemporary reports, those approaching this painting for the first time discovered 'at first sight something quite deformed'. Installed on its right side was an iron bar with a plate attached to it; visitors were encouraged to extend the bar and view the portrait through a 'small hole' cut in the plate, whereupon 'you see it in its true proportions'.[28] The striking anamorphosis would inform Shakespeare's point of view in *The Tragedy of Richard II*: 'Like perspectives, which rightly gazed upon/Show nothing but confusion; eyed awry/Distinguish form' (Act II, Scene ii, lines 18–20). It might also have inspired a similar reflection in *Henry V* about seeing 'perspectively' (Act V, Scene ii, line 315).

On at least one occasion Shakespeare earned money as a freelance writer. At celebratory tournaments held under both Elizabeth I and James I, courtiers greeted their monarch with an improvised *impresa* – a painted pasteboard shield with an enigmatic Latin motto. Despite his reputation for what Ben Jonson described as 'small Latin and less Greek',[29] Shakespeare was accomplished enough to create such a witty tag – who better to speak to an aristocrat's unarticulated desires? There is a payment recorded to him in 1613 by the Earl of Rutland for such an *impresa* (and Richard Burbage, Shakespeare's multi-talented fellow sharer, was paid for painting the shield).[30] It is unlikely to have been the first time Shakespeare worked for hire in this way – and in *Pericles* he all but advertised his talents with its half-dozen *imprese*.

With the coming of the Reformation, the age of Chaucer's pilgrims traversing the English countryside was over. Strolling players were among the very few people in early modern England who travelled widely (though itinerant actors without aristocratic patronage risked, like other vagabonds, being whipped and sent packing).

fig.9 **View of Hampton Court Palace**, 1558
Anthonis van den Wyngaerde
Watercolour with pen and ink, 300 × 200mm (11¾ × 78¾ in)
The Ashmolean Museum, Oxford

Shakespeare's professional activities thus extended well beyond London and its immediate environs. Touring records are patchy, but they indicate that the Chamberlain's Men played the provinces on a number of occasions, including touring through Faversham, Dover, Bristol, Bath and Marlborough (1596–7), through Shrewsbury, Coventry, Ipswich, Maldon and Oxford (1602–04), and through Folkestone, Oxford, Stafford and Shrewsbury (1613–14).[31] Shakespeare's exposure, while on the road, to the terrible conditions in the countryside, including the awful harvests that England suffered in the mid 1590s, must have been an especially sobering experience. Only someone who had seen the effects of crop failure could write so poignantly in *A Midsummer Night's Dream* of how 'the green corn/Hath rotted ere his youth attained a beard;/The fold stands empty in the drownèd field,/And crows are fatted with the murrain flock' (Act II, Scene i, lines 94–7).

It is tempting, but misleading, to see Shakespeare's career in binary terms: as foremost playwright or poet, court or popular dramatist, isolated or collaborative genius, concerned or careless about seeing his work published. His professional life was far more fluid and these binaries far too restrictive. It is more accurate to describe his creative universe as one of overlapping circles that included those Francis Meres (1565/6–1647) called Shakespeare's 'private friends'[32] – their names now lost to us – with whom he shared his sonnets; his fellow sharers and players; aristocratic patrons; printers, censors and booksellers; other playwrights whose plays he helped acquire and in which he acted; and playgoers of all social ranks, in the city, at court and in the countryside. Shakespeare also worked with musicians. The song 'It was a lover and his lass' that appears in *As You Like It* (Act V, Scene iii, line 15) was published shortly after it was first staged in Thomas Morley's *First Book of Ayres* in 1600. Morley (b.1556/7, d. in or after 1602), one of the leading composers of the day, had been Shakespeare's neighbour in Bishopsgate Ward. The likeliest explanation for the appearance of the same lyric in both their works is that it was a collaborative venture, with Shakespeare providing the words and Morley the musical setting.[33]

One of the most revealing images we have of Shakespeare in the course of his day-to-day professional affairs derives from a chance encounter with George Buc (1560–1622), a government servant and author who sought out Shakespeare's advice about the authorship of an anonymous play he had recently purchased.[34] Like everyone in the theatre community, Shakespeare knew that Buc was next in line for the position of Master of the Revels, so we can assume he would have done his best to help him. Buc, who was also one of the first serious collectors of Elizabethan drama, had purchased a copy of *George a Greene, the Pinner of Wakefield* (1599; fig.10) by an unknown author in the year it was published at Cuthbert Burby's bookshop near the Royal Exchange. Curious who had written the old play, he either ran into or sought out Shakespeare, who told him that it had been written by a minister, though at this point Shakespeare's memory failed him: he could not remember the minister's name. The lapse was excusable; it had been over a decade since the play was first staged. However, Shakespeare did volunteer an unusual bit of information: the minister had played the title role. A grateful Buc scribbled his findings on the title page of his copy (now at the Folger Shakespeare Library in Washington, DC): 'Written by

A
PLEASANT
CONCEYTED CO-
medie of George a Greene, the Pinner
of VVakefield.
As it was sundry times acted by the seruants of the right
Honourable the Earle of Sussex.
Imprinted at London by Simon Stafford,
for Cuthbert Burby: And are to be sold at his shop
neere the Royall Exchange. 1599.

fig.10 **Title page of *George a Greene*,** 1599
Inscriptions by George Buc
Folger Shakespeare Library, Washington, DC

... a minister, who acted the pinner's part in it himself. *Teste* [i.e., witnessed by] W. Shakespeare'.[35] He would have to fill in that blank another time. The encounter offers a glimpse of Shakespeare moving comfortably within a professional world capacious enough to embrace a minister who wrote and acted in his own play, an avid book collector who soon turned censor, and a glover's son from the provinces who would one day be celebrated as the world's greatest playwright.

Notes

1 Gurr 1996, p.279. See also S.P. Cerasano, 'The Chamberlain's–King's Men' in Kastan 1999, pp.328–45.
2 Gurr 1996, pp.270–71.
3 Gurr 2004, p.25.
4 For playhouse practice, including the staging of a different play every day, see Foakes and Rickert 1961, especially pp.16–37 and 47–60.
5 Scott McMillin, 'Professional Playwriting' in Kastan 1999, pp.225–38.
6 Gurr 1996, pp.292–4.
7 Gurr 2004, pp.34–7.
8 See, for example, Foakes and Rickert 1961, p.286; and Hotson 1931, pp.26–31.
9 Gurr 2004, p.14; Honan 1998, pp.110–11.
10 Harrison 1966, p.29. See also Wiles 1987, pp.116–35.
11 Wiles 1987, pp.136–63.
12 Harbage, Schoenbaum and Wagonheim 1989, pp.353–7.
13 Clare Williams (ed. and trans.), *Thomas Platter's Travels in England, 1599* (Jonathan Cape, London, 1937), p.170. Platter adds: 'How much time then they may merrily spend daily at the play everyone knows who has ever seen them play or act' (p.167).
14 See Butler 1984, pp.297–8; and Cook 1981, pp.176–91.
15 Roslyn Lander Knutson, 'Shakespeare's Repertory' in Kastan 1999, pp.346–61.
16 Vickers 2002.
17 For Thomas Dekker and others in 1599, see Foakes and Rickert 1961, pp.103–28.
18 G. Blakemore Evans (ed.), *The Riverside Shakespeare* (Houghton Mifflin Company, Boston, 1974), pp.1683–5.
19 Richard Dutton, 'Licensing and Censorship' in Kastan 1999, pp.377–91.
20 King 1992, pp.9–10.
21 Gurr 1992, pp.36–7.
22 Quotations from Shakespeare are cited from Wells and Taylor 2005.
23 Astington 1999, especially pp.215–20.
24 Chambers 1923, vol.4, p.325.
25 Chambers 1930, vol.2, pp.319–45.
26 See, for example, the descriptions in Clare Williams (ed. and trans.), *Thomas Platter's Travels in England, 1599* (Jonathan Cape, London, 1937) of the 'gold embroidered tapestry ... of the murder of Julius Caesar' that hung at Hampton Court (p.202).
27 Andrewes delivered a sermon 'Preached before Queen Elizabeth at Richmond, On the 21st of February, A.D., 1599, being Ash Wednesday, at What Time the Earl of Essex was Going Forth, upon the Expedition for Ireland', first published in *Ninety-Six Sermons* (London, 1629); the Chamberlain's Men had performed at Richmond Palace the previous evening (Chambers 1930, vol.2, p.322).
28 *Paul Hentzner's Travels in England, During the Reign of Queen Elizabeth*, trans. Horace, late Earl of Orford (London, 1797), p.23.
29 Ben Jonson, 'To the Memory of My Beloved, the Author Mr William Shakespeare', William Shakespeare, *Comedies, Histories and Tragedies* (London, 1623), sig. A4v.
30 Chambers 1930, vol.2, p.153.
31 Chambers 1930, vol.2, pp.319–45.
32 Francis Meres, *Palladis Tamia: Wit's Treasury* (London, 1598), as cited in Chambers 1930, vol.2, p.194.
33 Thomas Morley, *The First Book of Ayres or Little Short Songs* (London, 1600); Ernest Brennecke, Jr, 'Shakespeare's Musical Collaboration with Morley', *Publications of the Modern Language Association*, 54, 1939, pp.139–52.
34 Alan H. Nelson, 'George Buc, William Shakespeare, and the Folger *George a Greene*', *Shakespeare Quarterly*, 49, 1998, pp.74–83; and Mark Eccles, 'Sir George Buc, Master of the Revels' in *Sir Thomas Lodge and Other Elizabethans*, ed. C.J. Sisson (Harvard University Press, Cambridge, Mass., 1933), pp.409–506.
35 Alan H. Nelson, 'George Buc, William Shakespeare and the Folger *George a Greene*', *Shakespeare Quarterly* 49, 1998, p.74.

Lorde thow hafte a poynted owte my lyfe
In length lyke as a ſpan
Myne age is nothynge vnto thee
So vayne a thyng is Man
This myrrour meete for all mankynde
ſo viewe & ſtill to beare in myndе
And do not mys
Man walketh lyke a ſhade and dothe
In vayne hym ſelffe annoy
In gettinge goods and cannot tell
Who ſhall the ſame enioye
For tyme brynges youthfull youthes to ag
And age brings Deathe our herytage
When gods will ys
Confyder man howe tyme doth paſſe
And lykewyes knowe all fleſhe is graſſe
For tyme conſumes the ſtrongeſte oke
So deathe at laſte ſhall ſtryke the ſtroke
Thoughe luſtye youthe dothe bewtye beare
Yet youthe to age in tyme doth weare
And age at length a death will brynge
To Rytche, to Poore, Emprour, & Kynge
Therfore ſtill lyue as thow ſholdſt Dye
Thy Soule to ſaue, from Jeopardye
And as thow woldſt be done vnto
So to thy neyghbour alwayes doo
The heauenlye Joyes at lenghe to ſee
Lett fayth in Chryſte thyne Ancor bee
The Lorde that made us knoweth our ſhape
Our moulde and faſhion juſte
Howe weake and frayle our nature is
And howe webe but duſte
And howe the tyme of mortall men
Is lyke the wytheringe haye
Or lyke the flower righte fayer in feilde
That vadethe ſoone awaye

SILENT 'ORATORY'
PORTRAIT PAINTING IN ENGLAND AROUND 1600

TARNYA COOPER

From a distance of four hundred years it is difficult to determine whether the actor and playwright William Shakespeare ever sat for a portrait painter to record his likeness. Today only part of the evidence exists. The painting known as the Chandos portrait (cat.3), probably painted around 1600–10, has the strongest claim to being an authentic lifetime portrait of the playwright. Yet the identity of the sitter remains unproven: the debate is explored in detail on pp.54–61. The existence of this portrait – together with others depicting early seventeenth-century men of middle rank – provokes a broad set of questions allowing us to examine what motivated Londoners of the period, including Shakespeare.

This essay explores the context behind portrait painting in England around 1600. It asks what portraiture meant to men of Shakespeare's social background and what the motivation was for commissioning an artist to make a record of your own features. In making assessments about Shakespeare's likeness, we cannot alter the limited nature of available evidence, but we can cast our gaze as wide as possible in looking to understand the practice of portraiture in the years Shakespeare was most likely to have been portrayed, from 1590 to 1616. This essay therefore considers several portraits depicting men of Shakespeare's rank and provides evidence of portrait painting produced outside the sphere of the court and the nobility.

One problem in assessing the evidence about portraiture in this period is that the terminology for describing a portrait was not clearly defined. The word 'portrait' was far less frequently employed at this date, even though it appears to have had a similar meaning to the word we use today.[1] In legal documents (such as inventories of private houses) and in treatises and stage plays the words 'picture', 'image', 'table' or 'counterfeit' are far more commonly found when a portrait is described. For example, 'My Lord Leysters picture' is recorded in an inventory, and, in Shakespeare's *The Second Part of Henry VI*, Queen Margaret complains that her 'image' (i.e. her portrait) will be nothing more than 'an alehouse sign', while the King's likeness shall be remembered by a statue.[2] The term 'counterfeit' – and sometimes also 'shadow' – was used to refer to portraiture and refers to the portrait's task of duplicating the likeness of an individual in another form; the general usage of the word 'counterfeit', in different types of document, meant it must have been a reasonably well-understood term. The word appears in *Timon of Athens*, when Timon remarks to the Painter: 'Thou draw'st a counterfeit/Best

Emblematic tableau of Youth, Old Age and Father Time, c.1590–1610 (cat.31)

in all Athens'.[3] The word 'table' was also frequently used to refer to the physical characteristics of a painted image because most paintings at this time were made on flat wooden panels, not unlike the detachable boards or 'tables' placed upon trestles to serve food.

Apart from promoting the status of the individual, one of the main reasons that men and women of middle rank commissioned their own painted portrait was to own a likeness that captured their features at a specific moment in time. Since its earliest inception, portraiture had been intended to express this quest for personal immortality.[4] Consequently, for both sitter and their families, portraits served as memorials and aids to memory, both during the life and following the death of the sitter. Certain types of portraits also had a didactic purpose as moral exemplars or as champions of personal sentiments. English portraits in particular frequently included inscriptions such as Latin tags and verses or, at the very least, simple statements about the sitter's age at the date of portrayal, as in the Grafton portrait (cat.4). This type of text on the surface of the picture seems to have purposefully undermined the illusion of a physical presence – the very idea of the portrait as a lifelike replica or 'counterfeit' of the body. An elaborate example is the portrait of the English diplomat Sir Thomas Chaloner (1521–65; fig.11), which includes a long Latin inscription of his own invention on the transitory nature of all earthly things. Chaloner is shown acting out a role as an arbiter of worldly vanity by holding scales that indicate the higher value of intellectual and possibly spiritual endeavour (represented by a book) over worldly treasures and vanities (represented by jewels and a winged world).

This type of portrait makes sense of contemporary descriptions of paintings as 'dumb shows' or 'dumbe oratory' (i.e. silent speaking), the latter term used by Thomas Heywood (1573?–1641) to describe painting in his *Apology for Actors*, published in 1612.[5] Conversely, Heywood also describes plays themselves as 'speaking pictures', indicating an awareness of the link between both plays and painting as media expressing crafted narratives. This idea is evident in a small painting depicting an emblematic scene with Father Time hovering between the personified figures of Youth and Old Age (cat.31). This type of subject was common in printed imagery and wall paintings of the sixteenth century and was designed to serve as a reminder of the transience of human life. Yet here the composition might also owe much to Christian morality plays widely performed across England and Wales in the period before the flowering of English drama in the 1580s and 1590s. The image is full of text in a comic-book style. Indeed, the inscribed words might be understood as speech bubbles, with the static figures effectively playing out their moral message on a stage before the viewer.

At the turn of the seventeenth century, around the time that the Chandos portrait was painted, it was becoming fashionable for aspiring young gentlemen to commission their own portraits. Painted portraits of royalty, nobility and family members had already become a familiar feature in the domestic interiors of Elizabethan and Jacobean nobility and of some of the gentry, where they often hung in long galleries at the top of grand houses or in family rooms. Yet in London from around the 1550s and 1560s (and slightly later in other cities), a number of reasonably prosperous

fig.12 **A gentleman of the Terrick family**, 1590
Unknown English artist
Oil on panel, 451 × 356mm (17 3/4 × 14in)
Private collection

fig.11 **Sir Thomas Chaloner**, 1559
Unknown Netherlandish artist
Before conservation
Oil on panel, 1559
711 × 546mm (28 × 21½in)
National Portrait Gallery, London (NPG 2445)

aspiring city gentlemen, merchants, goldsmiths, lawyers, physicians and others among the civic élite began to commission their own portraits.[6] Most of these images were probably made for display in the sitter's own home, but occasionally portraits were also created as tokens to pass on to friends. One late sixteenth-century portrait of an unknown man at the age of twenty-five (fig.12) includes an inscription that might suggest the interests of a third party. Across the top of the panel the original inscription reads: 'TO PLEASE MY FREND AND NOT MY SELFE'. It is difficult to know whether this sentiment relates to the gift of the portrait or whether it was designed to dispel the charge of vanity. At a time when portraiture was a relatively recent phenomenon, many sitters were among the first in their family to be portrayed, and thus the inscription might simply have been designed to clarify its purpose as a record of likeness, rather than a celebration of self-worth.

The portraits of citizens, professionals, scholars and merchants that remain in existence from around this period are reasonably varied in type and format. However, many of these portraits are indistinguishable from those of the gentry, and, as Shakespeare's own career shows, it was possible for professional men to reconstruct themselves as gentlemen through the acquisition of a family coat of arms (cats 54, 55). Two examples provide an insight into who might be portrayed and in what format. A portrait of an Exeter merchant called Nicholas Spicer (1583–1647), painted in 1611 (fig.13), is a typical example not only of provincial portraiture, but also, more generally, of merchant portraiture produced in the major cities and trading centres of England and Wales. It shows a man soberly dressed in expensive black cloth. As in many merchant portraits of the period, Spicer displays his religious piety through various inscriptions and emblems, which help justify his right to be depicted as an individual who was not one of the nobility or gentry.[7] A London embroiderer, perhaps unsurprisingly, cuts a more glamorous figure in his portrait dated 1614

fig.13 **Nicholas Spicer**, 1611
Unknown English artist
Oil on panel, 1012 × 741mm (39⅞ × 29⅛in)
Royal Albert Memorial Museum and Art Gallery, Exeter

fig.14 **William Brodrick**, 1614
Unknown English artist
Oil on panel, 1118 × 838mm (44 × 33in)
Wandsworth Museum, London

fig.15 **Thomas Whythorne**, 1569
George Gower
Oil on panel, 508 × 241mm (20 × 9½in)
Beinecke Rare Book and Manuscript Library, Yale University

(fig.14). William Brodrick (1558–1620) was a highly successful member of the Broders' (or Embroiderers') Company, who had also purchased the post of the King's Embroiderer, and some time after 1603 he was wealthy enough to buy a country house in Wandsworth. Thus from artisanal roots he established himself as a gentleman.[8]

While many of these early portraits depicting men (and, less frequently, women) from outside the court environment have been lost, some additional evidence about portraiture appears in the personal diaries of citizens and professional men. One of the many references to lending money in the diary of Philip Henslowe (1555?–1616), owner of the Rose Theatre, concerns a loan to the actor William Bourne (or Bird) to pay a painter for his portrait in 1598.[9] An important source on commissioning portraits at this date is the autobiography of a musician, composer and dancing master called Thomas Whythorne (or Whithorne; *c.*1528–96). The account of his life was written in the mid to late sixteenth century and reveals that Whythorne commissioned his own likeness at least five times, in 1549, 1550, 1562, 1569 and 1596. Only the 1569 portrait survives, showing Whythorne aged forty-one (fig.15).[10] This portrait was the source for a woodcut that appeared alongside Whythorne's published verses in 1571.[11] Whythorne may have been unusual in showing an interest in portraiture. Yet the fact that a man of reasonably modest means chose to commission so many portraits of his changing features (the earliest when he was just twenty-one) suggests that more middle-ranking members of society had their portraits painted than has generally been perceived. We know this to be the case because, although survival rates are low, numerous examples still exist depicting aspiring London gentlemen, lawyers, physicians, merchants and other men of talent, wit and ambition.

Nevertheless, Elizabethan and Jacobean society was acutely hierarchical and it is unlikely that the right to portrayal in painted form was considered appropriate for individuals from all social orders. Across sixteenth-century Europe the theory that the purpose of portraiture should be to display virtue seemed self-evident. In sixteenth-century Italy there was a well-established idea that portraiture should depict only the élite, a model that derived from Aristotle, who defined the function of portraiture as the celebration of virtue inherent in individuals. Courtiers and the civic élite who sat for portraits at this period generally found a way of demonstrating their wealth, social station or professional calling. Distinctions in status were largely upheld via personal appearance, and dress, posture and manners were critical to establishing and maintaining the appropriate social standing of a gentleman.

Exactly what the clients of painters in cities such as London were expecting when they commissioned a portrait would depend on how much they chose to pay, and which artist they decided to employ. There is little evidence to explain how private individuals in London around 1600 sought out artists but it is highly likely that almost the whole process, including determining a composition, was directed by the paying patron, who in most cases was also the sitter or his or her kin. When Thomas Whythorne commissioned a portrait in 1549, his own account suggests he was responsible for determining the various elements of the composition, issuing highly specific instructions to the painter to include a figure depicting the muse of music and particular lines of painted text.[12] Most private individuals would have sat for an artist to draw their likeness, at least for the first preparatory drawing and possibly at later stages in the process. At the outset the sitter would probably have indicated the required size of the finished image, the format and potential composition. It is impossible to determine exactly how the process of negotiation between artist and patron took place, but the client was perhaps influenced by past portraits on show in the artist's studio.[13]

If Shakespeare did commission his own portrait and the Chandos portrait is that image, then he chose a competent English painter who could produce an honest likeness of his subject, instead of a foreign-trained artist, who generally offered a more sophisticated likeness and a greater degree of technical polish. At this period English painters were rarely as accomplished as their foreign counterparts, not only because of less intensive training, but also because of a lack of institutional patronage to encourage talent and specialization, for example from the church or local government. In turn, individual English patrons were frequently reluctant to pay the high prices for goods they regarded as simply brightly coloured wooden boards. Portraits were considered curious and endearing mementoes, but in a culture that was largely attuned to the value of materials, rather than the value of skill; painted pictures did not generally command high prices.

English patrons also had different expectations of portraiture from their counterparts in the rest of western Europe. Outside the court, most patrons would have expected little more from portraiture than a competent likeness of their features, as in the portrait of Nicholas Spicer (fig.13). This situation is well summarized by Richard Haydocke (1569/70–*c.*1642), the English translator of Giovanni Paolo Lomazzo's *Trattato dell'Arte della pittura* (1594), who provides two reasons for the decline in painting in England. The first was that the 'buyer' of paintings often refused to 'bestowe anie greate price on a peece of worke', because 'hee thinkes it is not well done'. The second was that the painter did not bother to use 'all his skill', nor take 'all the paines that he could' because of the 'slenderness of his reward'.[14]

In comparison to buying personal items such as jewellery, clothes, or silver or gilt tableware, purchasing a painted portrait was not expensive. It is difficult to guess exactly how much a painting such as the Chandos portrait cost when it was first made, but painters were typically paid less for their work than goldsmiths or tailors. The actor William Bourne borrowed 5*s.* to pay the painter of his portrait – though this sum might have been a final payment for his picture – far wealthier individuals such as Robert Cecil, Earl of Salisbury (1563–1612), paid up to £5 for a portrait in the period 1608 to 1610.[15] However, the price would have depended upon the choice of painter and size of panel and more research on the costs and values of pictures is needed. Even decades later prices of pictures were still low, and the writer Henry Peacham (b.1578, d. in or after 1644) informs us in 1622 that portraits could be bought for a 'triffle'.[16] There is little doubt that most artists working in England around 1600 saw themselves as craftsmen fulfilling a designated task for set fees. The majority of painters did not sign work to mark their creative input, and the idea of an artist as a creative individual intent on claiming authorship was not widespread. Italian art theorists such as Leon Battista Alberti (1404–72) had established that the purpose of representation was to imitate nature. Painting was itself akin to the act of creation and therefore in this sense the act of representation gave praise to God.[17] This theory associating artistic creation with the divine was contrary to Protestant ideology and filtered only slowly into English consciousness, becoming evident in some court circles through Italian influences at the end of the sixteenth century.[18]

The timing of commissioning a portrait could also be significant. Although there were any number of reasons why and when individuals chose to sit for portraits, illness or the death of family members sometimes provided the impetus. Perhaps such events encouraged the living to reflect on the passing of their own lives and gave them the stimulus to capture their appearance while remaining in good health. Numerous portraits of citizens or professionals also appear to have been produced at periods of prosperity, good fortune or upon the acquisition of property. The exact date of the Chandos portrait is not known. It seems likely that Shakespeare chose to be portrayed after 1598, after he had purchased the lease on his house in Stratford-upon-Avon and had been successfully granted a family coat of arms (cat.54).

The autobiography of the scholar and astrologer Simon Forman (1552–1611) provides an interesting comparison, as it refers to his decision to commission his portrait. Forman indicates that in the summer following his marriage to an Ann Baker of Kent in 1599, he 'had' his 'own picture drawen', a term that almost certainly refers to a painted portrait. Forman decided to commission a portrait just when he was increasing his assets, upgrading his wardrobe and personal appearance and generally feathering his nest. He recalled that at the same time he allowed his 'hear [hair] and berd' to grow, purchased leases on several houses, together with a gelding and an elaborate new suit of clothes (listed as a 'purple gowne', a 'cap', 'cote', velvet 'breches', a 'taffety cloke' and a hat), as well as new attire for his wife and many other 'pictures'.[19] Thus, for Forman, the act of commissioning a portrait became a rite of passage in fashioning his status as a gentleman.

Even if the monetary value and the broad appreciation of the visual arts in England did not compare with continental Europe during the sixteenth century, the art of capturing personal likeness via portraiture thrived. As in other parts of Europe, such as the Netherlands, portraiture in England evolved to depict new groups of sitters.[20] Yet, from 1590 to 1616, there was no fully established tradition of depicting poets, playwrights or actors, and the question of whether such individuals were worthy subjects for visual representation would have still been at issue. Of Shakespeare's friends and professional colleagues, there are only a few portraits that can be securely identified and they are mainly portraits of writers, such as Ben Jonson (cat.83) and John Fletcher (cat.84).[21] Like the sitter in the Chandos portrait, these men are generally shown in painted portraits without specific attributes, coats of arms or other identifying features.

Although little evidence has survived, it is clear that a genre of literary portraiture was emerging around the 1590s and 1600s. A highly unusual informal portrait of the metaphysical poet John Donne (1572–1631; cat.80) dates from 1595 to 1600, when Donne was writing amorous poetic verse on love and spiritual fulfilment. The picture shows the sitter in a self-conscious, contemplative and melancholic mood, wearing a broad-brimmed hat and an artistically composed array of lace collars, open to the neck. It is one of the earliest examples of this type of introspective author portrait, which does not champion the social status of the sitter but playfully presents him as individual, with a creative soul of hidden depths. It was bequeathed to Robert Ker, 1st Earl of Ancrum (1578–1654) in Donne's will, where it was described as 'that picture of mine which is taken in the shadows', indicating the poet's awareness of the curious nature of the composition.[22]

Recent research has authenticated another portrait depicting an English poet from the same period. This portrait of a 36-year-old man wearing a laurel wreath, dating from 1599 (cat.81), is probably the poet and playwright Michael Drayton (1563–1631), who collaborated with the Jacobean playwright Thomas Dekker (*c.*1572–1632) and dramatist John Webster (1578/80–1636?), among others. The laurel crown had associations with ancient victories but was used in Renaissance portraiture to herald literary and artistic achievement, and this image is one of the earliest examples of an English laureate portrait. Under Elizabeth I no official position of Poet Laureate existed, but Michael Drayton is depicted in later portraits wearing the laurel crown.[23]

Even before the emergence of author portraiture, what sort of contact might the poet William Shakespeare have had with visual imagery? When Shakespeare settled in London, probably in the late 1580s, he would have encountered examples of what was called 'curious painting' – what today we would understand as fine art – within the houses of his patrons, such as Lord Hunsdon (the Lord Chamberlain; cat.45) and the 3rd Earl of Southampton (cats 46, 47) and again when on tour, visiting the houses of nobility and wealthy gentry. As the Lord Chamberlain's Men (later the King's Men) performed at court, Shakespeare would probably have seen paintings hung in royal palaces in and around London, for example at Whitehall, Hampton Court and Greenwich, and also at the private homes of those entertaining the monarch. These opportunities must have increased after 1603, when Shakespeare and about eight to ten other company members became royal servants, wearing the livery of the Crown. For example, in November 1603 the King's Men performed at Wilton House (home of the Earl of Pembroke) and in December for four successive nights at Hampton Court, and the following year at Whitehall in February, November and December.[24] Shakespeare would undoubtedly have seen numerous portraits, tapestries and painted curiosities, perhaps, for example, the extraordinary anamorphic portrait of Edward VI (fig.16), which was seen at Whitehall by a number of different visitors from 1584 to 1613.[25] This image was a playful perspective device, which could only be resolved as a portrait in its correct proportions when viewed through a hole in the side of the frame. The author of the sonnets and *The Tragedy of King Richard II* was clearly aware of these types of devices, which could well have been more widespread than surviving examples suggest.[26]

A reasonable number of references to various portrait types, including miniatures, life-size paintings on panel and canvas, and statues, regularly appear in stage plays by Shakespeare and his contemporaries. Most of the audience at stage plays were familiar with the concept of a portrait (or perhaps, more accurately, the idea of painted

fig.16 **Anamorphic portrait of King Edward VI**, 1546
William Scrots
Oil on panel, 425 × 1600mm
(16¾ × 63in)
National Portrait Gallery, London
(NPG 1299)

heads); after all they could be seen hanging in the streets on painted inn signs and were also found as illustrations in popular printed broadsides and ballads sold by London stationers. In common with the prevailing view of the visual arts at this period, pictures were frequently described in plays in disparaging terms that focused on their static nature and the lack of skill in depiction, or, when well painted, their capacity to trick or deceive the viewer, in line with Protestant concerns about religious imagery. For example, Coriolanus' honour is, unless exercised, considered 'no better than picture-like to hang on th' wall' and, in *The Merchant of Venice*, Portia compares a man to a picture, and complains 'who can converse with a dumb show?'[27] Yet in plays such as *The Winter's Tale*, *Hamlet* and *The Merchant of Venice* portraits play parts in the narrative, beyond the role of props or simple curiosities, and subtly probe, or sometimes parody, the idea of deceptive likeness in a way that reflects tellingly on specific characters.[28]

The exchange of portrait miniatures as tokens of affection was reasonably common among Elizabethan and Jacobean courtiers and regularly appears in Shakespeare's plays and poetry. In the first lines of Sonnet 24, Shakespeare uses the idea of idolizing a lover in the 'table' or portrait within the author's imagination: 'Mine eye hath play'd the painter and hath stell'd/Thy beauty's form in table of my heart;/My body is the frame wherein 'tis held.'[29] This passionate language of possession casts light on the desire to own a likeness of a lover as a prelude to, or substitute for, bodily possession.

Although Shakespeare was familiar with the art of portraiture as an artistic genre and understood the roles that portraits might play, this alone does not necessarily mean that he would have sat for his own portrait. It is the existence of the posthumous engraving by Martin Droeshout the Younger (1601–after 1639) published in 1623 (cat.1) and the memorial bust erected in 1626 (cat.2) that makes this prospect highly probable, as these images must have been based on a lifetime portrait of Shakespeare, not an imaginary source. Exactly what this was is difficult to determine (see the discussion on the Flower portrait, cat.8), but the prototype has probably since perished. The Chandos portrait (discussed at greater length in cat.3) certainly had no link to the engraving, but a broad overall facial likeness, together with the development of author portraiture, means that its claim cannot be discounted. Like a number of other portraits produced around this time, such as the intimate portrait of a man, probably Nathan Field (cat.99), it shares an introspective mode of representation and appears to represent an individual who felt no need to make literal references to his status or professional calling.

It is very interesting that the idea of owning a portrait of the increasingly fashionable poet William Shakespeare is parodied in an anonymous play of 1599, *The Return from Parnassus*. Performed by the students of St John's College, Cambridge, the play has a foolish fop-like character called 'Gullio' who has become so enamoured of Shakespeare's erotic poems *Venus and Adonis* and *Lucrece* that he wants to own a portrait of the author as inspiration for his own literary endeavours. Thus Gullio declares: 'O' sweet Master Shakespeare, I'll have his picture in my study at court.'[30] This reference perhaps tells us more about conventions in drama and the practice of exchanging portrait miniatures than it does about the actual existence of portraits of Shakespeare in 1599. Gullio's desire to idolize a picture of an author of erotic poetry is evidence of his light, foolish and boastful character, and probably reflects the unknown author's view of 'wanton' poetry. Gullio's general behaviour satirizes the pretensions of gentlemen of the period, and he is little more than a generic character type, 'a Fly blowne gull that faine would be a Gallant', familiar from many plays of this period.[31] It is very unlikely that printed portraits of Shakespeare did exist at this date, as engraved portraits of authors were few and far between and were not apparently sold as single plates, but were designed to accompany published works as frontispieces.[32] Despite the many printed volumes of his plays that exist from Shakespeare's lifetime – creating a body of mass media – no examples of contemporary printed images survive.

We are unlikely ever to know whether the Chandos portrait is a true likeness of the actor, poet and playwright William Shakespeare. What we do know is that a man of Shakespeare's rank and social standing was likely to commission a portrait and that a genre of author portraiture was emerging around 1600. Not only is the Chandos portrait similar to other known portraits of writers, our knowledge of the portrait's provenance is also highly suggestive. Although the case remains unproven, by accepting the fragility of historical knowledge, we can begin to explore the wider frameworks in which portraits played their parts as household goods, emblems of status or sentiment, tokens of love and affection and objects of inspiration and desire.

Many pictures have undoubtedly perished, including, most probably, the original source for the posthumous engraving of Shakespeare by Martin Droeshout. This is also true of portraits of private individuals outside the nobility and the landed gentry. For those who did not have property to be passed down over generations, portraits of ancestors, especially those from three generations or more, could easily lose their meaning as the individuals concerned were not known to the current generation. Once outside the family circle, portraits of private citizens were of little financial value and were far more likely to be recycled as furniture or discarded. In an environment where paintings were considered as disposable goods, the Chandos portrait has survived the past four hundred years as a result of its early identification as a lifetime portrait of Shakespeare. Its iconic status has probably led to its current worn condition, and near relic-like state, and so, whoever the sitter is, its long history as a celebrated portrait of Shakespeare can never be unravelled.

Notes

1 In *The Merchant of Venice*, the Prince of Arragon chooses a 'casket' wherein an image of Portia is supposed to be 'contained' but he finds instead 'the portrait of a blinking idiot' (Act II, Scene ix, line 53). In reference to his uncle, Hamlet recalls: 'For by the image of my cause I see/The portraiture of his' (Act V, Scene ii, lines 78–9). In the latter context the word 'portraiture' is used to mean 'reflection' or 'vision'.

2 See Foister 1981, pp.273–82, and *The Second Part of Henry VI* (Act III, Scene ii, line 81).

3 *Timon of Athens* (Act V, Scene i, line 78). It also appears in *Hamlet* when the Prince confronts his mother with portraits of both his father and his uncle: 'Look here upon this picture, and on this,/The counterfeit presentment of two brothers./ See what a grace was seated on this brow' (Act III, Scene iv, lines 52–4).

4 See Foister 1995, pp.163–80 (p.168 on Pliny).

5 Thomas Heywood, *An Apology for Actors* (Nicholas Okes, London, 1612), fol. B3v. For a commentary on the uses of these terms, see M.E. Hazard, 'The Anatomy of "Liveliness" as a Concept in Renaissance Aesthetics' in *Journal of Aesthetics and Art Criticism*, vol.33, 1975, pp.407–18; and D. Chambers, '"A Speaking Picture": Some Ways of Proceeding in Literature and the Fine Arts in the late Sixteenth and Early Seventeenth Centuries' in Hunt 1971, pp.28–57.

6 See Tittler 2004. For a body of evidence of over seventy portraits of mostly non-court sitters, see Cooper 2002.

7 Cooper 2002, vol.2, pp.387–8.

8 The elaborate coat of arms on William Brodrick's portrait is a later addition – the Brodrick family did not acquire a coat of arms until 1649. See Cooper 2002, vol.2, pp.5–7; Ensing 1991, pp.1–5; and Tipping 1925.

9 The reference reads: 'lent vnto wm borne the 14 of July 1598 for to geue the painter in earneste of his pictor of the some of V s'. Foakes 2002, p.93. No evidence of this painting survives.

10 It is clear that this type of survival rate is not unusual and it is likely that between fifty and eighty per cent of paintings produced in the sixteenth century have not survived to the present day. Certain types of portrait have been more vulnerable to changes in taste.

11 Thomas Whythorne, *Medivs: Of Songes, for three, fower, and five voices,* and *Triplex: Of Songes for three…* and *Bassavs: Of Songs for three …* (John Day, London, 1571).

12 Whythorne writes: 'I caused a table to be made to hang in my chamber, whereon was painted, in oil colours, the figure and image of a young woman playing upon a lute, who I gave the name Terpsichore [the muse of music and dancing] …. I caused to be painted by and with her in the same table' the other elements of the composition, including further instruments and a book of 'pricksong' (music for singing). Whythorne's diary also reveals that he 'caused a pair of virginals to be painted [with] mine own counterfeit or picture, likewise playing upon the lute; and in the same virginals was written these verse following "The pleasures that I take, Now in my youthful years, The same shall me forsake when hoary age appears"'; Whithorne 1962, p.11.

13 When Thomas Whythorne visited an artist's studio in London, he saw many portraits of both young and old people, which presumably were either in progress or remained uncollected. Whithorne 1962, p.115.

14 Giovanni Paolo Lomazzo, *A Tracte containing the Artes of Curious Paintinge, Caruinge & Buildinge*, incomplete translation by Richard Haydocke, 1598, sig .V.

15 Hearn 1995, cat.119.

16 Henry Peacham, *The Compleat Gentleman* (John Marriott, London, sold by Francis Constable, 1634), p.8.

17 Leonardo da Vinci (1452–1519) considered the artist's creative energy or the individual creative force behind marks made on paper or canvas were implanted in the mind by God, and thus in turn the practice of drawing (and painting) was a re-enactment of creation. This idea led to an understanding of representation where the artist's own creative agency was perceived as inherent within the work. See Anthony Blunt, *Artistic Theory in Italy 1540–1600* (Clarendon Press, Oxford, 1940).

18 An anonymous English interlude published in 1600, entitled *The Wisdom of Doctor Dodypoll*, provides a rehearsal of the divine potential of artistic creation already familiar in Italian art theory. The play describes the antics of a German painter of noble birth called 'Lasingbergh' and a noble gentleman named 'Alberdure' (a version of Albrecht Dürer) and opens with an elaborate dialogue in praise of painting by Lasingbergh: 'Looke on the former fields adorn'd with flowers, How much is nature's painting honour'd there?… And to conclude, Nature her self diuine, In al things she hath made, is a meer Painter.' M.N. Matson (ed.), *The Wisdom of Doctor Dodypoll* c.1600 (Oxford University Press, Oxford, 1965), sig. A3v.

19 Simon Forman, *The Autobiography and Personal Diary of Dr. Simon Forman, The Celebrated Astrologer, From A.D. 1552 to A.D. 1602, from unpublished Manuscripts in the Ashmolean Museum, Oxford*, ed. James Orchard Halliwell (privately printed, 1849), p.31.

20 Woodall 1997, p.2.

21 It is interesting that the portrait of Ben Jonson appears to have been painted for a noble patron (possibly George Villiers, Duke of Buckingham), indicating the beginning of a demand for portraits of talented writers.

22 Strong 1969, vol.1, p.66.

23 See, for example, the portrait of Michael Drayton (1628) in the Dulwich Picture Gallery and the bust of Drayton (*c*.1631) in Westminster Abbey. See also Edward Kemper Broadus, *The Laureateship: A Study of the Office of the Poet Laureate in England, with some Account of the Poets* (Clarendon Press, Oxford, 1921), p.37.

24 Chambers 1923, vol.4, pp.116–19.

25 Strong 1969, vol.1, pp.89–90.

26 See, for example, *The Tragedy of King Richard II* 'Perspectives, which rightly gazed upon./ show nothing but confusion–eyed awry,/ Distinguish form' (Act II, Scene ii, lines 18–20). See also Allan Shickman, 'Turning Pictures in Shakespeare's England' in *The Art Bulletin*, vol.15, 1977, pp.67–70.

27 *Coriolanus* (Act 1, Scene iii, lines 10–11) and *The Merchant of Venice* (Act 1, Scene ii, lines 69–70).

28 For further commentary on Shakespeare's references to the visual arts, see Hunt 1985, pp.425–31, and Fairchild 1937, pp.104–36.

29 Sonnet 24, lines 1–3.

30 J.B Leishman, *The Three Parnassus Plays 1558–1601* (Ivor Nichols and Watson, London, 1949), Act IV, Scene i, line 1201. Later in this play Gullio declares: 'Let this duncified world esteeme of Spencer and Chaucer, I'll worship Sweet Mr. Shakespeare and to honoure him will lay his Venus and Adonis under my pillow.'

31 *Apology for Actors*, 1612, introductory address from John Taylor to Thomas Heywood, f.A7v.

32 Engraved portraits of poets and playwrights used as frontispieces were rare before 1610. See, for example, George Chapman (cat.90), and also Samuel Daniel's engraved portrait by Thomas Cockson in the quarto edition of *The Civile Wars betweene the Howses of Lancaster and Yorke…* (1609) and Robert Vaughan's engraved portrait of Ben Jonson (*c*.1625), later published as frontispieces in 1640. From the 1620s independent portraits of writers began to circulate independently.

Catalogue

Key to contributors and note to readers

ROBERT BEARMAN — RB
Shakespeare Birthplace Trust, Stratford-upon-Avon

BEATRIZ CHADOUR-SAMPSON — BCS
Independent scholar

TARNYA COOPER — TC
National Portrait Gallery, London

ANN DONNELLY — AD
Shakespeare Birthplace Trust, Stratford-upon-Avon

JANE EADE — JE
Schroder collection, London

EDWINA EHRMAN — EE
Museum of London

ERIN BLAKE — EB
Folger Shakespeare Library, Washington, DC

HAZEL FORSYTH — HF
Museum of London

ANDREW GURR — AG
University of Reading

SOPHIE LEE — SL
Victoria and Albert Museum, London

CATHARINE MACLEOD — CM
National Portrait Gallery, London

SUSAN NORTH — SN
Victoria and Albert Museum, London

ANGUS PATTERSON — AP
Victoria and Albert Museum, London

NICK DE SOMOGYI — NS
Independent scholar

JENNY TIRAMANI — JT
Costume designer

STANLEY WELLS — SW
Shakespeare Birthplace Trust, Stratford-upon-Avon

HENRY R. WOUDHUYSEN — HRW
University College London

The information in this catalogue has relied on primary sources, various published sources, museum records and physical examination *in situ*. The catalogue is a full record of objects shown at the National Portrait Gallery, London; not all the objects cited here are displayed at The Yale Center for British Art, New Haven (p.239).

A few other points regarding the catalogue entries may be helpful. Measurements of the paintings are given when unframed. It has not always been possible to measure paintings unframed and where stated some measurements are approximate. The convention of reproducing miniatures at actual size has not been observed in all cases for reasons of legibility. Inscriptions on paintings and translations have only been given where they add to the meaning of the object. For each entry, known provenance is given with gaps indicated by an ellipsis. Only selected literary references are cited. Literature cited in abbreviated form in the catalogue entries and essays is listed in full in the bibliography. Quotations from William Shakespeare correspond with Stanley Wells and Gary Taylor (eds), The Oxford Shakespeare – The Complete Works (Oxford University Press, Oxford, 2005). The main source for names and dates is *The Oxford Dictionary of National Biography* (Oxford University Press, Oxford 2005). Spellings have been modernized except for those of the original titles of publications. All dates are modernized following the calendar beginning on 1 January (i.e. the Gregorian 'New Style' calendar).

It is difficult to convey a sense of relative monetary values. It may be helpful to note, however, that in 1600 an average labourer's wage would have been about eight pence a week, and a craftsman might have received a shilling (twelve pence). Admission to a public theatre cost a minimum of one penny, and a printed play sold for about six pence.

SHAKESPEARE'S FACE

His known likeness

Determining what Shakespeare actually looked like is not straightforward. The most important evidence emerges after his death in 1616. Two posthumous portraits provide what must be a reasonably accurate likeness. Around 1620 a memorial bust showing a balding, solidly built citizen was installed in the parish church of Shakespeare's home town Stratford-upon-Avon. In 1623 a lively portrait engraving showing a younger man accompanied the first collected edition of his plays.

These two images must have been commissioned by Shakespeare's friends and family and provide a useful comparison in the search for a lifetime portrait of the poet.

1. William Shakespeare, from the First Folio, *c*.1623

Martin Droeshout the Younger (1601–after 1639)[1]

Engraving in the first state, bound into a printed book
340 × 225mm (13⅜ × 8⅞in)
Signed bottom left: 'Martin Droeshout sculpsit London'
The British Library, London, c.39 k.15, open at title page

Provenance Purchased by the British Library in 1922

Literature Friswell 1864, pp.38–45; A.M. Hind, *Engraving in England in the 16th and 17th Centuries*, vol.2 (Cambridge University Press, Cambridge, 1952), pp.341–66; Charlton Hinman, *Printing and Proof-Reading of the First Folio of Shakespeare* (Clarendon Press, Oxford, 1963); Fredson Bowers (ed.), *Elizabethan Dramatists, Dictionary of Literary Biography*, vol.62 (Gale Research, Detroit, 1987), p.338; Edmond 1991, pp.339–44; Schoenbaum 1981, pp.166–70; Christian Schuckman, 'The Engraver of the First Folio: Portrait of William Shakespeare', *Print Quarterly*, VIII, 1991, 1, pp.40–3; June Schlueter, 'Martin Droeshout Sculpsit: Reassessing the Folio Engraving of Shakespeare', *Shakespeare Quarterly*, forthcoming[1]

This engraved portrait appeared in the first printed edition of Shakespeare's plays, known as the First Folio, published posthumously in 1623. Alongside the Stratford funeral monument (cat.2), it is the only portrait that definitely provides us with a reasonable idea of Shakespeare's appearance. It was probably commissioned specifically for the title page by John Heminges (bap.1566, d.1630) and Henry Condell (1576?– 1627), Shakespeare's fellow actors, who were responsible for compiling the volume. It is likely that the surviving members of Shakespeare's family saw it, and Ben Jonson (1572–1637) praised the artist's ability to capture Shakespeare's 'face' (fig.17).

It is not clear what the original source of the engraving was, but the engraver must have based his likeness on an existing lifetime portrait, now lost. It has been suggested that the engraver copied an existing miniature, but there is no specific evidence to support this.[2] It is equally possible that the source for the Droeshout engraving was a small-scale panel or canvas painting, of which the probable portrait of Richard Burbage (1568– 1619; cat.51) is a good example. The historian Mary Edmond has proposed that the model for the Droeshout engraving was the 1595 portrait by Marcus Gheeraerts the Younger that antiquarian George Vertue mentioned in his notebooks of 1719 (figs 20, 21, p.55).

In comparison with other northern European countries, the art of printmaking in England was underdeveloped and there were relatively few skilled engravers. Yet even by the less exacting standards observed in England, the Droeshout engraving is poorly proportioned. In particular, the head appears slightly too large for the body, which suggests that the artist had access to an image of the head and shoulders alone and therefore was obliged to work on the costume independently, without the benefit of a model.

The clothing provides some clues that help to date the image. The wide starched linen collar is held out around the neck by a support known as a 'supportasse' (cat.41) stiffened with wire, whalebone or pasteboard. This type of collar with triangular sewn darts fanning out from the face appears in portraits that date from around 1604 to 1613, such as the painting of Phineas Pett (fig.18), although it was not until the 1630s that the starched collar or band went out of fashion. It is odd that the artist does not depict the supportasse under the collar on the left side which again suggests that he did not work from a life model or an image clearly showing the costume. The doublet dates from around 1610 to 1620 and is decorated with rows of silk and/or metal lace to provide a contrast with the darker fabric. The large number of close buttons (made of wood and covered in either metal or silk thread) ensured a tight fit to the body, and they are accurately depicted, all facing to the right, as a result of being pulled taut by the doublet as shown in the replica (fig.19). The artist, however, had some difficulty in depicting the costume on a body that is turned slightly to the left: the front panels and sleeves of the doublet are less accurately portrayed, particularly on the left side, where the braid fails to match the correct cut of the doublet and follow the curve under the arm.[3] As a consequence of these defects, the engraving has been regarded as a poor representation of Shakespeare.

In the printed folio the engraving is accompanied by a commentary written by Ben Jonson, which heralds the virtues of Shakespeare's wit over his physical likeness:

To the Reader.

This Figure, that thou here seest put,
It was for gentle Shakespeare cut;
Wherein the Grauer had a strife
with Nature, to out-doo the life :
O, could he but haue drawne his wit
As well in brasse, as he hath hit
His face ; the Print would then surpasse
All, that was euer writ in brasse.
But, since he cannot, Reader, looke
Not on his Picture, but his Booke.

B. I.

fig.17 **Ben Johnson's preface to the First Folio**, 1623
The British Library, London

MR. WILLIAM

SHAKESPEARES

COMEDIES,
HISTORIES, &
TRAGEDIES.

Publiſhed according to the True Originall Copies.

LONDON

Printed by Iſaac Iaggard, and Ed. Blount. 1623.

Playing down the value of visual representation was part of the standard rhetoric of this period. For example, in Thomas Heywood's *Apology for Actors*, published in 1612, the ability of poetry and plays to recreate experience is favourably compared to visual imagery: 'The visage is not better cut in brasse/Nor can the Carver so express the face/As doth the Poets Penne whose arts surpasse,/to give mens lives and virtues their due grace.'[4] Thus Jonson's verses draw our attention away from the image to Shakespeare's work, published here for the first time, precisely because no likeness could ever do justice to his literary achievement.

Some confusion surrounds the name of the engraver Martin Droeshout, who signs his name at the base. Two related artists of this name were alive at this date. Droeshout the Elder (*c.*1560s–1642) was the son of Protestant refugees who arrived in England from Brussels. He became a member of the Painter-Stainers' Company, settling in the parish of St Olave Hart Street in London around 1605. However, this engraving is more frequently ascribed to his nephew, known as Martin Droeshout the Younger (1601– after 1639). About twenty-three engravings, including portraits and frontispieces, are considered to have been produced by his hand. Around 1635, Martin Droeshout the Younger emigrated to Spain where he continued to work as an engraver.

fig.18 **Phineas Pett**, c.1612
Unknown artist
Oil on panel, 1187 × 997mm (46¾ × 39¼in)
National Portrait Gallery, London (NPG 2035)

fig.19 **Replica of buttons and braid**, 2005
The sample is one of many possible interpretations of the decoration on the doublet worn by Shakespeare in the Droeshout engraving. There is no clue as to the colour of the doublet, although the heavy engraved lines suggest a dark colour. Possible fabrics for the doublet are leather or wool, whilst other colours might be dark grey, brown or mulberry.

In the course of the seventeenth century the engraving was issued on four separate occasions to accompany versions of the Folio. As small changes to the engraved plate took place on several occasions, copies of the print exist in several different stages (called states). The first state is very rare and exists in only four impressions, of which this example from the British Library is one (the others are at the Bodleian Library, Oxford [cat.117], and the Folger Shakespeare Library, Washington, DC). The impressions of the first state were printed by the artist when the engraving was nearing completion, and may have been bound in some of the earliest printings of the book. The artist made some modifications to the image very soon afterwards and the second state includes darker cross-hatching upon the right collar, extending the shadowing along the jaw line out to the edge of the hair, as well as a broader, thicker moustache. The third state had only a very small amount of retouching, in particular, highlights in the eyes, probably done to improve the worn image, and is mostly found in the Second Folio of 1632 and the Third Folio of 1663–4. A fourth state dating from 1685 was greatly reworked. By this time the plate must have been very worn. TC

1 I am grateful to June Schlueter for allowing me to read a copy of her article on the Droeshout engraving before publication in the *Shakespeare Quarterly*.
2 While most surviving miniatures produced around 1600 depict exceptionally wealthy courtiers, there are several examples of unknown gentlemen and men of slightly more modest means by both Nicholas Hilliard (*c.*1547–1619) and Isaac Oliver (*c.*1565–1617). A small number of professional miniature painters, as well as trained amateurs, were perhaps painting for a wider audience than existing images indicate. Hilliard, the leading miniaturist of his day, commented that a number of artists who had trained with him now 'pleased the common sort [i.e. those outside the court] exceeding well'; see Mary Edmond, *Hilliard and Oliver: The Lives and Works of Two Great Miniaturists* (Hale, London, 1983), pp.72–3.
3 I am grateful to the costume historians Jenny Tiramani and Susan North for advice on the costume shown in this portrait.
4 Thomas Heywood, *An Apology for Actors* (Nicholas Okes, London, 1612), sig B3v.

2. Plaster cast of William Shakespeare's effigy, from part of the monument erected in his name in Holy Trinity Church, Stratford-upon-Avon, *c.*1620

Possibly by Garrat Johnson (Gheerart Janssen) the Younger (active 1612–23)

Plaster cast
806mm (31¾in) high
National Portrait Gallery, London (NPG 1735)

Provenance Purchased 1912 (cast from copy of a mould taken from the original in 1851)

Literature Chambers 1930, vol.2, pp.182–5; Schoenbaum 1981, pp.156–61

A monument in William Shakespeare's name was erected in the chancel of Holy Trinity Church, Stratford-upon-Avon, soon after his death in April 1616. Shakespeare left no money for a monument and we must assume that those who paid for it, whether family members or business colleagues, were satisfied that it was a good likeness. On this assumption, the bust, as one of the few authentic representations of Shakespeare's appearance, has attracted much attention over many years. In the mid eighteenth century some repainting was undertaken, but in the 1790s the vicar was persuaded by Shakespeare's biographer, Edmond Malone (1741–1812), to paint it white. In 1861, this process was reversed and the colouring restored on the basis of what was discovered beneath the recent paint layer.

A reference to 'thy Stratford Monument', which occurs in a poem by Leonard Digges (1588–1635) published in the First Folio of 1623, is usually taken as the latest date for its erection, but it no doubt dates from several years before that. According to a note made in 1653 by William Dugdale (1605–86), the author of *The Antiquities of Warwickshire*, the sculptor was 'Garrat Johnson', or Gheerart Janssen, son of the Dutch émigré of the same name who had settled in London in 1567. Dugdale may have been misinformed, as Garrat the Younger is otherwise recorded as having produced only an untraced marble basin for Hatfield House, Hertfordshire. However, the Johnson or Janssen family business was run from Southwark, not far from the Globe Theatre, and, given Dugdale's general reliability and assuming that Shakespeare's business associates in London would have been involved in commissioning the work, the attribution to Johnson remains a possibility. An impressive monument to John Combe (d.1614), now standing within a few feet of Shakespeare's, and which Dugdale also attributed to Johnson, should have been erected (if the terms of his will had been observed) by April 1615, a year before Shakespeare died. This raises interesting but unresolved questions about the relationship between the Combe and Shakespeare families, and the Johnson or Janssen family and Shakespeare's London friends. RB

LIKENESS AND MYTH

The search for Shakespeare's portrait

The search for an authentic portrait of William Shakespeare began in the mid 1600s and continues to the present day. The six portraits discussed in this section are among the many images once considered to represent him. They are now titled by the names of former owners or the presumed artist. New information based on recent technical analysis, published here for the first time, rules out some of the portraits as lifetime images, and provides fascinating new insights into others. But do any of them depict Shakespeare and what do we mean by an 'authentic portrait'?

It is highly probable that Shakespeare had his portrait painted during his lifetime. The bust and the engraving made after his death (cats 1, 2) almost certainly derived from earlier sources. Portraits exist of numerous other writers at this period (cats 80–91) and, as an acclaimed author, Shakespeare was both important and wealthy enough to have commissioned a likeness. The 'Chandos' portrait appears to have been regarded as authentic within living memory of the playwright. Apparently painted from life, it shows a gentle brown-eyed man, probably in his late thirties or early forties, staring out at the viewer. The 'Grafton' and 'Sanders' portraits were both made within Shakespeare's lifetime and show respectively a handsome grey-eyed young man of twenty-four and a slightly older man painted in 1603, when Shakespeare would have been forty. The 'Janssen' portrait is in a different, but equally fascinating, category as it is an original portrait of another man that was once fabricated to look more like other images of Shakespeare. Both the 'Soest' and the 'Flower' portraits date from after Shakespeare's death. They are not authentic likenesses, but they have provided highly convincing images of Shakespeare for their different viewers across the ages.

Together these images represent a visual history of interest in Shakespeare. Regardless of whether they represent him, they reflect our desire to encounter the expressive features and ponder the emotional character of the playwright whose work brilliantly reflects the universal passions of human nature.

cat.3 **William Shakespeare?, known as the Chandos portrait**

3. William Shakespeare?, known as the Chandos portrait, *c*.1600–10

Attributed to John Taylor (d.1651)

Oil on canvas
552 × 438mm (21¾ × 17¼in)
National Portrait Gallery, London (NPG 1)

Provenance Probably John Taylor, painter (and player?); Sir William Davenant; Thomas Betterton; certainly Robert Keck, FRS, Inner Temple (d.1719); Francis Keck of Great Tew; John Keck and his wife Margaret (née Poole); John Nichol of Southwick; James Brydges (3rd Duke of Chandos) in 1789; Marquess of Buckingham and his wife Anna Elizabeth Brydges in 1796; sold Stowe sale in 1848; bought by H. Rodd for Earl of Ellesmere and presented to the Gallery in 1856 as the founding portrait.

Literature Boaden 1824, pp.41–59; Friswell 1864, pp.28–37; M.H. Spielmann 1907, pp.7–9; Strong 1969, pp.276–84; Schoenbaum 1981, pp.175–80; Edmond 1982, pp.146–9; David Piper, *The Image of the Poet* (Clarendon Press, Oxford, 1982), pp. 18–22; Darren Emerson Lay, 'The Taylor of St Paul's Who Painted the Chandos Portrait', *Times Literary Supplement*, 24 May 1996, p.17

Illustrated on previous page

Early history and identification as a portrait of Shakespeare

This portrait was the first painting presented to the National Portrait Gallery in the year it was founded, 1856. Since the mid seventeenth century this simple image of a middle-aged Jacobean man has been considered to represent William Shakespeare. No other painting has had such a long history as a reputed portrait of Shakespeare. While there is much evidence to support this claim – such as the early history and provenance of the picture and the development of author portraiture in this period – there is no conclusive proof of the identity of the sitter.

The identification of a portrait of this date without an inscription or coat of arms is always complicated, and without an authenticated lifetime portrait of Shakespeare or further documentary evidence, the claim that the Chandos portrait represents Shakespeare is likely to remain unproven. We have instead only two posthumous sources, a stylized engraving and memorial bust (cats 1 and 2), to provide an approximate comparison. Furthermore, the Chandos portrait is in a damaged condition. Yet enough of the original image survives to show a brown-eyed man with an open and rather gentle face making direct eye contact with the viewer. It is these likeable features that have inspired numerous copies to be engraved (and painted), and generations of devotees to believe in the identity of the portrait.

Given the increasing popularity of portraiture among wealthy and aspiring Londoners, it is perfectly possible that Shakespeare, as a man of moderate wealth with an accepted claim to gentility, sat for a portrait during his years in London. The Chandos portrait is certainly a genuine early seventeenth-century picture and it does fit into an emerging tradition of author portraiture (see pp.33–43). Probably painted between 1600 and 1610, it appears to represent a man in his mid to late thirties or early forties. At this time Shakespeare would have been between thirty-six and forty-six years old, which fits the appearance of the sitter in this portrait.

The trail to identify the sitter leads back to a documentary source that records the early owners of the painting. The notebooks of the eighteenth-century writer and antiquarian George Vertue (1684–1756), written in 1719, provides two references to its early whereabouts. They read as follows, with slightly later insertions in bold:

> The picture of Shakespear ['the only' crossed out] **one** Original in Possesion/of Mr. Keyck of the Temple. he bought for forty guuines/of **Mr. Baterton** who bought it of Sr W. Davenant. **to whom it was left by will of John Taylor**. who had/ it of Shakespear. it was painted by one Taylor a Player and painter contemp: with Shakes and his intimate friend'. [The name 'Richard Burbridge' is crossed out in the margin; fig.20]

> Mr. Betterton told Mr Keck several times that the/ Picture of Shakespeare he had, was painted by one John Taylor/a Player, who acted for Shakespear and this John Taylor/in his will left it to Sr Willm. Davenant. & at/the death of Sir Will Davenant – Mr Betterton bought/it, & at his death Mr. Keck bought it in whose/poss. it now is'.[1] ['1719' in the margin; fig.21]

Vertue's evidence indicates that the ownership of the painting could be traced back to a contemporary of Shakespeare. Yet his comments date from over 100 years after Shakespeare's death and it is clear that the early history of the picture relies upon hearsay, half-remembered facts and assumptions by Robert Keck, the owner in 1719, and, significantly, upon the past reminiscences of those who had previously owned the picture: Thomas Betterton (1635–1710) and Sir William Davenant (1606–68). Vertue states that the picture passed into the hands of a painter called John Taylor (see 'Artist' below) either during the lifetime or at the death of Shakespeare. Vertue's narrative perhaps says as much about the growing interest in images of Shakespeare in the late seventeenth and early eighteenth century as it does about the actual identity of the sitter in this portrait.

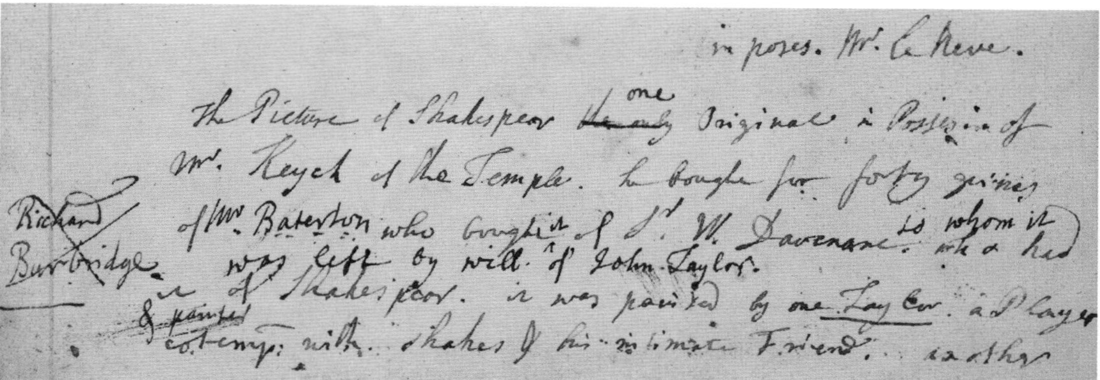
in posess. Mr. Le Neve.

Richard Burbridge

The Picture of Shakespear the one Original in Possession of Mr. Keyck of the Temple. he bought for forty guineas of Mr. Baterton who bought it of Sr. W. Davenant to whom it was left by will of John Taylor. who a ... of Shakespear. it was painted by one Taylor. a Player & painter contemp. with Shakes & his intimate Friend. another

Mr. Betterton told Mr Keck several times that the Picture of Shakespeare he had, was painted by one John Taylor a Player. who acted for Shakespear & this John Taylor in his will left it to Sr. Willm Davenant. & at the death of Sr Will Davenant Mr Betterton bought it, & at his death Mr. Keck bought it. in whose posess it now is.

1719

figs 20, 21
Extracts from George Vertue's notebook, 1719
The British Library, London

There are a number of unanswered questions and uncertain links that make us want to challenge the chain of events recorded by Vertue. For example, who decided this particular picture was a portrait of Shakespeare, and not another fashionable Jacobean urban dweller? William Davenant, who was only ten when Shakespeare died, is perhaps the weakest link in the narrative. Davenant claimed to be Shakespeare's godson and greatly admired the poet, but he was also known to embroider upon his association with Shakespeare. Was it perhaps wishful thinking on the part of Davenant that a portrait in his possession represented his celebrated godfather? Vertue states that the picture was given to Davenant in Taylor's will, but, as Mary Edmond has noted, the picture does not appear in the last will and testament of the John Taylor identified as a painter.[2] However, as paintings appear very infrequently in wills and inventories at this period, that is not surprising.

Even if we assume Vertue's facts to be correct, there are further questions to be answered. As John Taylor is not recorded as one of Shakespeare's associates, how did he come to have the picture 'of[f] Shakespeare'? No scholar would claim we have a perfect understanding of Shakespeare's life in London and he must have had many friends and associates whose names are not recorded. But why was the picture in the possession of a painter (and possibly player) rather than Shakespeare's family?[3] If the story about Taylor's ownership is true, could it indicate that the Chandos painting was an uncollected commission, or a rejected version, or even an early studio copy of another picture?

Vertue's notebooks are also important in recording the supposed existence of another lifetime portrait of Shakespeare in oil. This second picture was dated 1595 and also held within the collection of Mr Keck (or Kyke) of Temple, and was attributed by Vertue to 'M. Garrard', Marcus Gheeraerts the Younger (1561/2–1636), a celebrated artist whose name was improbably attached to many pictures of this date. A portrait of this description has not emerged and it is possible, as Vertue does not mention the picture again in his second entry, when he may have visited Keck, that he did not see the 1595 portrait or that he thought it unlikely to represent Shakespeare.

For Victorian and Edwardian critics, the Chandos portrait was censured for its depiction of the sitter's features in a way that was not fitting for a national hero; it was considered essential that Shakespeare, as the father of English literature, should appear in his portrait as a fair-faced and morally respectable idol. In 1864 J. Hain Friswell wrote: 'One cannot readily imagine our essentially English Shakespeare to have been a dark, heavy man, with a foreign expression, of decidedly Jewish physiognomy, thin curly hair, a somewhat lubricious mouth, red-edged eyes, wanton lips, with a coarse expression and his ears tricked out with earrings.'[4] M.H. Spielmann, another determined critic of the painting, held a similar view and commented in 1907 that 'it is hard to believe that this dark face, of distinctly Italian type, represents one of the pure English Shakespeare stock of the Midlands'.[5] This viewpoint tells us more about the values of the commentators than it does about the portrait itself, as portraits of many dark-haired Elizabethans and Jacobeans will bear out. Yet these critics were also partly deceived by the yellowing of the darkened varnish that covers the entire surface of the picture, including the flesh tones, and by patches of discoloured over-painting (see 'Condition' below).

Facial likeness and clothing

The question of the sitter's facial likeness to the two post-humous portraits of Shakespeare, the Droeshout engraving (cat.1) and the Stratford monument (cat.2), which were almost certainly based upon earlier images produced in Shakespeare's lifetime, has been frequently discussed. The features of the sitter in the Chandos portrait broadly agree with the man depicted in the engraving and bust. The Droeshout and the Chandos share a receding hairline with longer hair falling across the ears, a high forehead, moustache, prominent nose, heavy lidded eyes and full lips.

There are, however, significant problems in comparing likenesses in painted portraits, and yet further difficulties in comparing paintings and sculpture. Painted, engraved and sculpted portraits are artistic creations filtered through the interests of the sitter, and the skills and style of the artist. Likeness in portraiture is also subject to the peculiarities of technique and specific conventions of representation of a given period. Portraits are not, and can never be, forensic evidence of likeness, and comparison based upon the measurements of facial proportions of portraits does not therefore enhance our understanding of the various putative images of Shakespeare. It is also worth noting that native English artists at this time were often less skilled in capturing a realistic likeness than their European counterparts (p.40).

The impression provided by the costume is that the sitter was a reasonably wealthy member of what historians sometimes call 'the middling sort', one of the growing body of prosperous townspeople. The costume provides few specific clues, as the buttoned doublet or gown is a relatively plain example worn only with an undecorated white linen collar, a mode of dress in fashion from 1590 to 1615 (fig.25).

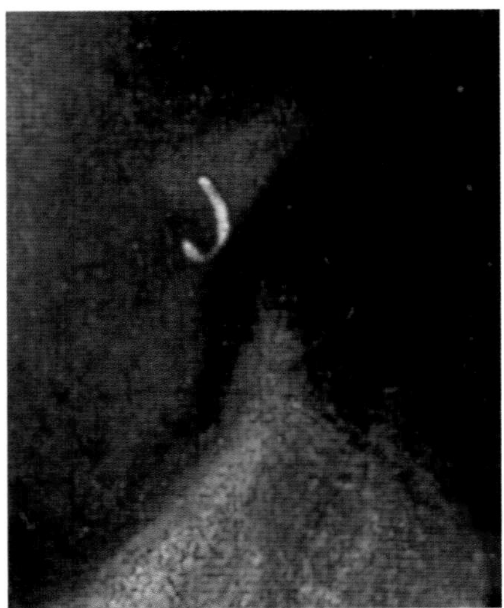
fig.22 **Earring of William Shakespeare?** (detail; cat.61)

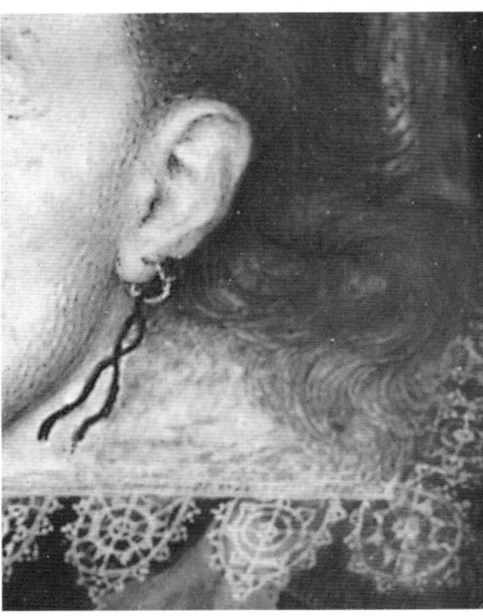
fig.23 **Earring of William Herbert, 3rd Earl of Pembroke** (detail; cat.86)

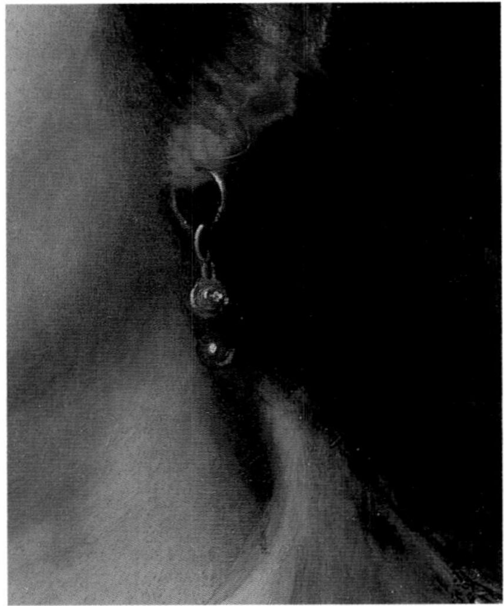
fig.24 **Earring of a man, probably Nathan Field** (detail; cat.52)

fig.25 **Portrait of a man with earring, possibly a poet**, *c.*1600
Unknown artist
Oil on canvas
Current location unknown

However, in line with other portraits of writers, including those of John Donne (cat.80) and the probable portrait of Nathan Field (cat.52), the collar is unusual in being untied, and the strings hang loose, providing a contrast with the plain black collar and creating an impression of informality. A gold hoop also appears in the sitter's left ear (fig.22). This feature was once considered to be a later addition but recent analysis has confirmed that the earring is an original part of the picture.[6] It is hard to assess what connotations single earrings worn by men may have had in the early seventeenth century. Certainly, wealthy gentlemen were as likely as women to adorn themselves with jewellery of all types, including gold chains, rings, hat badges and jewelled buttons, garters and sword belts. Earrings were not worn by all the male élite, however, and evidence from portraiture alone suggests they were worn by some courtiers and men of creative ambition, such as maritime adventurers including Francis Drake and Walter Ralegh (cat.89), literary patrons such as William Pembroke (fig.23) and, possibly, even writers and actors, see, for example, the portraits of a man, probably Nathan Field (fig.24) and of an unknown man, presenting himself in a melancholic pose with a sheet of paper on a desk, who is possibly a writer or poet (fig.25).[7] The simple gold earring perhaps provides a sense of someone who took pride in his individuality.

Artist and composition

The current condition of the portrait (discussed below) has meant it is difficult to know what it looked like when it was first painted. A painter named John Taylor was identified as a member of the Painter-Stainers' Company through the detective work of Mary Edmond (published in 1982).[8] As Edmond notes, John Taylor had at least six apprentices between 1626 and 1648, and each would have served for about seven years. Taylor became an important figure in the Painter-Stainers' Company, rising to Renter Warden from 1631 to 1632, Upper Warden from 1635 to 1636 and Master from 1643 to 1644. A portrait of John Taylor in his role as warden alongside two colleagues in 1632 (fig.28, p.59) remains in existence at the Painter-Stainers' Company. Whether John Taylor was also an actor – as Vertue states – was explored by Darren Emerson Lay, who identified a 'John Taylor as a boy chorister/actor of St Paul's Cathedral *c.*1598, who was probably aged between 11 and 14 years old'.[9] The link between the boy actor and the later painter has yet to be conclusively proved. If the two John Taylors were the same man, the painter would have been in his sixties at his death in 1651, when, according to his will, he still had an apprentice.

The Chandos portrait has previously been ascribed to Richard Burbage (cat.51), however, neither Burbage nor Taylor left any securely identifiable work with which a comparison can be made. The Chandos portrait was certainly painted by a different artist from the one who painted the portrait of Burbage himself. The feigned oval background surrounding the portrait seems to be original to the picture, and in 1610 this device would have been a relatively new format. It appears in the portrait of John Donne painted in the *c.*1595 (cat.80) and in a small number of other portraits around this date, such as a portrait of an unknown man (fig.32) and the portrait of William Sheldon (fig.33, p.57).[10] By 1615 the oval format had became a standard feature of British and continental portraiture.

Condition

The painting has been considerably damaged by cleaning and abrasion (noted in 1864) and might now be described as almost a relic. Successive cleaning and then overpainting, probably in the eighteenth and nineteenth centuries, have

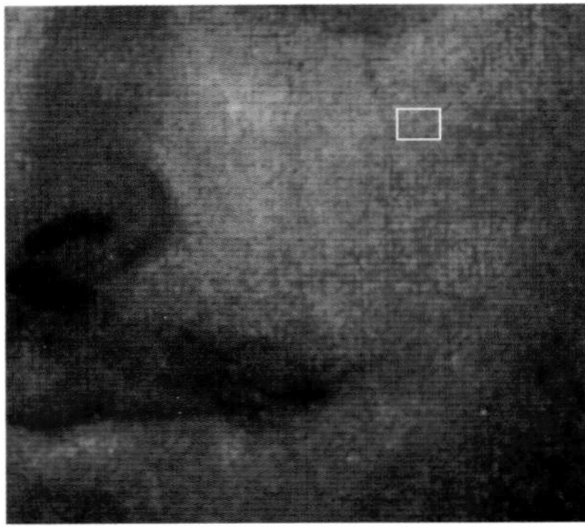

Area of sampling shown in fig.26
Paint sampling involves the removal of microscopic fragments from the paint surface for analysis.

fig.26 **Cross-section of paint from the cheek shown at ×1000 magnification**
This shows the extent of the dark overpaint in this area.

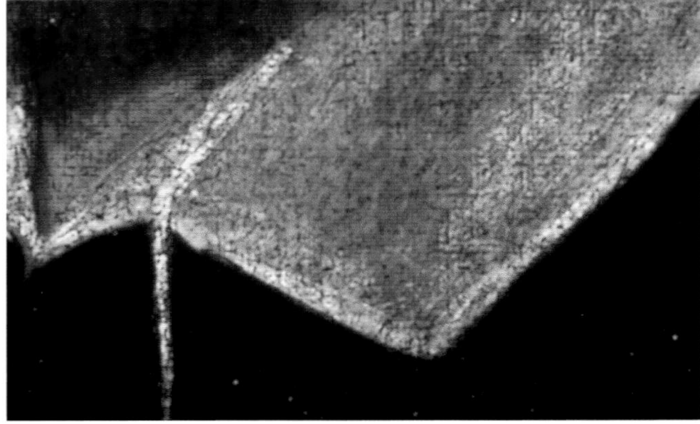

fig.27 **Detail of collar**
The white paint on the collar has been heavily abraded, exposing the original grey ground that primed the entire surface of the canvas.

obscured parts of the original surface. These retouched areas have since become discoloured and now make the visible surface patchy, particularly on the forehead. In some parts of the painting – such as across the white collar – the paint surface has worn down to the original grey ground that was used to prime the entire canvas (fig.27). In addition, the old varnish has discoloured, which gives the entire painting a darker, yellower hue. The original paint layers were probably sparsely applied, and so today only a very thin layer of the original paint remains. There have also been a number of additions to the portrait since it was first painted. In particular, the beard has been lengthened into a slightly more pointed shape and the hair has been extended down to the collar. An early copy of the portrait (fig.34, p.61) may give an indication of the original appearance.

The unusually worn condition of this picture can be clearly seen in the X-ray (fig.29), and it is apparent that only a small amount of pigment remains upon the surface of the canvas. The exception is the yellow paint used for the earring; as a metal-based pigment (known as lead tin yellow), it has withstood abrasion more successfully. The fact that the picture has been recognized as a portrait of Shakespeare since the seventeenth century has probably contributed to its worn surface and, apart from zealous cleaning, its appearance may be the result of persistent handling. If, as Vertue stated, the painting was owned by William Davenant, it was probably on display unglazed in the 1660s at the Duke's Theatre in Lisle Court, Lincoln's Inn Fields, where he and his family also had their lodgings.[10] Whether the picture was hanging in the theatre itself, or in Davenant's apartments, a portrait of the famous father of the London stage would have attracted dozens of devotees, who could well have wished to forge a link with the great writer by touching the surface of his portrait.

fig.28 **Master Painter-Stainer John Potkin and his Upper Warden, Thomas Carleton and Renter Warden John Taylor** (right), 1632
Oil on canvas, 1321 × 1575mm (52 × 62 in)
Worshipful Company of Painter-Stainers', London

fig.29 **X-ray of the Chandos portrait**

fig.30 **Micrograph of the sitter's right eye shown at ×10 magnification**
This photograph taken using a microscope shows the canvas texture and the grey ground showing through the worn paint surface.

fig.31 **Micrograph of the gold earring shown at ×10 magnification**
Examination under magnification confirmed that the earring is original to the portrait.

fig.32 **Micrograph of the collar and string shown at ×10 magnification**
This detail shows that brush strokes of original paint were used on both the collar and the string, proving the strings are original to the portrait.

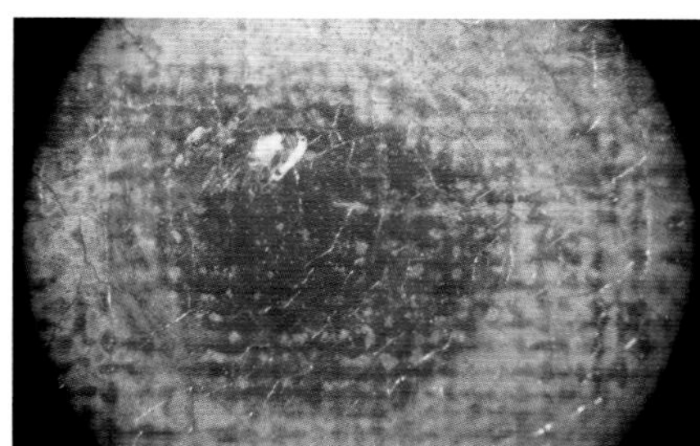

fig.30

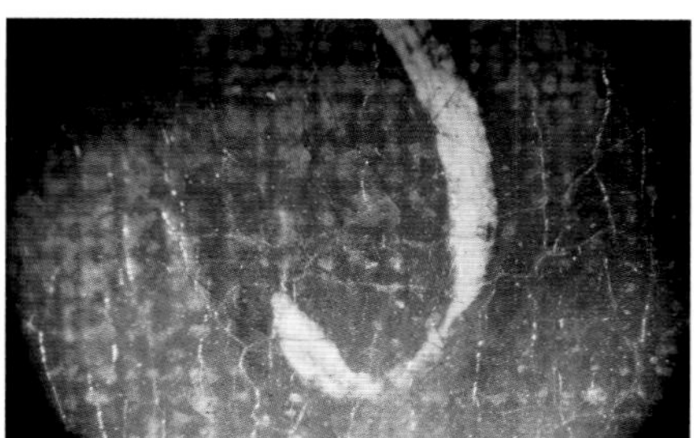

fig.31

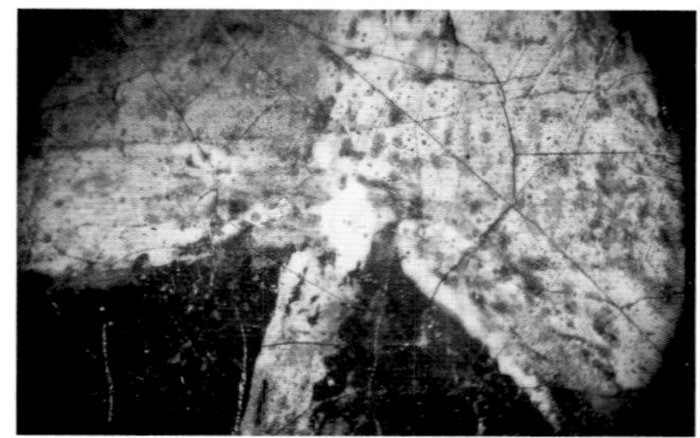

fig.32

fig.33 **William Sheldon**, dated 1590
Hieronymous Custodis
Oil on panel, 730 × 590mm (28¾ × 23¼in)
Private collection

fig.34 **Early copy after the Chandos portrait**, c.1670
Unknown English artist
Oil on canvas, 763 × 635mm (30 × 25in)
Private collection

Copies

The portrait has been frequently copied as an authentic portrait of Shakespeare and became familiar to eighteenth-century viewers via an engraving by Gerard Van der Gucht (1796–1779) that appeared in Nicholas Rowe's life of Shakespeare in 1709 and in an engraving by Houbraken in 1747. A considerable number of painted copies exist, including an early version from around 1689, once owned (not, as is usually stated, painted) by Godfrey Kneller (fig.34). TC

1 British Library, notebooks of George Vertue 1713–21 (Add ms 21, III, fol.30r–31v and fol.39v). Vertue also records that Mr Keck wrote some verses to put under the picture as follows: 'Sheakespear! Such thoughts imissible Shine. Own in thy words, thy fancy seems Divine;/Tis natures mirrour, whose she … each grace/and all the various features of the face' (fol.39v). For a full transcription, see George Vertue, notebooks, *Walpole Society*, vol.XXIV, 1936, p.48.
2 National Archives, PCC 132 Grey, Prob 11/217-132.
3 A player called Joseph Taylor is listed as an actor in the First Folio; he joined the King's Men in 1619, several years after Shakespeare's death.
4 Friswell 1864, p.31.
5 Spielmann 1907, p.7.
6 The earring is painted in a pigment identified as lead tin yellow, which was in common use in the early seventeenth century, falling out of use around the late seventeenth century. Conservation notes, registered packet no.1, Heinz Archive, National Portrait Gallery.
7 Many other examples exist, including John Croker of Hook Norton (*c.*1585), attributed to Robert Peake (see *Tudor and Stuart Portraits 1530–1660*, no.10, The Weiss Gallery, London, 1995); an unknown youth (1588) by Nicholas Hilliard (formerly Collection of Duke of Rutland); Prince Charles (1613) and William Herbert (1617; see Hearn 1995, nos 128, 138). James I also adopted the fashion in the second decade of the seventeenth century.
8 See Edmond 1982, pp.146–9.
9 Lay 1996 (see Literature).
10 Mary Edmond, *Rare Sir William Davenant* (Manchester University Press, 1987), pp.157–8.

4. A portrait of an unknown gentleman, known as the Grafton portrait, 1588

Unknown English artist

Oil on a single member of English oak panel
445 × 385mm (17½ × 15⅛in)
Inscribed top left: 'Æ SVÆ 24'; top right: '1.5.8.8'; on verso: 'W+S' (applied in the nineteenth century)
The John Rylands University Library, The University of Manchester

Provenance The Misses Ludgate, the Bridgewater Inn, Winston-on-Tees, Co. Durham, c.1907; bequeathed to the John Rylands Library, Manchester, in 1914 by Thomas Kay

Literature M.H. Spielmann, 'The Grafton and Sanders Portraits of Shakespeare', *The Connoisseur*, XXIII, February 1909, pp.97–102; Thomas Kay, *The Story of the Grafton Portrait of William Shakespeare* (S.W. Partridge & Co., London, 1914); Ernest Jarratt, 'The Grafton Portrait', *John Rylands Library Bulletin*, 1945–6, pp.225–9; Schoenbaum 1981, pp.191–4

fig.35 **The Grafton portrait before conservation**

There is no evidence that this portrait represents William Shakespeare, but throughout the twentieth century the painting had numerous champions expressing the hope that it did so.[1] The main reason for this attention is the original inscription that records the sitter's age as twenty-four in 1588, making him an exact contemporary of Shakespeare. The portrait depicts a rather beautiful youth with curly brown hair and grey eyes, wearing a sumptuous slashed scarlet doublet, painted in such a way as to depict silk or satin. As a portrait of an angelic-faced young man, this picture has fuelled interest in romantic notions of Shakespeare's youth prior to his life as an established playwright. The sitter has not been identified, but he must have been a man of considerable wealth. In particular, scarlet cloth was prohibited by sumptuary laws, reissued in 1579, for everyone except the nobility. On occasion, sitters may have borrowed or rented costumes, but this example would have been a very audacious choice. The Grafton portrait acquired its name in the early twentieth century, when the owners recalled an old family tradition that the portrait had been bequeathed by one of the Dukes of Grafton to their ancestor, a yeoman farmer in the village of Grafton, Northamptonshire, five or six generations previously.[2]

The technical examination, undertaken at the National Portrait Gallery in 2005, focused on confirming the date of the panel, and exploring an obvious alteration made to the last digit of the inscription, from 23 to 24, which can clearly be seen in the X-ray (fig.40, p.65). An examination using dendrochronology (tree-ring analysis) established that the earliest date at which the tree could have been felled was 1573. By matching chronologies and growing patterns of other examples of wood from this date, the panel has been determined as deriving from a tree grown in southern England, in particular in Surrey and London (fig.37, p.64).[3] As most wood used by professional painters for panel painting in Britain has been found to derive from the Baltic region, this example is unusual. The change in the lettering from 23 to 24 was confirmed by paint sampling as being contemporary with the rest of the picture, which indicates that the young man had probably passed his twenty-fourth birthday by the time the painting was completed and had requested that his age should be altered.[4]

It has not been possible to identify a specific artist, but the handling of the painting is in line with a controlled linear technique of English artists in the late sixteenth century.

Æ SVÆ · 24
1·5·8·8·

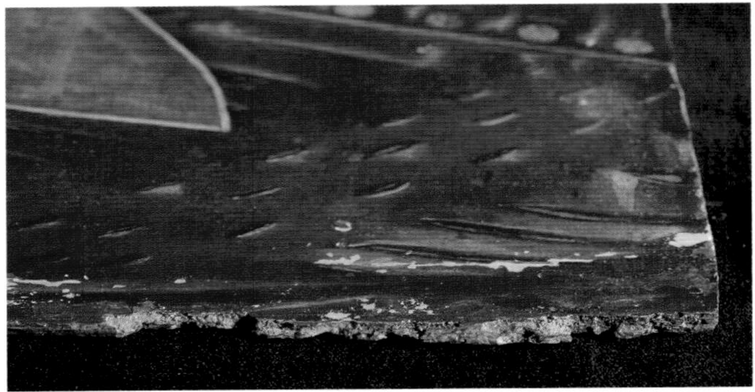

fig.36 **Detail of woodworm damage to the left side of the painting**

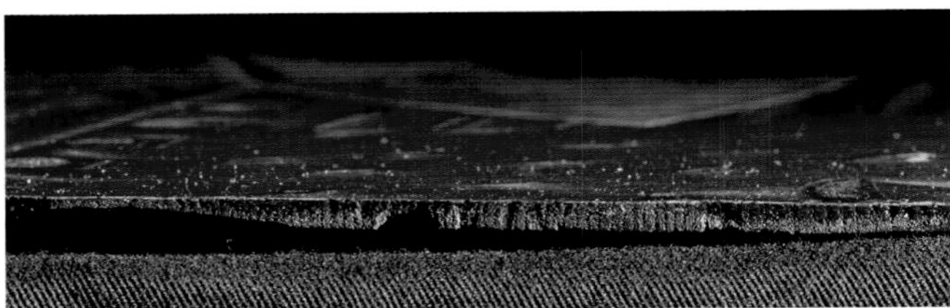

fig.37 **Detail of the panel end showing tree rings**
The rings were used to identify the date of the wood.

fig.38 **The Grafton portrait seen in ultraviolet light**
This treatment showed there was very little underpaint.

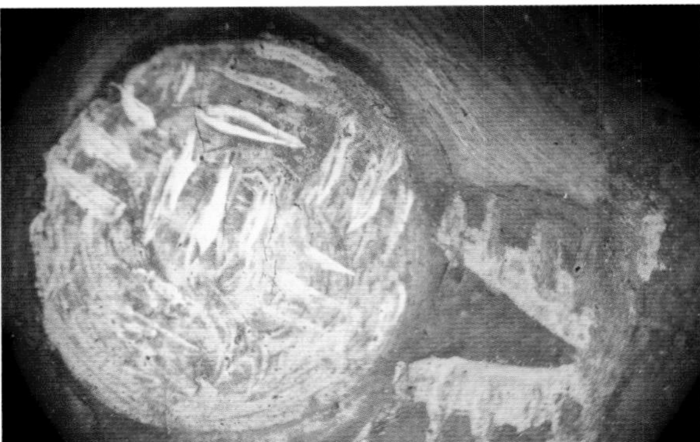

fig.39 **Detail of a button**

Prior to 1907 the picture suffered some damage, including significant woodworm scarring to the left side (fig.36). According to the scholar Samuel Schoenbaum, the painting was also subject to enthusiastic cleaning with caustic soda when in the possession of the Lydgate family. TC

1 The portrait has appeared as the frontispiece to numerous books of Shakespeare's collected works – see, for example; John Semple Smart, *Shakespeare: Truth and Tradition* (Edward Arnold & Co., London, 1928). The John Rylands Library does not uphold with the identification of this painting as William Shakespeare.
2 The picture was supposed to have been in a manor house at Grafton Regis, Northamptonshire, and removed after a siege in 1643. The 1st Duke of Grafton was Henry Fitzroy, formerly Palmer (1663–90); Philip Riden (assisted by Charles Insley), *A History of the County of Northampton*, vol.5 (Victoria County History, Boydell Press, 2002), p.145.
3 Ian Tyers, 'Tree-ring Analysis of a Panel Painting: The Grafton Portrait', February 2005, Icon notes (William Shakespeare: Grafton portrait), National Portrait Gallery Archive.
4 Libby Sheldon, technical report on the Grafton portrait, May 2005, Icon notes (William Shakespeare: Grafton portrait), National Portrait Gallery Archive.

fig.40 **X-ray of the Grafton portrait**
The X-ray reveals the single panel of wood, areas of paint loss on the face, damage to the left side and the change of the numerals from 23 to 24.

5. A portrait of an unknown gentleman, known as the Sanders portrait, 1603

Unknown English artist

Oil on panel
423 × 330mm (16 5/8 × 13 in)
Inscribed top right: 'AN? 1603'
Lloyd A. Sullivan, Ottawa, Ontario, Canada

Provenance John Sanders (d.1862); Thomas Sanders (1790–1862); Thomas Hale Sanders (1830–1915); Alloysius Sanders (b.1864); and by descent to the current owner

Literature M.H. Spielmann, 'The Grafton and Sanders Portraits of Shakespeare', *The Connoisseur*, XXIII, February 1909, pp.97–102; Stephanie Nolen, *Shakespeare's Face* (Alfred A. Knopf Canada, Toronto, 2002); Jenny Tiramani, 'The Sanders Portrait', *Costume, Journal for the Costume Society*, vol.39, 2005, pp.44–52

This painting appears to have a reasonably long history as a 'contender' portrait of Shakespeare. Like the Grafton portrait (cat.4), the Sanders portrait dates from within Shakespeare's lifetime. The image and the playwright have been linked through tradition and limited circumstantial evidence. A damaged label on the back of the portrait still exists and it was recorded by the scholar M.H. Spielmann in 1909 as follows: 'Shakpere/Born April 23 = 1564/Died April 23 – 1616/Aged 52/This likeness taken 1603/Age at the time 39 ys'. The paper of this label may date from as early as the mid seventeenth century, but the writing is probably later, particularly as Shakespeare's exact birth date – which is not known – came to be celebrated on St George's Day on 23 April only in the eighteenth century.[1]

Extensive technical analysis undertaken in Canada has confirmed the materials and pigments in use are consistent with an earlier seventeenth-century date. The panel has been identified as deriving from a tree felled around 1595. The portrait apparently depicts a man wearing a fashionable doublet with a falling lawn collar (or band) with sewn darts. The sitter is possibly in his late twenties or early thirties and appears to have soft grey eyes and light-brown hair. Although any assessment of age is subjective, the sitter appears too young to represent William Shakespeare, who was thirty-nine in 1603.

Like most paintings of this date, the portrait has suffered damage. An entire segment has been lost from the right side of the composition where the sitter's shoulder would have been. It is not unusual for parts of a panel to become detached due to ongoing movement within the structure of the wood and similar damage has occurred in another portrait of an unknown gentleman (fig.41). At this period the dates inscribed on portraits were frequently accompanied by the age of the sitter in the Latin form, AETATIS SUAE ('at the age of'), and it is possible that the lost segment of the panel in the Sanders portrait included the age of the sitter, helping to identify him.

By tradition the picture has been considered to be the work of a painter called John Sanders, who was supposed to be in some way connected with Shakespeare's company, although no evidence of this connection has been found. Over four decades later there is a record of an artist called John Sanders (or Saunders) in the Court Minutes of the Painter-Stainers' Company as a painter of coats of arms. He completed his apprenticeship on 13 July 1647 and was thereafter licensed to work as a professional painter.[2] At this date he would have been in his early or mid twenties and thus cannot be the painter associated with this picture, although a family link to an earlier painter of the same name cannot be discounted. TC

fig.41 **A portrait of an unknown gentleman**, 1590s
Unknown artist
Oil on panel, 476 × 346mm (18 3/4 × 13 5/8 in)
National Portrait Gallery, London (NPG 2613)

Both this portrait and the Sanders portrait have lost a portion of the original image to the right, making the sitters appear off-centre.

1 The inscription is now no longer as legible as Spielmann's transcript. According to the Canadian Institute of Conservation, it has been radiocarbon dated to the period from 1474 to 1640. See Alexander F. Johnston, Arleane Ralph and Abigail Anne Young, 'The Conundrum of the Label' in Stephanie Nolen 2002 (see Literature), pp.274–9.

2 Guildhall Library, London, ms 5667, 'John Sanders Servant to Mr. Babb', p.216. Thomas Babb was a member of the Court of Assistants within the company. John Sanders became Warden in 1674 and Master in 1680.

6. A portrait of an unknown gentleman, possibly Thomas Overbury (1581–1613), known as the Janssen portrait, *c*.1610

Unknown Anglo-Netherlandish artist

Oil on oak panel
564 × 435mm (22¼ × 17⅛ in)
Folger Shakespeare Library, Washington, DC (FPS 17)

Provenance In the collection of Charles Jennens of Gopsall Hall, Leicestershire, by 1770; purchased by Samuel Woodburn for the 9th Duke of Hamilton c.1809; thereafter by descent to Sir John Ramsden; his sale from 27 to 30 May 1932 at Christie's, lot 65; bought from Chas. J. Sawyer Ltd, in July 1932; purchased by R. Ward at a sale on 11 June 1947 at Sotheby's, lot 50

Literature William L. Pressly, *Catalogue of Paintings in the Folger Shakespeare Library* (Yale University Press, New Haven, 1993), no.160

From its emergence in the later eighteenth century, three key elements made this a compelling contender as a portrait of Shakespeare from life. First, the sitter's age and the date, inscribed 'AE^{te} 46 / 1610' in the upper-left corner, accord with Shakespeare's birth in 1564. Second, the uninterrupted curve defining the top of the sitter's high forehead matched the essential iconography provided by the Droeshout portrait and Stratford memorial bust (cats 1, 2). Third, the lace-trimmed collar and rich doublet with matching sleeves are not only consistent with the 1610 date, but also met nineteenth and early twentieth-century expectations of a gentleman's attire. This portrait provided an impression of Shakespeare the refined poet rather than the player or the provincial burgher.

fig.42 **The Janssen portrait before conservation**, 1970s
The hairline was modified at a later date.

In artistic terms, it remains a fine portrait, but Shakespeare is no longer regarded as the sitter, and Cornelis Janssen (1593–1661, also known as Cornelis Janssens van Ceulen or Cornelius Johnson) is no longer accepted as the artist. Janssen was only seventeen in 1610, and, except for a few paintings from 1617, his works all date from 1619 onwards, the year after he apparently returned to London following training in the Netherlands. As for the sitter, David Piper pointed out in 1964[1] that a portrait with the same face, pose and costume, but with a different hairline and no age or date, had appeared in the 1947 Ellenborough sale, and it might depict the courtier and author Sir Thomas Overbury, who became a victim of court intrigue in 1613.

Conservation work undertaken in 1988 proved conclusively that the original hairline and much of the hair had been overpainted to make the sitter 'Shakespearean' and that the 'AE^{te} 46 / 1610' inscription had been placed on top of this overpainting. During this recent work, overpainting on the forehead and hair was removed, returning the sitter's face to its original appearance (an exact match for the Ellenborough hairline), but the inscription remains as a testament to the portrait's later history.

Some questioned the attribution, the sitter's identity, or both, from the outset, but the Janssen portrait remained a strong contender as a portrait of Shakespeare well into the twentieth century. Over a dozen different prints and at least six oil paintings based on it appeared in the eighteenth and nineteenth centuries, fixing it in the public imagination as an image of the Bard. The Janssen portrait became popular from around 1770 as a result of a small mezzotint by Richard Earlom (1743–1822), which was published as the frontispiece to an edition of *King Lear*. The caption to the print read: 'William Shakespear. From an Original Picture by Cornelius Jansen in the Collection of C. Jennens Esq.' Charles Jennens (1700–73) was the anonymous editor (but named dedicatee) of the *Lear* volume. Descriptions of Jennens's famed art collection written between 1761 and 1766 do not mention a Shakespeare portrait, so it was presumably acquired in the late 1760s. When the Janssen portrait came on to the market in 1932, the Folger Shakespeare Library's Supervisor of Research, Joseph Q. Adams, urged that the library purchase it because 'next to the Chandos Portrait… and the Flower Portrait… this is the most famous portrait of Shakespeare' (cats 4, 8). EB

1 Piper 1964, p.36.

7. William Shakespeare, known as the Soest portrait, *c.*1667

Gerard or Gilbert Soest (*c.*1605–81)

Oil on canvas
725 × 610mm (28½ × 24in)
Shakespeare Birthplace Trust, Stratford-upon-Avon (SBT1994–19/183)

Provenance Sir Thomas Clarges?, *c.*1667; Thomas Wright, *c.*1685?–1725; William Doughlas Esq, *c.*1790; Sir John Lister Kay, *c.*1827; Sir J.F. Grey; Antiqualia Lda, Portugal until 1959

Literature Edmond Malone, *Shakespeare*, vol.1 (1790), p.127; Boaden 1824, pp.134–43; Wivell 1827, pp.157–64; Friswell 1864, pp.87–91; J. Parker Norris, *Portraits of Shakespeare* (1885), pp.201–3; Notebooks, *Walpole Society*, vol.XXIV, 1936, pp.13–14 (note of an actor sitting as Shakespeare, but to Lely rather than to Soest); Levi Fox, 'The Soest Portrait of Shakespeare', *Shakespeare Survey*, vol.15, 1962, p.130; David Piper, *The Image of the Poet: British Poets and their Portraits* (Clarendon Press, Oxford, 1982), pp.40–2

This portrait is one of the earliest examples of a memorial portrait of Shakespeare and was probably produced in the late 1660s as a constructed likeness of Shakespeare for the Restoration period. By this date the theatrical revival was well established, following the suppression and closure of playhouses from 1642 until the fall of Cromwell's Protectorate in 1659. As the diaries of Samuel Pepys (1633–1703), among much other evidence, make clear, Shakespeare's plays were regularly performed at this time, although initially they were not especially popular. The introduction of women playing the female roles, the often rather extreme changes that were made to the plots and language, and new, spectacular movable scenery helped to make the plays more palatable to the public, and gradually Shakespeare's reputation grew. Increasing respect for the original texts and for Shakespeare's creative genius was promoted by John Dryden (1631–1700), although even he believed that 'the tongue in general is so much refined since Shakespeare's time'.[1]

The features of the sitter derive partly from the Chandos portrait (cat.3), but the playwright is shown as a younger man with a pensive gaze, elegant bone structure, and without the bohemian earring, which was long out of fashion by the 1660s. The poet is thus reincarnated as an introspective man of fine manners and sensitive disposition. He is dressed in a black embroidered doublet that is clearly a late seventeenth-century approximation of earlier dress. The head of the figure is highly individual and it has been suggested that the portrait was based on an actor of the 1660s who was thought to resemble Shakespeare.[2] A reference to this episode appears in the notebooks of George Vertue, who describes the artist – perhaps mistakenly – as Sir Peter 'Lilly', probably Lely (1618–80), who apparently 'got a dress from the play house and with that picture [a copy after the Chandos portrait] and a man found so much in likeness to the countenance of Shakespear, he made a picture of him which still remains in the Family of Clarges'.[3] A number of other invented portraits of Shakespeare date from the Restoration period and are largely based upon the Chandos portrait, notably the Chesterfield portrait (Shakespeare Birthplace Trust), which shows the poet in a god-like pose as a great creator, with one hand upon a bound manuscript.

The painting was reproduced in a mezzotint by John Simon (1675–1751) in 1725, where it is recorded as having been painted by Soest. Gerard (or Gilbert) Soest was a Dutch-born, highly trained professional artist who worked in London from the 1640s until his death. The attribution to Soest seems plausible, as the picture has evidently been painted by a very competent artist, although, perhaps understandably, given the subject, Soest's very characteristic handling of drapery is not apparent here. The portrait was reproduced in engravings and oil copies, which ensured that it retained a popular following into the nineteenth century as a convincing portrait of Shakespeare. TC and CM

1 John Dryden, *Troilus and Cressida* (1679), sig. A4v.
2 James Boaden recounts an anecdote from *The Gentleman's Magazine* in Boaden 1824, p.137.
3 Notebooks, *Walpole Society*, vol.XXIV, 1936, p.13.

8. William Shakespeare, known as the Flower portrait, *c*.1820–40

Unknown English artist

Oil on wooden (poplar?) panel
590 × 445mm (23¼ × 17½in)
Inscribed top left in yellow paint: 'Willm Shakespeare, 1609'
Royal Shakespeare Company, Stratford-upon-Avon (STRPG: 1993.5)

Provenance In the possession of H.C. Clements of Peckham Rye, *c*.1840; purchased by Edgar Flower in 1892; presented to the Memorial Gallery, Royal Shakespeare Company in 1895

Literature Spielmann 1907, pp.13–17; Schoenbaum 1981, pp.172–5; Paul Bertram and Frank Cossa, 'Willm Shakespeare 1609: The Flower Portrait Revisited', *Shakespeare Quarterly*, vol.37, spring 1986, pp.83–97

Since its appearance in the 1840s this portrait has attracted considerable interest and has been variously considered as a lifetime portrait, the original source of the Droeshout engraving or a later copy. In the early twentieth century the scholar M.H. Spielmann thought it possible that the portrait might date from the early seventeenth century but that it was 'hardly consistent with a portrait from the life', and considered it a copy after the engraving partly because of the 'woodenness' of the composition.

The composition of the Flower portrait derives directly from the Droeshout engraving. Following detailed technical examination at the National Portrait Gallery in 2005, it was categorically identified as a product of the early nineteenth century. The portrait was painted on top of a sixteenth-century Italian painting depicting a Madonna and Child with John the Baptist (fig.43, p.74), dating from between 1540 and 1560. Spielmann had noted the existence of another image beneath the Flower portrait as early as 1907, but its full significance was not realized until an X-ray was made in the 1970s. At around this time the painting was cleaned and part of the Italian painting was exposed in the background (to the left of Shakespeare's head); the picture now remains in this semi-exposed state.

The recent technical analysis included looking through a microscope at the paint surface, infrared and ultraviolet examination, the production of a new X-ray and microscopic paint sampling. The crucial test was the use of paint sampling in ten separate areas across the surface of the picture.[1] Most of the pigments identified were in use across a reasonably wide period, yet the identification of a yellow pigment, known as chrome yellow, in the embroidered braid of the doublet indicated that the picture must date from after 1814, when this colour became commercially available to painters.[2] The cross-section of a microscopic paint sample taken from the yellow braid on the doublet (fig.45, p.75) shows the various layers, from the original priming or ground of the sixteenth-century Italian painting to the more modern yellow paint on the surface. To capture the appearance of the gold braid the artist used both yellow ochre (a natural yellow pigment in use in the seventeenth century) and chrome yellow as a type of glaze on the surface. The later pigment was very well integrated into the surface of the paint layers and could not have been added at a later date (fig.46, p.75). The presence of an ultramarine pigment was also detected and, although it cannot be categorically determined, it is probably French ultramarine, a pigment first available after 1828.

It is clear from the X-ray that the painting of the Madonna and Child was in a damaged state at the time it was reused as a surface for Shakespeare's likeness. It seems fairly likely that the panel was chosen by the nineteenth-century artist in order to give the painting a suitably aged appearance. If the Flower portrait was painted in Britain, as appears likely, the Italian panel may have arrived as a memento of the grand tour in the eighteenth century or early nineteenth century. The wooden panel has been tentatively identified as poplar wood, which was commonly used by artists in southern Europe during the Renaissance.

The nineteenth-century copyist was a reasonably accomplished artist and appears to have taken considerable care to ensure the painting was taken seriously as a lifetime portrait of the playwright. The artist attempted to copy some Jacobean painting techniques, notably in the depiction of the buttons and, despite the technical difficulties involved, chose to paint Shakespeare's features directly over the surface of the Italian painting without the benefit of a priming layer or ground between the two pictures.

The copyist also made some slight changes to the

fig.43 **X-ray of the Flower portrait**
The X-ray shows the three figures of the Madonna, Christ and John the Baptist beneath the portrait of Shakespeare. The original picture is Italian and dates from 1540 to 1560.

fig.44 **Close-up of face shown in raking light**
This detail reveals the surface damage that was probably present on the original picture before Shakespeare's face was painted. This provided a suitably aged appearance for the nineteenth-century artist.

composition of the Droeshout engraving, including the anatomy of the ear, the simplification of the embroidery and the addition of a painted inscription that was once gilded. It is possible that the early nineteenth-century owner H.C. Clements may have had some knowledge of the painting's recent production, though he claimed – according to the scholar Samuel Schoenbaum – that the painting had been presented to him by a descendant of the Shakespeare family. The early owner may also have attempted to fabricate a celebrated pedigree for the picture, as a note was attached to the original box stating that 'the picture was publicly exhibited in London seventy years ago [i.e. around 1770] and many thousands went to see it'. Needless to say, no evidence of this exhibition has been recorded. Despite its recently confirmed status as a nineteenth-century picture, the Flower portrait remains a fascinating object; a testament to the earnest desire to find a lifetime portrait of England's most famous poet and playwright. TC

1 Technical report dated 7 April 2005. Icon notes (William Shakespeare: Flower portrait), National Portrait Gallery Archive.
2 Chrome yellow (lead chromate) was discovered in the early nineteenth century and was first described in 1809. See Rutherford J. Gettens and George Stout, *Painting Materials: A Short Encyclopaedia* (Dover Publications, New York), p.106.

Areas of paint sampling shown in figs 45 and 46

a = fig.45
b = fig.46

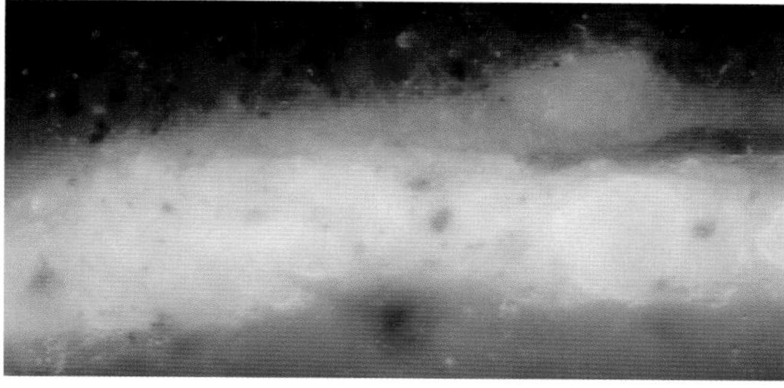

fig.45 **Cross-section of paint layers in yellow braid on doublet shown at ×400 magnification**
The pink flesh of the baby can be seen beneath the yellow braid.

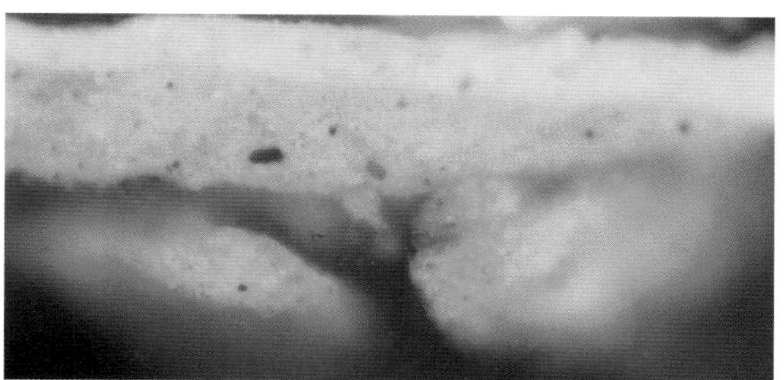

Two yellows well integrated

fig.46 **Cross-section of paint layers in yellow embroidery on doublet shown at ×400 magnification**
The nineteenth-century pigment chrome yellow is well integrated into the lower yellow layer proving they were painted at the same time.

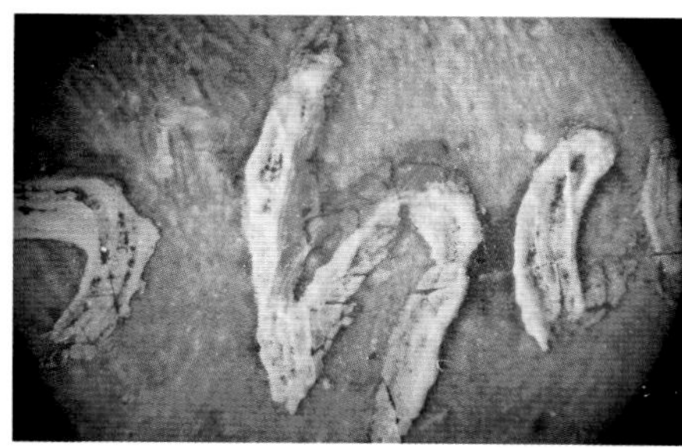

fig.47 **Micrograph of inscription shown at ×10 magnification**
Traces of gilding can be seen on the letters.

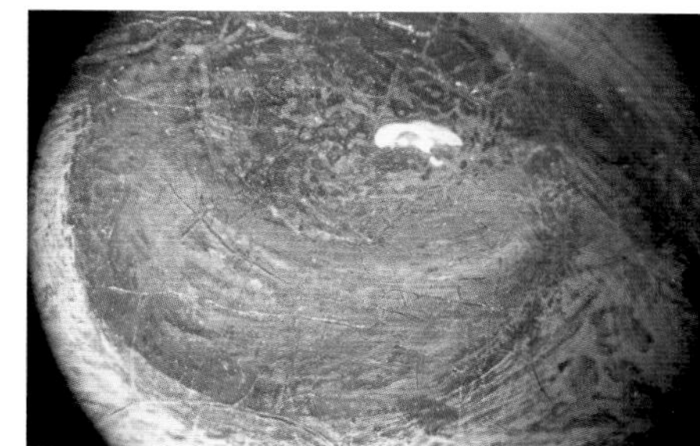

fig.48 **Micrograph of the eye shown at ×10 magnification**
This detail shows the red pigment of the Madonna's cloak beneath the painting of Shakespeare's eye.

THE EARLY YEARS

Shakespeare's family and his life in Stratford-upon-Avon

William Shakespeare was baptized in Stratford-upon-Avon on 26 April 1564 and was probably born a few days before. He was the eldest son of John Shakespeare (b. in or before *c.*1530, d.1601), a glove-maker who became bailiff (mayor) in 1568 and chief alderman of the town in 1571, and Mary Arden, the daughter of a local farmer.

One among six children who survived infancy, William Shakespeare grew up in a reasonably prosperous household and his father could have afforded to send his sons to school. It is likely that William Shakespeare attended the local grammar school where he would have learned Latin and studied the classics. Yet by the late 1570s the Shakespeare family was in financial trouble. Shakespeare's father was selling property and had virtually given up on his civic duties as an alderman. Any interest William may have had in furthering his formal education had to be put aside, and he probably left school at the usual age of fourteen or fifteen.

Dramatic events were to change Shakespeare's life. In November 1582, at the age of eighteen, he married Anne Hathaway (1555/6–1623), who was twenty-six. The difference in age was unusual by the standards of the period, but the reason for this swift early marriage is clear; only five months later Anne gave birth to a daughter, Susanna (d.1649). Less than two years later Shakespeare's family grew again, as Anne gave birth to twins Hamnet and Judith. It is likely that Shakespeare left Stratford-upon-Avon soon after their birth, although he probably kept in regular contact.

9. Map of Warwickshire and Leicestershire, 1576

Christopher Saxton (1542/4–1610/11)

Hand-coloured engraving
497 × 370mm (19½ × 14¾ in)
Shakespeare Birthplace Trust, Stratford-upon-Avon, 1993–31/444

Provenance Purchased 1912

Literature P.D.A. Harvey and Harry Thorpe, *The Printed Maps of Warwickshire 1576–1900* (Warwickshire County Council, Warwick, 1959), pp.1–5, 71–3

This is the earliest surviving topographical depiction of the county in which Shakespeare spent the first twenty years of his life. Christopher Saxton's map of Warwickshire and Leicestershire was part of a national project on which Saxton was engaged for several years, occasioned by the increasing demand during the sixteenth century for more detailed topographical information. His map of Warwickshire and Leicestershire was first published in 1576 and then re-issued in 1579 as part of a national atlas, the first to appear for any country.

Evidence for the height and form of the land is almost entirely confined to the southern border of the county, where humps indicate the prominent Cotswold scarp. Of more interest is the marked difference in woodland cover. The area to the north-west of the Avon, traditionally known as the Arden and once heavily forested, is still shown prominently dotted with tree symbols: in contrast, these symbols are largely absent to the south-east, across mainly arable country known as the Feldon, famed in Shakespeare's day for the growing of barley.

The river system, dominated by the River Avon, is clearly visible. Although no roads are shown, the main bridging points over the Avon, and its tributaries, are indicated. The most important settlements in the county, Coventry and Warwick, are depicted by large symbols, a smaller one, but with the same size lettering, reserved for other market towns, including, in the south of the county, Stratford, Alcester, Henley and Kineton. Below these towns, in smaller type, are villages, usually shown by means of a church, and hamlets simply indicated by a house. Parklands are portrayed as rounded areas enclosed by a fence symbol.

This map should only be used with care for the study of place names. Although some name forms are similar to those known to have been in circulation then, others are misleading, probably the result of Saxton's reliance on information supplied verbally. Charlecote, near Stratford, the home of the Lucy family, is given, for instance, in an otherwise unrecorded and very unlikely form, as 'Charleton', and Billesley as 'Bisley'. RB

10. Minute book of the Stratford-upon-Avon Corporation, showing the election of John Shakespeare as bailiff, 4 September 1568

Manuscript, ink on paper
Page of manuscript volume folio size 218 × 319mm (8½ × 12½in)
Shakespeare Birthplace Trust Records Office, Stratford-upon-Avon, BRU 2/1, p.368

Provenance From a collection deposited by the Stratford-upon-Avon Borough Council in 1862

Literature *Minutes and Accounts of the Corporation of Stratford-upon-Avon*, ed. Edgar I. Fripp (Dugdale Society, Stratford-upon-Avon, 1924), vol.2, pp.4–5, 12–14

This volume is shown open to record the proceedings of the Stratford-upon-Avon Corporation, when John Shakespeare was one of three candidates (listed on the right of the page) put forward for election as bailiff for the coming year.

The Stratford Corporation, comprising fourteen aldermen and fourteen chief burgesses, had come into being under the town's Charter of Incorporation of 1553. They served for life or until resignation or expulsion for misconduct. Each September they elected a bailiff from amongst their number, who then presided over their proceedings for the ensuing twelve months. With only fourteen senior figures from whom to choose, there was an expectation that each alderman would at some point serve as bailiff, and William Shakespeare's father, John, acted in this capacity.

Around 1560, the young John Shakespeare had been chosen as a chief burgess and he went on to hold a number of civic posts prior to his promotion to alderman in 1565. Two years later, on election day in September 1567, three names were put forward for bailiff: Robert Perrott (d.1589), John Shakespeare and Ralph Cawdrey (d.1588). Sixteen votes were cast for Perrott, three for Shakespeare and none for Cawdrey. At the next meeting, when the new bailiff was due to be sworn into office, neither Perrott nor Shakespeare attended and Cawdrey had to serve instead. The following year, September 1568, Perrott's and Shakespeare's names were put forward again, together with that of Robert Salisbury. On this occasion the votes were not recorded, yet John Shakespeare was later sworn in as bailiff. It is likely that he had not topped the poll, and his first act in his year of office was to vote through an order imposing fines on anyone refusing office. Thereafter Robert Perrott declined to attend any meetings at all and on 9 September 1569, the last over which John Shakespeare presided, Perrott was fined the massive sum of £20 (equivalent to a Stratford schoolmaster's annual salary). RB

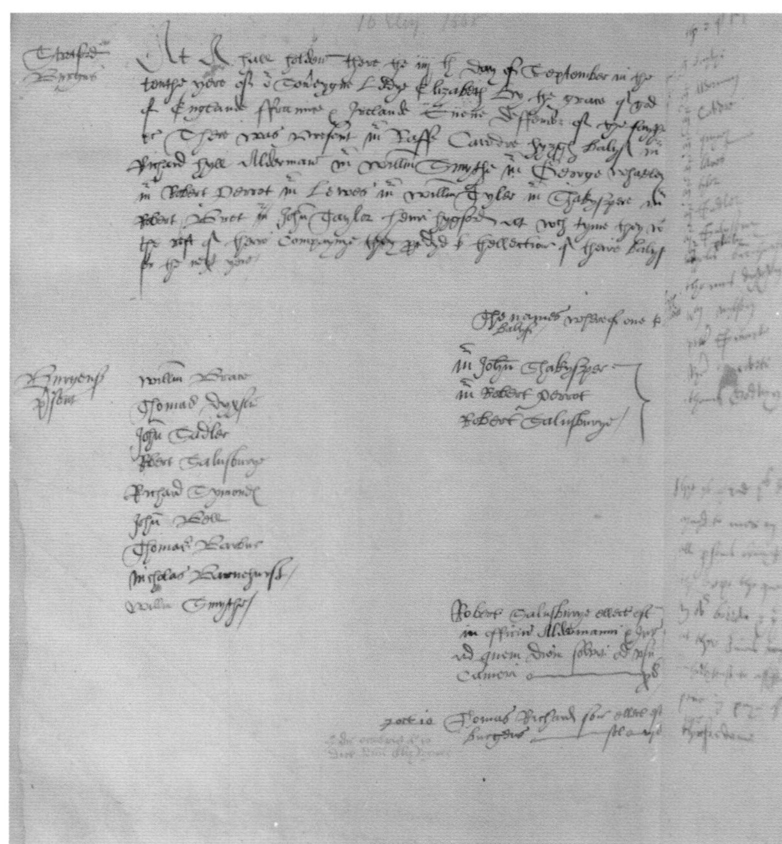

11. Parish register of Holy Trinity Church, Stratford-upon-Avon, showing the baptism of Susanna, daughter of William Shakespeare, 26 May 1583

Written in Latin
Manuscript, ink on parchment
Page of manuscript volume, folio size 450 × 210mm (17⅝ × 8¼in)
By kind permission of the Vicar and Parochial Church Council, Holy Trinity Church, Stratford-upon-Avon, DR 243/1, fol. 20v (baptisms)

Provenance Deposited by the Vicar and Churchwardens, Holy Trinity Church, Stratford-upon-Avon, 1964

Literature Robert Bearman, *Shakespeare in the Stratford Records* (Alan Sutton Publishing, Stroud, 1994), pp.1–14

This volume is the most important source of evidence for piecing together the various espisodes of Shakespeare's private life. It records his own baptism and burial and those of his three children, the marriages of his two daughters, the burial of his father and mother and similar information for his siblings.

These pages show that William Shakespeare's first child, Susanna (d.1649), was baptized on 26 May 1583, some six months after her parents' wedding. As Shakespeare had only just turned nineteen and is not known to have maintained his own establishment, the couple, with their new child, are assumed to have lodged in his family home in Henley Street, another indication that, by contemporary standards, the timing of the marriage was unfortunate. Anne conceived again, about a year later, giving birth in February 1585 to twins, Hamnet (d. 1596) and Judith (d.1662), but they proved to be the couple's last children.

The entries on these pages of the register were not made at the time the events actually took place. In 1538 priests had been instructed to keep a record of the baptisms, marriages and burials of their parishioners, but many had

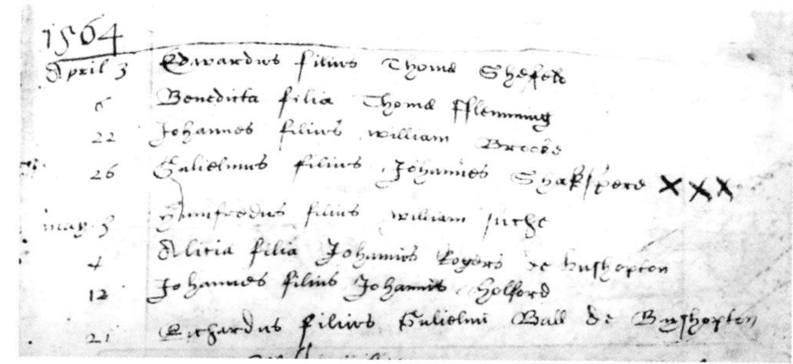

fig.49 **Parish register, photographed under ultraviolet light, showing the record of Shakespeare's baptism on 26 April 1564.**

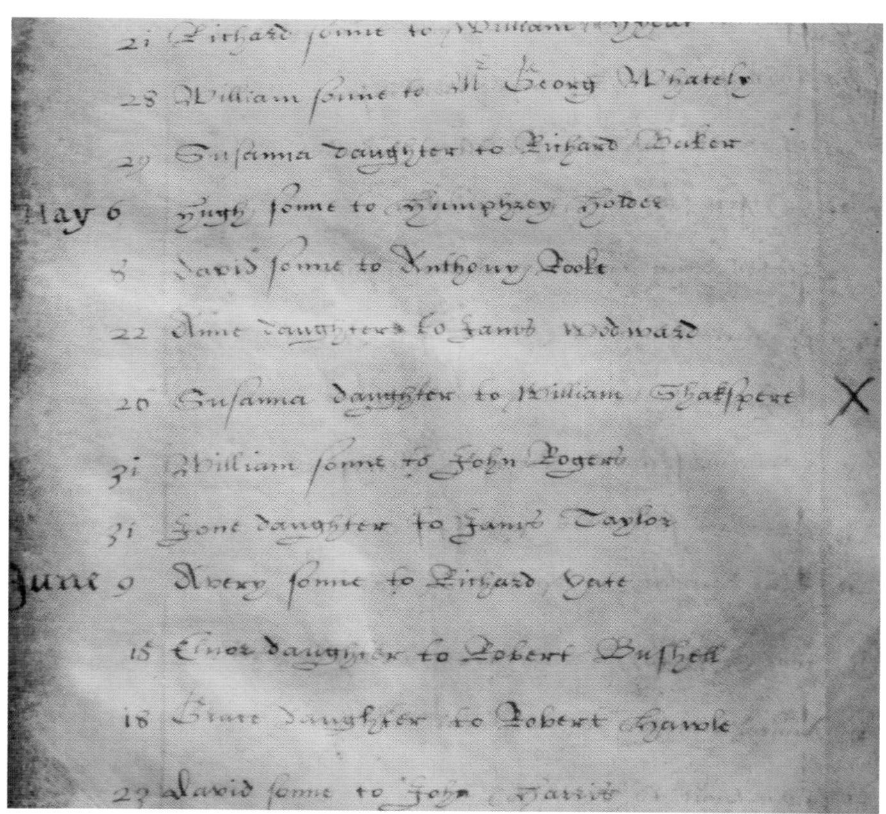

15 Richard a Bastard of Mr Phillip Mores servant
21 Thomas sonne to Mr Thomas Raynolds
31 William sonne to Edward Williams
February 2 Hamnet & Judeth sonne & daughter to William Shakspere X
3 Margret daughter to Hugh Piggette
10 John sonne to John Fisher
11 Thomas sonne to Richard Taylor
14 Richard sonne to John Elsome
21 Mary & Jone daughters to John Goodyeare
28 George sonne to Georges Carles
March 6 Josias sonne to Adrian Young
6 Margery daughter to John Hudsonne

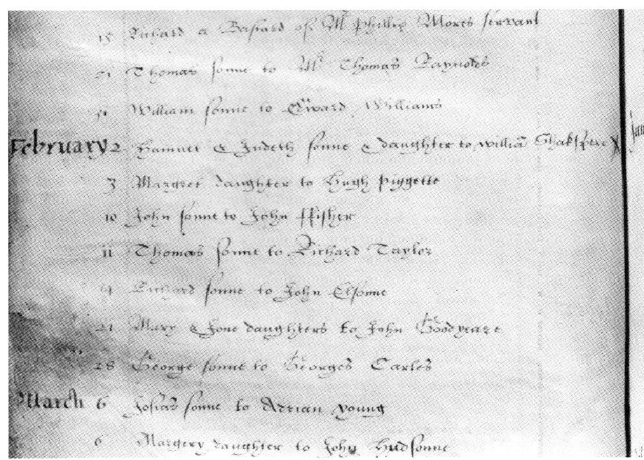

fig.50 **Parish register showing the birth of the twins, Hamnet and Judith, in 1585.**

31 An Infant of Mr Thomas Combes
August 10 Maria filia John Granams
11 Hamnet filius William Shakspere X
12 Margeria filia Georgij Singleton
13 Roger filius Jone Webbe
19 Bridged Rowles
September 3 Basill Burdet
16 Elizabet Aswell Alins woman

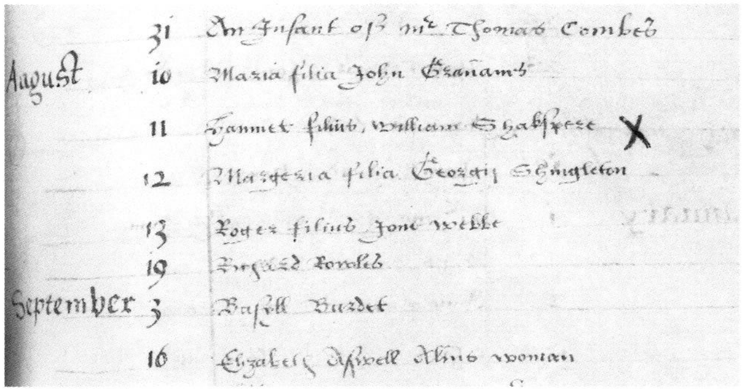

fig.51 **Parish register showing the burial of Hamnet in 1596.**

made their entries in paper volumes. By the end of the century, many of these volumes were in very poor condition. They were replaced by new parchment volumes by order of the Crown, and the entries from at least the beginning of Elizabeth's reign (1559) were copied into them. This is the volume that the Stratford churchwardens purchased. Its cover bears the date 1600 and all the entries down to 15 September of that year are in the neat and uniform hand of the copyist who was employed to transcribe the old register into the new. The names of the minister and churchwardens, who testify at the foot of each page to the accuracy of the copy, are also those holding office in 1600.

At some later date – probably in the early nineteenth century, when the sexton at the parish church regularly invited visitors to view the Shakespeare entries in the register – 'helpful' crosses were added to highlight them. RB

12. A list of Warwickshire recusants, including the name of John Shakespeare, 25 September 1592

Manuscript, ink on parchment
375 × 510 mm (14¾ × 20 in)
The National Archives, UK, SP 12/243/76

Provenance State Papers, Domestic, Elizabeth I

Literature David Thomas and Jane Cox, *Shakespeare in the Public Records* (Her Majesty's Stationery Office, London, 1985); Robert Bearman, 'John Shakespeare: A Papist or Just Penniless?', *Shakespeare Quarterly*, 56, no.4, winter 2005

One of the intriguing features in this list of those who had not been attending church in the county of Warwickshire is the inclusion of John Shakespeare's name. From 1580, the government was engaged in ever more determined attempts to seek out and punish 'recusants', that is, those who were obstinately persisting in their adherence to the Catholic faith. The process was considerably accelerated in 1591, when bodies of commissioners were appointed for each county to draw up detailed lists of such offenders. The Warwickshire commissioners got to work over the winter of 1591–2 and submitted a list in the spring, which did not meet with full government approval. A second survey was quickly carried out, and submitted to the government in October, of all those people 'presented to them ... to be Jesuits, seminary priests, fugitives or recusants ... or vehemently suspected to be such'.

There has been debate over the significance of this document as an indicator of John Shakespeare's religious beliefs. The list is divided into five sections, four of which concern varying degrees of recusancy, ranging from those who 'wilfully persist' in their obstinacy (including three from Stratford) to those who had conformed since the first return, or who were thought likely to do so (sixteen of whom were from Stratford). John Shakespeare's name occurs in a fifth category, those prevented from attending church for other reasons, such as illness or 'for feare of processe of debt'. As John Shakespeare is known, from other evidence, to have been in financial difficulties from the late 1570s until the year of this return, the stated reason for his failure to attend church cannot simply be written off as an excuse, especially as this would imply connivance by those who had had no hesitation in citing at least nineteen others from the town for failure to attend church on purely religious grounds. In cases of debt, however, the enforcement of legal action was very limited. RB

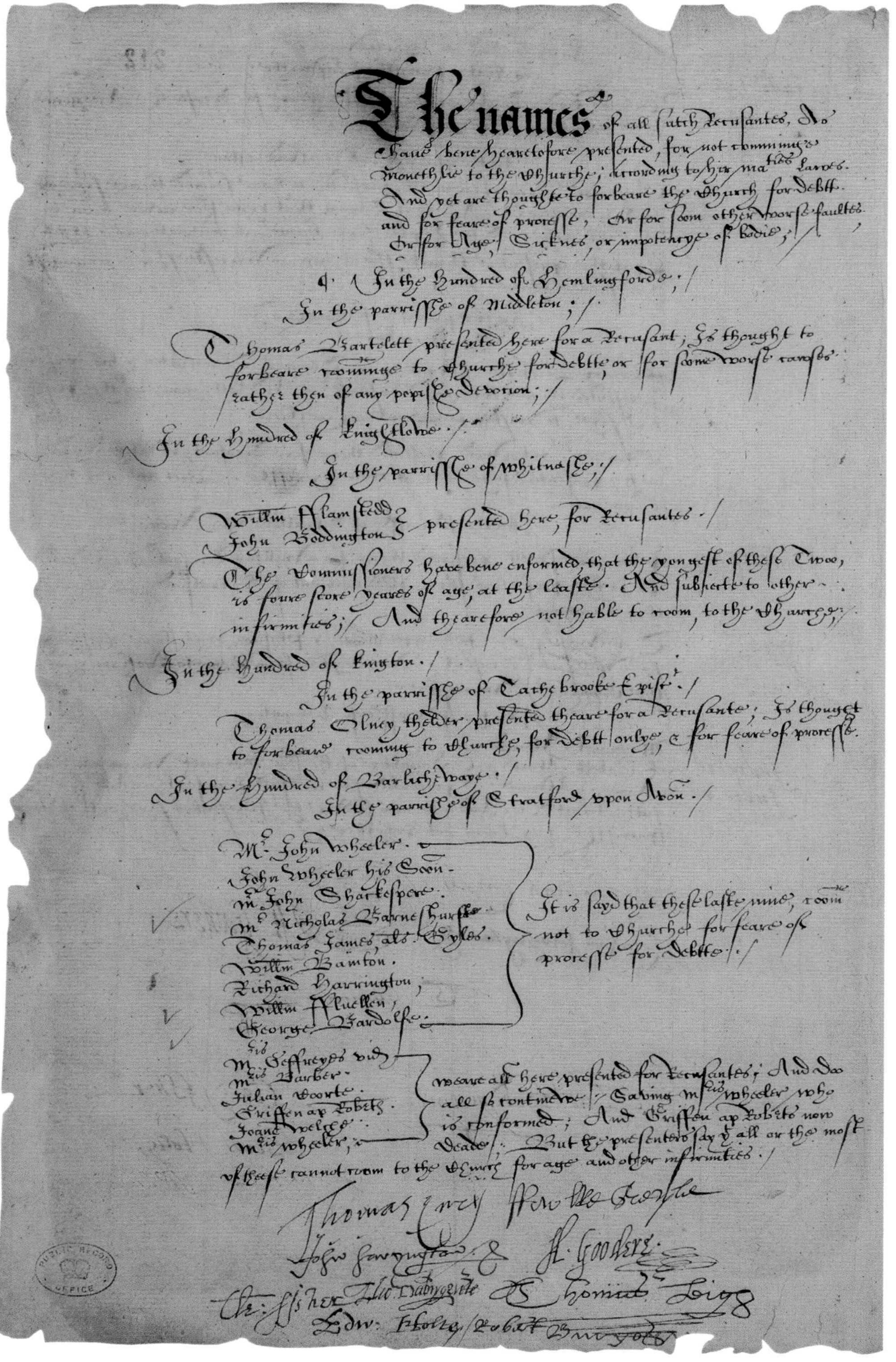

The names of all suche Recusantes, as have bene hearetofore presented, for not comminge monethlie to the Churche, acordinge to hir ma^ties lawes. And yet are thoughte to forbeare the Churche for debtt, and for feare of processe, Or for som other worse faultes. Or for Age, Sicknes, or impotencye of bodie;

In the Hundred of Hemlingforde;

In the parrishe of Midleton;

Thomas Bartlett presented here for a Recusant; Is thought to forbeare cominge to Churche for debtte, or for some worse cawses rather then of any popishe devotion;

In the hundred of Knightlowe.

In the parrishe of Whitnashe.

Willm Flamstedd
John Boddington } presented here, for Recusantes.

The Commissioners have bene enformed, that the yongest of these Twoo, is foure score yeares of age, at the leaste. And subiecte to other infirmities; And theare fore not hable to com, to the Churche;

In the hundred of Kington.

In the parrishe of Tachebrooke Episc.

Thomas Olney the elder presented theare for a Recusante; Is thought to forbeare cominge to Churche, for debtt onlye, & for feare of processe.

In the hundred of Barlichewaye.

In the parrishe of Stratford upon Avon.

Mr John Wheeler.
John Wheeler his Soon.
Mr John Shackspere.
Mr Nicholas Barneshurste.
Thomas James als Gyles.
Willm Bainton.
Richard Harrington.
Willm Fluellen.
George Bardolphe.
} It is sayd that these laste nine, coom not to Churche for feare of processe for Debtte.

Mris Jeffreys vid.
Mris Barber.
Julian Coorte.
Griffen ap Roberts.
Joane Welches.
Mris Wheeler,
} weare all here presented for Recusantes; And doo all so continewe; Saving Mris Wheeler who is conformed; And Griffen ap Roberts now deade; But the presenters say that all or the moste of theese cannot coom to the Churche for age and other infirmities.

Thomas Lucy   Fowlke Gresylle
John Haryngton   H. Goodere
Clem. Fisher   Tho. Dabrygecourte   Thomas Leigh
Edw. Holte   Robert Burgoyn

13. Man's cap, sixteenth century

English

Wool
Maximum diameter 303mm (12 in)
Museum of London, A5010

Provenance Found in Moorfields, London

Literature John Stow, *A Survey of London*, ed. Henry Morley (George Routledge, London, 1893), pp.445–6

John Stow (1524/5–1605), in his *Survey of London* written in 1598, records how the fashion for flat knitted caps, sometimes worn with chinstraps to prevent the wind blowing them away, spread from 'youthful citizens' to young aldermen during the reign of Henry VIII. It is possible that, as a sixteenth-century alderman of an important market town, John Shakespeare may have worn a cap similar to this rare example.

The popularity of the knitted cap had already waned by 1570 in favour, according to Stow, of caps and hats made of felt and therefore the following year a statute was passed for the 'Continuance of the Making of Caps'. This law ordered everyone over the age of six, except those of high rank, to wear a knitted woollen cap, made in England, on Sundays and holidays. Shakespeare's uncle was fined under the act, which was repealed in 1597. It was intended to boost sales of wool, which was England's principal commodity, and to safeguard employment. As many as twenty processes and up to fifteen trades could be involved in the manufacture of these often stylish, warm and waterproof felted caps. EE

14. Woman's glove, 1610–40

English

Leather (lamb skin) embroidered with silver and silver-gilt thread, cord wrapped with silver-gilt wire and silver-gilt purl, finished with a silver-gilt fringe
Length 310mm (12¼in)
Museum of London, 55.87/2a

Provenance The Hatchet family of Bedfont, Middlesex

John Shakespeare ran a business as a glover in the market town of Stratford-upon-Avon, which probably served townspeople and, occasionally, wealthy landowners. This embroidered one-piece leather glove is a relatively elaborate early seventeenth-century example of the type of work glovers produced for wealthy clients. The glover's skill, underpinned by his knowledge of leather, lay in his ability to select, prepare and cut dressed skins to maximize their elasticity and minimize wastage. He supervised the stitching of the gloves and, if they were to be decorated with embroidery, liaised between client and embroiderer. The most luxurious gloves were perfumed with oils, waters and spices such as musk, cedar, rose and cinnamon and many glovers carried out this service for an additional cost.

People of all classes wore gloves, which were, on the whole, undecorated. Even the very wealthy are usually depicted in portraits wearing or holding plain gloves, which were often finished with a turnover cuff of white leather or coloured silk. Embroidered gloves were worn, but they were primarily a symbol of wealth and status rather than a practical accessory. Many were commissioned as gifts, as an expression of the relationship between the giver and receiver, who might be a loved one, friend, business associate or patron. The gloves, carried like a favour, combined the personal and public perfectly, describing the attachment between donor and wearer. EE

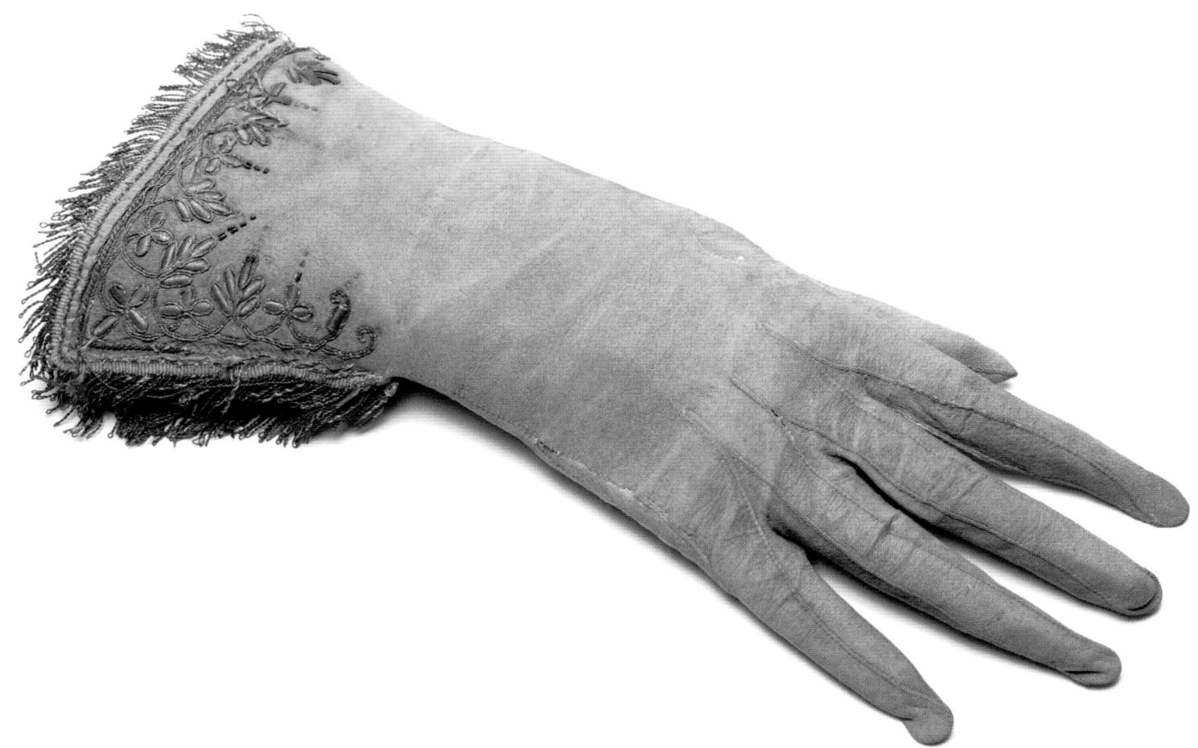

15. Early hornbook, *c.*1620

English

Horn, paper, wood
90 × 70mm (3½ × 2¾in)
The Bodleian Library, University of Oxford, Arch. A.f.11

Provenance Found at Brasenose College, 1881; presented to the Bodleian in 1882

In *The Two Gentlemen of Verona* (one of his earliest plays), Shakespeare compared a lover's petulant sadness to that of 'a schoolboy that had lost his ABC' (Act II, Scene i, line 21). This hornbook, now partially restored, demonstrates how easily such things could be lost. It is the earliest English example of this type of child's reading aid in existence, and was found in the grounds of Brasenose College, Oxford, in 1881.

At around the age of six, Shakespeare would have learned to recognize and pronounce his letters by memorizing the contents of hornbooks such as this. The printed sheet, here containing the alphabet, vowels and phonetic combinations, as well as the Lord's Prayer, was mounted in a handled wooden frame, and protected by a thin and highly polished layer of horn (hence the name). There were only twenty-four letters: 'i' and 'j', and 'u' and 'v', were considered identical, as in Latin. As the pupil indicated each letter with a fescue (or pointer), the schoolmaster would supply the correct pronunciation, which would then by learned by rote.

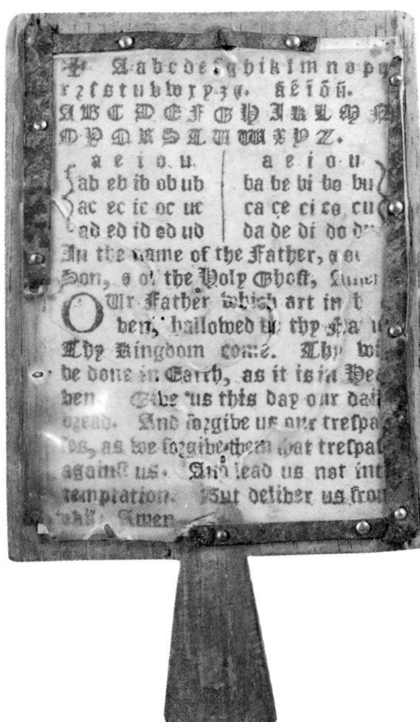

The celebrated dramatist and 'University Wit' George Peele (1556–96) sharpened this common childhood memory into a jingoistic point. Edward III's court spoke French, he wrote, because in those halcyon days, 'They went to school to put together towns,/And spell in France with fescues made of pikes' (*The Honour of the Garter*, 1590). In *Love's Labour's Lost* (Act V, Scene i, lines 44–5), Shakespeare fashioned a schoolboy joke from the same experience: *Question*: 'What is *a*, *b*, spelt backward, with the horn on his head?' *Answer*: 'Ba' (as in 'Baa, baa, black sheep'). NS

16. *A Shorte Introduction of Grammar*, 1567

William Lily (1468?–1522/3)

Printed book, 'Printed by Reyner Wolfe'
The Bodleian Library, University of Oxford, 4° A 17 Art, BS. open at sig. A2

Provenance Acquired 1835–47

Literature T.W. Baldwin, *William Shakspeare's Small Latin and Lesse Greeke*, 2 vols (University of Illinois Press, Urbana, Illinois, 1944)

William Lily, the first High Master of John Colet's newly founded St Paul's School, was largely responsible for producing what became the standard Latin grammar of the sixteenth century. It contained contributions by John Colet (1467–1519) and his friend the great humanist Desiderius Erasmus (*c.*1467–1536), and reached a more or less final form in 1548–9. A series of proclamations and injunctions issued by Edward VI, Elizabeth I and James I ensured that it became the only Latin grammar authorized for use in English schools and it remained the standard school text-book until at least the middle of the eighteenth century.

Like almost every schoolboy in the 1570s Shakespeare would have learned Latin using the grammar, in which poems and mnemonic verses show the importance attached to learning by heart at the time. Although Lily's *Shorte Introduction of Grammar* was once a very common book – it was regularly reprinted – very few examples of the early editions have survived because they were in constant use. Shakespeare makes fairly frequent allusions to the book, most famously in *The Merry Wives of Windsor* (Act IV, Scene i), in which the Welsh schoolmaster and parson Sir Hugh Evans quizzes his pupil Master William on its contents. Shakespeare evidently mastered the lessons it taught sufficiently well to have had little trouble reading works in Latin. HRW

AN INTRODVCTION OF THE EYGHT PARTES OF Latine Speache.

IN Speache be these eight partes folowinge:

Noune, Pronoune, Uerbe, Participle, } declined.

Aduerbe, Coniunction, Preposition, Interiection, } undeclined.

Of the Noune.

A Noune is the name of a thinge that may be seene, felt, hearde, or understande: As the name of my hande in Latine is Manus: the name of an house is Domus: the name of goodnes is Bonitas.

Of Nounes some be Substantiues, and some be Adiectiues.

A Noune Substantiue is that standeth by himselfe, & requireth not an other worde to be ioyned with him: as Homo *a man*. And it is declined with one article: as Hic magister, *a maister*. Or else with two at the moste: as Hic & hæc parens, *a Father or mother*.

A Noune Adiectiue is that can not stand by him selfe, but requireth to be ioyned with an other worde: as Bonus, *Good*. Pulcher, *Faire*. And it is declined either with three Terminations: as Bonus, Bona, Bonum: or else with three Articles: as Hic, Hæc, & Hoc Fœlix, *Happy*. Hic & hæc leuis, & hoc leue, *Lyght*.

A Noune Substantiue either is propre to the thing that it betokeneth: as Eduardus is my propre name. or else is commone to mo: as Homo, is a common name to all men.

Numbres of Nounes.

IN Nounes be two numbres, the Singular, & the Plurall. The Singular numbre speaketh of one: as Lapis, *a stone*. ye Plural

17. Bond for the marriage of William Shakespeare and Anne Hathaway, 28 November 1582

Written in Latin and English
Manuscript, ink on parchment
89 × 405mm approx (3½ × 16in)
Worcester Diocesan Archives (Worcestershire Record Office) X 797 BA 2783

Provenance From a collection deposited by the Worcester Diocesan Registry

Literature Chambers 1930, vol.2, pp.41–52; Schoenbaum 1975, pp.62–74

This is one of two records documenting the marriage of William Shakespeare and Anne Hathaway (1555/6–1623), which took place at the end of November 1582. It is a bond from two Stratford husbandmen, Fulk Sandells (1551–1624) and John Richardson (d.1594), to indemnify the bishop's officers should it later turn out that there was any legal obstacle to the marriage. On receipt of this bond, and other documents that have not survived, the bishop's court would then issue a licence to marry.

Marrying by licence was not the normal procedure. More common was marriage after three successive proclamations of banns in the parish church (or churches) of the betrothed. However, in Shakespeare's case there were complicating factors. Anne Hathaway was already three months pregnant. In addition, the calling of banns was not permitted during the period from Advent Sunday to the week after the feast of Epiphany (over the winter of 1582–3, from 2 December to 13 January). Some haste was therefore required. In the circumstances, the two families may also have wished to keep the affair low-key. In any event, it was decided to seek the consent of the bishop's court to marry by licence. The licence itself, which would have authorized a priest to carry out the ceremony, has not survived. The marriage did not take place in Stratford's parish church, another indication that the families were reluctant to draw attention to the match.

The situation is complicated further by the other surviving document of the marriage, an entry in the court register[1] recording the issue of the necessary licence: but the entry is dated 27 November and records the bride as Anne Whateley of Temple Grafton. These anomalies could partly be explained if the marriage had taken place at Temple Grafton, only a few miles from Anne's home at Shottery: this cannot be verified as its parish register for this early period has not survived. The name Whateley is now generally regarded as merely a clerical error.

Shakespeare was only eighteen when he married and Anne around twenty-six. By the standards of the time this was unusual and, given the poor state of the Shakespeare family finances in the early 1580s, suggests that the marriage was 'unplanned'. RB

1 Worcestershire Record Office, BA 2648/10.

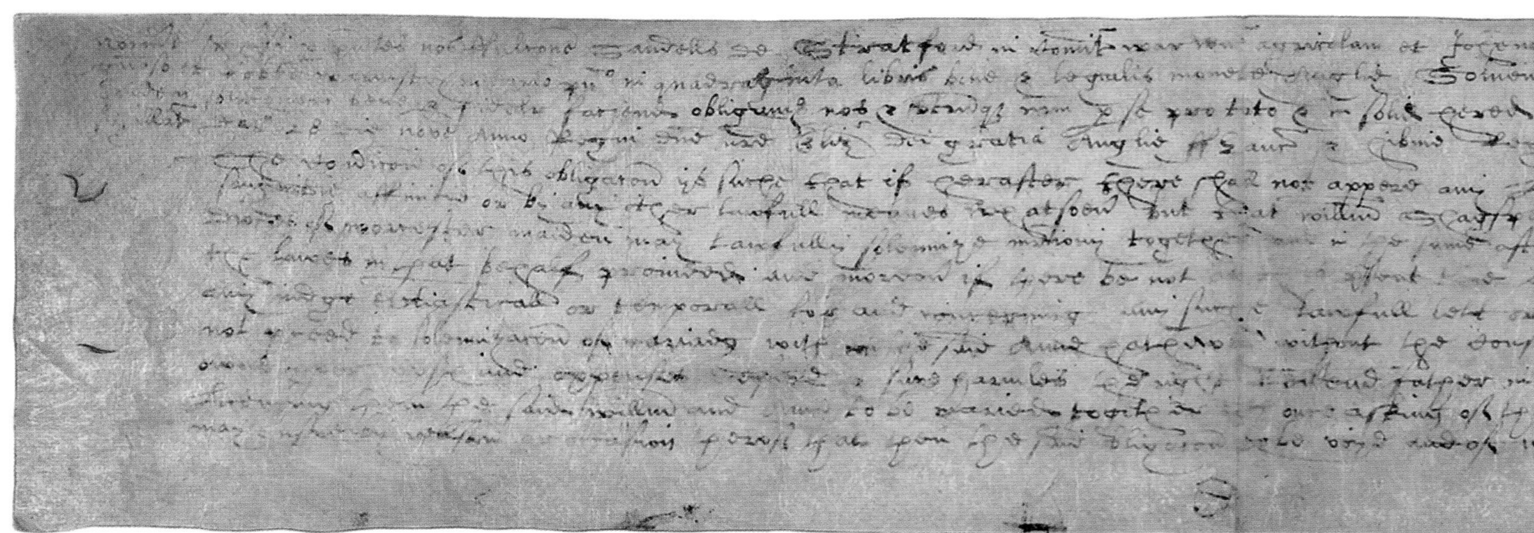

18. Gimmel ring, *c.*1600

English

Gold
Diameter 22mm (7/8in)
Inscribed: 'As handes doe shut, so hart be knit'
Museum of London, 62.121/10

Provenance Acquired by Sir John Evans in the 1850s; thereafter by descent; given to the Museum of London in 1962 from the collection of Dame Joan Evans

> I gave my love a ring and made him swear
> Never to part with it ...
> *The Merchant of Venice* (Act V, Scene i, lines 170–1)

We do not know what rings were given by Shakespeare when he married Anne Hathaway in November 1582, but simple gold bands, jewelled rings and gimmel rings were commonly exchanged as tokens of affection and at marriage. The gimmel ring (from the Latin *gemellus* meaning twin) was a perfect token of mutual fidelity and love, as it was constructed from two interlocking gold bands with a bezel 'made like ii handes one in an other'.[1] The message of union and affection is reinforced, in this example, by a small heart on the uppermost hand, and, when the rings are separated, a concealed motto is revealed on the inner face of each band, one reading 'AS HANDES DOE SHUT' and the other, 'SO HART BE KNIT': a secret shared between the wearer and her lover.

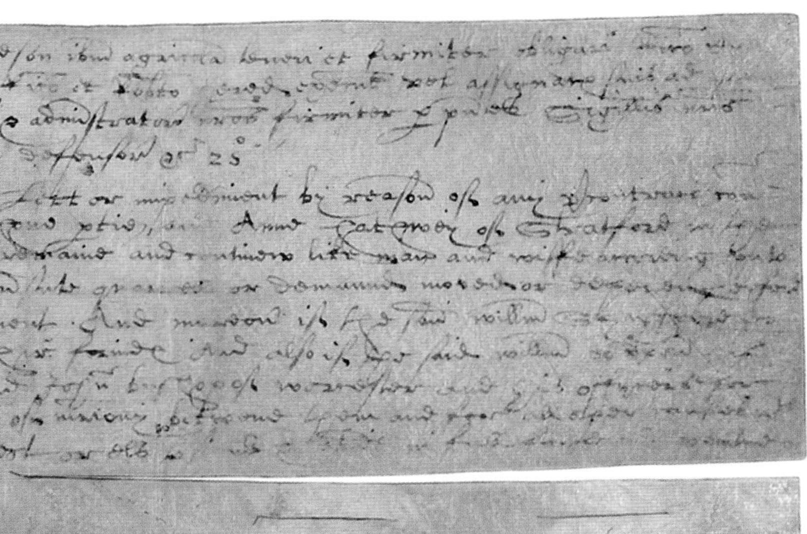

The overt symbolism of a gimmel ring with clasped-hand bezel would have been instantly understood in the Elizabethan and Jacobean period. Contemporary marriage practices required material proof of contract and gold rings were used to indicate marital intent or consent. Gimmel rings seem to have been used as tokens of 'goodwill' in courtship and, especially, as a material pledge or 'perfect Promise' during the marriage contract.[2] The union of the double band emphasized the binding agreement of the contract and the inscribed mottoes, taken from Latin and English compilations, helped to reinforce the marriage vow – 'What therefore God hath joined together, let no man put asunder'.[3] HF

1 London Metropolitan Archives, Diocese of London Consistory Court Records, Ms.DL/C/216/692/333r.
2 H. Swinburne, *A Treatise of Spousals or Matrimonial Contracts* (London, published posthumously in 1686, but probably written *c.*1600).
3 The Bible, Matt. 19:6.

19. Letter from Edward Alleyn (1566–1626) to Joan Alleyn (1572–1623), 1593

Manuscript, ink on paper
305 × 208mm (12 × 8in)
Dulwich College, Dulwich, London, MS I, fo.13

Provenance Dulwich College, Alleyn bequest, 1616

Literature Edmond Malone, *The Plays and Poems of William Shakespeare: Comprehending a Life of the Poet, and an Enlarged History of the Stage*, ed. James Boswell, 21 vols (London, 1821), vol.21, p.389; John Payne Collier, *Memoirs of Edward Alleyn, Founder of Dulwich College* (London, 1841), pp.25–6

Although we know few details about Shakespeare's marriage, the correspondence of one of his acquaintances provides a remarkable insight into the life of sixteenth-century newlyweds. This letter was written by Edward Alleyn, Shakespeare's near contemporary, and already a star of the London stage by the time Shakespeare arrived on the scene. On 22 October 1592, Alleyn secured a prosperous family business by marrying Joan Woodward, the step-daughter of Philip Henslowe (1555?–1616), the impresario in charge of the Rose Theatre. It was a love match, as this letter from Alleyn to his 'good sweet mouse' touchingly demonstrates; though the couple had no recorded children.

Within months of their marriage, Edward and Joan Alleyn were separated by a severe visitation of plague that shut down London's theatres, forcing Edward on tour. 'I received your letter at Bristol,' he writes, '. . . send to me by the carriers of Shrewsbury, or to West Chester, or to York.' A valuable resource for theatrical historians (naming a few of his fellow actors and one of the plays in their repertoire), Alleyn's letter is also both vividly domestic (the postscript concerns a pair of 'orange tawny stockings' and the plants in his kitchen garden) and anxiously pious ('hoping in God, though the sickness be round about you, yet by His mercy it may escape your house').

In Shakespeare's plays, marriage more often features as a long-promised conclusion than a lived experience. A list of his married couples makes bleak reading – a litany of jealousy between Leontes and Hermione in *The Winter's Tale*, alienation between Iago and Emilia in *Othello,* and worse (the Macbeths). As always with Shakespeare's plays, however, there are some glorious exceptions – the tender squabbles between Harry Hotspur and his wife in *The First Part of King Henry IV*, for instance, or Brutus and Portia's solicitous exchanges in *Julius Caesar*. Perhaps, after all – and despite the famous clause in Shakespeare's will bequeathing his 'second best bed' to his wife – our view of Shakespeare's marriage depends on the mere chance that none of his own personal letters have survived. NS

Emanuell

My good sweett mouse I comend me hartely to you And to my father my mother & my sister bess hoping in god though the sicknes be round about you yett by his mercy itt may escape your house which by the grace of god it shall therfor use this corse kepe your house fayr and clean which I knowe you will and every evening throwe water before your dore and in your bakesid and have in your windowes good store of rwe and herbe of grace and with all the grace of god which must be obtaynd by prayers and so doinge no dout but the Lord will mercifully defend you: now good mouse I have no newse to send you but this thatt we have all our helth for which the Lord be praysed I reseved your letter att bristo by richard couley for the which I thank you I have sent you by this berer Thomas popes kinsman my whit wascote because it is a trobell to me to cary it reseave it with this letter And lay it up for me till I com if you send any mor letters send to me by the cariers of shrowsbery or to west chester or to york to be keptt till my lord stranges players com and thus sweett hartt with my harty comenda to all our frends I sess from shrowsbery this wensday after saynt Jams his day being redy to begin the playe of hary of cornwall mouse do my harty comend to mr grigs his wif and all his houshold and to my sister phillyps

Your Loving housband E Alleyn

mouse you send me no newes of any things you should send of your domestycall matters such things as hapens att home as how your distilled watter proves or this or that or any thing what you will

and Jug I pray you lett my orayng tawny stokins of wolen be dyed a very good blak against I com hom to wear in the winter you sente me nott word of my garden but next tym you will but remember this in any case that all that bed which was parsley in the month of september you sowe it with spinage for then is the time: I would do it my sellf but we shall not com hom till allholand tyd and so swett mouse farwell and brook our Long Jorney with patience

ELIZABETHAN THEATRE

London playhouses in the 1580s

It is not clear where Shakespeare may have been between 1585 and 1592. He was already established on the London theatrical scene by 1592 when he is mentioned as an 'upstart' writer in London. By then he had written *The Two Gentlemen of Verona*, *The Taming of the Shrew*, *Titus Andronicus* and the three *Henry VI* plays. Whatever happened during the immediately preceding years is not clearly documented but later writers, some influenced by the desire to provide a romantic narrative, have speculated that he was a schoolteacher, lawyer, or even a soldier or a sailor. It is likely that at some point during that period he joined one of the many travelling theatre companies to learn the art of acting (see 'The lost years 1585–92', pp.226–7).

It is probable that Shakespeare had arrived in London by the late 1580s. At this period the city's population was rapidly expanding and the theatre was growing in popularity. Permanent public playhouses were being built just outside the city walls, both to the north in Shoreditch and to the south on the banks of the Thames, offering a different play every day. Writers like Christopher Marlowe (bap.1564, d.1593) and Thomas Kyd (bap.1558, d.1594) began to satisfy the demand for inventive drama and in 1587 Marlowe had his first major success with the tragedy *Tamburlaine*, followed by *Dr Faustus* in 1591. The theatres attracted huge crowds – sometimes up to 3,000 people – and Shakespeare must have been impressed and inspired by the potential for a young writer.

20. Plan of London from *Civitates Orbis Terrarum*, vol.1, 1572

Frans Hogenberg (*c*.1540–*c*.1590)

Engraving with hand-colouring
395 × 524mm (15 1/2 × 20 5/8 in)
Inscribed at top: LONDINVM FERACISSIMI AN:/GLIAE REGNI METROPOLIS;
at base: long description of London in Latin
UCL Art Collections, University College London, EPC 4787

Provenance Bequeathed by George Grote in 1872

Literature Arthur M Hind, *Engraving in England in the 16th and 17th Centuries. Part I: The Tudor Period* (Cambridge University Press, Cambridge, 1952); John Fisher, *An A–Z of Elizabethan London* (Topographical Society, London, 1979), pp.v–xi; James Elliot, *The City in Maps: Urban Mapping to 1900* (British Library, London, 1987), pp.26–37, Sanford 2002, pp.99–106 and 175

The most important map of late sixteenth-century London shows both sides of the river at a time when London's population had grown to around 90,000 people and the city had expanded beyond its medieval walls. The area on the south bank of the Thames known as Southwark shows the level of development before the major theatres of popular entertainment were built in the 1590s. Although this area is shown largely surrounded by green fields containing cattle and horses, it was already in use as a place for popular recreation and two circular arenas, for baiting animals such as bears and bulls with dogs, can be seen, sited on the South Bank. There were also a number of houses lining the main thoroughfares where inns, brothels and gaming houses were located. Within thirty years ever more

sophisticated audiences would flock to this area, not only to see brutal entertainments such as bear-baiting, but also to come to the newly built public theatres to be entertained by actors performing history plays, bawdy comedies and gripping dramatic tragedies.

Hogenberg's map served as the first plate in volume one of a German atlas of European cities, first published in Cologne in 1572 and written by George Braun (1541–1622). The print provides an intriguing bird's-eye view of London that allows viewers to trace the street plan and key monuments as though they were travelling through the city. In the foreground four figures are dressed in the costume of the principal inhabitants of the city: a gentleman and a merchant along with their wives. As a vibrant centre of trade, the river is shown busy with several different types of boat, including a royal barge at the centre, together with commercial merchant ships and personal water-taxis. The cartouche in the lower left-hand corner expounds: 'This is that royal city of all England London, situated on the River Thames, named, as many believe, by Caesare Trinobantes, made noble by the commerce of many races, adorned with houses, decorated with temples, elevated with arches, with famous ingenuity ... finally its wonderful excellence of wealth and abundance of all things; this same Thames carries into it the wealth of the whole world, a passageway for laden ships for 60 miles.'[1] TC

1 Sanford 2002, p.175.

21. A view from St Mary Overy, Southwark, looking towards Westminster, *c.*1638

Wenceslaus Hollar (1607–77)

Pen and black ink over graphite on two joined sheets of paper
127 × 306 mm (5 × 12 in)
Inscribed upper centre: 'East Part [crossed through] of ? West part o[f] Southwark towards Westminster' in artist's hand in graphite and brown ink; on verso: a list of towns and column of figures
Yale Center for British Art, Paul Mellon Collection (B1977.14.5548)

Provenance Sotheby's, 10 June 1931, lot 129 or 132

Literature Iolo A. Williams, 'Hollar: A Discovery by Iolo A. Williams', *The Connoisseur*, xcii, 1933, pp.309–13; I. A. Shapiro, *Shakespeare Survey 2*, Cambridge, 1949, pp.21–3; Richard T. Godfrey, *Wenceslaus Hollar: A Bohemian Artist in England* (Yale University Press, New Haven and London, 1994), cat.64

This exceptionally important study of Southwark shows the circular Globe Theatre in the middle distance, as it was rebuilt after a fire in 1613. From the late 1580s the South Bank of the Thames developed into a lively resort for popular entertainment. In 1603 John Stow described Southwark as an area of 'diverse streets, ways and winding lanes' full of inhabited buildings.[1] The area was home to five of London's prisons, numerous brothels (known as 'stew-houses') and the ever-popular bear-baiting house. In the midst of this colourful environment the public theatres were opened: the Rose in 1587 and the Swan in 1595. Shakespeare and his company members used the timbers of an earlier theatre in Shoreditch to erect the Globe Theatre on the South Bank in 1599.

This drawing was made while the artist Wenceslaus Hollar was resident in London between 1636 and 1644, as a study for his most ambitious panorama of London, an etching known as the *Long View of London from Bankside*, published in 1647 (fig.52). Hollar probably made numerous drawings for this printed view, which were taken on the spot, perhaps with the use of a drawing frame, from various high points across London.[2] The outlines were first laid in with graphite – a relatively new drawing medium – and later worked up in ink, probably in Hollar's studio. The clarity of Hollar's exacting drawing style allowed him to assimilate the complex three-dimensional space of mid seventeenth-century London into a brilliantly observed diagrammatic scheme.

In the resulting print, which was completed while Hollar was in Antwerp, some of the inscribed names of buildings are inaccurate. Once Hollar was outside England he would have been unable to check the topographical accuracy of his drawings and he may have consulted an earlier panorama of London by C.J. Visscher, published in 1616, which reverses the Globe and the bear-baiting house. In Hollar's printed panorama the actual Globe building is mislabelled the 'Beere bayting h[ouse]', while the circular building to the right, known to Londoners as the Hope Theatre (also used for bear-baiting) was wrongly described as 'The Globe'.

By the 1630s the South Bank was in decline as an area for popular entertainment: the Rose Theatre had been demolished and the Swan Theatre was in decay. TC

1 H.B. Wheatley, *Stow's Survey of London* (J.M. Dent, London and New York, 1956), p.359.
2 Another study of this view of Bankside, also showing the theatres, exists in a sketchbook at the John Ryland Library, University of Manchester. See Richard Pennington, *A Descriptive Catalogue of the Etched Work of Wenceslaus Hollar 1607–1677* (Cambridge University Press, 1982), cat.1014. A drawing for the far right side of the panorama exists at the Yale Center for British Art: *A View of the East Part of Southwark, Looking towards Greenwich*, B1977.14.4464.

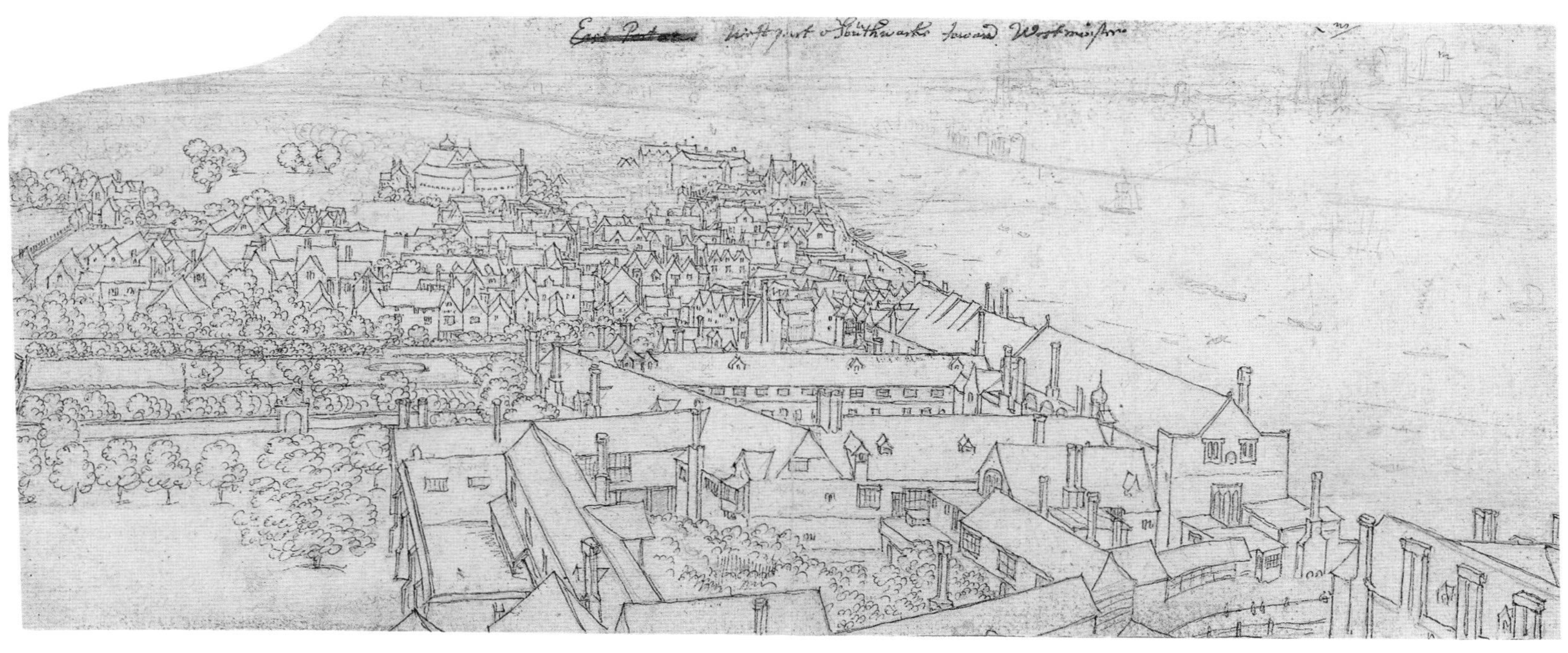

fig.52: **The *Long View of London from Bankside*,** *c.*1647
Lithograph copy of original etching by Wenceslaus Hollar,
455 × 2315mm (18 × 91⅛ in)
Museum of London

22. A portrait of an unknown man, called Christopher Marlowe (bap.1564, d.1593), dated 1585

Unknown Anglo-Netherlandish artist

Oil on panel
627 × 530mm (24⅝ × 20⅞in)
Inscribed top left: ANNO DNI ÆTATIS SVÆ 21/1585/QVOD ME NVTRIT/ME
The Masters and Fellows of Corpus Christi College, Cambridge

Provenance Discovered in the fabric of the Spencer Room, Master's Lodge (built 1823–7), Corpus Christi College in 1952

Literature 'B.D'., 'The Emergence of a College Portrait', *Letter of the Corpus Association*, no.45, Michaelmas, 1966, pp.24–5; Noel Purdon, 'Quod Me Nutrit Me Destruit', *Letter of the Corpus Association*, no.46, Michaelmas, 1967, pp.30–3; Fredson Bowers (ed.), *Elizabethan Dramatists Dictionary of Literary Biography*, vol.62 (Gale Research, Detroit, 1987), p.213; A.D. Wraight, *In Search of Christopher Marlowe: A Pictorial Biography* (Adam Hart Ltd, Chichester, 1999; first published 1965), p.68

Christopher Marlowe was a highly talented but reckless man whose attraction to the Elizabethan underworld led to his untimely and violent death. Like Shakespeare, Marlowe was the son of an artisan from a provincial town. Marlowe, however, was fortunate in gaining a scholarship to Corpus Christi College, Cambridge, where he studied at least intermittently from 1581 to 1587, when he received his MA. He probably began his literary career while at university, but he was also employed during this period as a government informer or agent, perhaps working for short periods in France. In the late 1580s Marlowe settled in London and had his first dramatic success with his play *Tamburlaine the Great* (cat.23). He went on to write a number of other plays of considerable psychological depth, including *Dr Faustus* and *The Jew of Malta*, which appear to have influenced the work of Shakespeare. On 30 May 1593, when he was only twenty-nine, Marlowe was stabbed to death following an argument with an associate at a house in Deptford.

No portraits of Christopher Marlowe from the period can be authenticated. Since its discovery in 1952 at Corpus Christi, Cambridge, this portrait of an educated and self-assured young man has been championed as a likeness of Marlowe. The sitter is described in the Latin inscription as being twenty-one in 1585, the age Marlowe would have been, along with a number of other wealthy, but less well-known, men.[1] The age of the sitter and the site of the picture's discovery do not provide enough evidence on their own to identify it as a portrait of Marlowe. Even the provenance is uncertain: it is not clear how or when the portrait came into the possession of the college.

The Latin inscription, which can be translated as 'that which nourishes me destroys me', is a version of a reasonably well-known Latin tag or *impresa* that appeared in various forms in emblem books of the period.[2] Versions of this expression appear in the works of Malowe and Shakespeare. As with the portrait of John Donne (cat.80), the motto must have had some personal significance that is now lost to us. The statement can probably be read as a plea from the sitter to a lover (or patron).

The painting has suffered serious damage in the past and has been extensively restored, but enough of the original paint remains to make a reasonable assessment of its original appearance. The costume of the sitter is very elaborate with over thirty gold buttons adorning the striking black slashed doublet. These clothes would have incurred large bills from a tailor and goldsmith. It is highly unlikely that Marlowe would have been able to afford such lavish attire as a young student, even if he did receive payments for undercover government work. This type of doublet would also have been an ostentatious outfit for a young man of limited means, even if the clothes were borrowed for the occasion. The picture was painted by a highly competent professional artist, who took particular care over the man's features – such as the extraordinary soft and buoyant hairstyle and downy facial hair – and the details of his costume. Such an acutely observed likeness must have been produced after several sittings from life. TC

1 There would have been over thirty other students at Corpus Christi College, Cambridge, in 1585, and there must have been a similar number who had since left the college but were aged 21 in 1585.

2 Purdon 1967, pp.31–2 (see Literature). For example, in Whitney's *Choice of Emblems* (1586), 'Qui me alit extinguit' is glossed 'Even as the waxe doth feede, and quenche the flame,/So loue gives life, and loue dispaire doth give'; *Geffrey Whitney: A Choice of Emblems* with introduction by John Manning (Scholar Press, Aldershot, 1989), p.183.

NO DNI ÆTATIS SVÆ 21
1585
ME NVTRIT
DESTRVIT

23. *Tamburlaine the Great*, 1590

Christopher Marlowe (bap.1564, d.1593)

Printed book, 'Printed by Richard Jones'
The Bodleian Library, University of Oxford, Mal.267(1), open at sigs. F2v–3r

Provenance Edmond Malone (1741–1812); Richard Malone, Lord Sunderlin (1738–1816); presented to the Bodleian Library in 1812

Literature Christopher Marlowe, *Tamburlaine the Great*, ed. J.S. Cunningham (Manchester University Press, Manchester, 1981); Ruth Samson Luborsky and Elizabeth Morley Ingram, *A Guide to English Illustrated Books 1536–1603* (Tempe, Arizona, 1999), vol.1, pp.442–6 and 568

This is one of only two known copies of the first edition of this very popular two-part play: it was reprinted in 1593, 1597 and 1605–6. *Tamburlaine* was published anonymously but is almost always assigned to Christopher Marlowe, one of Shakespeare's greatest contemporaries. The first part, probably dating from the summer of 1587, was Marlowe's first major success: the declamatory style of its blank verse would have suited Edward Alleyn (1566–1626), who was then a leading actor in the theatrical company called the Admiral's Men. It seems likely that the second part rapidly followed the first. By the end of the first part the Scythian shepherd and robber Tamburlaine (a character inspired by the exploits of the fourteenth-century warrior Timur) has won the crown of Persia, conquered the Turkish emperor Bajazet, captured Damascus and fallen in love with Zenocrate, the daughter of the Soldan (ruler) of Egypt. In the second part he conquers Babylon, has his chariot drawn by the kings of Trebizond and Soria among others – these are 'the pampered jades of Asia' to whom Pistol refers in *The Second Part of King Henry IV* – and finally dies with Zenocrate. Some of the play's power derives from its heroic rhetoric and spectacular effects. The exact nature of the relationship between Marlowe's works and Shakespeare's is uncertain, but *Tamburlaine*'s success on the stage as a two-part heroic drama may well have influenced Shakespeare's writing of the *Henry VI* plays and *The Tragedy of King Richard III*, as well as contributing to the imaginative power of the character Aaron in *Titus Andronicus*. Apart from their title pages, plays of the period were not usually illustrated. The woodcut displayed here is a generalized image of a knight and was first used in *The contemplation of mankinde* (1571) by Thomas Hill (1528–*c.*1574). HRW

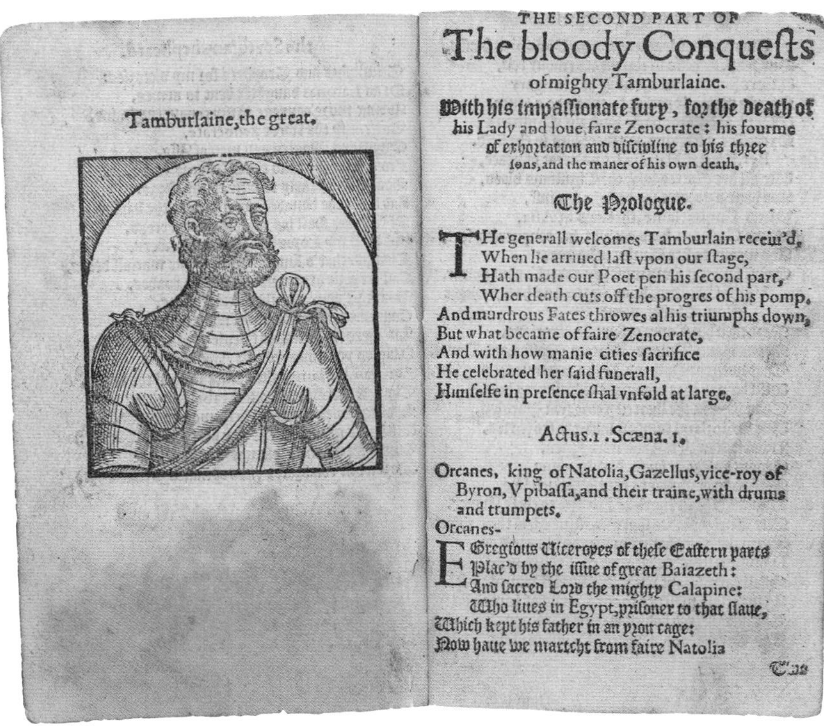

Tamburlaine,the great.

THE SECOND PART OF
The bloody Conquests
of mighty Tamburlaine.
With his impassionate fury, for the death of his Lady and loue faire Zenocrate: his fourme of exhortation and discipline to his three sons, and the maner of his own death.

The Prologue.

THe generall welcomes Tamburlain receiu'd,
When he arriued last vpon our stage,
Hath made our Poet pen his second part,
Wher death cuts off the progres of his pomp,
And murdrous Fates throwes al his triumphs down,
But what became of faire Zenocrate,
And with how manie cities sacrifice
He celebrated her said funerall,
Himselfe in presence shal vnfold at large.

Actus.1 .Scæna. 1.

Orcanes, king of Natolia, Gazellus, vice-roy of Byron, Vpibassa, and their traine, with drums and trumpets.

Orcanes-

EGregious Viceroyes of these Eastern parts
Plac'd by the issue of great Baiazeth:
And sacred Lord the mighty Calapine:
Who liues in Egypt, prisoner to that slaue,
Which kept his father in an yron cage:
Now haue we martcht from faire Natolia

24. *The Spanish Tragedy*, 1615 (first edition n.d., probably 1592)

Thomas Kyd (bap.1558, d.1594)

Printed book, 'Printed by W. White for I. White and T. Langley, and are to be sold at their Shop over against the Sarazens head without New-gate'
The British Library, London, C.117.b.36

Provenance Purchased 1838

The Spanish Tragedy by Thomas Kyd, perhaps the original 'one-hit wonder', was the single most influential play of the Elizabethan era and beyond. It was already a popular success during Shakespeare's early years in London and was still being printed long after his death. At least eleven editions are known between 1592 and 1633, out-stripping even Shakespeare's most popular plays. At the same time, it continued to attract new audiences. The *Diary* of box-office receipts at the Rose belonging to Philip Henslowe (1555?–1616) records nearly thirty performances between 1592 and 1597, presumably with Edward Alleyn in the leading role of Hieronimo – the public magistrate who contrives a private revenge on his son's murderer. The actor Richard Burbage (1568–1619; cat.51) was also famous in the part: 'old Hieronimo' is listed alongside 'young Hamlet', 'kind Lear', and 'the grievèd Moor' in an anonymous elegy to him in 1618 – the only non-Shakespearean role to be named.

Thomas Kyd's reputation has been overshadowed by that of Christopher Marlowe (cat.22), with whom he had shared lodgings, 'writing in one chamber' in around 1591. That association cost Kyd dear: hauled in for questioning – and, allegedly, torture – over Marlowe's scandalously subversive views, he died a broken man in August 1594, in the same year that *The Spanish Tragedy* was first reprinted. The play's posthumous reputation was as enduring as the Senecan ghost that presides over it, sponsoring imitations (including Shakespeare's *Titus Andronicus*), additions (some by Ben Jonson), parodies, allusions and even a 'prequel', *The First Part of Jeronimo*, published in a corrupt text in 1605. NS

The Spanish Tragedie:
OR,
Hieronimo is mad againe.

Containing the lamentable end of *Don Horatio*, and *Belimperia*; with the pittifull death of *Hieronimo*.

Newly corrected, amended, and enlarged with new Additions of the *Painters* part, and others, as it hath of late been diuers times acted.

LONDON,
Printed by W. White, for I. White and T. Langley, and are to be sold at their Shop ouer against the Sarazens head without New-gate. 1615.

25. *The Anatomie of Abuses*, 1583

Philip Stubbes (*c.*1555–1610?)

Printed book, 'Printed at London by Richard Jones'
Octavo, 160 × 140mm (6⅜ × 5½in) approximately
The British Library, London, 697.a.34, open at p.117

Provenance At foot of title page 'Tho: Wright/1606'?; purchased in 1841

Literature Alexandra Walsham, '"A Glose of Godlines": Philip Stubbes, Elizabethan Grub Street and the Invention of Puritanism', *Belief and Practice in Reformation England*, eds Susan Wabuda and Caroline Litzenberger (Ashgate, Aldershot, 1998), pp.177–206

Philip Stubbes was one of the leading pamphleteers and hack-writers of late sixteenth-century London, denouncing contemporary sins and practices in the hope of averting divine punishment. In the course of his immediately popular tract, *The Anatomie of Abuses* (twice printed in 1583 and again in 1584, 1585 and 1595), he provides detailed descriptions of the evils of the time in the form of a dialogue concerning 'a famous Ilande called Ailgna' (Anglia or England).

Among the many abuses surveyed are the way in which the theatres draw people away from churches and God's word towards 'ydlenes, vnthriftynes, whordome, wanton*n*es, drunken*n*es, and what not'. In Stubbes's view plays about divine matters are sacrilegious, while profane or secular plays dishonour God and breed vice; comedies and tragedies are all about sex and violence; the theatres encourage disgustingly amorous and erotic behaviour while teaching bad morals. In various accidents and earthquakes God has punished those who attend the theatre. Stubbes expresses the concerns about the theatre coming from civic and religious authorities. The moral issues raised by what was shown on the stage and by the outrageous behaviour of actors and audience were evidently important for them, but the theatre was also identified as a potentially dangerous site for riotous behaviour, leading to public disturbances. HRW

The Anatomie
of Abuſes:
Containing,
A DISCOVERIE, OR BRIEFE Summarie of ſuch Notable Vices and Imperfections, as now raigne in many Countreyes of the World: but (eſpeciallye) in a famous ILANDE called AILGNA: Together, with moſt fearefull Examples of Gods Iudgements, executed vppon the wicked for the ſame, aſwel in AILGNA of late, as in other places, elſewhere.
Very Godly, to be reade of all true Chriſtians: but moſt needefull to be regarded in ENGLANDE.
¶Made Dialogue-wiſe by Phillip Stubbes.
Seene and allowed, according to order.

Math. 3. Verſ. 2.
Repent, for the Kingdome of God is at hande.
Lvc. 13. Verſ. 5.
I ſay vnto you (ſaith Chriſt) except you repent, you ſhall all periſh.

¶ Printed at London, by Richard Jones. 16. Auguſt. 1583.

26. *A Ballad of the Lamentable and Tragical History of Titus Andronicus*, 1630s or 1640s

Unknown author
Printed sheet, 'Printed for F. Coles, T. Vere, J. Wright, and J. Clarke.'
283 × 356mm (11⅛ × 14in) approximately
The British Library, London, Huth 50 (69)

Provenance From the library of bibliophile Henry Huth (1815–78); bequeathed to the British (Museum) Library by his son Alfred Henry Huth in 1903

This exceptionally rare illustrated song sheet or ballad may have originally derived from Shakespeare's *Titus Andronicus*, published in 1594. Shakespeare's London was the centre of an emerging mass media world, supported by the three pillars of the pulpit, the printing press and the playhouse, each of which had an uneasy relationship with the others, and all of which were strictly regulated. International events were discussed in sermons, reenacted on the stage and reported in print, whether as front line testimony or jauntier ballads. Major events such as the Spanish Armada, for example, prompted printed sermons and prayers, as well as 'true discourses' of the battle in allegorical dramatizations and victorious songs.

Ballads such as this one were part of a burgeoning market for London's printers. Written 'to the tune' of a common stock of melodies, and often featuring a primitive illustration for those who could not read, they were a popular form of Jacobean and Elizabethan 'home entertainment'. They were also a useful marketing gimmick for plays – a theatre 'tie in' or penny 'taster' designed to attract new audiences. Kyd's *Spanish Tragedy* and Marlowe's *Tamburlaine the Great* and *Jew of Malta* were all issued in ballad form, as was Shakespeare's earliest triumph, *Titus Andronicus*.

The Stationers' Register of 6 February 1594 records John Danter's intention to publish both the play and ballad of the 'Noble Roman Historye of Tytus Andronicus'. The First Quarto of Shakespeare's play was printed that year, and so, presumably, was the ballad, though the earliest surviving text dates from around twenty-five years later. The example shown here may date from the 1630s or 1640s.[1] The exact chronology of Shakespeare's script, its printed texts, and the ballad version of the same story remain enormously complicated, and it seems unlikely that the truth will ever be known. Shakespeare himself makes his own comment on the genre. 'Pray now, buy some,' says one of Autolycus's customers in *The Winter's Tale* (Act IV, Scene iv, lines 261–2): 'I love a ballad in print a-life, for then we are sure they are true.' NS

1 This dating is based on the dates of the booksellers for whom the ballad was printed; Francis Coles (active before 1624–49), Thomas Vere (active before 1646–80), John Wright (active before 1605–58) and John Clarke (active before 1620–69). See Henry R. Plomer, *A Dictionary of the Booksellers and Printers who were at Work in England, Scotland and Ireland from 1641 to 1667* (London, 1907).

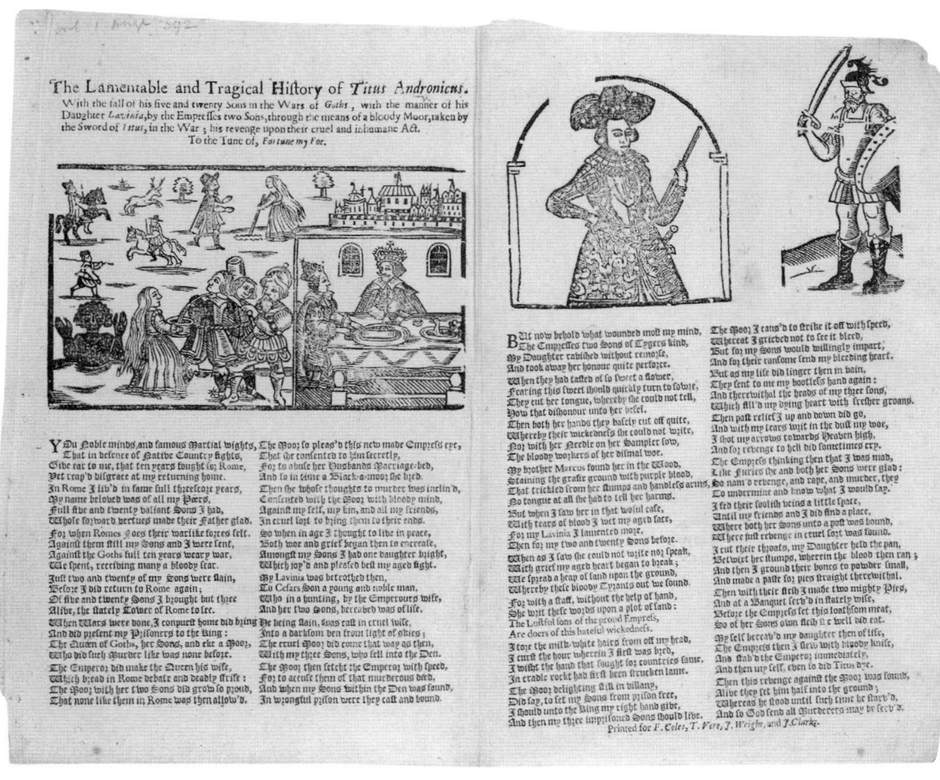

The Lamentable and Tragical History of *Titus Andronicus*.
With the fall of his five and twenty Sons in the Wars of *Goths*, with the manner of his Daughter *Lavinia*, by the Empresses two Sons, through the means of a bloody Moor, taken by the Sword of *Titus*, in the War; his revenge upon their cruel and inhumane Act.
To the Tune of, *Fortune my Foe*.

YOu Noble minds, and famous Martial wights,
That in defence of Native Country fights,
Give ear to me, that ten years fought for Rome,
Yet reap'd disgrace at my returning home.

In Rome I liv'd in fame full threescore years,
My name beloved was of all my Peers,
Full five and twenty valiant Sons I had,
Whose forward vertues made their Father glad.

For when Romes Foes their warlike forces felt,
Against them still my Sons and I were sent,
Against the Goths full ten years weary war,
We spent, receiving many a bloody scar.

Just two and twenty of my Sons were slain,
Before I did return to Rome again;
Of five and twenty Sons I brought but three
Alive, the stately Tower of Rome to see.

When Wars were done, I conquest home did bring
And did present my Prisoners to the King:
The Queen of Goths, her Sons, and eke a Moor,
Who did such Murder like was none before.

The Emperor did make the Queen his wife,
Which bread in Rome debate and deadly strife:
The Moor with her two Sons did grow so proud,
That none like them in Rome was then allow'd.

The Moor so pleas'd this new made Empress eye,
That she consented to him secretly,
For to abuse her Husbands Marriage-bed,
And so in time a Black-a-moor she bred.

Then she whose thoughts to murder was inclin'd,
Consented with the Moor with bloody mind,
Against my self, my kin, and all my friends,
In cruel sort to bring them to their ends.

So when in age I thought to live in peace,
Both woe and grief began then to encrease,
Amongst my Sons I had one daughter bright,
Which joy'd and pleased best my aged sight.

My Lavinia was betrothed then,
To Cesars Son a young and noble man,
Who in a hunting, by the Emperours wife,
And her two Sons, bereaved was of life.

He being slain, was cast in cruel wise,
Into a darksom den from light of skies;
The cruel Moor did come that way as then,
With my three Sons, who fell into the Den.

The Moor then fetcht the Emperor with speed,
For to accuse them of that murderous deed,
And when my Sons within the Den was found,
In wrongful prison were they cast and bound.

BUt now behold what wounded most my mind,
The Empresses two Sons of Tygers kind,
My Daughter ravished without remorse,
And took away her honour quite perforce.

When they had tasted of so sweet a flower,
Fearing this sweet should quickly turn to sowre,
They cut her tongue, whereby she could not tell,
How that dishonour unto her befel.

Then both her hands they basely cut off quite,
Whereby their wickedness she could not write,
Nor with her Needle on her Sampler sow,
The bloody workers of her dismal woe.

My brother Marcus found her in the Wood,
Staining the grasie ground with purple blood,
That trickled from her stumps and handless arms,
No tongue at all she had to tell her harms.

But when I saw her in that woful case,
With tears of blood I wet my aged face,
For my Lavinia I lamented more,
Then for my two and twenty Sons before.

When as I saw she could not write nor speak,
With grief my aged heart began to break;
We spread a heap of sand upon the ground,
Whereby these bloody Tyrants out we found.

For with a staff, without the help of hand,
She writ these words upon a plot of sand:
The Lustful sons of the proud Empress,
Are doers of this hateful wickedness.

I tore the milk-white hairs from off my head,
I curst the hour wherein I first was bred,
I wisht the hand that fought for countries fame,
In cradle rockt had first been strucken lame.

The Moor delighting still in villany,
Did say, to set my Sons from prison free,
I should unto the King my right hand give,
And then my three imprisoned Sons should live.

The Moor I caus'd to strike it off with speed,
Whereat I grieved not to see it bleed,
But for my Sons would willingly impart,
And for their ransome send my bleeding heart.

But as my life did linger then in vain,
They sent to me my bootless hand again:
And therewithal the heads of my three sons,
Which fill'd my dying heart with fresher groans.

Then past relief I up and down did go,
And with my tears writ in the dust my woe,
I shot my arrows towards Heaven high,
And for revenge to hell did sometimes cry.

The Empress thinking then that I was mad,
Like Furies she and both her Sons were glad:
So nam'd revenge, and rape, and murder, they
To undermine and know what I would say.

I fed their foolish veins a little space,
Until my friends and I did find a place,
Where both her Sons unto a post was bound,
Where just revenge in cruel sort was found.

I cut their throats, my Daughter held the pan,
Betwixt her stumps, wherein the blood then ran;
And then I ground their bones to powder small,
And made a paste for pies straight therewithal.

Then with their flesh I made two mighty Pies,
And at a Banquet serv'd in stately wise,
Before the Empress set this loathsom meat,
So of her Sons own flesh she well did eat.

My self bereav'd my daughter then of life,
The Empress then I slew with bloody knife,
And stab'd the Emperor immediately,
And then my self, even so did Titus dye.

Then this revenge against the Moor was found,
Alive they set him half into the ground;
Whereas he stood until such time he starv'd,
And so God send all Murderers may be serv'd.

Printed for *F. Coles, T. Vere, J. Wright*, and *J. Clarke*.

27. Drawing of the Swan Theatre in London, after 1596–7

Arendt van Buchell (Arnoldus Buchelius; 1565–1641), after a sketch by Johannes de Witt (1566–1622)

Manuscript, pen and brown ink on paper, bound into a book entitled 'Adversaria'
Size of page 198 × 158mm (7¾ × 6¼in)
Utrecht University Library, Utrecht (MS 842), open at fol.132r

Provenance Transferred in the nineteenth century from the Utrecht Municipal Archives to the University Library, Utrecht

Literature D.F. Rowan, 'The "Swan" Revisited', *Renaissance Drama*, 10, 1967, pp.33–48; J.B. Gleason, 'The Dutch Humanist Origins of the Witt drawing of the Swan Theatre', *Shakespeare Quarterly*, 32, 1981, pp.324–38; R.A. Foakes, *Illustrations of the English Stage 1580–1642* (Stanford University Press, 1985), pp.52–5; C. Walter Hodges, 'Van Buchel's Swan', *Shakespeare Quarterly*, 39, 1988, pp.489–94

This small drawing is the only surviving record of the interior of an Elizabethan theatre. It depicts the Swan Theatre, which was built in 1596, on the South Bank of the Thames in Southwark. By 1599, when the Globe was added to the two existing theatres and the Bear Garden, there were four large arenas for entertainment south of London Bridge.

The drawing survives in a copy by Johannes de Witt's friend, the Utrecht lawyer, historian and antiquarian Arendt van Buchell, who took it from the original, along with part of De Witt's description of the London theatres that existed at that date. Written in Latin, it translates as:

> There are four amphitheatres in London of notable beauty, which, from their diverse signs, bear diverse names. In each of them a different play is exhibited daily to the populace. The two more magnificent of these are situated to the south beyond the Thames, and from the signs suspended before them are called the Rose and the Swan.... Of all the theatres, the largest and most magnificent is that one of which the sign is called in the vernacular the Swan Theatre; for it accommodates in its seats three thousand persons, and is built of a mass of flint stones, and supported by wooden columns painted in such excellent imitation of marble that it is able to deceive even the most cunning. Since its form resembles that of a Roman work, I have made a sketch of it above.[1]

Although the drawing has been rendered in a sketchlike manner, its parts are carefully labelled in Latin to show the different uses of this enclosed space, including the projecting stage, three tiers of audience seating in the galleries, and the actors' tiring-house, the *mimorum aedes*, with two entrances onto the stage.

The main structure is a galleried polygon of twenty-four sides, with stepped *ingressi* from the yard to the lowest gallery. Two external staircases lead to the upper galleries. The *mimorum aedes* has two sets of double doors for the players to enter by, but no central opening between them for 'discoveries' of the sort that stage directions and other references in many plays call for. It has been suggested that De Witt was concerned to show the theatre's physical features, not the hangings that would have concealed the stage openings. The two huge Romanesque posts on the stage are striking, although they support a sharply inclined roof covering less than half the acting space.

Some of the drawing's features have raised doubts ever since it was first discovered in 1888. The tiles on the stage roof and the galleries, for instance, appear to be Dutch pantiles, not used in England for another fifty years. The roof structure is shown from two different perspectives, with the trumpeter outside the hut on the roof ridge viewed from the side. The stage is held up by two improbably curved trestles. The actors are located on stage, but some of the audience sit in a row of boxes on the stage balcony, usually assumed to be the area meant by '*above*' in a play. Even this identification of the 'lords' rooms' over the stage is less than reliable, as it shows six boxes, where a polygonal auditorium with twenty or twenty-four sides would have needed an uneven number, probably five.

The original drawing made by De Witt in London is lost, and it is impossible to estimate how accurate Van Buchell's copy may be. His interest in recording this unusual building probably relates to the similarity of its design to known examples from ancient Roman architecture. It is the only drawing to appear in Van Buchell's manuscript, which is made up principally of philosophical and ecclesiastical observations. AG and TC

1 Schoenbaum 1975, p.108

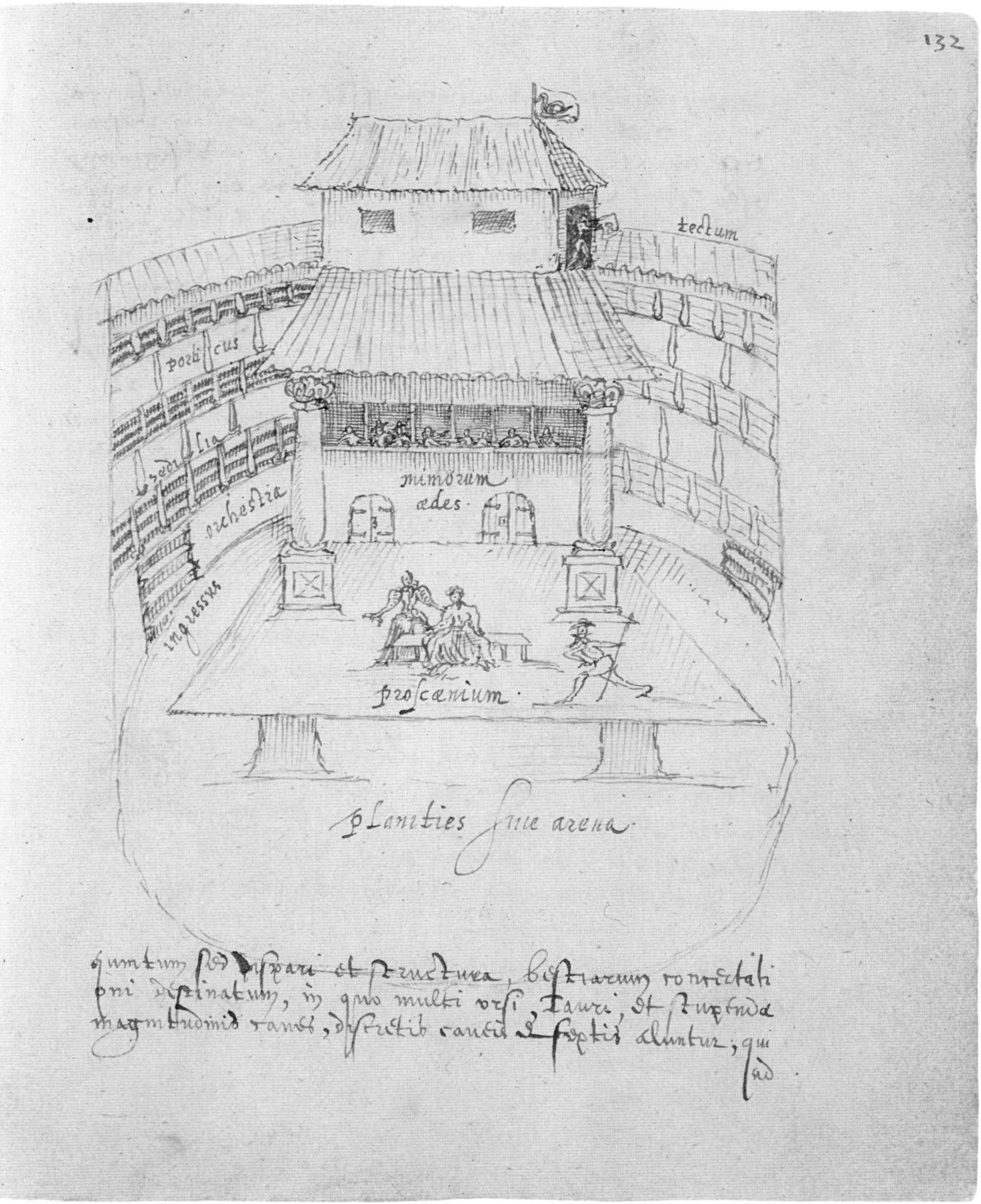
132
tectum
porticus
sedilia
orchestra
ingressus
mimorum
ædes
proscænium
planities sive arena

28. The Platt of 'The Second Part of the Seven Deadly Sins', *c.*1592

Unknown author

Manuscript, pen and ink on paper
586 × 386mm (23 × 15¼ in)
Dulwich College, London, MS XIX

Provenance Philip Henslowe and his son-in-law Edward Alleyn; by inheritance to the Master and Fellows of Alleyn's College of God's Gift

This extraordinary document, one of a handful of its kind to have survived from the period, was discovered in the eighteenth century. It had been folded in half and used in the binding of another manuscript. As its name suggests, a 'platt' or 'plot' was a play's schematic outline, designed to be hung backstage – by the square hole visible a third of the way down this sheet – for reference by its cast during performance. The plot listed the characters, cast members, props (for example, a head in a dish), stage effects ('A Larum wth Excurcions', i.e. the noise and bustle of a battle) and essential action ('Mercury comes and all vanish') required in each of its scenes.

A 'play of the seven deadly sins' by the comedian Richard Tarlton (d.1588) was already 'famous' in 1592. To judge from the actors named in it, the plot probably relates to some sort of revival at Henslowe's Rose Theatre at around that time. No text of the play itself has survived, but it seems to have been made up of seven separate episodes (drawn from a variety of historical and classical sources), each illustrating one of the deadly sins: Envy, Sloth and Lechery preside over the action here, in the play's 'Second Part'. Many of the actors listed – 'R Burbadg', 'R Cowly', 'Mr Phillipps', 'Mr Pope', 'Mr Bryan' and 'W Sly' – later reappeared among 'The Names of the Principall Actors in all these Playes' that prefaced the 1623 First Folio of Shakespeare's works (fig.55,p136). Indeed, the plot's 'Harry' has been plausibly identified as Henry Condell (1576?–1627), one of the Folio's co-editors. NS

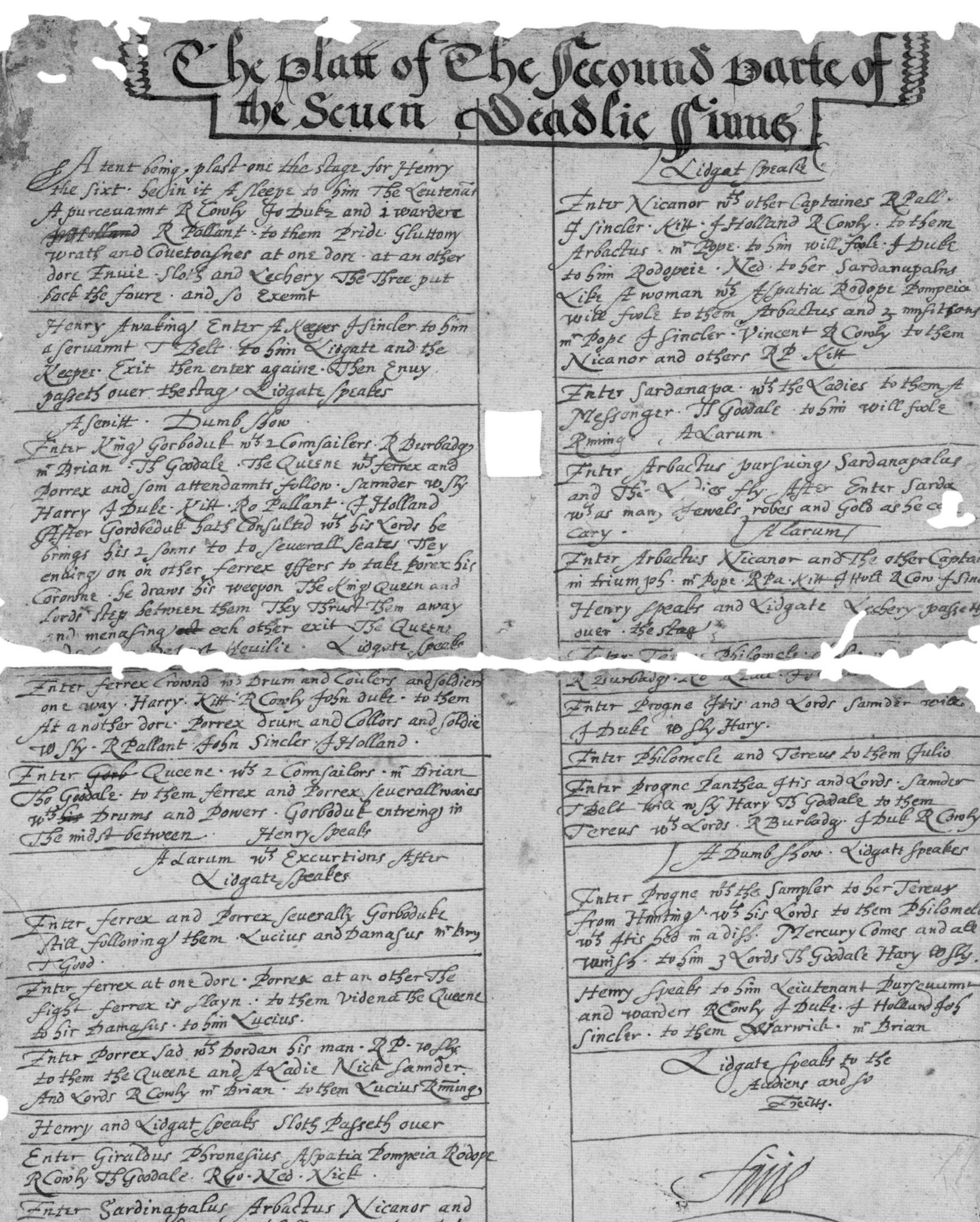

The platt of The Secound parte of the Seuen Deadlie Sinns

A tent being plast one the stage for Henry the sixt he in it A sleepe to him The Leutenant A purceuant R Cowly Jo Duke and 1 warder ~~J Holland~~ R Pallant · to them Pride Gluttony wrath and Couetousnes at one dore at an other dore Enuie Sloth and Lechery The Three put back the foure and so Exeunt

Henry Awaking Enter A Keeper J Sincler to him a seruant T Belt to him Lidgate and the Keeper · Exit then enter againe · Then Enuy passeth ouer the stag · Lidgate speakes

A senitt · Dumb show

Enter King Gorboduk wth 2 Counsailers · R Burbadg mr Brian Th Goodale · The Queene wth ferrex and Porrex and som attendaunts follow · Saunder wth Harry J Duke · Kitt · Ro Pallant · J Holland · After Gordbeduk hath Consulted wth his Lords he brings his 2 sonns to to seuerall seates They enuing on on other ferrex offers to take Porex his Corowne · he draws his weapon The King Queen and Lords step between them They Thrust Them away and menasing ~~ech~~ ech other exit The Queene and Lords Depart Heuilie · Lidgate speaks

Enter ferrex Crownd wth Drum and Coulers and soldiers one way · Harry · Kitt · R Cowly John duke · to them At another dore · Porrex drum and Collors and soldie wth Sly · R Pallant John Sincler J Holland ·

Enter ~~Gorb~~ Queene · wth 2 Counsailors · mr Brian Tho Goodale · to them ferrex and Porrex seuerall waies wth ~~his~~ Drums and Powers · Gorboduk entreing in The midst between · Henry speaks

Alarum wth Excurtions After Lidgate speakes

Enter ferrex and Porrex seuerally Gorboduke still following them Lucius and Damasus mr Bry T Good ·

Enter ferrex at one dore · Porrex at an other The fight ferrex is slayn · to them Videna the Queene to hir Damasus · to him Lucius ·

Enter Porrex sad wth Dordan his man · R P · wth sly to them the Queene and A Ladie Nick Saunder And Lords R Cowly mr Brian · to them Lucius Running

Henry and Lidgat speaks Sloth Passeth ouer

Enter Giraldus Phronesius Aspatia Pompeia Rodope R Cowly Th Goodale R Go · Ned · Nick

Enter Sardinapalus Arbactus Nicanor and Captaines marching · mr Phillipps mr Pope R Pa Kit J Sincler · J Holland ·

Enter A Captaine wth Aspatia and the Ladies Kitt

Lidgat speake

Enter Nicanor wth other Captaines R Pall · J Sincler · Kitt · J Holland R Cowly · to them Arbactus · mr Pope · to him will foole J Duke to him Rodopeie · Ned · to her Sardanapalus Like A woman wth Aspatia Rodope Pompeia will foole to them Arbactus and 3 musitions mr Pope J Sincler · Vincent R Cowly to them Nicanor and others R P · Kitt

Enter Sardanapa · wth the Ladies to them A Messenger · Th Goodale · to him will foole Running · A Larum ·

Enter Arbactus pursuing Sardanapalus and The Ladies fly · After Enter Sarda wth as many Jewels robes and Gold as he ca cary · Alarum

Enter Arbactus Nicanor and The other Captain in triumph · mr Pope · R Pa · Kitt J Holl R Cow J Sinc

Henry speaks and Lidgate Lechery passeth ouer · the stag

Enter Tereus Philomele [...] R Burbadg · Ro Pall · [...]

Enter Progne Itis and Lords Saunder · will J Duke wth Sly Hary ·

Enter Philomele and Tereus to them Julio

Enter Progne Panthea Itis and Lords · Saunder T Belt will wth Sly Hary Th Goodale to them Tereus wth Lords · R Burbadg · J Duke R Cowly

A Dumb show · Lidgate speakes

Enter Progne wth the Sampler to her Tereus from Hunting wth his Lords to them Philomele wth Itis hed in a dish · Mercury Comes and all vanish · to him 3 Lords Th Goodale Hary wth Sly ·

Henry speaks to him Leiutenant Pursuiuant and warders R Cowly J Duke · J Holland Joh Sincler · to them Warwick · mr Brian

Lidgate speaks to the Audiens and so Exitt.

29. Baluster, dress pins, manicure pin and buttons from the Rose Theatre, *c*.1592–*c*.1604

Wood, copper alloy, bone and pewter
Museum of London

Provenance The Rose Theatre, Southwark. Excavated by the Museum of London Archaeology Service from 1988 to 1989

Literature J. Bowsher, *The Rose Theatre: An Archaeological Discovery* (Museum of London, London, 1998)

> 'A stage, where every man must play a part,'
> *The Merchant of Venice* (Act I, Scene i, line 78)

The London theatres attracted vast audiences. In the jostle to find a good seat, many people seem to have lost belongings on the floor of the playhouse yard. These objects were among an assortment of buttons, pins and other personal items recovered during excavation at the Rose Theatre from 1988 to 1989. The excavations revealed the footings of the building, and other structural features, including part of a turned oak baluster that presumably came from the safety rail around the upper galleries or stage. Payments for two-dozen 'turned ballesters' at 2¼*d*. each and a further two-dozen with a farthing discount are recorded in Philip Henslowe's *Diary* for February 1592.[1]

Henslowe opened the Rose Theatre as a business investment with his partner John Cholmley (biography unknown) in 1587. The playhouse began to attract large audiences and Henslowe encouraged acting companies to the Rose by advancing loans to cover production costs, paying performance licences and keeping the theatre in good repair. The commercial enterprise was not without risk, but in 1592 Henslowe speculated further, by refurbishing and enlarging the Rose to accommodate a capacity crowd of nearly 2,000. Much is known about the day-to-day running of the Rose because Henslowe kept meticulous records of his business and financial transactions. They survive in a series of account books, known as the *Diary*, which provide a unique insight into the workings of an Elizabethan theatre. The entries include debts owed by the Lord Strange's Men, who performed at the Rose and who put on the first performance of a play by Shakespeare – *Henry VI* – on 3 March 1592. Although the Rose was successful for a number of years, the theatre closed in 1604 and was demolished the following year. HF

1 Foakes and Rickert 1961, f4, p.10 and f5, p.12.

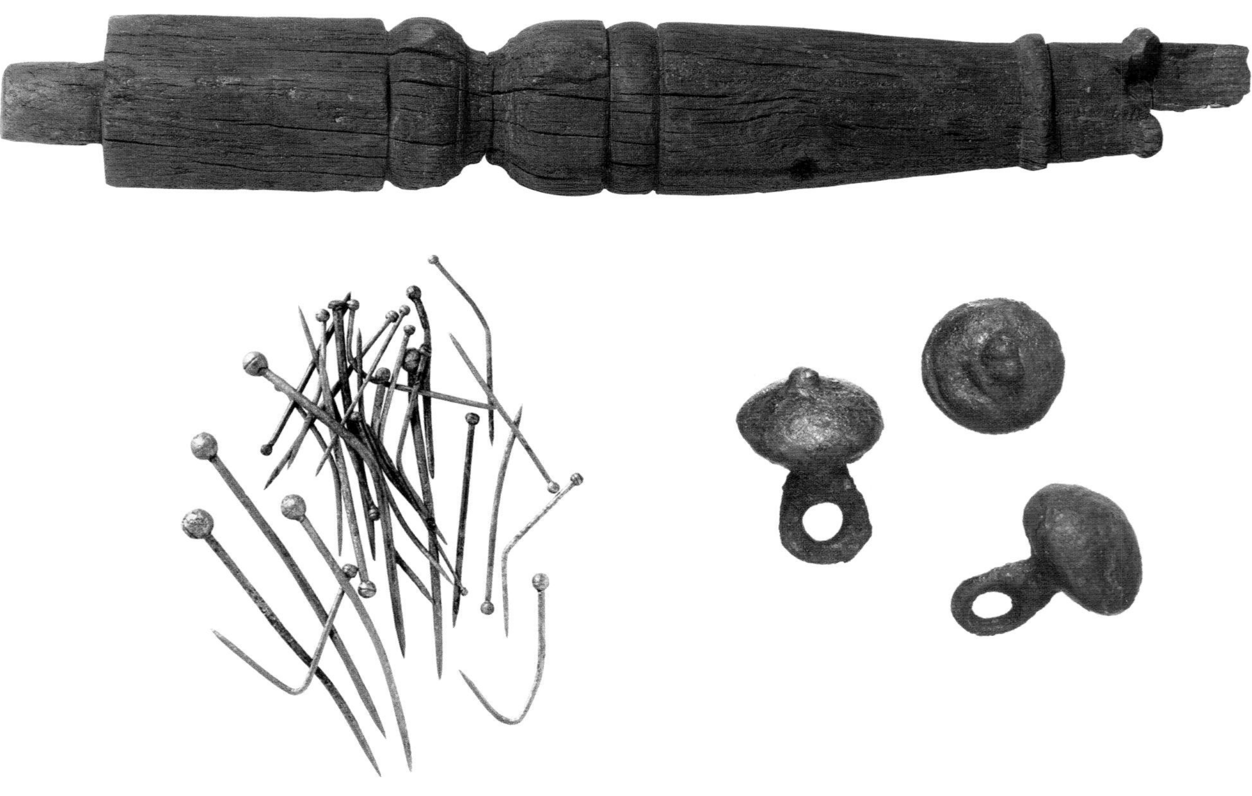

30. Bear skull

Bone
135 × 180mm (5¼ × 7in)
Dulwich College, London

Provenance Excavated from the Globe foundations during the 1980s

Shakespeare's Globe competed for trade on Bankside with a wide range of rival attractions, 'houses of resort in the suburbs' (*Measure for Measure*, Act I, Scene ii, line 93) that included pubs, brothels, gambling dens, and other 'wooden Os' devoted to cockfighting, bullfights and bear-baiting. After building the Rose in 1587, the impresario Philip Henslowe developed a portfolio of such ventures which in time he shared with his son-in-law, the actor Edward Alleyn (1566–1626). They were granted the joint mastership of the King's Bears, Bulls and Mastiff Dogs in 1604, a lucrative post they held for the rest of their lives.

This grim exhibit was excavated from the site of the reconstructed Globe in 1989 – the approximate site of the original Bear Garden, where stables for around twelve brown bears and kennels for over one hundred dogs once stood. A 'course' of baiting – a series of which supplied the afternoon's entertainment – involved chaining a bear to a stake in the centre of the arena and setting dogs, singly or in groups, upon it. Variations included using blinded bears, and, to round things off, an ape would be tied to a horse's back and sent riding through a pack of dogs. The bear skull shown here has been identified by the Natural History Museum, London, as that of a mature female brown bear; the skull has suffered a blow to the back of the head, which may have been the cause of death.

The spectacle seems to have been designed to sponsor in its audience an appreciation of vicious tribulation, heroically borne. Individual bears, whose names survive – Sackerson, 'Monsieur Hunks', George Stone, Little Bess of Bromley – earned a degree of celebrity rivalled only by the heroes and actors of Elizabethan and Jacobean tragedy. 'They have tied me to a stake; I cannot fly,' says Macbeth. 'But bear-like I must fight the course' (Act V, Scene vii, lines 1–2). If all the world was a stage in the Globe play-house, the neighbouring Bear Garden presented an equivalent theatre of universal suffering. It was one which repeatedly impinged on Shakespeare's imagination, as his most famous stage direction, in *The Winter's Tale* (Act III, Scene iii, line 57), indicates: 'Exit, pursued by a bear'. NS

31. Emblematic tableau of Youth, Old Age and Father Time, *c.*1590–1610

Unknown English artist

Oil on panel
566 × 432 mm (22¼ × 17 in)
Inscribed: *top left*: 'Lorde thow haste a poynted owte my lyfe/In length lyke as a span/Myne age is nothynge unto thee/So vayne a thyng is Man'; and *below*: 'This myrrour [mirror] meete for all mankynde/To viewe & still to beare in mynde/And do not mys' [miss]; *centre panel*: 'Consyder man howe tyme doth passe/And lykewyes [likewise] knowe all fleshe is grasse/For tyme consumes the strongeste oke [oak]/So deathe at laste shall stryke the stroke/Thoughe lustye youthe dothe bewtye [beauty] beare/Yet youthe to age in tyme doth weare./And age at length a death will brynge/To Rytche [rich] to Poore, Emprour & Kynge/Therfore still lyue [live] as thow sholdst Dye/Thy Soule to saue [save] from Jeopardye/And as thow woldst be done vnto/So to thy neyghbour alwayes doo/The heauenlye [heavenly] ioyes [joys] at lenghe to see/Lett fayth in Chryste thyne Ancor bee.'; *top right*: 'Man walketh lyke a shade and dothe/In vayne hym selffe annoy/In gettinge goods and cannot tell/Who shall the same enoye [annoy]'; *and below*: 'For tyme brynges [brings] youthfull youthes to age/And age brings Deathe our herytage/When gods will ys [us]'; *at base*: 'The Lorde that made us knoweth our shape/Our moulde and fashion juste/Howe weake and frayle our nature is/And howe we be but duste/And howe the tyme of mortall men/Is lyke the wytheringe [withering] haye [hay]/Or lyke the flower righte fayer [fair] in feilde/That vadethe [fadeth] soone awaye.'
Norwich Castle Museum and Art Gallery, Norwich, NWH COL: 1953.134.2:F

Provenance Purchased Christie's, 4 February 1949, lot 174

This panel is one of a small number of emblematic paintings produced for a secular domestic market in the late sixteenth and early seventeenth centuries. It shows the personified figures of 'Youth', 'Age' and 'Old Father Time' raised above eye level, as if upon a stage, and was designed to have a moralizing function. The composition may also relate to an earlier tradition of Christian morality plays, in which figures such as Youth, Death and the Devil appeared upon stage to shock the audience with graphic depictions of the appalling punishments for a sinful life. Until the 1560s and 1570s these types of plays (or interludes) were commonly performed around England by troupes of travelling players, who would have been familiar to Shakespeare and his contemporaries from their youth. In this image the text is painted upon plaques nailed to the wall which relate to the figures directly below, much in the manner of a speech bubble. This turns the figures into speaking players and the picture into what the writer Thomas Heywood called 'dumbe oratory'.[1]

This composition must have been reasonably common as at least five different versions of it still exist, dating from *c.*1590 to 1610.[2] It is possible that the initial source for the design may have been an illustrated print (or broadsheet), as all the existing versions include roughly the same set of lengthy inscriptions, with a few variations. These images were probably painted as ready-made objects for sale and, like religious treatises, may have been given as gifts for the instruction of young adults. The text defines their function as a mirror suitable for 'all mankynde/To view' and keep continually in mind, as an aid to understanding the perils of pride. The young and old man stand upon marks on the floor, representing the span of a human life. Pictorial allegories and emblematic devices on the theme of death and worldly transience were reasonably common and are found in inventories of pictures in the royal household and in the houses of the nobility, gentry and wealthy merchants in London. TC

1 Thomas Heywood, *An Apology for Actors* (Nicholas Okes, London, 1612), sig. B3v.
2 See, for example, *Memento Mori*, English, *c.*1590, Brighton City Art Gallery, (000101; OW: 540/435).

Lorde thow hasste a poynted owte my lyfe
In length lyke as a span
Myne age is nothynge vnto thee
So vayne a thyng is Man
This myrrour meete for all mankynde
To viewe & still to beare in mynde
And do not mys
Man walketh lyke a shade and dothe
In vayne hym selffe annoy
In gettinge goods and cannot tell
Who shall the same enioye
For tyme brynges youthfull youthes to age
And age brings Deathe our herytage
When gods will ys
Consyder man howe tyme doth passe
And lykewyes knowe all fleshe is grasse
For tyme consumes the strongeste oke
So deathe at laste shall stryke the stroke
Thoughe lustye youthe dothe bewtye beare
Yet youthe to age in tyme doth weare
And age at length a death will brynge
To Ryche, to Poore, Emprour, & Kynge
Therfore still lyue as thow sholdst Dye
Thy Soule to saue, from Jeopardye
And as thow woldst be done vnto
So to thy neyghbour alwayes doo
The heauenlye Joyes at lenghe to see
Lett fayth in Chryste thyne Ancor bee
The Lorde that made us knoweth our shape
Our moulde and fashion iuste
Howe weake and frayle our nature is
And howe webe but duste
And howe the tyme of mortall men
Is lyke the wytheringe haye
Or lyke the flower righte fayer in feilde
That vadethe soone awaye

32. Purse, 1600–25

English

Linen embroidered with silk and metal threads
145 × 126mm (5¾ × 5 in)
Victoria and Albert Museum, London, T.127–1992

Provenance Given by Margaret Simeon in 1992

Literature Claire Wilcox, *Bags* (V&A Publications, London, 1999), p.27

Of the many commercial venues in sixteenth- and early seventeenth-century English society, the market and theatre were exceptional in requiring cash for payment. In the 1590s entrance to public London theatres such as the Globe was charged at a penny, which gave access to the yard before the stage, while the covered seated area cost a further penny and cushioned seats in the galleries above three pence.

Coins were probably carried in simple leather pouches and luxurious purses such as this example were rarely used for that purpose. One of the few occasions when embroidered purses did hold money was when a coin was given as a gift. The embellished bag served as a form of gift wrapping, perhaps worth more than the cash inside. These bags might also contain items for personal grooming, such as combs and mirrors, or needlework tools, such as scissors and pincushions. They often held dried flowers and perfumed powders, essential at a time when daily washing and bathing were not widely practised. In a crowded theatre, a purse filled with powdered orris root or rose petals must have been indispensable.

This exquisitely embroidered purse is one of many such items from the early seventeenth century that survive in museum collections, illustrating a wide range of materials and decorative techniques. Simple in shape and construction, this example is made of linen canvas with ground embroidered in silver thread. A raised pattern of scrolling chains of silver-gilt purl surrounds a variety of flowers and plants, including honeysuckle, borage, rose, gilly flower, rosehips, grapes and peapods, as well as a butterfly. They are worked in high relief with detached leaves, petals and wings in coloured silks, silver-gilt thread, silver thread, purl and spangles. The purse is lined with salmon-pink silk taffeta. The plants depicted here are universally found in Elizabethan and Jacobean embroidery, influenced in design by the popular herbals. They also relate to the symbolism of flowers, fruits and herbs found in English literature of the period, particularly Shakespeare's plays. SN

33. Gaming purse, 1590–1620

French

Cream leather covered with silk velvet and embroidered silver and silver-gilt metal threads
Diameter of base 95mm (3¾ in)
Museum of London, A13387

Illustrated base side up

Provenance The Isham Collection, Lamport Hall, Northamptonshire; Seymour Lucas R.A.

Literature Vanda Foster, *Bags and Purses* (Batsford, London, 1982), p.13, fig.7

Although clergymen and moralists condemned pastimes such as cards and dice as idle, wasteful pursuits, especially when played for money, they were popular with every class of society. In *The Gull's Hornbook* (1609) Thomas Dekker (*c.*1572–1632) alleged that cards were played at the playhouse before the performance began. Many of the games are now obscure. While Falstaff played Primero, James I favoured a game called Maw; another game called Post and Pair was played for the highest stakes.

The wealthy carried their money or tokens to the gambling tables in gaming purses designed for the purpose. These purses have circular stiffened bases and straight sides, which are gathered together with a drawstring threaded through the top edge. This typical example is made of leather covered with crimson silk velvet and lined with pink silk. The base is decorated with a pair of shields bearing coats of arms, surmounted by a coronet and encircled by laurel sprays. The sides of the purse are embroidered with four different patterns of stylized floral sprays worked in silver and silver-gilt thread and cord. The drawstring is a replacement; the original would have been longer and finished with tassels. EE

34. *The Groundworke of Conny-catching*, 1592

Anonymous author, after Thomas Harman (active 1547–67)

Printed book, 'Printed at London by John Danter for William Barley, and are to be sold at his shop at the upper end of Gratious Streete over against London-hail'
Quarto
The British Library, London, C.27.b.21, open at title page

Provenance Thomas Hearne, given to him on 28 June 1726 by Mr Bartholomew of University College, Oxford; acquired between 1787 and 1812

Literature *Cony-Catchers and Bawdy Baskets: An Anthology of Elizabethan Low Life*, ed. Gàmini Salgàdo (Penguin, Harmondsworth, 1972); Ruth Samson Luborsky and Elizabeth Morley Ingram, *A Guide to English Illustrated Books 1536–1603* (Tempe, Arizona, 1999), vol.1, pp.427–8

Towards the end of his short and prolific life, the writer and Cambridge graduate Robert Greene (1558–92) turned to writing accounts of 'true' crime. He seems to have made up the term 'conny-catching' to describe the activities of those who cheat, dupe and steal from their victims (called conies or rabbits). In a series of pamphlets – *A notable discouery of coosenage* (1591), and two further parts dealing with *Conny-catching* (1591, 1592), and *A disputation between a hee conny-catcher, and a shee conny-catcher* (1592) – Greene described the activities of tricksters and fraudsters, both male and female. The pamphlets are written in vivid colloquial prose and provide entertaining and rather sympathetic accounts of those who lived by their wits and traded on the foolishness of simple people and those new to the city.

As the pamphlets offer important evidence of the activities of urban criminals, drawing attention to their links with areas such as Southwark and Shoreditch, where the theatres were, so the playwrights saw their dramatic potential for the stage. Autolycus is probably the most famous of these rogues in *The Winter's Tale*, which is based on Robert Greene's romance *Pandosto, the Triumph of Time* (1588). In drawing upon this source, Shakespeare may have been taking some sort of revenge for an attack on him that appeared in the pamphlet *Greenes, groats-worth of witte* (1592). The author (who was almost certainly not Greene himself) accuses Shakespeare of being 'an upstart Crow, beautified with our feathers, that with his *Tygers hart wrapt in a Players hyde*, supposes he is as well able to bombast out a blanke verse as the best of you: and beeing an absolute *Iohannes fac totum* [Jack of all trades] is in his owne conceit the onely Shake-scene in a countrey.'

The pamphlet displayed here is not by Greene but is based on *A caueat for commen cursetors vulgarely called vagabones* by Thomas Harman, JP. The earliest surviving edition dates to 1567. The woodcut on the title page shows a range of emblems, including rabbits dressed in contemporary costume, and was designed to suggest a link with similar pictures on the title pages of Greene's pamphlets. HRW

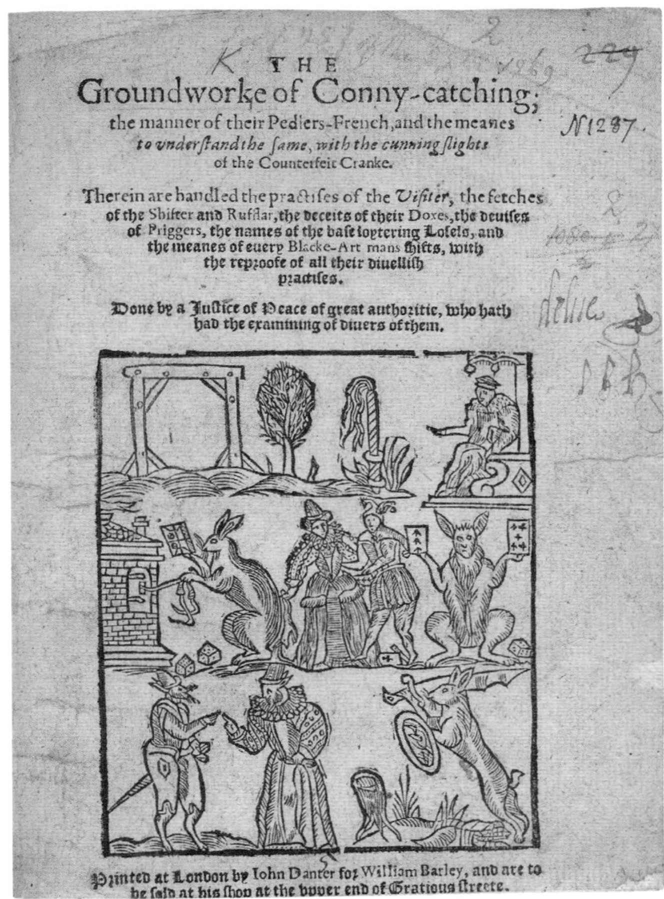

THE
Groundworke of Conny-catching;
the manner of their Pediers-French, and the meanes
to vnderstand the same, with the cunning slights
of the Counterfeit Cranke.

Therein are handled the practises of the *Visiter*, the fetches
of the Shifter and Rufflar, the deceits of their Doxes, the deuises
of Priggers, the names of the base loytering Losels, and
the meanes of euery Blacke-Art mans shifts, with
the reproofe of all their diuellish
practises.

Done by a Iustice of Peace of great authoritie, who hath
had the examining of diuers of them.

Printed at London by Iohn Danter for William Barley, and are to
be sold at his shop at the vpper end of Gratious streete.

COSTUME AND THE THEATRE

Detail of cat.77

Unlike the costumes used on the modern stage, theatrical dress in the period 1574 to 1642 primarily followed the current fashion in English society at the period. It was considered particularly important to distinguish the social rank and occupation of characters through their dress. The association of fine clothing with social status during the Shakespearean age was very clearly marked, indeed by sumptuary laws until 1604. These laws dictated who was allowed to wear various luxurious fabrics and trimmings, such as velvets, silks, laces and embroideries of silver and gold, as well as particular colours. In order to identify himself as King Lear or Richard III, a player had to wear garments associated with the court. Correspondingly the minor working-class parts were dressed in appropriately humble attire.

As a result, the wardrobes of Shakespearean theatre companies were valuable assets. Recent research on this subject has noted the importance of the theatres as a stimulus for the costume trade.[1] The cost of clothing in the late sixteenth and early seventeenth centuries was far higher in relation to other essentials, such as food and property, than it is today. A frequently quoted example is the purchase by Edward Alleyn (1566–1626), a leading actor of the day, of a black velvet cloak with gold- and silver-embroidered sleeves for £20 10*s.* 6*d.*, over a third of the price Shakespeare paid for his house in Stratford.[2] Although some garments for the stage were ordered from tailors, theatre companies relied principally on the second-hand clothing market for their stage costumes. During this period, a far smaller proportion of the population was wealthy enough to buy new clothing than today. Except for the wealthiest élite, most people bought at least some of their clothes second-hand. A very common practice was for members of the aristocracy to give their cast-offs to their servants. As they were often too fine for servants to wear, they were pawned or sold to second-hand clothing merchants.

The activities of Philip Henslowe, both as manager of the Rose and Fortune Theatres and as a pawnbroker, illustrate the reliance of a successful theatre company on a continuing supply of second-hand clothing to furnish new plays.

As anyone who works in contemporary theatre knows all too well, costumes do not last long. Characters lunge and leap around in their clothing, fight, die and are dragged across the wooden stage. Buttons are lost, embroidery worn away, applied lace abraded and seams give way. It was common practice to have one actor playing multiple minor characters and the numerous speedy changes of costume these parts entailed caused considerable wear and tear. Henslowe's *Diary* indicates the money invested in the maintenance and upkeep of the wardrobe, and also reveals not all the damage was done by the actors. In November 1601, he paid 7*s.* 6*d.* for the repair of a tawny coat 'eaten by rattes'![3] It is highly unlikely any clothing from the Shakespearean stage would survive to this day. With the closure of the theatres in 1642, the companies' playing apparel would have been sold. Back on the second-hand market, the garments continued their downward spiral of reuse until, too ragged and worn for anyone's wear, they were recycled into paper or shredded to stuff mattresses. SN and JT

1 Ann Rosalind Jones and Richard Stallybrass, *Renaissance Clothing and the Materials of Memory* (Cambridge University Press, 2000).

2 Gurr 1970, p.128.

3 R.A. Foakes, *Henslowe's Diary* (2nd ed., Cambridge University Press, 2002).

35. List of apparel belonging to the Lord Admiral's Men, *c.*1602

Edward Alleyn (1566–1626)

Manuscript, ink on paper
205 × 305 mm (8 × 12 in)
Dulwich College, London, MS I/30

Provenance Philip Henslowe and his son-in-law Edward Alleyn; by inheritance to the Master and Fellows of Alleyn's College of God's Gift

This inventory of the most valued costumes in the stock of the theatre company known as the Lord Admiral's Men provides a unique record of actors' clothing at the turn of the seventeenth century. The inventory, which is in the hand of Edward Alleyn, a leading player in the company, demonstrates that actors were directly involved in the purchase and care of their stage clothes. There are no such surviving records from Shakespeare's company, the Lord Chamberlain's Men, but the playing practices of these two companies are directly comparable.

The list is laid out in columns, categorizing the clothes in order of importance from left to right, starting with outer garments such as cloaks and gowns on the left, and ending with leg garments on the right. Most of the clothes described in the list are items of contemporary dress, made of silk and decorated with gold and silver embroidery or laces. In everyday life such luxurious garments were strictly reserved for the various ranks of the aristocracy. Queen Elizabeth I made a very detailed proclamation outlining these privileges in 1597, just before this list was compiled. The actors, most of whom were below the social rank entitled to wear such clothes in the street, were exempted from these laws while on stage in order to present themselves to the audience recognizably dressed as the nobility, so often represented in contemporary plays. It is not surprising that the majority of the garments mentioned in the list are items of men's clothing, as most plays of this period have far fewer female characters than male ones. Missing, however, are many items of clothing such as shoes, shirts, ruffs and hats – either because they were stocked but were less valuable or because the actors were expected to provide these items themselves. In some cases the association of a particular garment with a character is so strong that it is described not by its colour, fabric or decoration, but rather as 'Hary ye viii gowne' or 'Faustus Jerkin his clok'.

Alongside the modern clothing there is an intriguing column in the centre of the list devoted to 'Antik sutes'. This may refer to old-fashioned garments from the early sixteenth century or to the clothes of the ancients – the Greeks, Romans and Eygptians – who were so often depicted in the plays of Shakespeare and his contemporaries, or indeed to a mixture of both. Edward Alleyn's father-in-law Philip Henslowe was the owner of the Fortune Theatre where the Admiral's Men played at this time. In his accounts, which have survived alongside this inventory, there are several entries made in 1602 that may directly relate to items in this section of the list. For example:

> Lent vnto Thomas downton the 27 of maij [May] 1602 to bye [buy] wm someres cotte [William Sommers's coat][1] & other thinges for the 2 pt of wollsey [*Cardinal Wolsey* the play] the some [sum] of iij li. [2]

As these entries demonstrate, the actors were constantly adding to their clothing stock. Some items were bought second-hand, while others were commissioned from tailors. The actors dealt with suppliers such as silk merchants personally and there are many entries naming 'the cope lace man' who sold lace to decorate both new garments and to re-furbish old ones. The inventory is therefore a 'snapshot' of a particular moment in the everyday life of the company. At this point in its history it had accumulated a considerable clothing stock worth an enormous amount of money, which was essential for it to mount increasingly spectacular productions in the early seventeenth century. JT

1 William Sommers was a court jester to Henry VIII (r.1509–47). This entry may refer to the purchase of a coat that had belonged to William Sommers, of a surviving mid-sixteenth-century garment or a newly reconstructed *c.*1540 coat.

2 Foakes 2002, p.201.

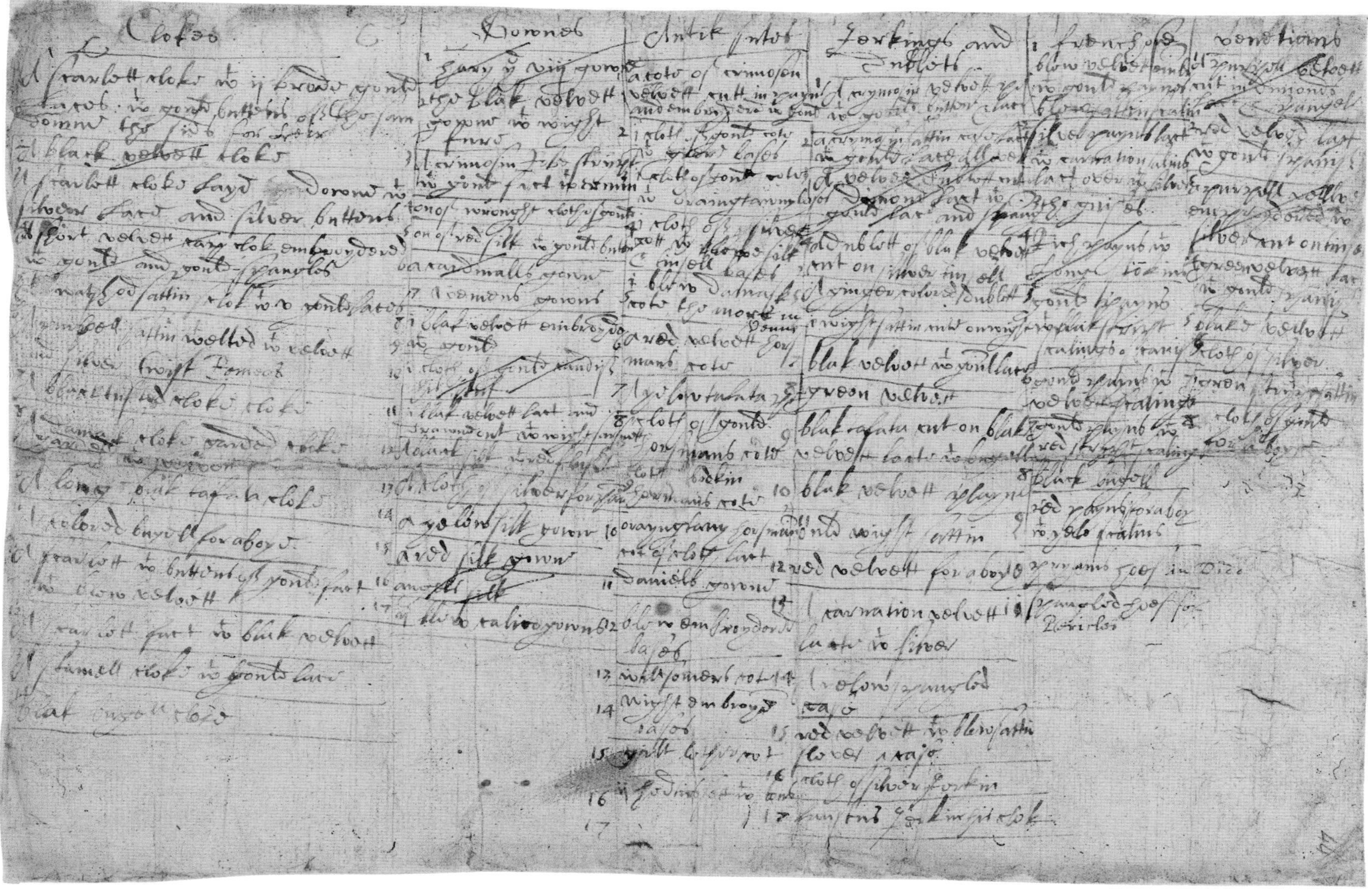

CLOKES

1. A scarlett cloke wt ij brode gould laces: wt gould buttens of the sam downe the sides (for *Leir*)
2. A black velvett cloke
3. A scarlett cloke layd downe with silver lace and silver buttens
4. A short velvett cap clok embroyded wt gould and gould spangles
5. A watshod sattin clok wt v gould lace
6. A purpell sattin welted with velvett and silver twist (*Romeos*)
7. A black tufted cloke cloke
8. A damask cloke garded cloke garded wt velvett
9. A longe blak tafata cloke
10. A colored bugell for a boye
11. A scarlett with buttens of gould fact with blew velvett
12. A scarlett fact with blak velvett
13. A stamell cloke with gould lace
14. Black bugell cloke

GOWNES

1. Hary ye viii gowne
2. The blak velvett gowne with wight fure
3. A crimosin Robe strypt with gould fact with ermin
4. On of wrought cloth of gould
5. On of red silk with gould butens
6. A cardinalls gowne
7. Wemens gowns
8, 9. i blak velvett embroydered wt gould
10. i cloth of gould candish his stuf
11. i blak velvett lact and drawne out with wight sarsnett
12. A black silk with red flush
13. A cloth of silver for par
14. A yelow silk gowne
15. A red silke gowne
16. Angels silk
17. ij blew calico gowns

ANTIK SUTES

1. A cote of crimosen velvett cutt in payns and embroydered wt gould
2. i cloth of gould cote wt grene bases
3. i cloth of gould cote wt orang tawny bases
4. i cloth of silver cott with blewe silk & tinsell bases
5. i blew damask cote the more (in *Venus*)
6. A red velvett horsmans cote
7. A yelow tafata pes
8. Cloth of gould horsmans cote
9. Cloth of bodkin hormans cote
10. Orayng tany horsmans cot of cloth lact
11. Daniels gowne
12. Blew embroyderd bases
13. Will somers cote
14. Wight embroyd. bases
15. Gilt lether cot
16. ii hedtirs sett wt stons

JERKINGS AND DUBLETS

1. A crimosin velvett pes wt gould buttons and lace
2. A crymosin satin case lact wt gould lace all over
3. A velvett dublett cut dimond lact with gould lace and spangles
4. A dublett of blak velvett cut on sillver tinsell
5. A ginger colored dublett
6. i wight satin cute on wight
7. Blak velvett with gould lace
8. Green velvett
9. Blak tafata cut on blak velvett lacte with bugell
10. Blak velvett playne
11. Ould wight satin
12. Red velvett for a boy
13. A carnation velvett lacte with silver
14. A yelow spangled case
15. Red velvett with blew satin sleves and case
16. Cloth of silver Jerkin
17. Faustus Jerkin, his clok

FRENCH HOSE

1. Blew velvett embr. wth gould paynes, blew satin scalin
2. Silver payns lact wt carnation salins lact over wt silver
3. The guises
4. Rich payns with long stokins
5. Gould payns wt blak stript scalings of canish
6. Gould payns wt velvett scalings
7. Gould payns wt red strypt scaling
8. Black bugell
9. Red payns for a boy wt yelo scalins
10. Pryams hoes (in *Dido*)
11. Spangled hoes (for *Pericles*)

VENETIANS

1. A purpell velvett cut in dimonds lact & spangels
2. Red velved lact wt gould Spanish
3. A purpell vellvet emproydered wt silver cut on tinsell
4. Green velvett lact wt gould Spanish
5. Blake velvett
6. Cloth of silver
7. Gren strypt satin
8. Cloth of gould for a boy

36. Man's cloak, 1560–75

European

Silk velvet embroidered with silver-gilt and silver thread, purl, cord and coloured silks
Maximum length 750mm (29½in), maximum width 1530mm (60¼in)
Museum of London, C2116

Provenance In the collection of M. Larcarde, 1909; purchased by John G. Joicey

Literature *Société de l'histoire du costume* (exh. cat., Musée des Arts Décoratifs, Paris, 1909), salle 113, vitrine 6; Zillah Halls, *Men's Costume 1580–1750* (Museum of London, London, 1970), p.35, pl.2

The list of apparel belonging to the Lord Admiral's Men (cat.35) includes 'A scarlet cloke w^t^ ij brode gould laces; w^t^ gould buttens of the sam downe the sides' which, while not as lavishly or subtly decorated as this surviving cloak, would have been similarly showy in its combination of colours and use of metal thread. Sumptuously embroidered cloaks, many of which were cut in a full circle like this example, were fashionable in the second half of the sixteenth century. In *The Anatomie of Abuses* published in 1583 (cat.25) Philip Stubbes vividly describes their vibrant colours and costly decoration:

> They have clokes . . . of diverse and sundry colours, white, red, tawnie, black, greene, yellow, russet, purple, violet and infinite other colours: some of cloth, silk, velvet, taffetie and such like, wherof some be of the Spanish, French and Dutch fashion. Some be short, scaresely reaching the gyrdlestead, some to the knee, and othersome traylinge uppon the ground . . . . These clokes must be guarded, laced and thorowly faced: and sometimes so much lined, as the inner side standeth almost in as much as the outside. . . .

According to the sumptuary laws, only men above the rank of gentleman could wear cloaks, but these laws were notoriously difficult to enforce and largely ineffective. Cloaks were expensive, however. The front edges and hem of this cloak are decorated with a broad border outlined by parallel lines of silver-gilt cord enclosing two looped lines of silver purl lying back to back. The border is filled by a bold pattern of C-shaped foliate branches in interlocking pairs, with an upright spray of three feathers or exotic leaves between each alternate pair. At the bottom of each vertical border is a large letter 'M' beneath a coronet. The embroidery is skilfully executed, and two shades of blue silk, green and yellow silk are used to shade the gold work. The effect of the embroidery is enhanced by the contrasting textures of the metal thread and the combination, for example, of silver thread wrapped loosely around the laid lines of silver-gilt thread. EE

37. Gown, 1600–10

English

Italian silk brocade
Length 1475mm (58in)
Victoria and Albert Museum, London, 189–100

Provenance Purchased in 1899 from Captain Charles Vere, part of the Isham collection of seventeenth-century dress

Literature Natalie Rothstein, *Four Hundred Years of Fashion* (V&A Museum, London, 1984, 1992), pp.12, 15 and 121; Marie Channing Linthicum, *Costume in the Drama of Shakespeare and his Contemporaries* (Clarendon Press, Oxford, 1936), p.184, pl.VII

The gown was the principal garment in a woman's wardrobe in the late sixteenth and early seventeenth centuries. This particular style with a loose, pleated back and open front formed part of a formal day ensemble. A bodice and petticoat of equally luxurious, although not necessarily matching, materials would have been worn underneath. Such a combination can be seen in the portrait of Mary, Lady Scudamore, by Marcus Gheeraerts the Younger (1615) in the National Portrait Gallery, London.

Edward Alleyn's list of playing apparel (cat.35) includes a group of gowns for both men and women, including one for Henry VIII, an angel and a cardinal. Open gowns similar in style to this one were also worn by men for informal wear in private. Black wool or silk gowns lined with fur became part of official dress for doctors, lawyers and religious and government ministers. The entry 'women's gowns' may well have accounted for an open gown such as this example.

Once part of the theatre wardrobe, a woman's gown would have been worn by one of the boys or young men who played the female parts on the Shakespearean stage. Its unstructured style would not have required much alteration for a masculine figure. In her analysis of Shakespearean dress, Marie Channing Linthicum notes the innuendo that surrounded this style of gown in references found in plays of the period.[1] This usually equated the looseness of the garment to the wearer's morals. In Shakespeare's *The First Part of King Henry IV* (Act III, Scene iii, lines 1–3), it was used to humorous effect in the words of Sir John Oldcastle: 'Russell, am I not fallen away vilely since this last action?/Do I not bate? Do I not dwindle? Why,/my skin hangs about me like an old lady's loose gown.'

In this example, the imported Italian silk is brocaded in a pattern of repeating floral motifs worked in green, pink, yellow and blue silk. Between the woven motifs, the fabric has been slashed, that is, deliberately cut in measured diagonal incisions. This was a popular decorative technique that had originated in the early sixteenth century and remained fashionable well into the 1660s. Salmon-pink corded silk ribbon, now disintegrating, once adorned the shoulder seams and tabs of the shoulder wings, with a silver lace. The lace was later removed, leaving a tiny remnant with a single silver spangle in the crease of a seam. At the centre back of the gown's small upright collar are two eyelets for fastening a supportasse (cat.41) to support a ruff or collar. The design of the silk dates from about 1600, although the style of the gown indicates the period 1605 to 1610. Evidence of previous stitching and the piecing of the silk at the back hem suggest that it was probably restyled and remade at the later date. This was very common practice, given the extremely high cost of clothes and their fabrics. As well as being commercially recycled, clothing was continually reused domestically, restyled into new fashions and made over into children's clothes and furnishings.

Detail of the slashed silk brocade

Silk was the most expensive and highly desired fabric in late sixteenth- and early seventeenth-century England. Velvet cost the most, due to its dense pile, followed by brocades (listed as 'damask' in the Henslowe and Alleyn inventories) with intricate patterns that made time-consuming technical demands.

All silks were imported from France and Italy, mainly by piece. Although James I made valiant efforts to encourage the cultivation of silkworms in England, no economically viable sericulture industry developed, due most likely to the inhospitable climate.[2] SN

1 Linthicum 1936 (see Literature), p.183.
2 John Feltwell, *The Story of Silk* (St Martin's Press, New York, 1990), pp.20–22.

38. Doublet, 1615–20

English

Wool and silver-gilt lace
655mm (25¾in)
Victoria and Albert Museum, London, T.147–1937

Provenance Given by Lady Spickernell in 1937 and said to have belonged to the Cotton family of Etwall Hall in Derbyshire

The doublet (a close-fitting upper garment) was a basic item of clothing for men during the late sixteenth and early seventeenth centuries. It was worn over a linen shirt, with breeches and a cloak. The fabric of this particular example looks very much like watered silk or moiré, but a close examination of the warp and weft reveals that it is made of wool. The yarn has been spun extremely tightly to make it very smooth and fine, giving a silk-like sheen. Wool was one of England's primary manufactures. Second only to silk, wool was costly and a sign of wealth and social status. This doublet has been further enhanced by the application of a narrow lace (braid) made of silver-gilt and silk. Not quite luxurious enough for court dress, a doublet like this would have served as formal daywear for a member of the gentry or urban élite.

The style of the doublet did not change radically between 1580 and 1630. Characteristics such as the high collar, shoulder wings, long sleeves, front buttoning and waist tabs remain constant. Variations appear in the length of the waistline, fullness of the sleeves and dimensions of the waist tabs. This particular example was probably made in the five years following Shakespeare's death. The only notable change in style between a doublet fashionable during the playwright's last years and this one is the raising of the waistline above the natural level. Indeed, the decoration of this example is similar to that on the doublet seen in the Droeshout engraving (cat.1). Lines of lace cover the shoulder and sleeve seams, and edge the individual tabs of fabric that make up the shoulder wings. Lace also parallels each front edge beside the buttons and buttonholes.

The reddish-brown colour suggests 'a ginger colored dublett' in the list of 'Dublets' owned as playing apparel by the Lord Admiral's Men (cat.35). The variety and the imaginative names of colours in this list are characteristic of early seventeenth-century clothing. Before the invention of chemical dyes in the mid nineteenth century, fabrics were coloured with a wide range of natural substances. The vibrancy and richness of hues seen in surviving garments indicates what has been lost in adopting chemical substitutes. Also lost are some of the descriptive terms for colours observed on the Shakespearean stage: watchet, puke, goose-turd green, ash, murrey, peach-flower and horse-flesh are just a few of the shades no longer seen.

Colours were often symbolic in the early seventeenth century, relating sometimes to the exclusivity of the dyestuff and sometimes to emotions associated with certain hues. Purple was traditionally connected with royalty. Scarlet required cochineal, imported from the Spanish colonies in Central America, and was therefore very expensive. The dye process to produce black was unpredictable, resulting more often in a dark brown, hence the preference for the deepest midnight hue. Colours associated with personal qualities or feelings included green for joy and young love, tawny for sadness and certain shades of yellow for treachery. SN

39. Doublet and breeches, 1625–30

English

Wool twill
Length of doublet 660mm (26 in), length of breeches 710mm (28 in)
Victoria and Albert Museum, London, T.29&A-1938

Provenance Given by Lady Spickernell in 1938 and said to have belonged to the Cotton family of Etwall Hall in Derbyshire

This suit of plain serge (wool twill), probably once black and now faded to brown, is a rare example of the dress of the urban middle class or yeoman in the early seventeenth century, who would have made up part of the audience in London playhouses. Both doublet and breeches are lined for warmth with a linen pile fabric, similar to modern towelling. The centre front and sleeve openings are faced with shot purple and pink silk, as were the waist tabs originally. These facings would have flashed as the wearer moved, perhaps to deceive a casual observer that the whole garment was lined with a more luxurious fabric. The buttons are made from a round core of wood, covered with plaited black silk thread. The practicality of the ensemble extends to the breeches' pockets, four in number, which were originally lined with durable chamois leather. The style may represent the rather old-fashioned tastes of someone from a rural area or an older man. By 1625 slashed sleeves or paned sleeves (made from strips of fabric sewn together but left open in areas to show a lining or shirt underneath) were coming into fashion and a longer, slimmer cut of breeches replaced the baggy style seen here.

This outfit is certainly far less grand than the doublets and hose listed in the accounts by Philip Henslowe and Edward Alleyn (cat.35), which comprise velvets and silks elaborately embroidered and applied with metal laces. It may have been expected for actors to provide their own costumes of everyday clothing. Such a modest suit would have been appropriate dress for a character such as Master Frank Ford or Master George Page, the husbands in *The Merry Wives of Windsor*. Documentation indicates that Shakespeare's plays were still being performed in the 1630s and given the fairly short lifespan of theatre costume and its constant replacement, these later productions would have been presented in 1630s fashions. SN

40. Doublet, 1620–5

English

Kid skin embroidered with silk
766mm (30⅛in)
Victoria and Albert Museum, London, T.146-1937

Provenance Given by Lady Spickernell in 1937 and said to have belonged to the Cotton family of Etwall Hall in Derbyshire

Literature Avril Hart and Susan North, *Historical Fashion in Detail: The 17th and 18th Centuries* (V&A Publications, London, 1998), p.152

Leather was a material much used in Shakespeare's time for footwear, hats, gloves and other clothing. Resistance to abrasion and windproof qualities made it the natural choice for outdoor wear, particularly when riding and travelling. A variety of skins were worn, including the common cowhide. Buff or oxhide was favoured by soldiers for its protection against sword cuts, while deer and elk skin might represent the wearer's hunting prowess. This example made of kid (young goat) probably dates from the early 1620s. A waist-line above the natural level and deep waist tabs are typical of the decade, although the sleeve has not been paned or left open at the front seam, a characteristic of the late 1620s.

The embroidery on this doublet suggests something more formal than riding gear. A variety of stitches have been used: raised satin stitch, French knots, couching and stem stitch, worked in black silk twist over brown linen under-stitching. The design of stylized flowers and leaves is arranged in narrow rectangular panels.

The degeneration of the embroidery thread indicates the use of iron in the dyeing process. It was a preferred mordant for black, as it obtained the darkest colour. Over time, however, the iron oxidizes, causing the threads to disintegrate. Most natural dyes are not colourfast, as the silks and wools they tinted were never meant to be washed. The question regarding a doublet such as this is whether the black colour of the embroidery would have run in the rain, restricting its use to occasional outdoor wear in fine weather and informal indoor dress. On the Shakespearean stage, an embroidered leather doublet might serve to distinguish a nobleman in a hunting or outdoor scene. SN

41. Supportasse, 1600–25

English

Card covered with silk
260 × 304mm (10¼ × 12in)
Victoria and Albert Museum, London, 192–1900

Provenance Purchased in 1899 from Captain Charles Vere, part of the Isham collection of seventeenth-century dress

Literature Natalie Rothstein, *Four Hundred Years of Fashion* (V&A Museum, London, 1984, 1992), p.15

The elaborate neckwear of the late sixteenth and early seventeenth centuries included a variety of ruffs and bands (collars). The most casual versions were 'falling', that is, unstarched and draping over the collar of the doublet or gown. Formal ruffs and bands were heavily starched. In order to frame the face properly, they required support underneath to hold them up at the back of the neck. A variety of materials were used to make such supports, including wire and whalebone. They were also called a range of different names: 'supportasse', 'underpropper', 'pickadil' (with a multiplicity of spellings) or 'rebato'. The *Oxford English Dictionary* suggests that the London street known as Piccadilly may have been named after the house 'Piccadilly Hall', owned by a tailor who made his fortune selling pickadils.

This particular example is constructed of card – layers of paper glued together – cut in a wide U-shape. The card has been moulded when damp to fit the curve at the back of the neck. The upper inside edge is padded lightly and the whole covered with pale-blue satin. Around the outer edge, the satin has been cut in strips and sewn to fit the curving shape. Through the two holes on the underside the supportasse was laced to corresponding eyelets at the back of the collar of a gown or doublet. The ruff or starched collar was then pinned on top.

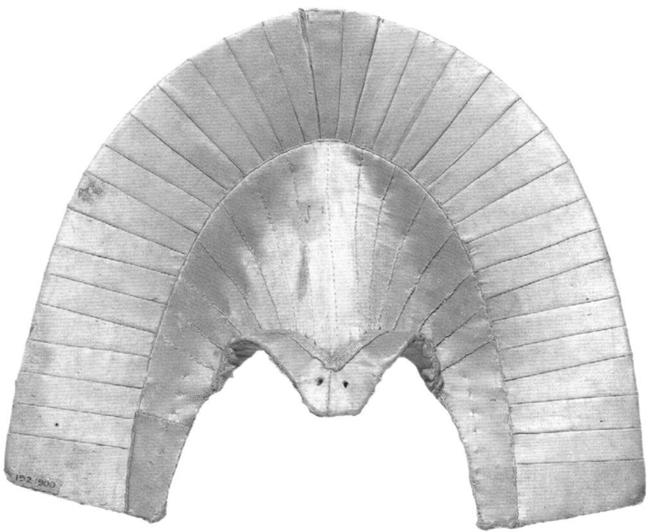

When an underpropper such as this one was worn under a very fine starched linen band, its outline was often visible through the nearly transparent fabric, as seen in the portrait of Phineas Pett in the National Portrait Gallery, London (fig.18, p.50). This helps to explain one of the curiosities seen in the engraving of Shakespeare by Martin Droeshout in the First Folio of 1623 (cat.1). The strange markings on his collar depict the narrow darts made on the inside of the linen band to shape it to the neck. On such sheer linen, the pleating of the fabric is visible, and, underneath it, the outline of a pickadil similar to this example can be seen, although curiously it is only shown on one side. SN

42. Man's hat, *c.*1600–10

European

Buff leather embroidered with silk and silver thread
Height 195mm (7⅝in), diameter 285mm (11¼in)
Museum of London, C2113

Provenance Purchased by John G. Joicey

Literature Janet Arnold, *Patterns of Fashion. The Cut and Construction of Clothes for Men and Women c.1560–1620* (London, 1985), pp.34 and 94

The coat of arms that adorns the front of this hat suggests that it was part of a page's livery. Visiting the playhouse was a popular tourist activity and such hats might have been seen in London's theatres, worn by the liveried servants of a foreign noble household.

The rigid leather hat has a narrow brim and a high crown, which tapers towards the dome-shaped top, finished with a leather-covered button. The hat is decorated with lines of chain stitch worked in gold-coloured silk, small leaf shapes and a central fleur-de-lis worked in satin stitch and embellished with silver thread. A padded shell-shaped leather socket for a feather plume is attached to the left side of the brim. The inside of the crown is interlined with linen and lined with silk, glued to the linen.

Two similar hats were presented to the London Museum in 1913 by John Joicey. He probably acquired them in France or Italy, where he frequently spent November and

December hunting for costume, jewellery and *objets de vertu*. Comparable hats survive at the Stibbert Museum, Florence, Museo Parmigianino in Reggio Emilia, Germanisches Nationalmuseum, Nuremberg, and Deutsches Ledermuseum in Offenbach. EE

42. Shoes, *c.*1600

Western Europe

Alum-tanned leather
Length 180mm (7in), width 60mm (2in), height 90mm (3½in)
The Ashmolean Museum, Oxford, 1685 B310

Provenance Tradescant collection

Literature Janet Arnold, *Queen Elizabeth's Wardrobe Unlock'd* (W.S. Maney & Son, Leeds, 1988), p.213; June Swann, *Shoes* (Costume Accessories Series, Batsford, London, 1982), p.13

In the late sixteenth and early seventeenth centuries, decorative shoes were a luxurious form of footwear for the aristocracy. Shoes of this sort would not have been worn in the mucky London streets, where only boots and clogs were practical. The style seen here – with heels and open sides – was popular for both men and women. Narrow latchets (straps) were fastened over the arch of the foot, providing a base for the spectacularly elaborate 'shoe rose', a large dense knot of silk ribbon loops, often embellished with precious metal laces and spangles (sequins) or pearls. Leather was a fashionable material for boots and shoes, particularly cordovan, from Cordoba in Spain, considered the best quality. Leather shoes were frequently slashed and pinked, that is, perforated with decorative holes, as seen in this example. More casual styles of footwear, such as slippers or pantobles (mules), were often covered with velvet or silk, laced and embroidered.

Few accessories, apart from stockings, are mentioned in the *Diary* kept by Philip Henslowe, although shoes, hats and gloves would have been essential to the costumes worn on stage. Quantities of linen appear in the *Diary*, probably for ruffs and bands made up by the seamstresses who sewed linen underwear and accessories, household goods and baby clothes. It might have been difficult to share shoes, however, as they had to fit the individual actors. It is conceivable that actors had to supply the appropriate accessories for their parts.

The short trunk hose or breeches worn by men made their legs and feet highly visible. Contemporary portraits show considerable lengths of silk-covered calf and thigh with very decorative garters, shoes and shoe roses. Women's footwear also appears in portraiture, for only in court dress were women's feet completely covered. In formal daywear and masque costume, the petticoats skimmed the ankles, revealing pinked leather shoes and ornate ribbon roses. On the Shakespearean stage, shoes would have had a more immediate focus, particularly for the groundlings. Those standing in the yard of the public playhouses found themselves at eye-level with the actors' feet. One surviving play from the period is of particular relevance to Elizabethan footwear and how it was made. *The Shoemaker's Holiday* (1598–9) by Thomas Dekker is a romantic comedy of thwarted love and upward social mobility in urban London, set in the milieu of a shoemaker. SN

THE ESTABLISHED PLAYWRIGHT

Patrons and players, wealth and reputation

Shakespeare had established himself as an accomplished playwright by the early 1590s. His reputation as a talented writer grew and during this decade he wrote many of his most acclaimed plays including *Love's Labour's Lost*, *A Midsummer Night's Dream*, *The Merchant of Venice* and *Richard II*. In 1598 he was described by the author Francis Meres as a 'hony-tongued' poet, the equal of Ovid and the rival of Plautus and Seneca for both comedy and tragedy.

In 1593–4 Shakespeare dedicated two long poems to the glamorous and wealthy young courtier Henry Wriothesley, 3rd Earl of Southampton (1573–1624), who became his patron. He probably also worked for other theatrical companies before joining the Lord Chamberlain's Men in 1594 as both an actor and principal dramatist. The company proved highly successful, frequently performing at court, and in 1599 Shakespeare and eight or so of his fellow actors, including Richard Burbage (1568–1619), became sharers in a financial partnership to fund the building of the Globe Theatre on the South Bank of the Thames, Southwark.

The success of Shakespeare's plays brought lucrative rewards and in 1597 Shakespeare was able to purchase a large family house in Stratford-upon-Avon. Around the same time he was also attempting to improve his social standing by applying for a family coat of arms that would bring with it the title 'gentleman'.

44. Ferdinando Stanley, 5th Earl of Derby (1559?–94), dated 1594

Unknown English artist

Oil on two joined oak panels
914 × 711 mm (36 × 2 in)
Inscribed below coat of arms on a banner: 'savns changer ma verriti';
and beneath: 'Ferdinand Earl of Derby/Æ 35. AD 1594'
Private collection

Provenance Possibly William Farrington, Worden Hall; sold Worden Hall, Lancashire, 1951, lot 749

Illustrated overleaf

Ferdinando Stanley, Lord Strange and later Earl of Derby, was the patron of a highly successful theatrical company known as 'Lord Strange's Men' who frequently performed at court in the late 1580s and early 1590s. As many of the actors who later became the core of the Lord Chamberlain's Men (Shakespeare's company from 1594) were part of Strange's troupe, it is considered likely that Shakespeare was also one of their number.[1]

The Stanley family was distantly related to the royal line through Mary Brandon (1496–1533), the younger sister of Henry VIII, and received preferment under Edward VI, Mary I and Elizabeth I. Ferdinando Stanley was educated at St John's College, Oxford, and spent part of his teenage years in the royal household, later becoming mayor of Liverpool and a member of the House of Lords. He was a committed patron of literature, particularly poetry and drama, and throughout the 1580s and early 1590s numerous authors dedicated work to him, including Robert Greene and George Chapman (1559/60–1634; cat.90).

The last year of his life was worthy of an act in a Shakespearean tragedy. On his father's death in 1593 Ferdinando succeeded to the title Earl of Derby and soon became subject to the demands of Catholic plotters, notably Richard Hesketh (d.1593/4), to overthrow the Queen and claim the Crown. Derby refused to be drawn into the plan and Hesketh was executed. Only months later in April the same year, Derby suddenly fell ill and, according to John Stow, died a slow and painful death afflicted by hallucinations and strange dreams, the result probably of poisoning, or witchcraft.[2]

This portrait is one of the few surviving images of Stanley painted in his lifetime. It shows him with a lance and helmet, perhaps as a record of one of his performances before the Queen at the accession day tilts on 17 November each year. In 1591 his performance at the tiltyard was celebrated in a poem by George Peele (1556–96), who describes Lord Strange as the 'Brave Ferdinand' the 'valiant son and heir' of Lord Derby, dressed in white armour with a 'costly ship' bearing an eagle as his pageant that bowed before the Queen.[3]

The portrait is painted in a workmanlike late Elizabethan style, with careful delineation of the facial features, including a noticeable mole above his left eye, and significant attention paid to details of costume, such as the elaborate lace collar and jewelled and pearl-embellished sword belt. The artist seems to have had some trouble with the proportions of the body and particularly with the helmet. TC

1 Richard Burbage, George Bryan, Will Kemp, Augustine Phillips, Thomas Pope and William Sly were all at some time associated with Lord Strange's Men. See Gurr 2004.
2 John Stow, *The Annales of England* (Ralph Newbury, London, 1600), pp.1275–7.
3 Roy Strong, *The Cult of Elizabeth. Portraiture and Pageantry* (Thames and Hudson, London, 1977), pp.146 and 152; see *Polyhmnia* in A.H. Bullen, *The Works of George Peele*, 2 vols (John C. Nimmo, London, 1888), p.281.

cat.44 **Ferdinand Stanley, 5th Earl of Derby**

cat.45 **Henry Carey, 1st Baron Hunsdon**

45. Henry Carey, 1st Baron Hunsdon (1526–96), dated 1591

Unknown Anglo-Netherlandish artist

Oil on oak panel
900 × 750mm (35½ × 29½in)
Inscription top right: ATATIS SVÆ 66 AN. 1591; top left: 'Henry Carey/ Lord Hunsdon/Mark Gerards' (later, probably eighteenth century)
Berkeley Will Trust

Provenance By descent

Illustrated on previous page

In the office of Lord Chamberlain, Baron Hunsdon became the patron of a highly successful company of players – including Shakespeare – known as the Lord Chamberlain's Men, who regularly performed at court. A cousin of Elizabeth I, Carey swiftly rose to power and was knighted, raised to the peerage and awarded the prestigious honour of Knight of the Order of the Garter soon after Elizabeth's accession. As a loyal and hard-working royal servant and talented foreign diplomat, he became a highly influential statesman, rising to privy counsellor and, in 1585, to Lord Chamberlain. As Lord Chamberlain, Carey took charge of the potentially lucrative task of arranging audiences with the Queen.

In 1594 Hunsdon licensed two theatrical companies to perform at theatres just outside the official city limits. Under his own patronage the Lord Chamberlain's Men had the right to perform at the Theatre to the north of the city, while the Lord Admiral's Men, under the patronage of Charles Howard, Earl of Nottingham (1536–1624), performed at the Rose Theatre on the South Bank. This arrangement appeased the London authorities, who wanted to keep unruly theatregoers out of the confines of the city. However, with their lease on the Theatre coming up for renewal, the Lord Chamberlain's Men were soon trying to evade the ban on staging plays in London and sought a site in the centre that would have the advantage of attracting a wealthier and more discerning audience and allow them to play indoors in the winter. With the apparent support of Lord Hunsdon, the company manager James Burbage (?1531–97) invested heavily in remodelling a new site in Blackfriars, building a new hall theatre with curved viewing galleries on an upper floor.[1] When Hunsdon died in July 1596, the patronage of the company was eventually taken over by his son George Carey, who was far less sympathetic to the plans for a theatre at Blackfriars, perhaps not least because the site was near his own home. Hundson's death was thus a disaster for the Lord Chamberlain's Men, who found the plans for their new theatre blocked and their investment tied up in an unusable site. These circumstances eventually proved fortunate for Shakespeare and some of his fellow actors, who, in return for financial investment to establish a new theatre, became 'sharers' in the management and income of the company.

This portrait shows Hunsdon wearing a fur-trimmed cloak and holding his badge of the Order of the Garter and his rod of office. The picture was previously ascribed to Marcus Gheeraerts the Younger (1561/2–1636), an anglicized version of whose name appears in the later inscription to the top left. It was certainly painted by a very competent artist, possibly a Netherlandish émigré or an artist trained by a Netherlander in England. The facial features are most carefully depicted and the portrait would appear to be taken from life. This skilled artist has captured the translucency of the flushed cheeks and the mass of individual hairs upon Hunsdon's head and in his beard, which are rendered in single strokes. Particular attention has been paid to the quality and richness of the black doublet of slashed silk or satin cloth, embroidered with thick bands of gilt thread. There are several other roughly contemporary or slightly later versions of this painting. TC

1 Gurr 2004, p.5.

46. Henry Wriothesley, 3rd Earl of Southampton (1573–1624), dated 1594

Nicholas Hilliard (*c.*1547–1619)

Body colour on vellum, stuck to a playing card with three hearts showing at the reverse
Oval 75 × 62 mm (3in × 2½)
Inscribed in gold on either side of the head, left: ANO DM 1594; right: ETATIS SUAE 20
Syndics of the Fitzwilliam Museum, University of Cambridge (3856)

Provenance Cunliffe Bequest

Literature Robert Bayne-Powell, *Catalogue of Portrait Miniatures in the Fitzwilliam Museum* (Cambridge University Press, Cambridge, 1985), p.114; Fredson Bowers (ed.), *Elizabethan Dramatists Dictionary of Literary Biography*, vol. 62 (Gale Research, Detroit, 1987), p.289; Susan Doran (ed.), *Elizabeth* (exh. cat., National Maritime Museum, Greenwich, 2003), cat.116

Henry Wriothesley has become renowned as the only known literary patron of William Shakespeare. The extent of Shakespeare's direct involvement with the flamboyant, literature-loving 3rd Earl of Southampton is not clear, and many of the assumptions about their relationship are conjectural.

Southampton succeeded to the earldom in 1581, just before the age of eight, following the death of his father, Henry Wriothesley, and he became a royal ward under the guardianship of William Cecil, Lord Burghley (1520/21–98). At Cecil House in London, Southampton grew up with other young noblemen around the pinnacle of political power. He was tutored there in the classics, history and literature, as well as in modern languages, drawing and dancing. From the ages of twelve to sixteen he continued his education at St John's College, Cambridge, and thereafter at the Inns of Court, where plays and satires were frequently performed by both the students and professional actors. Despite financial difficulties, Southampton attracted the attention of numerous poets and writers who sought his patronage and he received dedications from a wide range of authors, including Gervase Markham (1568?–1637), Barnabe Barnes (1571–1609) and Michael Drayton (1563–1631; cat.81).

It is not clear when Shakespeare met Southampton, but the author dedicated to him the narrative poems *Venus and Adonis* (cat.48) in 1593 and *Lucrece* (cat.49) in 1594. This miniature dates from around this time. The first dedication is written in a way which may indicate that Shakespeare had not yet met Southampton or was not yet well-acquainted with him, but the tone of the dedication to the later poem, *Lucrece*, is far more personal and whole-hearted in its appreciation: 'The loue I dedicate to your Lordship is without end. . . . What I haue done is yours, what I haue to doe is yours, being part in all I haue, deuoted yours.' Yet by the summer of the same year, Shakespeare's energies were probably engaged elsewhere when he became a member of the Lord Chamberlain's company of players (cat.45).

Hilliard's miniature shows Southampton as an effete, 20-year-old, fresh-faced youth, with soft blue eyes and luscious curling brown locks carefully arranged to fall across his shoulder towards his breast; the epitome of the feminized romantic hero. Southampton was particularly fond of his appearance and throughout his life had numerous portraits painted. In the 1590s he was famous at court for wearing his long hair loose – like a female virgin – and he was one among a number of courtiers who favoured flamboyant feminized dress. His beauty, physical prowess and interest in literary pursuits may have enchanted the older playwright. TC

47. Henry Wriothesley, 3rd Earl of Southampton (1573–1624), 1603

Attributed to John de Critz (*c.*1551/2–1642)

Oil on canvas
1044 × 876mm (41⅛ × 34½in)
Inscribed upon a pillar top right: IN VINCULIS INVICTUS [unconquered though in chains] Februa 8; 1600; 601; 602; 603: - Apri'
The Duke of Buccleuch & Queensberry, KT

Provenance By descent from the sitter to Elizabeth Wriothesley, daughter of the 4th Earl of Southampton, who took as her second husband Ralph Montagu, 1st Duke of Montagu; thereafter by descent

Literature Richard W. Goulding, 'Wriothesley Portraits Authentic and Reputed', *Walpole Society*, vol.VIII, 1919–20, pp.17–94; Strong 1969, pp.298–300; Roy Strong, *The English Icon: Elizabethan and Jacobean Portraiture* (Routledge and Kegan Paul, London, 1969), p.261; Tessa Murdoch, *Boughton House: The English Versailles* (Faber and Faber, London, 1992), p.184

From 1596 Southampton succeeded in pursuing an ambitious and impetuous young courtier's true employment – military and naval ventures abroad – and he served alongside Robert Devereux, Earl of Essex (cat.68) on expeditions to Cadiz, the Azores and, later, Ireland. In 1598, however, Southampton disgraced himself at court by a hasty marriage to the pregnant maid of honour, Elizabeth Vernon (1576–1612) and the pair were briefly imprisoned. His lack of favour at Court did not appear to encourage more regular attendance and in 1599 he was described, along with Lord Rutland, probably Roger Manners, 5th Earl of Rutland (1576–1612), as passing 'way the tyme in London merely in going to plaies euery Day'.[1]

This portrait apparently commemorates Southampton's period of imprisonment in the Tower of London following the part he played in the rebellion led by the Earl of Essex in February 1601 (see pp.156–8). The inscription notes the period of his incarceration between February 1601 and April 1603 (recorded in the 'Old Style' calendar). Unlike Essex, Southampton had his sentence commuted from execution to life imprisonment, and he was only released following the accession of James I. Southampton is represented wearing his hair characteristically long and hanging loose about his shoulders, while behind him, seated upon the window sill, is an unusual companion, a black-and-white pet cat. Although there is no further evidence from the period, this indignant-looking cat may have accompanied the prisoner during his years of incarceration in the Tower. A later tradition, first published in the 1790s, asserts that this was Southampton's favourite cat, which had climbed down the chimney to reach him in the Tower.[2] He is shown in a room with mullioned windows and a view of the Tower to the right. This room may represent an approximation of his prison quarters, which consisted of at least two rooms on a top floor near the Queen's gallery, including a sitting room and bedchamber, which were whitewashed and remodelled for his use in the spring of 1601. Southampton suffered from ill health at this period and in August 1601 his terms of imprisonment were eased. His mother and those in charge of his estate were allowed to visit and he was given access to the lead rooftops above his apartment for recreation.[3]

The painting is tentatively attributed to John de Critz, serjeant painter to James I but, as there are no signed paintings by this artist and only a few other pictures are linked to his workshop, attributions to de Critz are problematic. A surviving bill of 1607 indicates that de Critz had painted a portrait of Robert Cecil, 1st Earl of Salisbury, along with three other portraits, each of which were charged at £4. De Critz must have run a reasonably large studio, which may account for the range of styles that are attributed to him, and he was also undertaking decorative work for the Crown, as well as portraits of merchants and city fathers.[4] TC

1 Goulding 1920, p.30 (the Hatfield papers, IX, 341); see Literature.
2 Thomas Pennant, *Of London* (R. Faulder, London, 1790), p.272.
3 Mary Ann Everett Green (ed.), *Calendar of State Papers, Domestic Series, of the Reign of Elizabeth 1601–1603* (Longman, London, 1870), p.89; Charlotte Carmichael Stopes, *The Life of Henry, Third Earl of Southampton, Shakespeare's Patron* (Cambridge University Press, Cambridge, 1968), p.246.
4 Mary Edmond, 'Limners and Picturemakers – New light on the lives of miniaturists and large-scale portrait-painters working in London in the sixteenth and seventeenth centuries', *Walpole Society*, vol.XLVII, 1978–80, pp.140–55; Hearn 1995, pp.173–5; Robert Tittler, 'Three portraits by John de Critz for the Merchant Taylors' Company', *Burlington Magazine*, CXLVII, July 2005, pp.491–3.

IN VINCVLIS
INVICTVS.
FEBRVA: 8: 1600: 60
602: 603: APRI:

48. *VENVS AND ADONIS*, 1593

William Shakespeare

Printed book, 'Imprinted by Richard Field, and are to be sold at the signe of the white Greyhound in Paules Church-yard'
Quarto
The Bodleian Library, University of Oxford, Arch. G. e. 31 (2), open at title page

Provenance Frances Wolfreston (1607–76), one of the earliest known female English book collectors; bought by Edmond Malone (1741–1812) in 1805 from William Ford, a Manchester bookseller

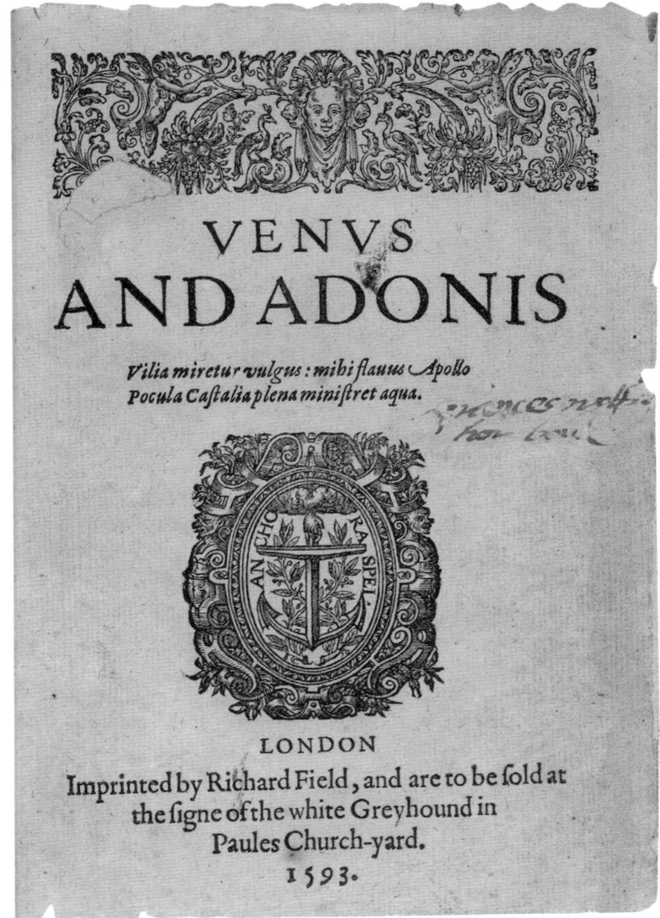

VENVS
AND ADONIS

Vilia miretur vulgus: mihi flauus Apollo
Pocula Castalia plena ministret aqua.

LONDON
Imprinted by Richard Field, and are to be sold at the signe of the white Greyhound in Paules Church-yard.
1593.

Venus and Adonis is the first of the two long narrative poems that Shakespeare composed in 1593 and 1594, during which the London playhouses were closed in an effort to reduce the spread of plague. The second is *Lucrece* (cat.49). A witty and graceful erotic poem with a tragic conclusion, *Venus and Adonis* adapts a story from the Roman poet Ovid's longpoem *Metamorphoses*. Shakespeare would have studied this at school in Stratford-upon-Avon, and he also knew it in a popular English translation of 1567 by Arthur Golding (cat.64).

This, the first edition, was printed and published in London by Richard Field (1561–1624), who, like Shakespeare, was born in Stratford-upon-Avon, and was probably a friend. It is of especial interest in relation to Shakespeare's biography because of its dedication to Henry Wriothesley, 3rd Earl of Southampton (cats 46, 47). The highly intelligent and immensely attractive nobleman was the only person to whom Shakespeare dedicated any of his writings.

The poem tells how the goddess Venus strives in vain to seduce the beautiful youth Adonis, who cares more for the hunt than for love. 'Hunting he lou'd, but loue he laught to scorne.' But his love of the sport is his undoing: he is gored to death by a wild boar. Venus grieves eloquently over his body, and he is metamorphosed into a flower.

The poem was immensely popular, especially with young people, no doubt partly because of its humorous eroticism. It was the most frequently reprinted of all Shakespeare's writings, running through at least sixteen editions by 1636.
SW

49. *Lucrece*, 1594

William Shakespeare

Printed book, Printed by Richard Field for John Harrison
Quarto
The British Library, London, Q1, 1594, C.21.c.45, open at dedication page A2

Provenance Possibly from the library of Benjamin Heywood Bright (1787–1843), purchased 1845

This is the second of Shakespeare's long narrative poems and, like its predecessor *Venus and Adonis*, was composed at a time when the London theatres were closed because of plague. It appeared in 1594 and, also like *Venus and Adonis*, was printed in London by Shakespeare's fellow townsman Richard Field, this time for the publisher John Harrison (active 1566–1617).

Lucrece is a powerfully rhetorical poem, often dramatic in tone. Like *Venus and Adonis*, it is dedicated to Henry Wriothesley, 3rd Earl of Southampton, but in far warmer terms. Shakespeare declares: 'The loue I dedicate to your Lordship is without end: whereof this pamphlet without beginning is but a superfluous Moity. . . . What I haue done is yours, what I have to doe is yours, being part in all I haue, deuoted yours.' It is often supposed that Southampton figures as the 'louely boy' of Shakespeare's sonnets (cat.50).

The narrative is based on a story told by Ovid (43 BC–AD 18) in his *Fasti* ('Chronicles') and it appears to be deliberately designed as a tragic counterpart to the earlier poem. It is preceded by a prose 'Argument' outlining the story. Tarquin and his friend Collatinus, engaged in the siege of the city of Ardea, resolve to test their wives' virtue by riding back to Rome to see how they are behaving. All except Collatinus's wife Lucrece are enjoying themselves, whereas she is virtuously spinning with her maids. Tarquin, inflamed with desire, returns on a later occasion and is welcomed, but in the dead of night he creeps to Lucrece's chamber and rapes her. Next morning she summons her father and husband, tells them what has happened, and stabs herself to death. SW

TO THE RIGHT
HONOVRABLE, HENRY
VVriotheſley, Earle of Southhampton,
and Baron of Titchfield.

THE loue I dedicate to your Lordſhip is without end: wherof this Pamphlet without beginning is but a ſuperfluous Moity. The warrant I haue of your Honourable diſpoſition, not the worth of my vntutord Lines makes it aſſured of acceptance. VVhat I haue done is yours, what I haue to doe is yours, being part in all I haue, deuoted yours. VVere my worth greater, my duety would ſhew greater, meane time, as it is, it is bound to your Lordſhip; To whom I wiſh long life ſtill lengthned with all happineſſe.

Your Lordſhips in all duety.

William Shakeſpeare.

A 2

50. *SHAKE-SPEARES SONNETS*, 1609

William Shakespeare

Printed book; 'Printed At London by G. Eld for T.T. [Thomas Thorpe] and are to be sold by John Wright, dwelling at Christ Church gate'
Quarto
The British Library, London, G11181, C.21 c.44, open at the title page

Provenance Possibly from the library of Benjamin Heywood Bright (1787–1842), purchased 1845

'Neuer before Imprinted' proclaims the title page of the 1609 edition of Shakespeare's sonnets, implying that their existence was already well known. It is likely that he had written many, if not all of them, in the sixteenth century, perhaps as early as 1593, and versions of two of them, numbers 138 and 144, appeared in print in 1599, in a pirated little volume called *The Passionate Pilgrim* (fig.2, p.15) purporting to be by Shakespeare but made up mostly of poems by other writers. Whereas the narrative poems, *Venus and Adonis* and *Lucrece* of 1593 and 1594 respectively (cats 48, 49), were immensely successful, being frequently reprinted throughout Shakespeare's lifetime and for many years after he died, the sonnets were not reprinted until 1640. Even then they were published only partially, in altered form, and along with many poems by other writers, in John Benson's (active 1635–67) fraudulent 'POEMS: WRITTEN BY WIL. SHAKES-PEARE. Gent.'.

Whereas the narrative poems carry dedications written by Shakespeare himself, the curiously laid-out dedication of the 1609 sonnets is signed with the initials of the publisher, Thomas Thorpe (fig.3, p.16). Shakespeare may have had nothing to do with the publication of his most intimately revealing writings, and the deliberately cryptic dedication conceals far more than it reveals. What exactly does 'THE ONLIE BEGETTER' mean? Above all, who is 'Mr W.H.'? Is he the 'sweet boy' addressed in some of the poems? Among men known to Shakespeare the initials are those of William Herbert, and, reversed, of Henry Wriothesley, but neither was properly addressed as 'Mr.': Herbert was Earl of Pembroke, Wriothesley was Earl of Southampton. This dedication presents one of the most tantalizing mysteries of Shakespeare scholarship and biography. SW

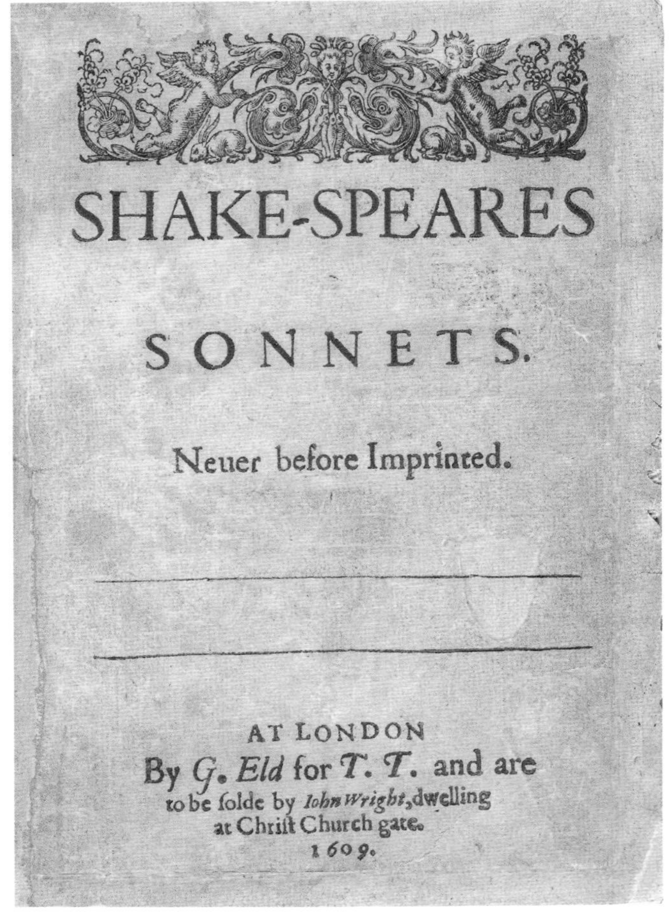
SHAKE-SPEARES

SONNETS.

Neuer before Imprinted.

AT LONDON
By G. Eld for T. T. and are
to be solde by Iohn Wright, dwelling
at Christ Church gate.
1609.

51. A portrait of a man, probably Richard Burbage (1568–1619), 1619[1]

Unknown English artist

Oil on canvas
303 × 262 mm (12 × 10¼ in)
The Trustees of Dulwich Picture Gallery, London (DPG 391)

Provenance Cartwright Bequest, 1686

Literature Jean Paul Richter and John C.L. Sparkes, *Catalogue of the Pictures and Portraits in Dulwich College Gallery* (Spottiswoode and Co., London, 1880), pp.27–9; Peter Murray, *Dulwich Picture Gallery: A Catalogue* (Philip Wilson Publishers for Sotheby Parke Bernet Publications and the Governors of Dulwich College, London, 1980); Dulwich Picture Gallery, *Mr Cartwright's Pictures: A Seventeenth-century Collection* (Dulwich Picture Gallery, London, 1987), no.25; Richard Beresford, *Dulwich Picture Gallery: Complete Illustrated Catalogue* (Unicorn Press, London, 1998), no.395, p.279

The actor Richard Burbage was a close friend and professional associate of Shakespeare. Burbage came from a theatrical family and his father James Burbage (*c.*1531–97) had been a touring player, who, in 1576, financed one of the earliest permanent public playhouses in London, known as the Theatre, in Shoreditch.

Richard Burbage began his career as an actor with his father and probably acted with Lord Strange's Men (cat.44) in the early 1590s. He became one of the Lord Chamberlain's Men in 1594 and established a reputation as that company's leading actor. By the time the company became the King's Men in 1603 he was a famous face on the London stage. Burbage played many of Shakespeare's key dramatic heroes, including Richard III, Hamlet, Othello and King Lear, as well as taking leading parts in plays by Ben Jonson (cat.83) and John Webster (1578/80–1636). He took a key role in the company, not only as its star actor but also in the arrangements for playing at court, as a reference to his organization of the performance of *Love's Labour's Lost* indicates in a letter to the King's principal Secretary of State, Robert Cecil (1563–1612) in 1605. When Shakespeare wrote his will in 1616 (cat.92), he named Richard Burbage as one of only three friends from his life in London and bequeathed him 26*s.* 8*d.* to buy a ring of remembrance.

This painting has traditionally been identified as a portrait of Burbage because of the inventory of the actor and bookseller William Cartwright (1606–86), written in his own hand in the early 1680s. The entry reads: '105 Mr Burbig his head in a gilt frame a small closet pece [piece]'.[2] Cartwright's extensive collection was made up of 239 paintings, including still-lifes, religious images, landscapes, mythological and allegorical paintings and portraits of past monarchs, nobility, family members and friends. Not all of the paintings listed in the inventory survive and it is difficult to match existing pictures with entries in the inventory. While the brief description of the Burbage picture does seem to correspond with this small painting the evidence is not definitive. It is not clear who first linked the individual paintings with the inventory records.

Nevertheless, the Cartwright collection inventory is particularly interesting in several respects. It documents the existence of numerous portraits of early seventeenth-century writers and actors, such as Michael Drayton, Nathan Field and, notably, the actors William Sly and Tom Bond, who may be represented by the portraits shown overleaf (figs 53, 54).

The Burbage picture provides an unusual example of a style of painting – perhaps produced for temporary decorative purposes – that was at one time more widespread. It has suffered from considerable surface abrasion but, even in this damaged condition, it is clear that it was executed with some speed. Because of the painting's small size and the position of the head on the canvas, it has the appearance of having

fig.53 **A portrait of an unknown man, called William Sly**
Unknown English artist
Oil on panel,
388 × 278mm (15¼ × 11in)
Dulwich Picture Gallery, London

fig.54 **A portrait of an unknown man, called Tom Bond**
Unknown English artist
Oil on panel,
390 × 310mm (15⅜ × 12¼ in)
Dulwich Picture Gallery, London

been cut down but the identification of the canvas selvedge on the left and bottom edges indicates that the picture was almost certainly painted in this format. It may have originally been designed to be sewn into a larger canvas; if so, this never happened.[3]

It is not known who painted the portrait, although it differs considerably in style from the Chandos portrait (cat.3), which was once attributed to Burbage himself. It should be noted that there is no specific evidence to support the theory that this picture is a self-portrait. Although Burbage historically has a reputation as a painter, his abilities may have been limited to theatrical banners and coats of arms. He is known to have painted an *impresa* (or emblem) for the Earl of Rutland (1578–1632), which accompanied a motto written by Shakespeare in March 1613.[4] TC

1 I am grateful to John Ingamells for allowing me to read a draft of his entry on this picture for his forthcoming catalogue on British paintings at Dulwich Picture Gallery, prior to its publication.
2 Dulwich Picture Gallery 1987, p.24 (see Literature).
3 I am grateful to Sophie Plender for her invaluable advice on the condition of this portrait and on the condition of cat.52.
4 Gurr 2004, p.223.

cat.52 **A portrait of a man, probably Nathan Field**

52. A portrait of a man, probably Nathan Field (1587–1619/20), *c*.1615[1]

Unknown Anglo-Netherlandish artist

Oil on panel
546 × 422mm (21½ × 16⅝ in)
The Trustees of Dulwich Picture Gallery, London (DPG 385)

Provenance Cartwright collection, 1686

Literature John Charles Lewis Sparkes and Alfred Carver, *Catalogue of the Cartwright Collection and other Pictures and Portraits at Dulwich College* (Spottiswoode and Co., London, 1890), p.30; Peter Murray, *Dulwich Picture Gallery: A Catalogue* (Philip Wilson Publishers for Sotheby Parke Bernet Publications and the Governors of Dulwich College, London, 1980), no.27; Dulwich Picture Gallery, *Mr Cartwright's Pictures: A Seventeenth-century Collection* (Dulwich Picture Gallery, London, 1987), no.25; Richard Beresford, *Dulwich Picture Gallery: Complete Illustrated Catalogue* (Unicorn Press, London, 1998), no.395, p.277

Illustrated on previous page

The actor and playwright Nathan Field joined the King's Men in 1616 and is listed as a 'principal player' in the First Folio of 1623 (fig.55). Field, the son of a puritan minister who held strong opinions against public entertainment, was educated as St Paul's School and went on to become a boy chorister and player. He wrote at least eight plays, including *A Woman is a Weather-Cocke* and *An Honest Man's Fortune*, frequently working in collaboration with the playwrights Philip Massinger (1583–1640) and John Fletcher (1579–1625; cat.84). He was also a good friend of Ben Jonson, who called him his 'scholar'. He never married, but is noted as the subject of gossip about his relationship with the Countess of Argyll, with whom he apparently fathered a child. In 1613 Field became the court payee and representative of Lady Elizabeth's Men, though in 1616 – the year of Shakespeare's death – he left to join the King's Men.

If this highly unusual portrait does represent Field, it is particularly important as an early example of a portrait of an actor/playwright, and a man of similar social standing to William Shakespeare. As with the portrait of Richard Burbage, identification rests with the Cartwright inventory (see p.133), which reads: '167 master fields pictur in his shurt [shirt] on a bourd [board i.e. wooden panel] in a black frame filited with gould [gold] an actour 10s'.[2]

The portrait dates from around the same time as the Chandos portrait (cat.3). It was not painted by an artist trained solely in England, however, but appears to be by a Netherlandish émigré or an English artist trained by a Netherlander. The painter appears to have altered the position of the sitter's ear – an earlier rendering can still be faintly seen above the final position. The sitter wears a shirt embroidered with a delicate 'blackwork' design, datable between 1600 and 1625, which would have been worn under a simple doublet. He also has a gold hooped earring with a gold and pearl pendant, a more elaborate version of the plain gold earring worn by the sitter in the Chandos portrait. The composition of this portrait is unusually expressive for this period and, as in several miniatures from around the same time, the sitter wears costume that is too informal to appear in public. The portrait may have been painted as a private image for a friend or sweetheart.[3] TC

1 I am grateful to John Ingamells for allowing me to read a draft of his entry on this picture for his forthcoming catalogue on British paintings at Dulwich Picture Gallery prior to its publication.
2 Dulwich Picture Gallery 1987, p.25 (see Literature).
3 See, for example, miniatures by Nicholas Hilliard, particularly *Young Man Against a Flame Background*, V&A P.5-1917, illustrated in Katherine Coombs, *The Portrait Miniature in England* (V&A Publications, London, 1998), p.36.

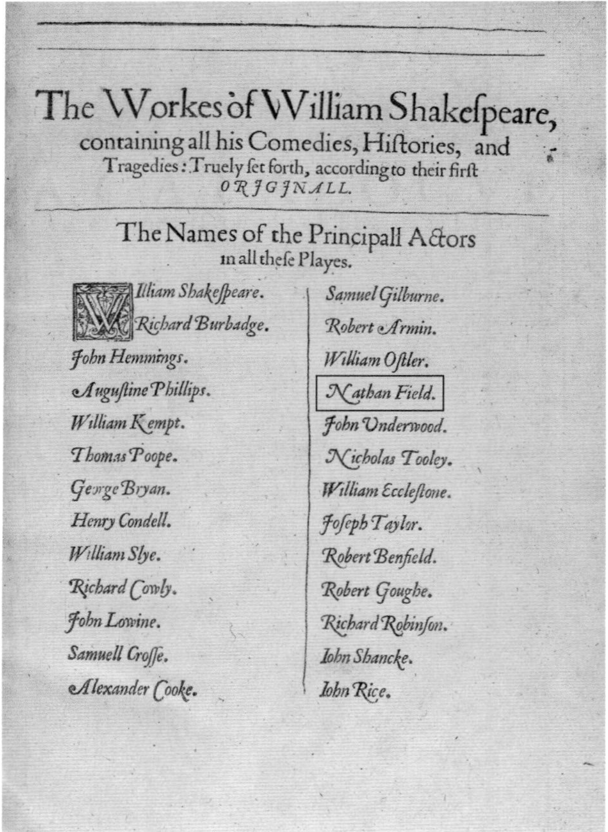

The Workes of William Shakeſpeare,
containing all his Comedies, Hiſtories, and
Tragedies: Truely ſet forth, according to their firſt
ORIGINALL.

The Names of the Principall Actors
in all theſe Playes.

William Shakeſpeare.	Samuel Gilburne.
Richard Burbadge.	Robert Armin.
John Hemmings.	William Oſtler.
Auguſtine Phillips.	Nathan Field.
William Kempt.	John Underwood.
Thomas Poope.	Nicholas Tooley.
George Bryan.	William Eccleſtone.
Henry Condell.	Joſeph Taylor.
William Slye.	Robert Benfield.
Richard Cowly.	Robert Goughe.
John Lowine.	Richard Robinſon.
Samuell Croſſe.	Iohn Shancke.
Alexander Cooke.	Iohn Rice.

fig.55 **A list of twenty-six names of the principal actors in all the plays, from the First Folio.** The British Library, London, c. 39.k.15

53. Letter from Nathan Field to Philip Henslowe, 1613

Manuscript, ink on paper
207 × 154mm (8⅛ × 6 in)
Dulwich College Archive, London, MS I, 168

Provenance Philip Henslowe and his son-in-law Edward Alleyn; by inheritance to the Master and Fellows of Alleyn's College of God's Gift

Literature John Payne Collier, *Memoirs of Edward Alleyn, Founder of Dulwich College* (printed for the Shakespeare Society, London, 1841), p.120; facsimile reproduced in Vickers 2002, p.31

Written from the 'unfortunate extremity' of debtors' prison in 1613, this letter from Nathan Field begs the loan of £5 from the theatrical impresario Philip Henslowe. The loan was to be secured on the promise of the new 'play of Mr Fletcher & ours' – the same John Fletcher (cat.84) who had recently completed work on another collaboration, this time with Shakespeare: *The Famous History of the Life of King Henry VIII*. At one time or another, most of Shakespeare's fellow dramatists saw the inside of a prison-cell, whether for writing 'seditious and slanderous' plays (Ben Jonson, John Marston, Thomas Middleton), counterfeiting coins (Christopher Marlowe), manslaughter (Jonson again) or for simple debt – evidently an occupational hazard. The letter includes postscripts by his co-authors Robert Daborne (*c*.1580–1628) and Philip Massinger (1583–1640), illustrating the perilous hand-to-mouth existence playwrights endured. To the many dramatists who worked for Henslowe, he was both part-producer and part-banker, as the detailed set of financial accounts preserved in his *Diary* makes clear. While Victorian scholars over-emphasized Henslowe's mercenary strain, it remains true that (rather as in modern Hollywood) the status of writer was far outranked by that of the star-actor. So, when his son-in-law the famous actor Edward Alleyn started investing his massive wealth in the charitable foundation of Dulwich College in 1616, their old friend Thomas Dekker wrote a letter of congratulation – from the King's Bench prison: 'poor testimonies of a more rich affection'.[1] Shakespeare, too, earned a fortune from the stage – not from the sale or publication of his plays, but as a shareholder in the Globe. NS

1 Dulwich College Archive, MS I, fol.154.

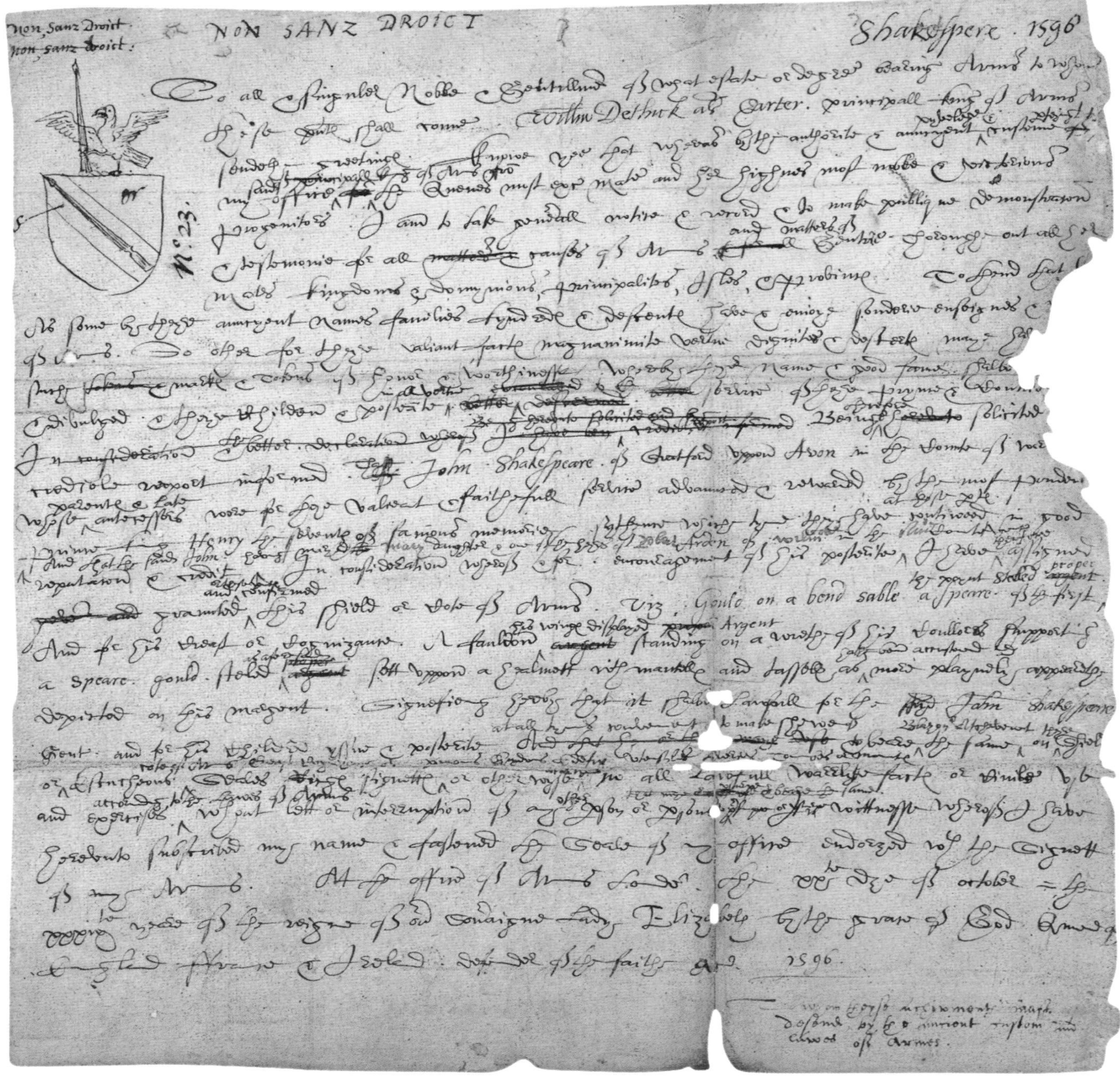

cat.54a **Grant of arms to John Shakespeare (draft)**

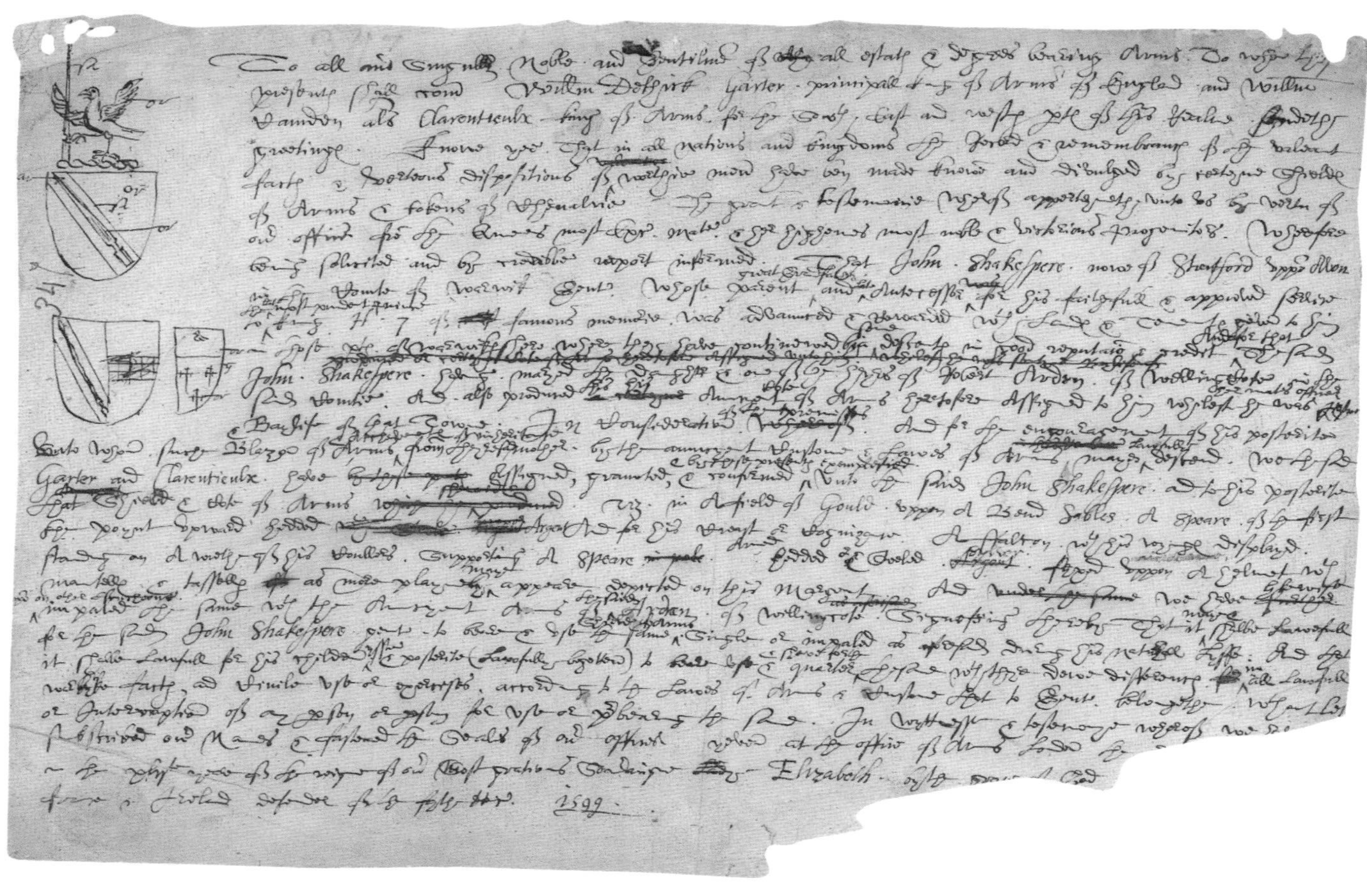

cat.54b **Grant of arms to John Shakespeare (draft)**

54a, b. Grant of arms to John Shakespeare (drafts), 20 October 1595

William Dethick (1543–1612)

Manuscripts, ink on paper
a 292 × 293mm (11½ × 11½in), b 205 × 315mm (8 × 12in)
The College of Arms, London, Shakespeare Grants 1 and 3

Literature Chambers 1930, vol.2, pp.18–32; Schoenbaum 1975, pp.166–73; Katherine Duncan-Jones, *Ungentle Shakespeare* (Arden Shakespeare, London, 2001), pp.91–103

Illustrated on pp. 138–9

These two documents are drafts produced by the Garter King-of-Arms, Sir William Dethick, as part of the process of granting a coat of arms to John Shakespeare of Stratford-upon-Avon in 1596. The fair copy made from these drafts has never come to light, but later documents, and the controversy over the original grant, establish that a coat of arms was indeed granted. This marked an important change in the fortunes of the Shakespeare family. There is much evidence to suggest that in the late 1570s and early 1580s, John Shakespeare's affairs were in serious crisis and there are indications that he was still in financial difficulties in the early 1590s. It is more than likely, therefore, that, although this grant was made to John, at that date still the nominal head of the family, the instigator of the application was his son, William, whose financial success as a poet and play-wright encouraged him to take steps to re-establish his family's reputation in his native town. He was, in any case, better placed, in London, to enter into negotiations with the heralds.

To obtain a grant of arms, entitling the bearer to style himself a gentleman, a very substantial fee – typically between £10 and £20 – was payable. There was a significant increase in the number of applications by wealthy members of an emerging class of merchants and entrepreneurs in the late sixteenth century, although some had difficulties in making a sufficient case for gentry status. In John Shakespeare's case, a vague reference was made to the activities of an unnamed grandfather in the service of Henry VII and to the fact that he had married into the family of Arden, allegedly then already of gentry status. Be this as it may, the real significance of the grant is that, by late 1595, the Shakespeares were clearly of sufficient means to embark on this expensive exercise. Three years later, they made a further application to Dethick for permission to quarter (or 'impale') the Arden arms with their own.

The words, twice repeated, at the head of one of the documents (NON SANZ DROICT; cat.54a) are usually taken to be the family motto (and translated as 'not without right'), although there is no indication that it was ever used and the omission of the comma in one rendering has led to confusion over its meaning. The choice of device, a spear, is a direct reference, of course, to the family name (an inversion of 'spear shaker'), which presumably originated as a nickname. RB

55. The York Herald's complaint against William Dethick (1543–1612), 1602

Ralph Brooke (*c.*1553–1625)

Manuscript, ink on paper
199 × 150mm (7¾ × 5⅞in)
Folger Shakespeare Library, Washington, DC, Ms V.a.350, open at p.28

Literature Chambers 1930, vol.2, pp.18–32, pp.166–73; Schoenbaum 1975; Katherine Duncan-Jones, *Ungentle Shakespeare* (Arden Shakespeare, London, 2001), pp.91–103

The willingness of William Dethick to grant coats of arms without careful regard to the suitability of the applicants – allegedly for financial gain – provoked criticism from his brother heralds. In 1602, Ralph Brooke, York Herald, listed twenty-three cases in which Dethick had, in his view, abused his authority by elevating base persons or assigning to applicants devices already in use. William Shakespeare's name was included in the list – he was now head of the family following his father's death in 1601 – and the description of him here as 'Shakespeare ye Player' does indeed suggest his status may have been an issue. The other individuals whose coats of arms are disputed by Brooke include 'Tey the Hoiser', 'Dunyan Clarke a plasterer', 'Robt Young a ropemaker of London' and 'Smith an Innkeeper in Huntingdon'.

Other documents reveal that the objection to Shakespeare's coat of arms was linked, at least in part, to the similarity between his arms, as granted by Dethick, and the arms of Lord Mauley; but Dethick also justified his grant on the grounds that John Shakespeare had been a man 'of good substance and habilitie', suggesting that the criticism had included a reference to the family's lack of gentlemanly status.

RB

56. William Shakespeare's purchase of New Place, Stratford-upon-Avon, May 1597

Written in Latin
Manuscript, ink on parchment with tag bearing large fragment of the seal of the Court of Common Pleas
372 × 221 × 40mm (14⅝ × 8¾ × 1½ in)
Shakespeare Birthplace Trust, Stratford-upon-Avon, ERSBT 27/49

Provenance From the papers of Robert Bell Wheler, presented 1863

Literature Robert Bearman, *Shakespeare in the Stratford Records* (Alan Sutton, Stroud, 1994), pp.16–21

In May 1597, William Shakespeare purchased from William Underhill (d.1597), a member of the local gentry, a substantial house in Stratford known as New Place. Built in the 1490s, and reputedly the second largest house in the town, this was Shakespeare's first known investment. It provides striking evidence not only of his financial success but also of his intention to acquire property in his native town for the benefit of his family.

We do not know how much the property cost. The Underhills had paid £110 when they bought New Place in 1567 and so Shakespeare might be expected to have paid a higher sum thirty years later. However, it may have been in bad repair. Its owner, William Underhill, lived mainly at his principal residence, in nearby Idlicote, and, at the time of the purchase, was keeping a low profile as a result of his recusancy (adherence to the Catholic faith) and financial difficulties.

The surviving documentation is unusual. The normal arrangement then, as today, was for a conveyance from one party to the other to be drawn up, including details of the purchase price and the property, which was then signed. If there was such a deed, it has since been lost. It was also possible, as a protection against fraud, to have the transaction recorded in the Court of Common Pleas by means of a fictitious legal action, or a 'fine', a copy of which would then be kept with the title deeds. In this document, the property would be described in a highly formal (and historically unhelpful) manner and a sum of money mentioned that was much less than the actual purchase price.

The document displayed here originated in this way, although it is not the usual copy, but the less common official confirmation – an 'exemplification' – issued in Queen Elizabeth's name and once bearing the seal of the Court of Common Pleas. It was found amongst the deeds to Shakespeare's estate. RB

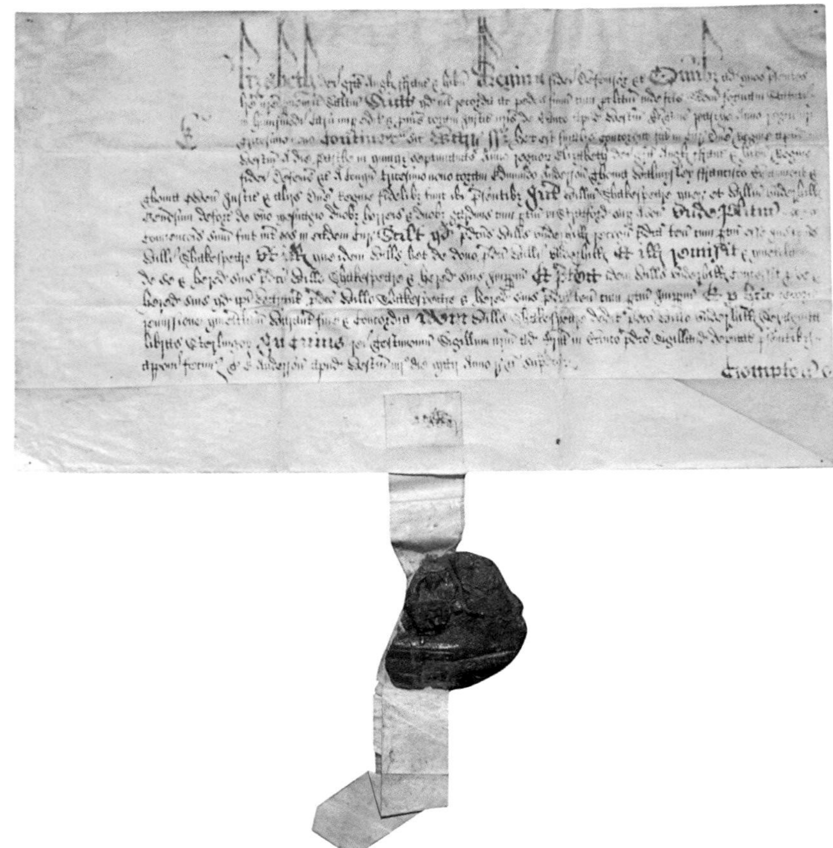

57. Signet ring, bearing the initials 'WS', *c.*1600

English

Gold
19 × 16.5mm (3/4 × 5/8 in)
Shakespeare Birthplace Trust, Stratford-upon-Avon (STRST SBT 1868-3/274)

Provenance Purchased from the finder, a Mrs Martin, by Robert Bell Wheler on the day of its discovery in the mill close field, adjoining the churchyard of Holy Trinity Church, Stratford-upon-Avon, 16 March 1810; donated to the Shakespeare Birthplace Trust by R.B. Wheler's sister Anne in 1868

Literature R.B. Wheler, *Guide to Stratford-upon-Avon*, 1814; *The Catalogue of Books, Manuscripts, Works of Art and Relics at present exhibited in Shakespeare's Birthplace* (Trustees of the guardians of Shakespeare's Birthplace [2nd pages], Stratford-upon-Avon, 1868); Schoenbaum 1991, p.47; S. Wells, 'The God of Our Idolatry' in Stephanie Nolan, *Shakespeare's Face* (A.A. Knopf, Toronto, 2002), pp.24–5; Wood 2003, p.337

This heavy gold finger ring is neatly engraved with the initials 'WS' intertwined with a tasselled knot, a device typically used on Elizabethan gold signet or 'seal' rings. It would have been owned by a man of considerable wealth and social standing.

Since its discovery in 1810, there has been much speculation that the ring might have belonged to William Shakespeare. In a letter to John Keats (1795–1821), the artist Robert Haydon (1786–1846), who was convinced of the authenticity of its ownership, wrote: 'I shall certainly go mad! In a field at Stratford upon Avon, in a field that belonged to Shakespeare; they have found a gold ring and seal, with initial thus – W.S. and a true lover's knot!! As sure as you breathe, & he that was the first of beings the Seal belonged to him – Oh Lord!'

The early owner, Robert Bell Wheler (1785–1857) argued in conversation with Edmond Malone (1741–1812), Shakespeare's biographer, that there were few men of sufficient means living in Stratford at the time with the correct initials. Malone suggested that there was one candidate: William Smith (*c.*1550–1618), a wealthy local draper. Smith's seal was already documented, however, and its design did not correspond to the one on the ring. One piece of circumstantial evidence that might point towards it having been owned, but then lost, by Shakespeare, is to be found in his will of 1616 (cat.92). At the bottom of the document, the phrase 'In Witness whereof I have hereunto put my Seale' has been altered, and the word 'hand' substituted for 'Seale'. AD

58. Letter from Richard Quiney (d.1602) to William Shakespeare asking for his help in obtaining a loan of £30, 25 October 1598

Manuscript, ink on paper
167 × 135mm (6½× 5¼in), once folded to 72 × 53mm (2⅞ × 2in)
Shakespeare Birthplace Trust, Stratford-upon-Avon, ER 27/4

Provenance From the papers of Robert Bell Wheler, presented 1863

Literature Robert Bearman, *Shakespeare in the Stratford Records* (Alan Sutton, Stroud, 1994), pp.24–6

In the autumn of 1598, Richard Quiney, a leading Stratford townsman, was in London, pursuing legal business on behalf of the Stratford-upon-Avon Corporation. While there, he penned this famous note to William Shakespeare – the only item of the poet's correspondence to have survived – asking for help in securing a loan of £30. He explains it is to help him pay off his debts in London, but we also know that a few days earlier Quiney had received a letter from a Stratford friend, Abraham Sturley (1551–1614), begging for his help in raising £25 in order to meet the demands of pressing creditors. In addition, on the day that Quiney wrote to Shakespeare, he penned another letter to Sturley to explain what he had done.

We are not certain whether Shakespeare responded to Quiney's appeal, nor indeed whether the letter was ever sent; for, although it was clearly folded, sealed and addressed to Shakespeare, it was later found in Quiney's own papers. The real point of interest is Quiney's confidence that Shakespeare had the means to assist him in raising this very substantial sum of money. At a time when a small Stratford house could change hands for £30 and the Stratford schoolmaster's annual salary was £20, Shakespeare's credit must have been thought very sound.

The other interesting feature of the letter is its air of familiarity, confirming that the two men knew each other well. There is no formality in Quiney's greeting – 'Loveinge Contreyman, I am bold with you as with a frende' – and this is quickly followed by a bald statement of his request. Quiney was often in London, and he is known to have met Shakespeare on at least one other occasion. Even if Shakespeare visited Stratford only infrequently at this time, his financial success would have been well known in his native town as the result of such contacts. RB

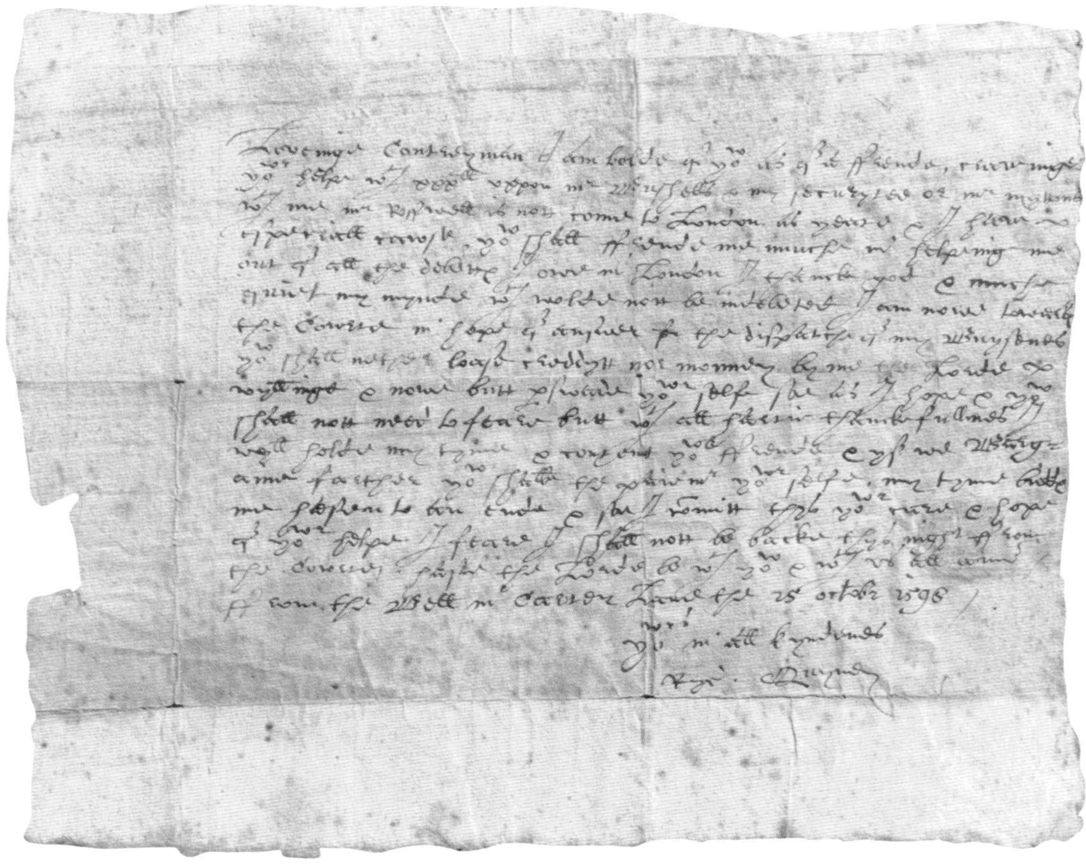

Loveinge Contreyman I am bolde of yowe as of a ffrende, craveinge yowe[r] helpe with xxxli vppon Mr Bushells & my securytee or Mr Myttons with me. Mr Rosswell is nott come to London as yeate & I have especiall cawse. Yowe shall ffrende me muche in helpeinge me out of all the debettes I owe in London, I thancke god, & muche quiet my mynde which wolde nott be indebeted. I am nowe towardes the Cowrte in hope of answer for the dispatche of my Buysenes. Yowe shall neither loase creddytt nor monney by me, the Lorde wyllinge, & nowe butt perswade yowe selfe soe as I hope & yowe shall nott need to feare butt with all hartie thanckefullenes I will holde my tyme & content yowe ffrende, & yf we Bargaine farther yowe shalbe the paiemaster yowe self. My tyme biddes me hasten to an ende & soe I committ thys [to] yowe[r] care & hope of yowe[r] helpe. I feare I shall nott be backe thys night ffrom the Cowrte. Haste. The Lorde be with yowe & with vs all Amen. ffrom the Bell in Carter Lane the 25 October 1598.

Yowes in all kyndenes
Ryc. Quyney

59. *Palladis Tamia Wits Treasury Being the Second Part of Wits Common wealth*, 1598

Francis Meres (1565/6–1647)

Printed book, 'Printed by P. Short, for Cuthbert Burbie, and are to be solde at his shop at the Royall Exchange'
Octavo
The British Library, London, G. 10375, open at fols 281v–2r

Provenance Bequest of Thomas Grenville (1755–1846), statesman and book collector, *c.*1846

Literature D.C. Allen, 'Francis Meres's Treatise "Poetrie": A Critical Edition', *University of Illinois Studies in Language and Literature*, 16, 1933, pp.345–500; D.C. Allen, Introduction in Francis Meres, *Palladis Tamia* (facs. ed. 1938)

In the same year that Shakespeare's name first appeared on the title page of one of his plays (*Love's Labour's Lost*), Francis Meres, a Cambridge graduate, published *Palladis Tamia*, which contains an early indication of Shakespeare's growing fame.

The book consists of a long series of similitudes or *exempla*, comparing the natural and the spiritual worlds and drawing on biblical and classical sources. Much of it consisted of translations from well-known writers, such as Desiderius Erasmus (*c.*1467–1536) and Roger Ascham (1514/15–1568), but part of the material Meres included was original. In particular the chapter called 'A comparative discourse of our English poets, with the Greeke, Latine, and Italian poets' contains a series of comparisons between Greek and Roman writers and modern English ones. Shakespeare is mentioned, along with Philip Sidney (1554–1586), Edmund Spenser (1552?–1599), Samuel Daniel (1562/3–1619), Michael Drayton (cat.81), William Warner (1558/9–1609), Christopher Marlowe (cat.22) and George Chapman (cat.90) as writers who have 'mightily enriched, and gorgeouslie inuested [the English tongue] in rare ornaments and resplendent abiliments'.

In two further passages Shakespeare is praised as a poet, the 'mellifluous & hony-tongued' equal to Ovid, and as a dramatist, the rival of Plautus and Seneca for comedy and tragedy. Meres knows of the two narrative poems, and also of poems, 'sugred Sonnets' (not necessarily sonnets, but any short poems), which circulated 'among his priuate friends', presumably in manuscript or as songs. He lists six comedies and six tragedies and histories. Some of them, like *The Life and Death of King John*, had not yet been printed, but he does not mention *The Taming of the Shrew* or *Much Ado about Nothing*. His reference to a play called *Love's Labour's Won* has occasioned much debate about its identity and very existence. In 1953 a reference was found to a play with this title in the stock of an Exeter stationer, Christopher Hunt (active 1592–1606), in August 1603; if the play had been printed by then, no copy has survived, and it does not appear in the first Folio under that title. HRW

The secondpart of

mong al writers to be of an honest life and vpright conuersation:so *Michael Drayton* (*quē toties honoris & amoris causa nomino*) among schollers,souldiours,Poets, and all sorts of people,is helde for a man of vertuous disposition,honest conuersation, and wel gouerned cariage,which is almost miraculous among good wits in these declining and corrupt times, when there is nothing but rogery in villanous man, & whē cheating and craftines is counted the cleanest wit, and soundest wisedome.

As *Decius Ausonius Gallus in libris Fastorum*,penned the occurrences of ỹ world from the first creation of it to his time,that is,to the raigne of the Emperor *Gratian*:so *Warner* in his absolute *Albions Englande* hath most admirably penned the historie of his own country from *Noah* to his time, that is,to the raigne of Queene *Elizabeth*; I haue heard him termd of the best wits of both our Vniuersities,our English *Homer*.

As *Euripedes* is the most sententious among the Greek Poets:so is *Warner* amōg our English Poets.

As the soule of *Euphorbus* was thought to liue in *Pythagoras*: so the sweete wittie soule of *Ouid* liues in mellifluous & hony-tongued *Shakespeare*,witnes his *Venus and Adonis*,his *Lucrece*, his sugred Sonnets among

Wits Common-Wealth. 282

among his priuate friends,&c.

As *Plautus* and *Seneca* are accounted the best for Comedy and Tragedy among the Latines: so *Shakespeare* among ỹ English is the most excellent in both kinds for the stage;for Comedy, witnes his *Gētlemē of Verona*,his *Errors*,his *Loue labors lost*,his *Loue labours wonne*,his *Midsummers night dreame*,& his *Merchant of Venice*:for Tragedy his *Richard the 2.Richard the 3.Henry the 4.King Iohn*,*Titus Andronicus* and his *Romeo* and *Iuliet*.

As *Epius Stolo* said,that the Muses would speake with *Plautus* tongue,if they would speak Latin:so I say that the Muses would speak with *Shakespeares* fine filed phrase,if they would speake English.

As *Musæus*,who wrote the loue of *Hero* and *Leander*,had two excellent schollers, *Thamaras* & *Hercules*:so hath he in England two excellent Poets,imitators of him in the same argument and subiect,*Christopher Marlow*,and *George Chapman*.

As *Ouid* saith of his worke;

Iamq; opus exegi,quod nec Iouis ira,nec ignis,
Nec poterit ferrum,nec edax abolere vetustas.

And as *Horace* saith of his;*Exegi monumentū ære perennius;Regaliq; situ pyramidū altius;Quod non imber edax; Non Aquilo impotens possit diruere; aut innumerabilis*

Oo2. *annorum*

60. The performance of *Titus Andronicus*, 1594

Henry Peacham (1578–in or after 1644)

Manuscript, pen and ink on paper from a folio manuscript
296 × 403mm (11 5/8 × 15 7/8 in)
Inscribed vertically at left between the folds: 'Henrye Peachams Hand/1595';
below the drawing lengthy speeches from the play
The Most Hon. Marquess of Bath, Longleat House, Warminster, Wiltshire, Portland Papers, vol.I, f.159v

Provenance From the first volume of the Portland Papers, by descent from the 1st Marquess of Bath

Literature R.A. Foakes, *Illustrations of the English Stage 1580–1642* (Stanford University Press, California, 1985), pp.48–51; Herbert Berry, 'The Date on the "Peacham" Manuscript', *Shakespeare Bulletin*, 17, 1999, pp.5–6; June Schlueter, 'Rereading the Peacham Drawing', *Shakespeare Quarterly*, 50, 1999, pp.171–84; Richard Levin, 'The Longleat Manuscript and *Titus Andronicus*', *Shakespeare Quarterly*, 53, 2002, pp.323–40

Henry Peacham, author of *The Art of Drawing* (1606) and *The Compleat Gentleman* (1622), was a student at Cambridge in 1594. This drawing by Peacham is the first known illustration of a scene from Shakespeare and derives from a folio page manuscript with quotations from Shakespeare's *Titus Andronicus*. The image appears to show a version of a staged performance and is placed above a set of quotations copied from the play as it was published in 1594. Peacham signed and dated his work in that year, although confirmation of the date has proved contentious.

The verses are principally a long speech from the play, beginning with a stage direction, 'Enter Tamora pleadinge for her sonnes going to execution'. This direction is apt for the illustration, but does not exist in either the 1594 Quarto text of the play or the Folio text of 1623. The next forty lines comprise Tamora's speech to Titus from the opening scene, followed by a compressed version of Titus's five-line reply. The verses end with a version of Aaron's boast from Act V, which may explain his distinctive pose in the illustration, except that in Act V he speaks from a ladder while about to be hanged, where he could not wield his sword as he does in the drawing.

The clothing in the drawing is particularly notable, because, although it shows Titus in what seems to be a version of a Roman toga, and Tamora in a masque-like flowing dress, the ordinary soldiers are in Elizabethan clothing and carry Elizabethan halberds (combined spears and battleaxes). This implies that while the leading characters wore special clothing to suit their roles, the mutes and other walk-on characters were dressed in standard gear from the company stockroom.

The date of the drawing and the inscription appear as a set of numbers at the bottom left of the page. Although it is in distinctively odd hieroglyphs, the date does appear to signify 1594, the year of the play's first publication. In that year the newly created Shakespeare company first started performing at the Theatre in Shoreditch. *Titus Andronicus* is already on record as being staged at the Rose Theatre in late 1593 and early 1594, where it was performed by Sussex's Men, some of whom probably joined the Shakespeare company when it was formed that May. Peacham's illustration must derive from performances at the Rose, since the Quarto text of the play appeared in the Stationers' Register on 6 February 1594 and came on sale soon afterwards. AG

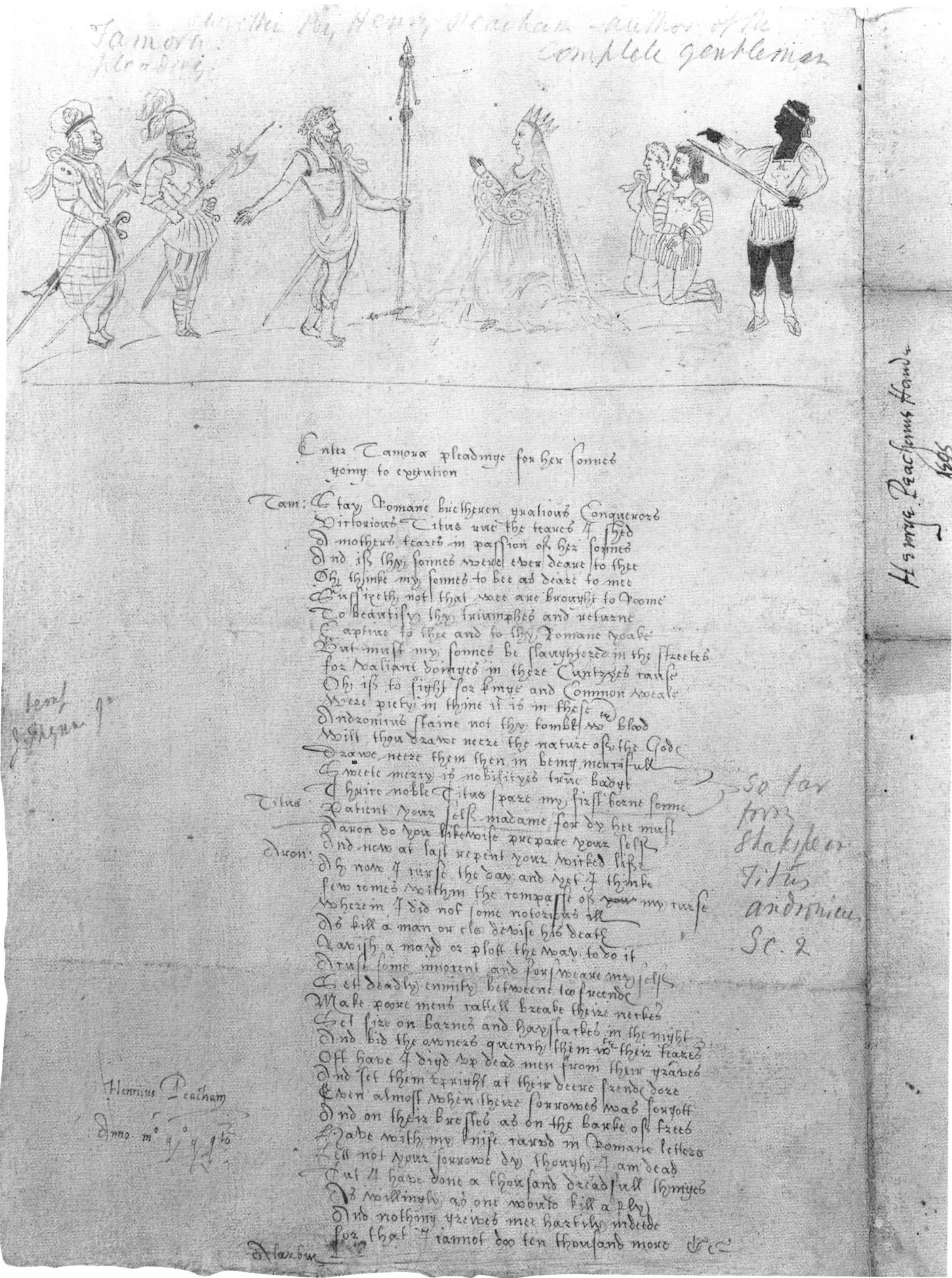
Tamora pleading
written by Henry Peacham - author of the Complete gentleman
Enter Tamora pleadinge for her sonnes going to execution
Tam: Stay Romane bretheren gratious Conquerors
Victorious Titus rue the teares I shed
A mothers teares in passion of her sonnes
And if thy sonnes were ever deare to thee
Oh thinke my sonnes to bee as deare to mee
Suffizeth not that wee are brought to Rome
To beautify thy triumphes and returne
Captive to thee and to thy Romane yoake
But must my sonnes be slaughtered in the streetes
for valiant doinges in there Cuntryes cause
Oh if to fight for kinge and Common weale
Were piety in thine it is in these
Andronicus staine not thy tombe wth blood
Wilt thou drawe neere the nature of the Gods
Drawe neere them then in being mercifull
Sweete mercy is nobilityes true badge
Thrice noble Titus spare my first borne sonne
Titus: Patient your self madame for dy hee must
Aaron do you likewise prepare your self
And now at last repent your wicked life
Aron: Ah now I curse the day and yet I thinke
few comes within the compasse of my curse
Wherein I did not some notorious ill
As kill a man or els devise his death
Ravish a mayd or plott the way to do it
Acuse some innocent and forsweare myself
Set deadly enmity betweene too freendes
Make poore mens cattell breake theire neckes
Set fire on barnes and haystackes in the night
And bid the owners quench them wth theire teares
Oft have I digd vp dead men from their graves
And set them upright at theire deere frendes dore
Even almost when theire sorrowes was forgott
And on theire brestes as on the barke of trees
Have with my knife carved in Romane letters
Let not your sorrowe dy though I am dead
But I have done a thousand dreadfull thinges
As willingly as one would kill a fly
And nothing greeves mee hartily indeede
for that I cannot doo ten thousand more &c.
Alarbus
Henricus Peacham
Anno mo qo qo qto
So far from Shakspear Titus andronicus Sc. 2
Henrye Peachams Hand 1595

61. Simon Forman's *Diary* recording a performance of Shakespeare's *Winter's Tale*, 1611

Manuscript, ink on paper
Approximately 300 × 200mm (11 3/4 × 7 7/8in)
The Bodleian Library, University of Oxford, MS Ashmole. 208, open at fol.201

Provenance Elias Ashmole (1617–92); transferred to the Bodleian in 1860

Literature A.L. Rowse, *Simon Forman: Sex and Society in Shakespeare's Age* (Weidenfeld and Nicolson, London, 1974); Barbara Howard Traister, *The Notorious Astrological Physician of London: Works and Days of Simon Forman* (University of Chicago Press, Chicago and London, 2001)

Simon Forman (1552–1611) was one of the most colourful characters of Elizabethan London. An astrologer, magician and physician, he left voluminous notebooks, written often in Latin and in code, which offer astonishingly intimate glimpses into the lives of many of his contemporaries. Thousands of men and women of all walks of life consulted him about their health, things they had lost, anxieties about what might happen to friends and relatives and for insight into the future. He noted their symptoms and their horoscopes, recorded the advice that he gave, chronicled innumerable sexual encounters with his women patients, and recounted his dreams, in one of which he propositioned Queen Elizabeth. In 1597 he was consulted by Maria, wife of Christopher Mountjoy, in whose house Shakespeare lodged, probably between 1602 and 1604. Another patient was Emilia Lanier, whom the historian A.L. Rowse believed to be the so-called 'dark lady' of Shakespeare's sonnets. Forman was also consulted by Shakespeare's printer Richard Field (cats 48, 49), who had swallowed a coin.

Most excitingly of all, Forman made notes on performances of *Cymbeline*, *Macbeth* and *The Winter's Tale*, which he saw at the Globe Theatre in 1611. Although they are partial and raise many questions, these are by far the fullest contemporary accounts of performances of any of Shakespeare's plays. Forman was interested in drawing morals from what he saw. In his record of *The Winter's Tale*, shown here, he reminded himself how the rogue Autolycus 'feyned him sicke & to haue bin Robbed of all that he had and how he cozened [tricked] the por man of all his money. And after cam to the shep sher [shep shearing] with a peddlers packe & ther cozened them Again of all their money . . .' From this Forman drew the (rather obvious) moral 'beware of trustinge feined beggars or fawning fellouse [fellows]'.
SW

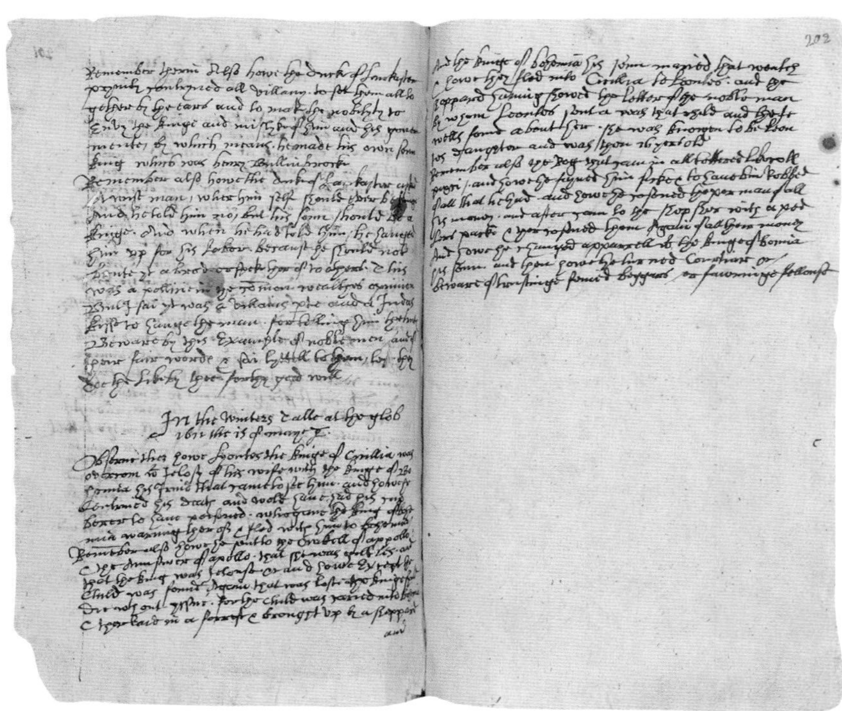

62. *THE Third volume of Chronicles*, 1587

Raphael Holinshed (*c.*1525–80)

Printed book, 'Printed by '[H. Denham] at the expenses of J. Harrison, G. Bishop, R. Newberie, H. Denham and T. Woodcocke'.
Folio
The British Library, London, 674.i.7, open at the title page

Provenance Top of title page 'liber ?gidij Martij 22 1627'; bequest of Rev. Clayton Mordaunt Cracherode (1730–1799)

Literature R.B. McKerrow and F. S. Ferguson, *Title-page Borders Used in England & Scotland, 1485–1640* (The Bibliographical Society, London, 1932), no.131; Annabel Patterson, *Reading Holinshed's Chronicles* (University of Chicago Press, Chicago and London, 1994)

Illustrated overleaf

Shakespeare drew on two important sources for his plays: Raphael Holinshed's *Chronicles* and Thomas North's translation of Plutarch's *Lives* (the 1595 edition; see below). Holinshed's *Chronicles*, the work of several men, provided readers with the first continuous and more or less full account of the entire history of the British Isles. The book was first published by Holinshed in two volumes of just under 3,000 pages in 1577 and reissued in an edition revised and augmented by John Hooker, alias Vowell (*c.*1527–1601), and Francis Thynne (1545?–1608) in three substantial volumes in 1587. This was the edition that Shakespeare seems to have used, and he may well have owned a copy of this expensive publication. From Holinshed's nationalist account Shakespeare took much of the material that he dramatized in the history plays, as well as in *Macbeth*, parts of *Cymbeline* and *King Lear* (but not in *The Life and Death of King John*). Shakespeare also drew on the *Chronicle* of 1548 written by Edward Halle (1497–1547) and Richard Grafton (*c.*1511–73) for the *Henry VI* plays.

The title page of the third volume of Holinshed's *Chronicles* shown here is framed by a border that was first used in Richard Grafton's *A chronicle at large* (1569). At the top in the centre are Moses and Brute, the legendary founder of Britain; at the foot in the central panel Queen Elizabeth is enthroned and accompanied by courtiers; the figures in the left-hand border are supposed to be Saul, David, Solomon and William I; in the right-hand border they are Locrine (the subject of a play first printed in 1595 and attributed to 'W.S.'), Albanact (Albany in *King Lear*), Camber and Henry VIII. HRW

63. *The liues of the noble Grecians and Romanes*, translated by Thomas North (1535–1603?), 1579

Plutarch

Printed book, 'Imprinted at London by Thomas Vautrouillier and John Wight'
Folio
The British Library, London, C.38.k.24, open at p.763

Provenance On upper endpaper, 'James Wrightwick/his Book'; 'John Sheldon' ; on title page: 'Tho Wightwick. . .'; purchased in 1873

Literature *Shakespeare's Plutarch*, ed. T.J.B. Spencer (Penguin, Harmondsworth, 1964)

Illustrated on p.151

When at the turn of the sixteenth century Shakespeare chose to dramatize ancient history, he drew on Plutarch's forty-six lives of famous Greeks and Romans, almost all of which were arranged in pairs. He read the work in the translation by Sir Thomas North, first published in 1579 and reprinted in 1595 and 1603 by Shakespeare's fellow Stratfordian Richard Field. It is possible that Shakespeare used the 1595 edition. North made his translation from the French version of Jacques Amyot (1513–93), printed at Lausanne in 1574, and Shakespeare's debt to him in *Julius Caesar*, *Timon of Athens*, *Antony and Cleopatra* and *Coriolanus* was first recognized by Samuel Johnson (1709–84) in the Preface to his 1765 edition of Shakespeare ('he dilated some of Plutarch's lives into plays'). Not only did Shakespeare use the lives generally as sources for the plays, but he also sometimes turned North's vigorous prose into blank verse with few changes or adjustments. The most famous example of this is Enobarbus's description of Cleopatra's arrival at Cydnus: 'The barge she sat in like a burnish'd throne . . .'. Plutarch's exploration of history through biography evidently appealed to Shakespeare, who found inspiration in his investigation of individual character and action. This biographical approach may well have influenced the writing of *The Life of King Henry V*, and Plutarch's interest in the inner lives of his subjects may be reflected in such plays as *Hamlet* and *Macbeth*. HRW

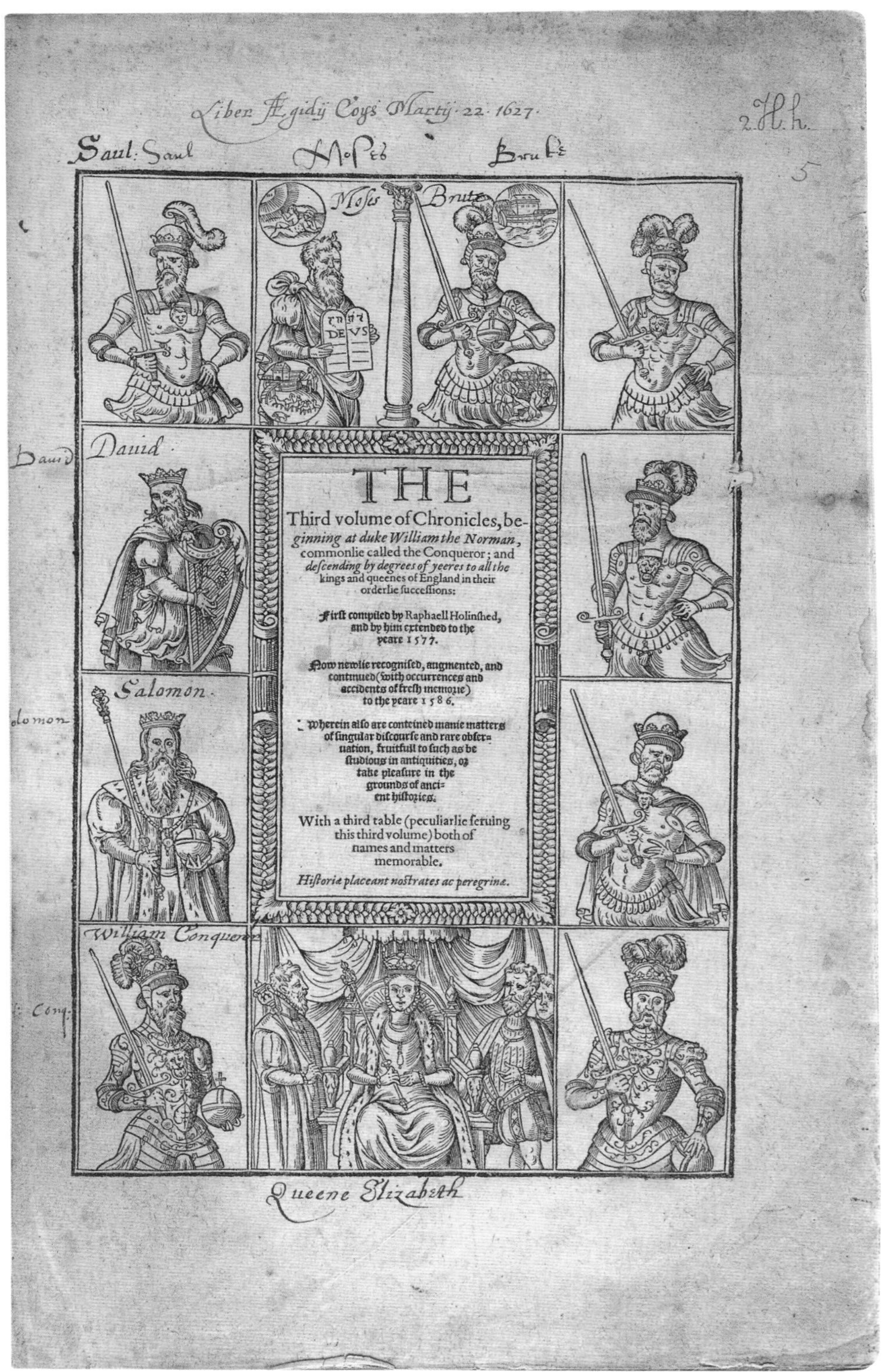

cat.62 **The third volume of Holinshed's *Chronicles***

A faire corps as could be. *Alexander* left *Roxane* great with childe, for the which the Macedonians did her great honor: but she did malice *Statira* extreamely, & did finely deceiue her by a counterfeat letter she sent, as if it had comen from *Alexander*, willing her to come vnto him. But when she was come, *Roxane* killed her and her sister, and then threw their bodies into a well, and filled it vp with earth, by *Perdiccas* helpe and consent. *Perdiccas* came to be king, immediatly after *Alexanders* death, by meanes of *Aridæus*, whom he kept about him for his gard and safety. This *Aridæus*, beeing borne of a common strumpet and common woman, called *Philinna*, was halfe lunaticke, not by nature nor by chaunce: but, as it is reported, put out of his wits when he was a young towardly boy, by drinkes, which *Olympias* caused to be geuen him, and thereby continued franticke.

Statira slaine by Roxane.

Aridæus, Alexanders bastard brother.

B

The end of Alexanders life.

THE LIFE OF *Iulius Cæsar.*

C

D

AT what time *Sylla* was made Lord of all, he would haue had *Cæsar* put away his wife *Cornelia*, the daughter of *Cinna* Dictator: but when he saw, he could neither with any promise nor threate bring him to it, he tooke her ioynter away from him. The cause of *Cæsars* ill will vnto *Sylla*,
E was by meanes of mariage: for *Marius* thelder, maried his fathers own sister, by whom he had *Marius* the younger, whereby *Cæsar* & he were cosin germaines. *Sylla* being troubled in waightie matters, putting to death so many of his enemies, when he came to be cōqueror, he made no reckoning of *Cæsar*: but he was not contented to be hidden in safety, but came and made sute vnto the people for the Priesthoodshippe that was voyde, when he had scant any heare on his face. Howbeit he was repulsed by *Syllaes* meanes, that secretly was against him. Who, when he was determined to haue killed him, some of his frendes told him, that it was to no purpose to put so young a boy as he to death. But *Sylla* told them againe, that they did not consider that there were many *Marians* in that young boy. *Cæsar* vnderstanding
F that, stale out of Rome, and hidde him selfe a long time in the contrie of the Sabines, wandring still from place to place. But one day being caried from house to house, he fell into the handes of *Syllaes* souldiers, who searched all those places, and tooke them whom they found

Cæsar ioyned with Cinna & Marius.

cat.63 ***The Lives of the Noble Grecians and Romans***

64. *The Essayes or Morall, Politike and Millitarie Discourses. Done into English* [by John Florio], 1603

Michel de Montaigne (1533–92)

Printed book, 'Printed by Val. Sims [Simmes] for Edward Blount dwelling in Pauls Churchyard'
Folio
The British Library, London, C.21.e.17, open at endpaper and title page

Provenance Owned by the Rev. Edward Patteson of Smethwick, Staffordshire; by descent to his son the Rev. Edward Patteson of East Sheen, Surrey; through Mr Barnwell inspected by Frederic Madden of the British Museum in 1836; sold at auction by R.H. Evans; bought by the book dealer William Pickering for £100; purchased by the British Museum June 1838

Literature Frederic Madden, 'Observations on an Autograph of Shakspere and the Orthography of his name', *Archaeologia* 27, 1838, pp.113–23; Edward Maunde Thompson, *Shakespeare's Handwriting* (Clarendon Press, Oxford, 1916); Edward Maunde Thompson, 'Two Pretended Autographs of Shakespeare', *Library* 3rd ser., 8 (1917), pp.193–217; Schoenbaum 1981, pp.102–4

The absence of identifiable books from Shakespeare's library has encouraged a certain amount of wishful thinking by scholars, and some forgeries. Shakespeare's use of the version of Montaigne by John Florio (1553–1625) as a source for his plays (for example, *The Tempest*) had been established as early as 1780. This copy of the work contains what is generally accepted to be a forged Shakespeare signature. 'Willm Shakspere' is written on the verso of the endpaper facing the book's title page. A copy of Ovid's *Metamorphoses* (1502) in the Bodleian Library has another forged signature. The Montaigne volume is supposed to have an eighteenth-century Midlands (Staffordshire) provenance; it was bought by the British Museum in 1838 from a book dealer who had paid £100 for it at auction. Several examples of Shakespeare's genuine signatures exist, for example in his last will and testament (cat.92). Here, the 'W' is quite out of proportion, the 'p' is uncharacteristically lacking a loop and many of the letters are written individually rather than continuously, indicating that it is almost certainly an accomplished forgery. The same forger may also have been responsible for another Shakespeare signature in a copy of John Rastell's *Statutes.*

A copy of William Lambarde's account of Anglo-Saxon ecclesiastical law, *Archaionomia* (1568), now in the Folger Shakespeare Library, has possibly the best claim to have belonged to Shakespeare, although unlike the Montaigne and Ovid, its subject matter is rather remote from the plays and poems. HRW

65. *The.xv. Bookes of P. Ouidius Naso, entytuled Metamorphosis, translated oute of Latin into English meeter, by Arthur Golding* (1535/6–1606), 1567

Ovid

Printed book, 'Imprinted at London, by Willyam Seres'
Quarto in 8s
The British Library, London, G.17529, open at title page

Provenance Bequest of Thomas Grenville (1755–1846), book collector and statesman, *c.*1846.

Literature *Shakespeare's Ovid: Being Arthur Golding's Translation of the Metamorphoses*, ed. W.H.D. Rouse (Alexander de la More, London, 1904); Jonathan Bate, *Shakespeare and Ovid* (Clarendon Press, Oxford, 1993)

Publius Ovidius Naso, better known as Ovid (43 BC–AD 17), was Shakespeare's favourite Latin poet, and perhaps his favourite writer in any language. In 1598 Francis Meres (cat.59) specifically associated Shakespeare with Ovid, and Shakespeare returned to his works, especially the mythological transformations described in the *Metamorphoses*, again and again. For example, the story of Venus and Adonis was taken from it, while Imogen is shown to have been reading it in *Cymbeline* and Prospero's farewell to his own art, 'Ye elves of hills, brooks, standing lakes, and groves', is also closely related to the account of Medea's recantation in Ovid. Shakespeare probably had enough Latin to read Ovid in the original, but he may well also have made use of Arthur Golding's popular translation into rhyming couplets, each line made up of fourteen syllables. This, the first translation of the whole poem into English, was first published in 1567 and again in 1575, 1584, 1587, 1593, 1603 and 1612. It is not known which edition of Ovid in Latin or in English Shakespeare used.

Golding translated works by classical and Protestant writers (including Calvin) into English, explaining that Ovid's tales of divine misbehaviour were allegorical and could be given a Christian, moral interpretation. He dedicated his version of Ovid to Robert Dudley (1532/3–88), who had recently been created Earl of Leicester: the woodcut of his badge, the bear and ragged staff, on the title page in this copy has been coloured by hand and the volume contains some particularly interesting handwritten notes in the margin (known as marginalia). HRW

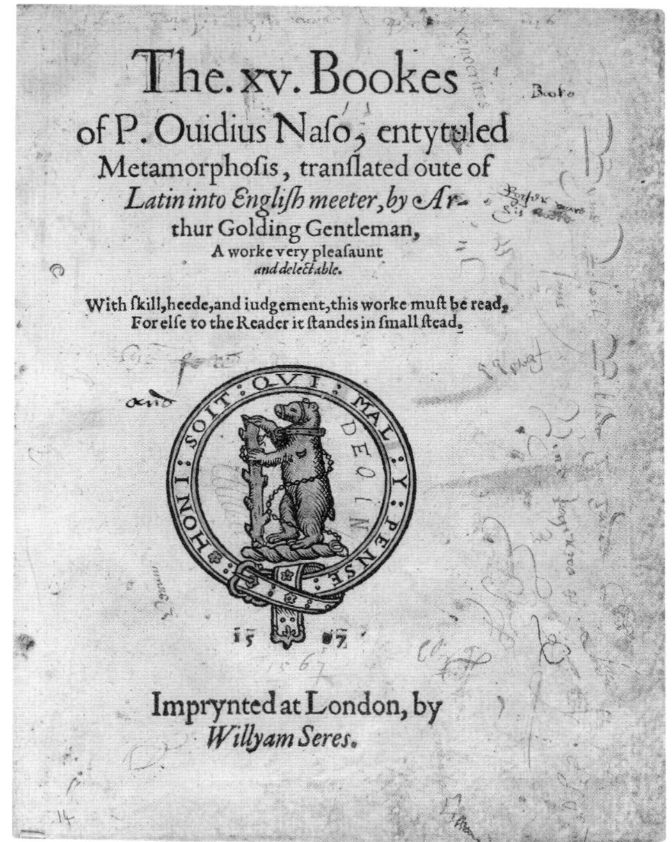
The.xv. Bookes of P. Ouidius Naso, entytuled Metamorphosis, translated oute of Latin into English meeter, by Arthur Golding Gentleman, A worke very pleasaunt and delectable.

With skill, heede, and iudgement, this worke must be read, For else to the Reader it standes in small stead.

HONI SOIT QVI MAL Y PENSE

DEO LN

15 67

Imprynted at London, by Willyam Seres.

66. *The Booke of Sir Thomas Moore*, *c.*1592–*c.*1604

?Anthony Munday (1560–1633) and Henry Chettle (d.1603–7)

Manuscript, ink on paper
Approximately 370 × 270mm (14½ × 10⅝in)
The British Library, London, Harley MS 7368, fol.f9

Provenance Seen by Thomas Hearne in 1727 in the collection of John Murray (1670–1748); acquired by Robert Harley, second Earl of Oxford; acquired by the British Museum in 1753

Literature Richard Simpson, 'Are there any Extant MSS. in Shakespeare's Handwriting?', *Notes and Queries*, 183, 1871, pp.1–3; *The Booke of Sir Thomas Moore*, ed. W.W. Greg (Malone Society, Oxford, 1911), rev. Harold Jenkins (Malone Society, Oxford, 1961); *Shakespeare's Hand in the Play of Sir Thomas More*, ed. A.W. Pollard (Cambridge University Press, Cambridge, 1923); *Shakespeare and 'Sir Thomas More': Essays on the Play and its Shakespearian Interest*, ed. T.H. Howard-Hill (Cambridge University Press, Cambridge, 1989); Anthony Munday *et al.*, *Sir Thomas More*, eds Vittorio Gabrieli and Giorgio Melchiori (Manchester University Press, Manchester, 1990)

Of all the theatrical manuscripts that have survived from the late sixteenth and early seventeenth centuries, the one that preserves the play generally known as *Sir Thomas More* may have the closest links to Shakespeare. The manuscript originally consisted of sixteen leaves (thirty-two pages), of which the last is blank. The play shows evidence of having being censored by Edmund Tilney (1535/6–1610), Master of the Revels from 1579 to 1610, and then of being revised. In the course of these changes three leaves were removed and seven new leaves and two fragments were added. Six different hands have been detected at work in the manuscript: the original authors of the play seem to have been Anthony Munday and Henry Chettle; they were joined, when it came to revising the manuscript, by Thomas Dekker (*c.*1572–1632), Thomas Heywood (1573?–1641), by a professional theatrical scribe whose hand has also been identified in two Elizabethan stage plots (Hand C), and by another hand (Hand D), which may be Shakespeare's.

The play was probably written for the theatrical entrepreneur Philip Henslowe (1555?–1616) and may have been performed by the Admiral's Men. As with many other aspects of the play, there is uncertainty about its date: it might originally date from 1592 to 1595, with the revisions prepared from 1603 to 1604. The suggestion that Shakespeare was involved in the play was first made in 1871. He may have been responsible for the 140 or so lines of the play that describe the incident in which Sir Thomas More (1478–1535) as sheriff of London seeks to pacify a city mob of rebellious apprentices during the anti-alien or immigrant riots ('Ill May Day') of 1517: the episode almost certainly had a topical significance for Shakespeare's contemporaries. The lines have been attributed to Shakespeare on several grounds: the hand-writing; the distinctive spellings (in particular 'scilens' for 'silence' as in the name of the Justice in *The Second Part of King Henry IV*); and the imagery and expression of ideas, which have been found to match works that can be more firmly assigned to Shakespeare.

The manuscript is important because it demonstrates to some extent how the writing of plays during Shakespeare's lifetime was a collaborative activity. However, Hand D does not seem to have paid very close attention to what his fellow authors had written. Similarly, although Tilney, the censor, demanded certain changes to the original text of the play, the revisers tended to do little to meet his demands. Some of the handwriting in the manuscript is hard to read and the book is generally in poor condition. The page displayed is one of the more legible and shows some characteristics of dramatic manuscripts of the period: speech prefixes were generally written in the margin after the speeches had been composed (note the change in the penultimate prefix from 'all' to 'Linco[ln]'), and speeches were separated by horizontal lines. The deletions and revisions the author makes suggest he may have been composing as he wrote, or at least revising as he transcribed copy composed elsewhere. There is no evidence that, despite the alterations, the play was ever performed in Shakespeare's day, but more recent productions show that it has considerable dramatic power and interest.
HRW

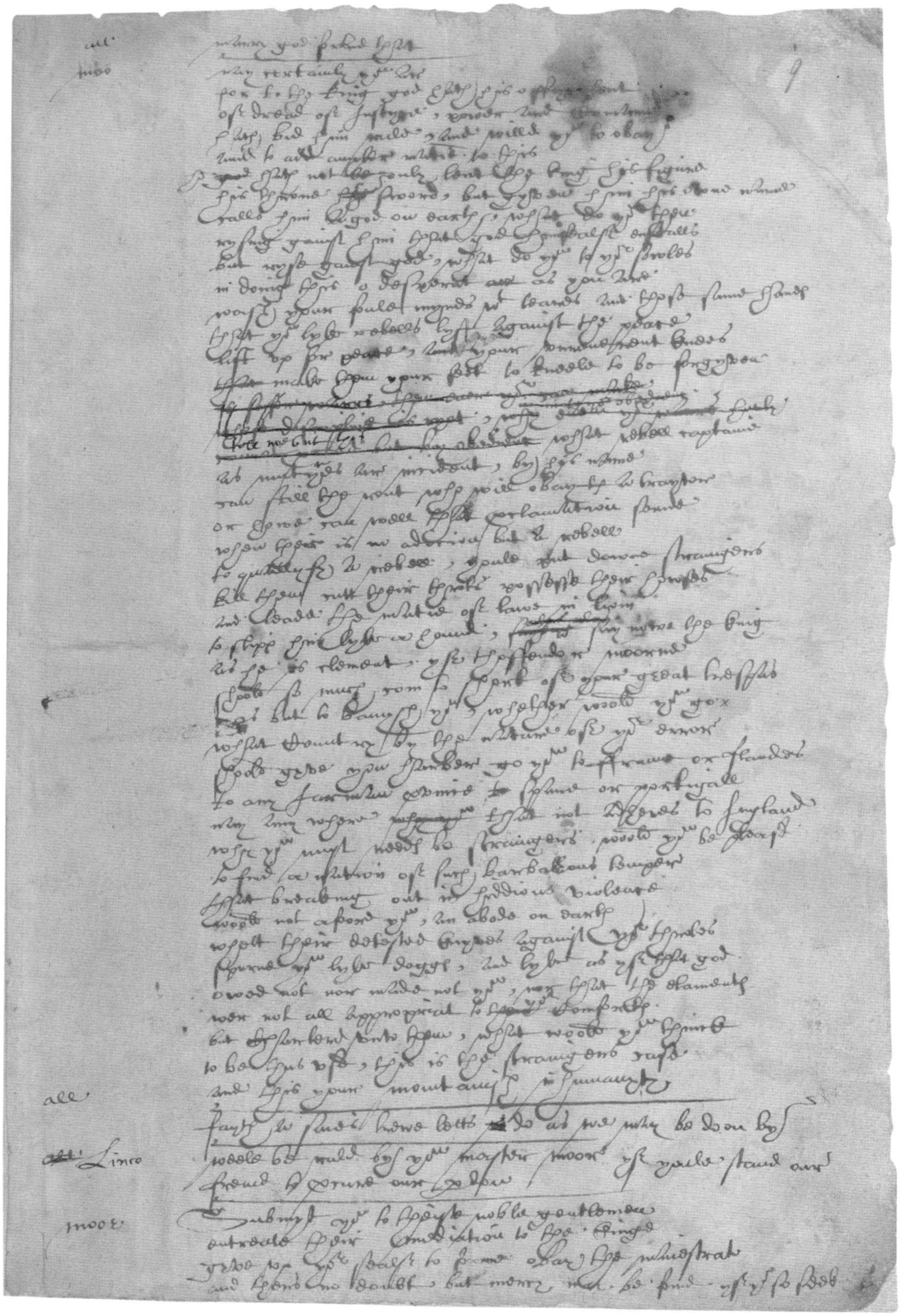

9

all — marry god forbid that
moo — nay certainly you ar
for to the king god hath his offyce lent
of dread of Iustyce, power and Comaund
hath bid him rule, and willd you to obay
and to add ampler maiestie to this
he hath not only lent the king his figure
his throne and sword, but gyven him his owne name
calls him a god on earth, what do you then
rysing gainst him that god himsealf enstalls
but ryse gainst god, what do you to your sowles
in doing this o desperat as you are.
wash your foule mynds with teares and those same hands
that you lyke rebells lyft against the peace
lift vp for peace, and your vnreuerent knees
make them your feet to kneele to be forgyven
~~is safer warrs, then euer you can make~~
~~whose discipline is ryot;~~ why euen your ~~warrs~~ hurly
~~cannot proceed but by obedienc~~ what rebell captaine
as mutyes ar incident, by his name
can still the rout who will obay a traytor
or howe can well that proclamation sounde
when ther is no adicion but a rebell
to quallyfy a rebell, youle put downe straingers
kill them cutt their throts possesse their howses
and leade the matie of lawe in liom
to slipp him lyke a hound; ~~sayeng~~ say nowe the king
as he is clement, yf thoffendor moorne
shoold so much com to short of your great trespas
as but to banysh you, whether woold you go.
what country by the nature of your error
shoold gyve you harber go you to ffraunc or flanders
to any Iarman prouince, to spane or portigall
nay any where ~~why you~~ that not adheres to Ingland
why you must needs be straingers, woold you be pleasd
to find a nation of such barbarous temper
that breaking out in hiddious violence
woold not afoord you, an abode on earth
whett their detested knyves against your throtes
spurne you lyke doggs, and lyke as yf that god
owed not nor made not you, nor that the elamentes
wer not all appropriat to ~~their~~ your Comforts.
but Charterd vnto them, what woold you thinck
to be thus vsd, this is the straingers case
and this your mountanish inhumanyty

all — fayth a saies trewe letts ~~vs~~ do as we may be doon by
~~all~~ Linco — weele be ruld by you master moor yf youle stand our
freind to procure our pardon

moor — Submit you to theise noble gentlemen
entreate their mediation to the kinge
geve vp yoursealf to forme obay the maiestrate
and thers no doubt, but mercy may be found yf you so seek

AT COURT

The Essex Rebellion and the King's Men

As one of the Lord Chamberlain's Men, Shakespeare performed at the court of Elizabeth I on many occasions. From the mid 1590s he was known to the Queen and her courtiers as the author of numerous plays performed during the Christmas season at Elizabeth's royal palaces at Greenwich, Whitehall, Richmond and Hampton Court.

In the last years of Elizabeth's reign Shakespeare's company unwittingly played a supporting role in a major political event. Part of the preparations by the supporters of Robert Devereux, 2nd Earl of Essex (1565–1601) for an armed march on the Queen's palace included the staging of a special performance by Shakespeare's company. *Richard II*, the play requested, had a politically charged message, as it charts the story of the monarch's forced abdication. In the event the rebellion was unsuccessful and Essex was executed. By March 1603 the Queen was dying, and the public theatres closed as a mark of respect for their monarch.

With the accession of James I (1566–1625) to the English throne, Shakespeare's fortunes improved further. Within weeks of his arrival in London James I took on the patronage of Shakespeare's company, who now became known as the 'King's Men'. Shakespeare and his fellow actors officially became servants of the Crown and were each awarded several yards of valuable scarlet velvet and wool cloth to make into their personal livery.

cat.67 **Queen Elizabeth I**

67. Queen Elizabeth I (1533–1603), c.1585–90

Unknown English artist

Oil on panel
953 × 819mm (37½ × 32¼ in)
National Portrait Gallery, London (NPG 2471)

Provenance Possibly from Cowdray House; built into the wall of a cottage at Coolham Green, Shipley, Sussex in 1890; acquired by Robert Downing, Surveyor to Lord Leconfield; by 1910 in the collection of Sir Aston Webb, who bequeathed the picture to the Gallery on his death in 1930

Literature Strong 1969, p.104

Illustrated on previous page

As one of the Lord Chamberlain's Men, Shakespeare performed before Elizabeth I at numerous royal palaces on several occasions, from December 1594 to February 1603. The ageing Queen would have known Shakespeare as an actor and playwright of one of the many entertainments that were part of the Christmas and New Year festivities at court. For example, in the season of 1600–01, the year of the Essex Rebellion, the Lord Chamberlain's Men performed twice at Richmond Palace in January and February and twice at Whitehall in December. Indeed, the Privy Council defended the public performance of plays in London, by claiming to the ever-conservative London authorities that such performances were essential if a proper standard was to be maintained to entertain the Queen, 'to which end they have been cheeflie licensed and tollerated'.[1] Under Elizabeth I performances at public theatres were therefore officially considered to be rehearsals for royal entertainment.

At the end of the 1570s Elizabeth had centralized the system of censorship of theatrical performances by creating an office of the Master of the Revels to control the licence of plays performed in public. The Queen had also been a personal patron of players at least since 1583, when a group of talented actors was drawn from a number of other companies to become known as the 'Queen's Men', who then regularly performed at court (see pp.230–31). By the mid 1590s, however, the Queen's Men were being outshone by Shakespeare's own company, which was invited in 1596–7 to perform all the plays at court.

Elizabeth I was greatly dismayed by the betrayal of the Earl of Essex, but her resolve had already begun to harden against her last favourite courtier in 1599, when Essex had disobeyed orders in Ireland. Within days of the rebellion Essex was found guilty of treason before his peers and, despite their previously close relationship, Elizabeth proved resolute and reluctantly sanctioned his execution.

This image was painted towards the end of Elizabeth's reign, and was frequently copied in the 1590s. Yet, as with nearly all late images of her, it is not a portrait in the conventional sense. It was not painted from life: while her clothes followed the changing fashions over the decades, the Queen's face was frequently modelled on an earlier recorded likeness in portraits. The 'face pattern' in this portrait is a reversed version of the one used in a portrait painted c.1575, known as the Darnley portrait (fig.56). This type of flat, almost diagrammatic style of representation, which makes little attempt at capturing figures in three dimensions, is typical of native late Elizabethan painting. TC

1 Gurr 2004, p.168.

fig.56 **The Darnley portrait of Queen Elizabeth I**, c.1575
Unknown artist
Oil on panel, 1130 × 787mm (44½ × 31 in)
National Portrait Gallery, London (NPG 2082)

68. Robert Devereux, 2nd Earl of Essex (1565–1601), *c.*1596

Unknown artist after Marcus Gheeraerts the Younger (1561/2–1636)

Oil on canvas
635 × 508mm (25 × 20 in)
National Portrait Gallery, London (NPG 180)

Provenance Purchased by the National Portrait Gallery from Colnaghi in 1864

Literature Strong 1969, pp.115–17

Despite being Elizabeth's favourite for more than ten years, and a committed soldier and politician, Essex fell dramatically from favour in 1601. His final appointment was as Lord Lieutenant of Ireland in 1599, when he was sent to subdue the rebellion of Hugh O'Neill, 2nd Earl of Tyrone (*c.*1550–1616). Essex negotiated a truce with Tyrone, the conditions of which were felt to be unfavourable to England, and on his return he was arrested and imprisoned on charges of intriguing against the Crown. Released, he was subsequently re-arrested in the wake of the publication of an engraving of him mounted on a horse that declared him 'Vertue's honour' and 'God's elected'. At the point when his political career and finances were ruined, Essex's supporters conspired to return the Earl to his former influence and favour.

On Saturday, 7 February 1601 Essex failed to appear before the Privy Council. On the same day his followers spent the afternoon at the Globe Theatre, where they had paid Shakespeare's company to perform *Richard II*. To use the theatre to rally support in this way was a dangerous political act. However inspiring the play may have been, the following day's march through London – which aimed to restore Essex, claim allegiance to Elizabeth and declare James I her successor – was a failure. Essex was found guilty of treason and condemned to death. On 25 February 1601 he was beheaded in the courtyard of the Tower of London.

This portrait of Essex, in a pinked white satin doublet and with the pendant Lesser George on a ribbon about his neck, is after a full-length portrait by Marcus Gheeraerts the Younger at Woburn Abbey (collection of the Dukes of Bedford). The original was painted shortly after the expedition to Cadiz in 1596, from which Essex had returned a national hero. It was widely copied and this portrait is one of several contemporary versions in existence. JE

69. King Richard II (1367–1400), late sixteenth century

Unknown English artist

Oil on oak panel
603 × 457mm ($23\frac{3}{4}$ × 18in)
National Portrait Gallery, London (NPG 565)

Provenance Presented to the British Museum by John Goodman in 1766; transferred to the National Portrait Gallery in 1879

Literature Strong 1969, pp.259–62

Shakespeare's play *The Tragedy of King Richard II* was probably written in 1595, about the time this portrait was painted. This likeness of Richard II, wearing an ermine mantle and jewelled collar and crown, is based on the life-size portrait that the King himself commissioned for Westminster Abbey around 1395. It became a standard image of the monarch and towards the end of the sixteenth century was reproduced in several portrait sets of early English kings and queens that were fashionable among the nobility. Painted for the long galleries of country houses, these sets were intended as a visual chronicle of England's rulers and reflected the growing interest in history and antiquarianism in this period.

Shakespeare's play charts the narrative of Richard II's forced abdication by Henry Bolingbroke in 1399. During Elizabeth's reign writers were still drawing lessons from the King's fate. His deposition and death had introduced an element of uncertainty into the concept of dynastic inheritance which had a lasting impact on the monarchy. With the issue of the Elizabethan succession not yet resolved, the dramatization of the deposing of a monarch was viewed as so politically sensitive that Edmund Tilney, the Queen's Master of the Revels from 1578 (cat.73), censored the first three editions of the play text, all of which were published without the abdication scene. The theatre's potential for subversion was demonstrated in February 1601 when associates of the Earl of Essex financed a performance of *Richard II* in order to rally support for their cause. Richard II had been accused of allowing his favourites too much authority and a parallel with Elizabeth's dependence on Sir Robert Cecil (1563–1612) and Sir Walter Ralegh (1554–1618), both enemies of Essex, was presumably intended. Six months after the failure of the so-called Essex Rebellion, the Queen famously remarked to her archivist, William Lambarde (1536–1601), 'I am Richard II, know ye not that?'[1] JE

1 John Nichols, *The Progresses, and Public Processions, of Queen Elizabeth* vol.II (Society of Antiquaries, London, 1788), p.41

70. Examination of Augustine Phillips (d.1605); testimony at the trial of the Earl of Essex, 18 February 1601

Manuscript, ink on paper
310 × 210mm (12¼ × 8¼in)
The National Archives, UK, SP 12/278/85

Provenance State Papers Domestic, Elizabeth I

Literature *Calendar State Papers, Dom. 1598–1601*, 1869, p.578; J. Leeds Barroll, 'A New History for Shakespeare and his Time', *Shakespeare Quarterly* 39, 1988, pp.441–64

On 8 February 1601 the 2nd Earl of Essex (cat.68) attempted to depose the ageing Queen Elizabeth I by a coup of his followers, especially the gentlemen who had fought with him on his Irish campaign. The evidence at his trial included a report that some of Essex's followers had asked Shakespeare's theatre company, the Lord Chamberlain's Men, to perform their play *Richard II* at the Globe on the afternoon before the coup, 7 February. They evidently asked for it because the play's central scene shows the Earl of Lancaster deposing King Richard and thus making himself King Henry IV. At the trial, a representative of the company's sharers, Augustine Phillips, was asked why they had performed the play. Phillips said that they had objected that the play was so long out of use that they would not get a good audience and the conspirators had paid them £2 to make up for it. The court accepted this as a good enough reason, and did not punish the players. AG

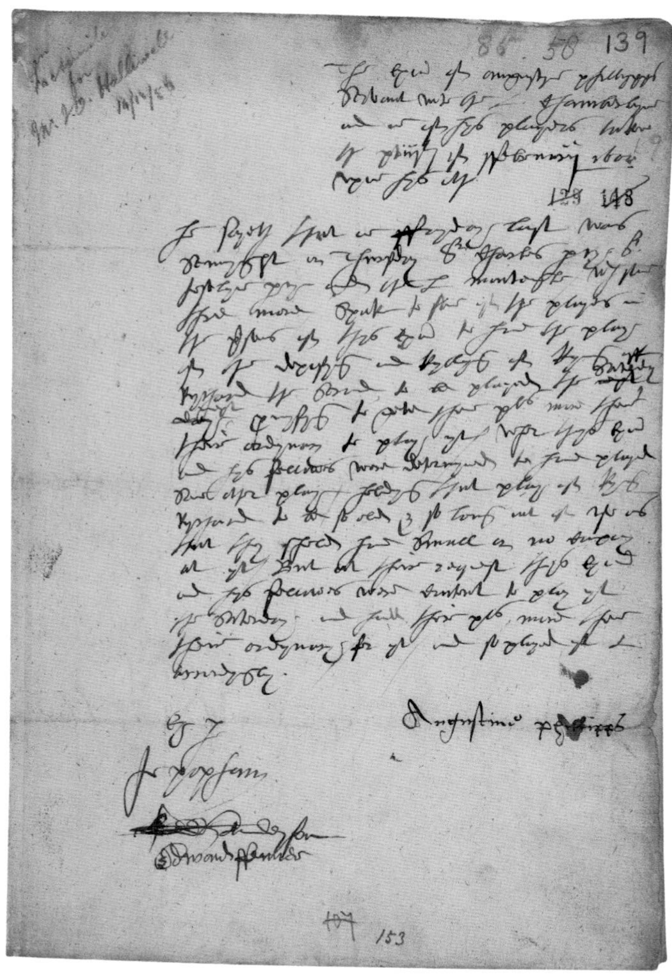

71. King James I of England and VI of Scotland (1566–1625), *c.*1606–15

Unknown English artist

Oil on canvas
2010 × 1040mm (79⅛ × 41in)
The Chancellor, Masters and Scholars of The University of Cambridge

Provenance Early history unknown; University of Cambridge by 1776

Literature J.W. Goodison, *Catalogue of Cambridge Portraits* (Cambridge University Press, 1955), vol.1, pp.15–16, no.16; Strong 1969, vol.1, p.179

The son of Mary, Queen of Scots, James came to the throne of Scotland at the age of thirteen months on his mother's abdication. His early tutelage by George Buchanan (1506–82) and Peter Young (1544–1628) engendered a genuine love of literature and scholarship that remained with him throughout his life. His enormous literary output over his lifetime included poetry, poetic theory, translations of the Psalms, theology, political theory, speeches and letters.

James's reign in Scotland was characterized by a struggle to control powerful aristocratic factions, but in this difficult context he oversaw and contributed to a huge flowering of Scottish poetry, particularly in the 1580s. In the late 1590s he wrote two famous works on kingship, *Basilikon Doron* and *The Trew Law of Free Monarchies*. At this time he also showed a distinct interest in English drama and English players, asking Elizabeth I for six maskers and six torch-bearers, as well as English actors for the celebrations in 1590 of his marriage to Anne of Denmark (cat.76), which had taken place the previous year. In 1594 he again invited English actors to Edinburgh.

In 1603 James inherited the crown of England from his cousin Elizabeth I. In the bigger English political arena his interest in literature was still striking. Probably his most significant act of literary (and of course theological) patronage during this period was the new English translation of the Bible, the Authorized or 'King James' Version, published in 1611, which both reflected and stimulated the astonishing heights achieved by English prose and poetry in the Jacobean period.

James's interest in the theatre was less marked than that of his wife, but one of his first official acts as king of England was to take over the patronage of the Chamberlain's Men, who became the King's Men. It is striking that the patent (cat.72) explicitly stated the theatre company was not only for the pleasure of the king, but also for the people, contrasting with Elizabeth I's view that the companies existed to serve her.[1] The company performed frequently at court, putting on eleven different plays between November 1604 and October 1605, including seven works by Shakespeare. Between the establishment of the new company in 1603 and Shakespeare's death in 1616 they performed at court at least 107 times.

Some of Shakespeare's plays reflect political events and concerns of James's reign: the division of the kingdoms in *King Lear*, for example, must have had particular resonance to the audience of the period whose new monarch reigned for the first time over England, Scotland, Wales and Ireland, and there are references to the Gunpowder Plot and James's claim of descent from Banquo in *Macbeth*. Issues of the role of the ruler are explored in *Measure for Measure*, whose first recorded performance was at James's court in 1604.

In contrast to his fascination with literature, James showed little interest in the visual arts and was apparently reluctant to sit for his portrait. This highly decorative image of him is one of a number of full-length portraits painted in the early years of his reign in England, which show similarities in pose but differences in costume and jewels. Some of this group (the portrait at Dulwich Picture Gallery, for example) have been plausibly attributed to the King's serjeant-painter John de Critz (*c.*1551/2–1642), who was paid for a portrait of James in 1606. It has been suggested that the present painting may be associated with the King's first visit to Cambridge in 1615, but it seems likely that this was not a new portrait taken from life but one derived from the de Critz-associated images of *c.*1606.[2] With its strong emphasis on rich decorative surfaces and magnificent jewels, including the famous diamond 'Feather' jewel in his hat, it has echoes of some of the portraiture of James's predecessor Elizabeth I (cat.67), presenting James's kingship as a thing of glamour, magnificence and, in a broad sense, theatricality. CM

1 Gurr 2004, p.168 and note 3.
2 Goodison 1995, p.16, see Literature. The present painting shows some distinct differences in the handling of the face and uncertainties in the placing of the figure in space, compared with the paintings attributed to de Critz. Its general appearance of not being taken from life is perhaps strengthened by the fact that the motto around the King's garter is misspelled.

72. The first Royal Patent for the King's Men, 19 May 1603

Manuscript, ink on parchment
Approximately 300 × 250mm (11⅞ × 9⅞in)
The National Archives, UK, C66/1608 M 4

Provenance Chancery and Wardrobe, Royal Household, Exchequer, Commissions of Chancery and Supreme Court of Judicature; Patent Rolls

Literature Chambers 1923, vol.2, pp.208–9; *Malone Society Collections*, ed. E.K. Chambers and W.W. Greg (Oxford, 1909), vol.1, part 3, p.264; Gurr 2004, pp.168–72

King James arrived in London to take up his long-awaited inheritance on 4 May 1603. The patent licensing the King's company of players was written out and given the Privy Seal on 19 May 1603, the same day that James announced the union of his two kingdoms, England and Scotland. Thus within two weeks of his arrival in London he had made himself the official patron of London's leading theatre company.

His new troupe of players, formerly the Lord Chamberlain's Men, had Richard Burbage (cat.51) as its leading actor and Shakespeare as one of its ten 'sharers'. Along with the Lord Admiral's Men, it had been formed as half of a duopoly in 1594, the two companies licensed to perform at the Theatre and the Rose in the suburbs of London. The idea was to keep them out of the city itself, a concession to the Lord Mayor who for the last twenty-five years had been complaining about playing in the city. The Lord Chamberlain, protecting the companies from the Lord Mayor, used to claim that it was essential for them to perform in front of a London audience if they were to maintain their quality and fulfil their principal duty, entertaining the Queen. The King James Patent for the first time added 'the recreation of our lovinge Subjectes' as the reason for granting them their licence to perform.

The name of Lawrence Fletcher (d.1608), listed first in the licence, reflects James's personal interest in the company. Fletcher was an English player who came south from Edinburgh with the King. He is not mentioned in the company records subsequently, although Augustine Phillips left him a small bequest as 'my fellow' along with Shakespeare, Burbage, Henry Condell (1576?–1627), John Heminges (bap.1566–d.1630), Robert Armin (1563–1615), Richard Cowley (1568? –1619) and other members of the company, in his will dated 4 May 1605. AG

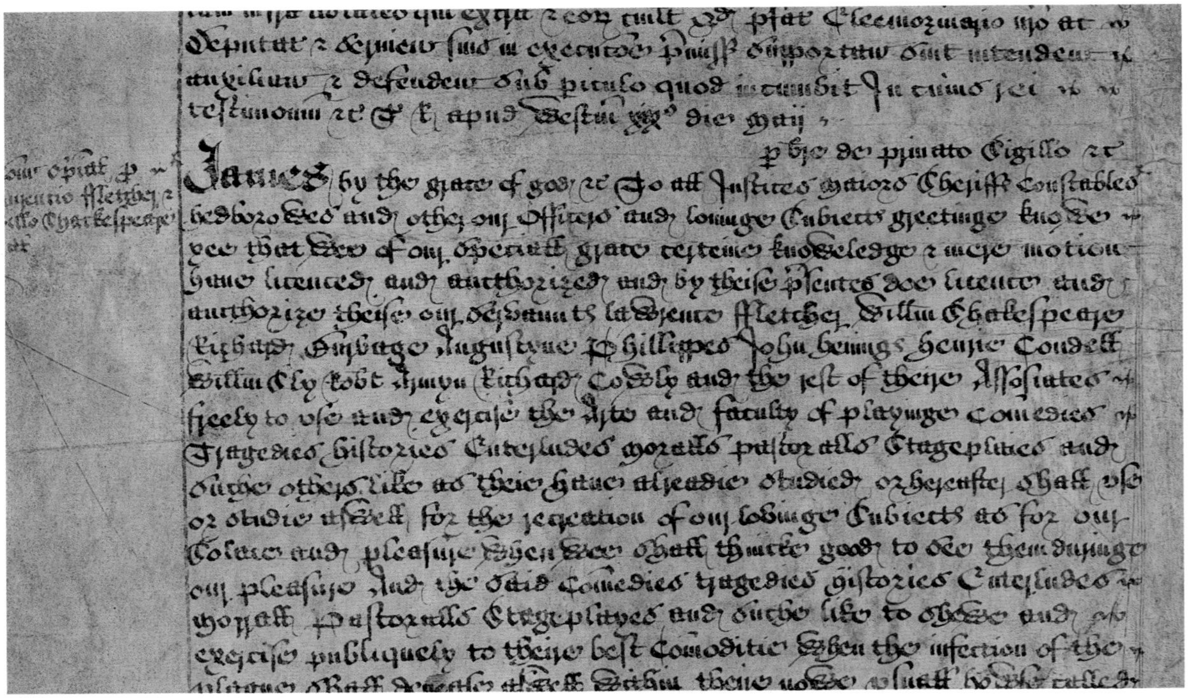

Detail of cat.72

cat.73 **'Londinivm' from *Arches of Triumph***

73. 'Londinivm', from Stephen Harrison, *Arches of Triumph*, 1604

William Kip (before 1588–1618)

Engraving
267 × 232mm (10½ × 9⅛ in)
The British Museum, London, 1906-7-19-11-6

Literature A.M. Hind, *Engraving in England in the Sixteenth and Seventeenth Centuries* (Cambridge University Press, 1955), vol.2, pp.17–29; Eileen Harris, *British Architectural Books and Writers 1556–1785* (Cambridge University Press, 1960), p.323; Antony Griffiths, *The Print in Stuart Britain 1603–1689* (exh. cat., British Museum Press, London, 1998), no.3

Illustrated on previous page

King James VI of Scotland succeeded to the English throne in March 1603 but, due to a renewed outbreak of plague, his coronation in July was a low-key affair and his formal welcome into the City of London – the 'Magnificent Entertainment' – had to be postponed until 15 March 1604. This sumptuous pageant, mostly co-scripted by Ben Jonson (cat.83) and Thomas Dekker (*c.*1572–1632), took the form of a procession from the Tower of London to Temple Bar. As Grooms of the Royal Chamber, Shakespeare and his eleven fellow actors may have walked in the procession in their official livery of red velvet cloaks, doublets and breeches. The King and his retinue passed by seven intricately constructed ceremonial arches devised by Stephen Harrison (active 1604–5), a 'joyner and architect' and 'the sole inventor of the architecture'. As the King approached the first of these, the 'Arch of Londinium' at Fenchurch, a 'curtain of silk' was pulled away revealing Harrison's magnificent *tableau vivant*, a painted wooden structure, staged with living actors and musicians. Beneath a stunning model of London, the 'Genius of the City' – played by the great actor Edward Alleyn (1566–1626) – formally addressed the new King and delivered Jonson's lines 'with excellent action and a well tuned, audible voice'.

Jonson and Dekker quarrelled so violently over their collaboration that they published separate accounts of the day's events, each truncating the other's contribution. A third account featured William Kip's superb engravings of Harrison's arches. James I himself was solemnly reported to have 'endured this day's brunt with patience' – characteristics that probably found their way into the play Shakespeare was then writing for his newly promoted company, the King's Men. 'I love the people,' says the Duke in *Measure for Measure* (Act I, Scene i, lines 69–71), 'But do not like to stage me to their eyes . . . I do not relish well/Their loud applause and '*Aves*' vehement [cries of praise].' NS

74. Account of Edmund Tilney (1535/6–1610), 1605

Manuscript, ink on paper
Approximately 430 × 164mm (16⅞ × 6½in)
The National Archives, UK, AO3/908/13

Provenance Auditors of the Impress, Commissioners of Audit Exchequer

Literature *Malone Society Collections*, vol.XIII, ed. E.K. Chambers and W.W. Greg (Oxford, 1910), pp.8–9; Richard Dutton, *Mastering the Revels. The Regulation and Censorship of English Renaissance Drama* (Macmillan, London, 1991)

Under the Tudor and Stuart monarchs the Office of the Revels was responsible for the production of all types of entertainments performed at court. Edmund Tilney (or Edmond Tyllney) was appointed Master of the Revels by Elizabeth I in 1578, and ran the Office of the Revels until his death in 1610. He was the first Master of the Revels to make extensive use of plays performed by the professional

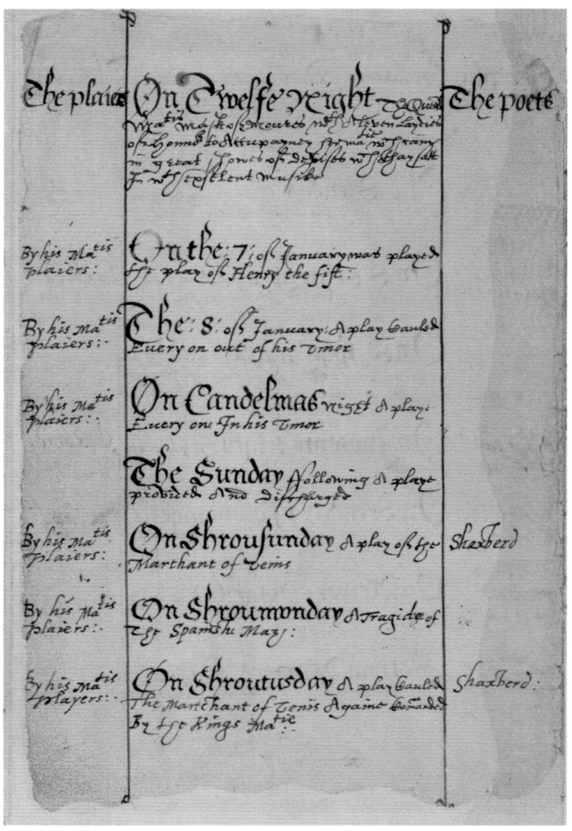

The plaiers | On Twelfe Night | The poets

By his Maties plaiers: On the 7 of January was played the play of Henry the fift.

By his Maties plaiers: The 8 of January A play Cauled Euery on out of his Umor.

By his Maties plaiers: On Candelmas night A playe Euery one In his Umor.

The Sunday ffollowing A playe provided And discharged.

By his Maties plaiers: On Shrousunday A play of the Marthant of Venis | Shaxberd

By his Maties plaiers: On Shroumonday A Tragidye of The Spanishe Maz:

By his Maties plaiers: On Shrovtusday A play Cauled The Martchant of Venis Againe Comanded By the Kings Matie | Shaxberd

companies, which grew in status and quality through his first years in office. Tilney welcomed professionally staged plays because they were much cheaper to produce than elaborate court masques or other shows, which involved large sets or expensive costumes. His accounts for the first years of Christmas festivities under James I, especially the 1604–5 season, show a marked increase in the number of plays compared with those chosen to be performed for Elizabeth. They also show the impressive range of comedies, tragedies and history plays that were performed for the assembled audience of the King, courtiers and political élite. Many of the plays were by Shakespeare.

These plays were the first to be recorded not only by the acting companies but also by the names of their authors, which appear under a special heading 'The poets wch [which] mayd the Plaies [plays]'. In the accounts submitted on 19 December 1605 this extra column noted that a new play by the King's Men, 'Mesur for Mesur', was by an author 'Shaxberd', so spelled by a scribe trying to normalize the sounds he heard (the column is in a different hand from the original inscriptions, raising the question whether it was a later forgery). It followed two older plays, *Othello* and *The Merry Wives of Windsor*, and in turn was followed by *The Comedy of Errors*, also listed as by 'Shaxberd'. Two plays were attributed to Thomas Heywood (1573?–1641), inscribed as 'Hewood', and George Chapman (cat.90), whose name was, perhaps, more familiar to the scribe than 'Shakespeare'. A few evenings later the court saw *Love's Labour's Lost*, *Henry V*, the two '*Humour*' plays by Ben Jonson, and *The Merchant of Venice*, again noted as by 'Shaxberd', which played twice, the second performance 'Commanded By the Kings Majestie'. AG

75. Record of plays performed at the wedding of Princess Elizabeth and Frederick, Elector Palatine, from the accounts of Lord Stanhope (1583/4–1656), 1613

Manuscript, ink on paper
440 × 560 ($17\frac{5}{8} \times 22$ in)
The Bodleian Library, University of Oxford, MS.Rawl.A239, open at A47v

Provenance Samuel Pepys (1633–1703); the Bowdler family of Canterbury; sold for waste paper, but purchased in 1749 by Richard Rawlinson (1690–1755); bequeathed in 1756

Literature *Malone Society Collections* vol.VI, ed. David Cook (Oxford University Press, Oxford, 1961), pp.55–6

For the celebration of the wedding of Princess Elizabeth to Frederick, Elector Palatine, Shakespeare's company performed fourteen plays listed in this court account book, of which five or six were by Shakespeare. They were 'Pilaster' (Beaumont and Fletcher's *Philaster*), 'The Knott: of Fooles', 'Much adoe about nothinge', 'The Mayeds Tragedy' (Beaumont and Fletcher's *The Maid's Tragedy*), 'The merye Dyvell of Edmonton', 'The Tempest', 'A King and no Kinge' (another by Beaumont and Fletcher), 'The Twins Tragedie', 'The Winters Tale', 'Sr Iohn Falstafe' (either *The First Part of Henry IV* or *The Merry Wives of Windsor*), 'The Moore of Venice' (*Othello*), 'The Nobleman' (a play, now lost, by Cyril Tourneur), 'Caesars Tragedye' (probably Shakespeare's *Julius Caesar*), and 'Love Lyes a bleedinge' (the subtitle of

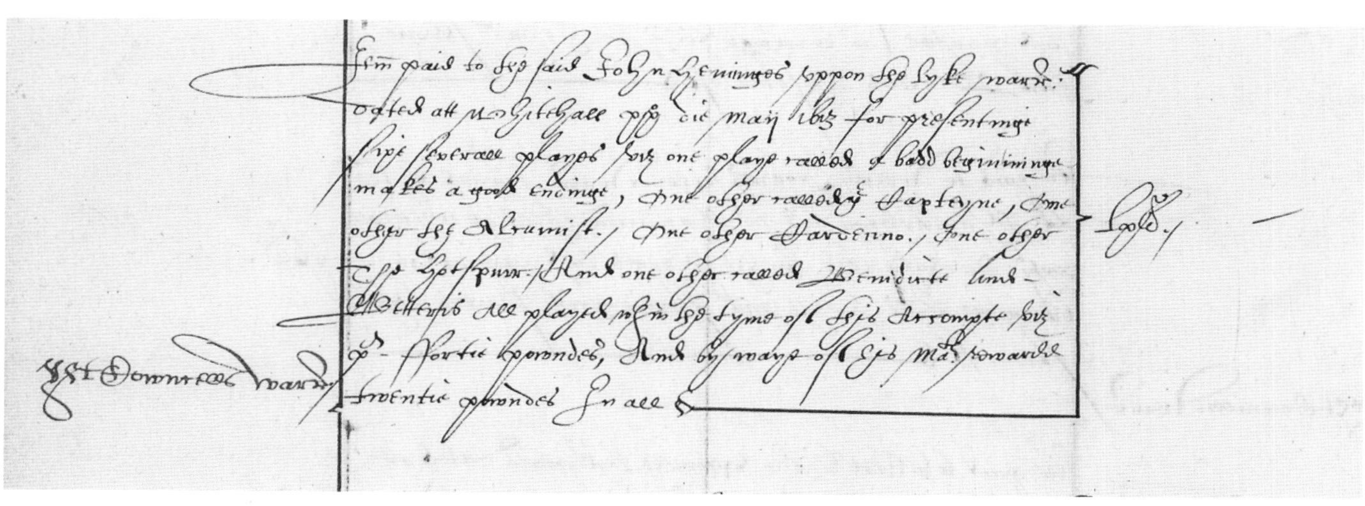

Detail

the first play listed, *Philaster*; this repeat may indicate that it was performed twice, if it was not a mistake by the accountants).

This page shows that on behalf of the whole company, Shakespeare included, John Heminges (1566?–1630) was paid for the wedding entertainments on 20 May 1613. At the same time he was also paid £20 for six other plays, including the lost play *Cardenio*, and Ben Jonson's *The Alchemist*, which were performed at court at unspecified times.

Lord Stanhope served as the Treasurer of the Chamber between 1596 and 1618 and these accounts include numerous references to payments made to the professional playing companies for their performances at court over each Christmas period, and on other special occasions, often when visiting royalty was entertained. The official opening of the winter festivities was always Boxing Day (St Stephen's Night, 26 December), but, under James I from 1603 onwards, these evening entertainments might include as many as thirty plays performed from Michaelmas (29 September) onwards through the whole winter. With James I as their patron, Shakespeare's company always gave the majority of the Christmas performances. During the three lengthy festive seasons between 1611 and 1614 they staged fifty-eight plays, as against thirty-nine by all the other London companies together. In these years, while new playwrights such as Beaumont and Fletcher were growing in esteem, Shakespeare's plays still took pride of place. AG

76. Anne of Denmark (1574–1619), *c.*1612

Unknown artist

Oil on panel
572 × 438mm (22½ × 17¼ in)
National Portrait Gallery, London (NPG 4656)

Provenance Possibly Elizabeth of Bohemia; possibly bequeathed to 1st Earl of Craven (or possibly to Prince Rupert; bequeathed to Ruperta Howe; purchased at her sale by 1st Earl of Craven); Collection of the Earls of Craven, Coombe Abbey, by 1866 (cat.14); by descent to Cornelia, Countess of Craven; sold at Sotheby's, 15 January 1969, lot 11; Leggatt Brothers; given by Dr Esmond S. De Beer to the National Portrait Gallery, London, in 1969

The daughter of Frederick II of Denmark, Anne was married to James VI of Scotland (later James I of England) in 1589 at the age of fifteen. Her education and experience at the Danish court had given her a taste for culture, and she became an important patron of poets, musicians and players. Like James, she had her own company of players, and also a company of child actors, the Children of the Revels to the Queen. However, her most important cultural contribution was the patronage of masques, lavish court entertainments combining dance, music and allegorical drama performed in spectacular costumes before elaborate sets. Anne commissioned and performed in six masques at court, two of which were written by Samuel Daniel (cat.91) and four by Ben Jonson (cat.83). The great architect and designer Inigo Jones (1573–1652) designed the sets and costumes for most of the Stuart court masques, and later worked on architectural projects for the Queen.

This portrait shows Anne wearing deep mourning and is likely to have been painted shortly after the death of her son Henry, Prince of Wales, in the winter of 1612; this date also fits well with the Queen's costume and hairstyle. The portrait may originally have been produced for the Queen's daughter, Elizabeth, many of whose paintings subsequently belonged to the Earls of Craven.

The painting was at one time attributed to William Larkin (*c*.1580–1619), but this idea was discounted when a thorough technical examination was undertaken on works more securely ascribed to the artist.[1] It has since been attributed to Marcus Gheeraerts the Younger (1561/2–1636), the leading portrait painter of his day, who was patronized by Anne at about this time. However, the smooth and polished way in which the flesh, in particular, is depicted, is not very close to Gheeraerts's style at this time, and it seems more likely that the portrait is by an accomplished painter yet to be identified. Anne became increasingly interested in painting, and her patronage of painters was more adventurous than that of her husband. She also became a keen collector. CM

1 Sarah Cove, 'The Materials and Techniques of Paintings Attributed to William Larkin 1610–1620', Dip. Conservation of Paintings, Courtauld Institute, London, 1985.

77. Princess Elizabeth, later Queen of Bohemia (1596–1662), 1613

Unknown artist

Oil on panel
784 × 622mm (30⅞ × 24½in)
Inscribed: '1613' top left
National Portrait Gallery, London (NPG 5529)

Provenance Mrs J.B. Coulthurst sale, Gargrave House, on 26 October 1982, Sotheby's, lot 51; purchased by the National Portrait Gallery, London

Illustrated overleaf

Elizabeth was the only surviving daughter and second child of James VI of Scotland and I of England and his queen, Anne of Denmark. Considered beautiful, charming and intelligent, she was seen as a real asset in furthering James's diplomatic and political ambitions. At the age of sixteen, she was married to Frederick V, Count Palatine of the Rhine and Elector of the Holy Roman Empire, at Whitehall Palace; this portrait dates from about this time. The wedding had been delayed by the death of Elizabeth's beloved brother, Henry, Prince of Wales, but it finally took place with much accompanying festivity on 14 February 1613. The lavish wedding celebrations, lasting several weeks, included the performance of fourteen plays by the King's Men, the theatrical company to which Shakespeare belonged (cat.75). At least five of these plays were Shakespeare's own works. Among them *The Tempest* must have seemed particularly appropriate, with its wedding masque celebrating the marriage of Ferdinand and Miranda.

Elizabeth is shown in the portrait in an elaborate silver dress that recalls, but is apparently not identical to, the dress in which she was married.[1] The detail with which the costume is depicted, compared with the rather schematic rendering of the face, suggests that, while the artist may not have had sittings from Elizabeth herself, he may have had access to her dress. Her status as an English royal princess is emphasized by the prominent royal coats of arms and heraldic lions, unicorns and fleurs-de-lis in the lace of her collar and around her neckline, perhaps indicating that the painting was produced for an important diplomatic context abroad. Elizabeth also wears a mourning armband for her brother Henry and may carry his miniature in the black locket pinned to her dress. The panel support, unusual for an English painting of this date, suggests that the portrait may be by a Netherlandish artist.[2] CM

1 According to John Chamberlain, writing at the time: 'The bridegrome and bride were both in a sute of cloth of silver, richly embrodered with silver .... The bride was married in her haire that hung downe long, with an exceeding rich coronet on her head.' John Chamberlain, *Letters*, 18 February 1613. Norman Egbert McClure (ed.), *The Letters of John Chamberlain*, vol.1 (The American Philosophical Society, Philadelphia, 1939), pp.423–4.

2 In spite of the fact that it is approximately the size of a standard English canvas of the later seventeenth or eighteenth century, and the uncomfortable way in which the Princess's arms and the farthingale of her dress are cut off, the painting does not appear to have been cut down, but retains what seem to be the original edges of the panel. The date at the top left is apparently contemporary with the rest of the painting.

cat.77 **Princess Elizabeth, later Queen of Bohemia**

78. Princess Elizabeth and Frederick, Elector Palatine (1596–1632), *c.*1613

Renold Elstrack (b.1570; last recorded 1625)

Engraving
263 × 200mm (10³/₈ × 7⁷/₈ in)
Inscribed with the sitters' names, titles, dates of birth and marriage, and details of the publisher and printmaker
The British Museum, London (1849-9-11-490)

Provenance Purchased from Mr Tross in Paris in 1864

Literature Arthur M. Hind, *Engraving in England in the Sixteenth and Seventeenth Centuries*, vol.2, *The Reign of James I* (London, 1955), no.22, p.175; Roy Strong with contributions by V.J. Murrell, *Artists of the Tudor Court: The Portrait Miniature Rediscovered 1520–1620* (Victoria and Albert Museum, London, 1983), no.250, p.150; Antony Griffiths, *The Print in Stuart Britain 1603–1689* (exh. cat., British Museum, London, 1998), no.7, pp.47–9

This magnificent engraving shows Elizabeth, daughter of James I, with her husband Frederick V, Elector Palatine, at the time of their wedding in February 1613 (given on the print in the 'Old Style' calendar form of 1612). Frederick, the most important of the German Protestant princes, was the same age as the Princess, and, according to reports at the time, slightly shorter than her. He made a very favourable impression on all who met him at court, particularly the Princess. After the death of Henry, Prince of Wales, he took on the patronage of the Prince's company of players, which became the Palsgrave's Men.

Although arranged for political purposes, the marriage was a great success and at first all seemed to augur well for the future of the Elector and Electress Palatine. Elizabeth gave birth to her first son a year after her marriage, and subsequently had twelve more children, most of whom lived to adulthood. She and Frederick lived happily in Heidelberg, the capital of the Palatinate, for six years. In 1619, however, Frederick was offered the throne of Bohemia by its Protestant nobility, in defiance of the traditional rulers, the imperial, Catholic, Habsburg family. Much to the concern of James I (and others), Frederick accepted, and he and Elizabeth were installed in Prague as King and Queen of Bohemia. Their reign lasted only one year, after which they were ousted by the armies of the Catholic League, and in the process also lost their lands in the Palatinate. From that point on they lived in exile in the Low Countries, Frederick periodically fighting with the Protestant allies against the Habsburg troops in what became the Thirty Years War. He died in 1632 and Elizabeth spent the remainder of her life fighting – by all the diplomatic and political means at her disposal – for the return of the Palatine lands to her family.

This is one of a series of three large engravings of members of the Stuart family made by Renold Elstrack at about the same time, and is one of the finest prints he made. Roy Strong has suggested that the designs for these prints may have come from Nicholas Hilliard.[1] Throughout her life Elizabeth in particular was the subject of portraiture, at first celebrating her youth and beauty and later, when she was living in poverty and exile, promoting her cause in Protestant Europe as a beleaguered heroine in need of military and financial help. CM

1 Strong and Murrell 1983, p.150 (see Literature).

79. Accounts of various payments to the King's Men from 1603

Manuscript, ink on parchment
450 × 500mm ($17^3/_4$ × $19^5/_8$in)
The National Archives, UK, AO1/388/41, open at folio 20 r

Provenance Auditors of the Imprest, Commissioners of the Audit Exchequer, declared accounts in rolls

Literature *Malone Society Collections* vol.VI (Oxford, 1961), p.38; Gurr 2004, pp.51–3

These court account payments bound onto a roll provide significant evidence of the many occasions the King's Men performed before James I, both at royal palaces and while the King was visiting courtiers around the country. This page indicates that the King's Men, almost certainly including Shakespeare, were summoned from Mortlake in Surrey to perform before 'his Majestie' at Wilton House near Salisbury, the home of William Herbert, Earl of Pembroke (1580–1630; cat.87) in December 1603. John Heminges (bap.1566?, d.1630) is paid 'for the paynes [pains] and expenses of himself and the rest of his company' for their travel costs (undertaken by cart and on horseback in mid-winter) and the performance of plays before the assembled court.

The same manuscript shows that the twelve sharers of the King's Men, again most likely including Shakespeare, were paid to attend the delegation from Spain throughout its eighteen-day stay at Somerset House between 9 and 27 August 1604, while the Spanish ambassador signed the peace treaty to bring the long-running war in the Low Countries between England and Spain to an end. It is odd that the sharers were not called on to perform any plays to entertain the noble guests while they were in attendance at Somerset House. On 15 March the Great Wardrobe had issued all the company with official royal livery made from four and a half yards of 'bastard scarlet' for their cloaks and a quarter-yard of crimson velvet for their capes. AG

fig.57 **Wilton House**
The original Tudor House, taken from a vellum scroll containing a survey of the lands for the 1st Earl of Pembroke, 1566
Wilton House Trust, Wiltshire

signed by Mr Secretarie dated at the Courte primo die Octobr 1603 for his Chardges and
paynes in bringinge of lres for his Maties service from Parris in ffraunce sent by Sr
Thomas Parrie knight his Maties Embassador resident there xli To **John**
Hemynges one of his Maties players uppon the Councells warrant dated at the
Courte at wilton iido die Decembr 1603 for the paynes and expences of himselfe and the
rest of his companye in cominge from Mortelacke in the Countie of Surrie unto the Courte
aforesayde and there presentinge before his Matie one playe on the seconde of December last
by waye of his Maties reward xxxli To **Fraunceis Raweworth** uppon
a warrant dated at the Courte at wilton xio die Decembr 1603 for his chardges and paynes
in bringinge of lres for his Maties service from Dover and for returninge back againe
wth answere iiijli To **Sir Wyllm Evers** knighte uppon the Councells
warrant dated at the Courte at wilton xio Decembr 1603 for his chardges and
expences beinge imployed by his Maties speciall direction uppon the arryvall of the
Embassador of fflorence wth lres unto him to Dover and by his Maties like order and
direction for accompanyinge him not onelye in his iorney hether but also contynuallie
since his repaire unto the Courte till this tyme lxli To **Thomas watt**
servaunt to Mr Roland white post of the Courte uppon the Councells warrant dated
at the Courte at wilton xio die Decembr 1603 for his chardges and paynes beinge
sente of late in extraordynary hast wth lres to the Shreife of Southton at winchester
Castle in wch service he was at hier for post horses xxs To **Peter Hardye**

POETS AND PLAYWRIGHTS

Shakespeare's contemporaries

Shakespeare's genius was recognized in his lifetime, but he was one amongst many other celebrated poets and dramatists working in London. This was a period of unrivalled literary creativity. Poetry, drama, prose, histories and translations from classical texts streamed from the printing presses, the work of writers including courtiers, university-trained men and others of talent, wit and ambition.

Writers such as the metaphysical poet John Donne (1572–1631) and the playwright Ben Jonson (1572–1637), like Shakespeare, have retained their high reputation to the present day. Yet many other Elizabethan and Jacobean authors who were highly acclaimed in their own time, such as Samuel Daniel (1562/3–1619) and Michael Drayton (1563–1631), are not now widely read. Given the high demand for new plays many writers chose to work together, contributing different parts of the same play. Shakespeare occasionally worked collaboratively with other writers including John Fletcher (1579–1625), particularly towards the end of his career, but the extent to which he did so remains disputed.

From the 1590s some writers, such as John Donne, began to commission painted portraits to record their likeness. The existence of these portraits provides further evidence of the likelihood that Shakespeare commissioned his own image in his lifetime. However, the development of author portraiture was in its early stages and not all writers would have chosen to be portrayed. Many portraits from this period have been lost, and the gallery of writers displayed here lacks some key literary figures including, for example, the poet Edmund Spenser (1552–99).

80. John Donne (1572–1631), *c*.1595

Unknown English artist

Oil on panel
724 × 600mm (28½ × 23⅝in)
Inscribed around the edge of the oval: ILLUMINA TENEBR[AS]/NOSTRAS DOMINA
Executors of the late Lord Lothian

Provenance Robert Ker, 1st Earl of Ancrum; by descent to the Marquesses of Lothian

Literature Strong 1969, pp.65–6; Geoffrey Keynes, *A Bibliography of Dr John Donne Dean of Saint Paul's* (Clarendon Press, Oxford, 1973), pp.373–4; David Piper, *The Image of the Poet: British Poets and their Portraits* (Clarendon Press, Oxford, 1982), pp.24–31; Kate Gartner Frost, 'The Lothian Portrait: A Prologmenon', *John Donne Journal*, 15, 1996, pp.95–125; Annabel Patterson, 'Donne in Shadows: Pictures and Politics', *John Donne Journal*, 16, 1997, pp.1–35; Maureen Sabine, 'Illumina Tenebras Nostras Domina – Donne at Evensong', *John Donne Journal*, 19, 2000, pp.19–44; D. L. Edwards, *John Donne: Man of Flesh and Spirit* (Continuum, London and New York, 2001), pp.38–40

Illustrated overleaf

One of the most talented writers of his age, Donne produced a remarkable body of work encompassing metaphysical poetry, verse letters, essays and sermons that came to be widely celebrated following general publication after his death. Born into a devout Roman Catholic family, he was educated from before the age of twelve at the University of Oxford. In 1592, he was admitted to the Inns of Court, where he undertook legal training and began to write poetry that drew on both spiritual and classical sources. Ben Jonson held the view that Donne had written all his best poetry before the age of twenty-five: this dramatic portrait of Donne, playing the role of a melancholic lover, dates from this early period of intense creativity.

In 1601, he entered into a clandestine marriage with Ann More (1584–1617), the niece of his employer Thomas Egerton (1540–1617). Although the marriage was a love match, the union was a disaster for Donne's career. He found himself briefly imprisoned and stripped of his post as Egerton's secretary and for several years the couple survived on charity from friends and relatives. Some time in the 1590s he gradually became drawn to the Protestant religion. In 1615 he was ordained as a minister of the Church of England and he later became the Dean of St Paul's, London.

This remarkable image, one of the earliest surviving examples of an Elizabethan author portrait, owes much to the Italian style of self-presentation. It shows Donne in a self-conscious pose, his head set back in the shadows, topped by a wide-brimmed hat. Expensive lace collars are left open and untied at the neck, perhaps in a pun on the author's name (that is, 'unDonne') and as an affectation of the fashionable literary disposition of melancholy.[1] Donne was closely involved in commissioning the composition and it has been argued that the painting 'is as much a product of Donne's creative imagination as . . . the Satires and the early Elegies.'[2] The X-ray reveals that his lip and an eye were repainted in a lower position – early changes made by the original artist.

That the composition may have originally been painted for a lover or close friend is suggested by the inscription, itself a reworking of a psalm, 'O Lady, lighten our darkness'. Donne's friend Thomas Morton, Bishop of Durham (1564–1659), noted a portrait of Donne in the chambers of one of Donne's close friends at Lincoln's Inn, 'all envelloed with a darkish shadow, his face and feature hardly discernable' with an inscription DOMINE ILLUMINE TENEBRAS MEAS.[3] This encounter probably occurred before 1596 when Donne and his friends apparently left the Inns of Court, and although the inscription does not exactly match the existing one on this portrait, it seems likely that Morton's description relates to this image or another early version of it. One theory is that the portrait was in the chamber of Donne's close friend and fellow student Christopher Brooke (*c*.1570–1628). As has been noted, around this time Donne wrote several verse letters to friends (including Brooke) referring to 'loves hot fires, which maryr [martyr] my sad minde' and the object of his attentions is described as a woman residing in the north of England, who Donne refers to as the 'saint of his affection'.[4] It has been suggested that this may have been Brooke's sister who was then living in York.[5]

A similar picture, described in Donne's will, was left to his friend Robert Ker, later 1st Earl of Ancrum (1578–1654): 'I give to my honourable and faithful friend Mr Robert Karr of his Majesties Bedchamber that Picture of myne wch is taken in Shaddowes and was made very many yeares before I was of this profession [i.e. a minister].' For many years the portrait was lost, but in 1959 it was rediscovered in the Ancrum family collection after it had been mislabelled as the medieval poet 'Duns Scotus'. TC

1 See Roy Strong, 'The Elizabethan Malady. Melancholy in Elizabethan and Jacobean Portraiture', *The Tudor and Stuart Monarchy: Pageantry, Painting, Iconography*, vol.2: *Elizabethan* (Boydell Press, Woodbridge, 1995; originally published in the *Shakespeare Quarterly*).
2 Kate Gartner Frost 1996, p.95 (see Literature).
3 Keynes 1973, p.373 (see Literature). See also Richard Baddeley, *Life of Dr Thomas Morton* (Stephen Buckley, York, 1666), p.101. The picture is also mentioned by William Drummond (cat.81), see Sabine 2000, p.21 (in Literature).
4 Roy Booth, *The Collected Poems of John Donne* (Wordsworth Poetry Library, Ware, 1994), pp.150 and 155.
5 Edwards 2001, pp.39–40 (see Literature).

cat.80 **John Donne**

cat.81 **A portrait of a poet, probably Michael Drayton**

81. A portrait of a poet, probably Michael Drayton (1563–1631), dated 1599

Unknown Anglo-Netherlandish artist

Oil on panel
597 × 457 mm (23½ × 18 in)
Inscribed top left in a later hand: 'Æ SVÆ 36'; top right: 'A.D. 1599'
National Portrait Gallery, London (NPG 776)

Provenance Offered to Horace Walpole in 1781 as a portrait of Drayton by Canon William Mason; Lady Mary Thompson, daughter of 5th Earl Fitzwilliam and widow of Leonard Thompson of Sheriff Hutton Park; sold Christie's, lot 108, on 2 July 1887; presented to the Gallery in 1888 by Thomas H. Woods

Literature Strong 1969, p.72

Illustrated on previous page

Drayton was a versatile poet working in the tradition of Edmund Spenser (1552–99). Like Shakespeare, he came from relatively humble origins in Warwickshire, where his father may have been a butcher or a tanner. Although there is no record of his education, it is possible that Drayton studied at the University of Oxford; if so, he did not complete a degree and he served in the household of Sir Henry Goodere, where he later claimed that he received the 'most part' of his education.[1] The subjects of his poetry derived from historical and classical sources: *Morimeriados* (1596), for example, was based on the civil wars under Edward II and *England's Heroicall Epistles* (1597), a text on English historical lovers, which used Ovid as a literary model. By the late 1590s Drayton was a respected published poet who styled himself as a London gentleman, and, around the same time, he also turned to playwriting. He wrote more than twenty plays for the Lord Admiral's Men, collaborating with Anthony Munday (1560–1633), Henry Chettle (d.1603–7) and Thomas Dekker (*c.*1572–1632). Yet his real interest lay in his poetry and he probably saw his plays – which were not included in his published works of 1619 – as a form of ephemera.[2]

Under Elizabeth I no official position of Poet Laureate existed. However, Edmund Spenser had informally fulfilled that role, and, in recognition of his epic poem *The Faerie Queen*, Elizabeth I granted him an annual pension of £50. Following Spenser's death in 1599, Drayton was certainly one of the main contenders (along with Samuel Daniel; cat.91) for the unofficial role of Poet Laureate, and this portrait with a laurel crown dates from that year. In fact, Drayton never gained the approval of James I, but worked for the rest of his life for a range of minor patrons.

This portrait was acquired by the National Portrait Gallery, London, in the late nineteenth century as an

fig.58 **X-ray of cat.81**

authentic likeness of Drayton. During a reappraisal in the 1960s, the authenticity of the painted wreath was questioned, leading to doubts about the identity of the sitter.[3] Recent technical evidence has proved that the wreath is contemporary with the rest of the picture and it seems likely that the sitter is Michael Drayton.[4] The painting has suffered damage to the right edge: it appears to have lost one or two centimetres. The background has been completely repainted and the X-ray (fig.58) reveals fragments of an old inscription under the surface, apparently replicated by the later visible text. In line with the inscription, Drayton was aged around thirty-six in 1599: the year before he appeared as a witness in court, expressing his age as 'xxxv or thereab[ou]ts'.[5] The portrait also strongly resembles other later acknowledged images of Drayton, particularly the portrait at Dulwich Picture Gallery, dated 1628, where he also appears with a laurel wreath.[6] The Dulwich painting was employed as a model for the bust monument of Drayton in Westminster Abbey, London. TC

1 Ezekiel Sanford, *The Works of the British Poets with the Lives of the Authors* (Mitchell, Ames and White, Philadelphia, 1819), p.323; Anne Lake Prescott, 'Michael Drayton', ODNB 2005, vol.16, pp.894–8.
2 Only one play, *The First Part of Sir John Oldcastle*, survives.
3 See Strong 1969, p.1972.
4 Technical report by Libby Sheldon, 2005. Registered packet 776, Heinz Archive, National Portrait Gallery, London.
5 Alan B. Coban, ODNB 2005, vol.16, p.894.
6 Dulwich Picture Gallery, London (DPG 430).

82. William Drummond of Hawthornden (1585–1649), 1612

Attributed to Abraham van Blyenberch or Blijenberch (1575/6–24)

Oil on panel
604 × 485mm (23¾ × 19in)
Scottish National Portrait Gallery, Edinburgh (SNPG 1096)

Provenance Formerly in the possession of Earl of Home at the Hirsel, Coldstream; bought by Sir Hugh Drummond at the Home sale in 1919; purchased by the Leggatt Brothers, London, on behalf of the Scottish National Portrait Gallery at Christie's, lot 91, on 8 June 1928 (at the time attributed to George Jamesone)

Literature Helen Smailes (ed.), *The Concise Catalogue of the Scottish National Portrait Gallery* (National Galleries of Scotland, Edinburgh, 1990), pp.91 and 93; *A Companion Guide to the Scottish National Portrait Gallery* (National Galleries of Scotland, Edinburgh, 1999), p.31

A poet and author of pamphlets and historical treatises, Drummond was over twenty years younger than Shakespeare and grew up in the privileged environs of the court of James VI of Scotland (later James I of England) in Edinburgh. He was the eldest legitimate son of Sir John Drummond (1553–1610), a gentleman usher to King James. He was educated, first at Edinburgh University and later at Paris and Bourges, where he studied law and began to collect what became a large private library of literature in French, Spanish, Italian and Latin. According to his early biographer, his travels in France, where he saw pictures by a range of continental masters, stimulated a taste for the visual arts.[1]

This portrait was painted after he became Laird of Hawthornden on the death of his father and had abandoned law in order to return to Scotland and take up literature. His first independent published work was an elegy on the death of Prince Henry in November 1612, entitled *Teares on the Death of Meliades*, and in 1616 he published a collection of romantic sonnets, lyric and spiritual poems, and madrigals. Drummond maintained friendships with poets and play-wrights in London, including Michael Drayton (cat.81), with whom he corresponded and Ben Jonson (cat.83), who visited him in Scotland from 1618 to 1619. Drummond compiled an account of their conversations soon after, describing Jonson as 'a great lover and praiser of himself' and, among many recollections, he recorded Jonson's comment that Shakespeare 'wanted art' in his writing.[2]

Blyenberch, a highly talented Flemish painter, is recorded as working in London from 1617 to 1621. If this portrait is to be considered his work, it is not clear where Drummond would have met the painter. Blyenberch was responsible for painting several portraits, including those of Ben Jonson, of Charles I as Prince of Wales (*c*.1617–20) and William Herbert, 3rd Earl of Pembroke (1580–1630). In his own distinctive style he managed to convey a sense of direct presence through his remarkable rendering of three-dimensional form. This portrait is not the source for an engraved portrait of Drummond that appeared as the frontispiece to his published works in the 1614 edition of his poems. Yet the facial likeness presented in this portrait, together with the elaborate lace collar, bears a broad similarity to the authorized engraving. This painted composition was popularized through several engravings produced by J. Rogers (1808–88) and W. Birch (biography unknown) in the nineteenth century. Other painted portraits insecurely identified as Drummond are held in the collections of the Scottish National Portrait Gallery, Edinburgh, and the National Portrait Gallery, London. TC

1 See French Rowe Fogle, *A Critical Study of William Drummond* (King's Crown Press, Columbia, NY, 1952), p.22; Thomas Ruddiman and John Sage, *The Works of William Drummond of Hawthornden* (James Watson, Edinburgh, 1711), pp.139–41.
2 Philip Sidney, *Conversations of Ben Jonson with William Drummond of Hawthornden* (Gay and Bird, London, 1904), p.13.

83. Ben Jonson (1572–1637), *c.*1617

Abraham van Blyenberch or Blijenberch (1575/6–24)

Oil on canvas
470 × 419mm (18½ × 16½in)
National Portrait Gallery, London (NPG 2752)

Provenance Probably George Villiers, 1st Duke of Buckingham (this portrait is likely to be the painting recorded in the inventory of his son in 1635); probably George Villiers, 2nd Duke of Buckingham; . . .; said to have been in Oldstock House, Wiltshire, seat of the Webb family; with Henry Bates of Salisbury; sold by him in 1915 to Sidney Wise of Duke Street, London; purchased by the National Portrait Gallery, London, in 1935

Literature Strong 1969, vol.1, pp.183–4; Oliver Millar, *The Age of Charles I* (exh. cat., Tate Gallery, London, 1972), p.13; Hearn 1995, p.204

The posthumous son of a clergyman and stepson of a building contractor and bricklayer, Ben Jonson rose to become the most celebrated literary figure of his age, the subject of fame and admiration, rivalling, and perhaps even outshining, Shakespeare in his lifetime. In addition to numerous plays (many of which are now lost), he wrote many masques, a large body of poetry, court entertainments and works of history and rhetoric. A close friend as well as rival of Shakespeare, he wrote a poem, 'To the memory of my beloved, the author Mr. William Shakespeare', in the First Folio of Shakespeare's works (cats 1 and 117).

Like Shakespeare, Jonson began his career in the theatre as an actor, although he was apparently not highly regarded in this capacity and he soon abandoned acting as his career as a writer took off. His first really significant dramatic success was *Every Man in his Humour*, first performed in 1598 by the Lord Chamberlain's Men, with Shakespeare in a leading role. Yet it was after the accession of James I in 1603 that his career really began to flourish, and his first court masque, *The Masque of Blackness*, commissioned by Queen Anne (cat.76), was performed in 1605. More theatrical successes followed, including Jonson's comic masterpiece *Volpone* or *The Fox* (first performed 1606) and *The Alchemist* (1610), which sealed his reputation as a dramatist.

In 1616, the year of Shakespeare's death, Jonson published his *Workes*. This was a new departure for an English writer, creating a sense of authorial ownership and identity comparable to that of a modern writer, and providing a model for later publications of this kind. Technically his plays, regarded as ephemeral works, belonged to the theatre companies that staged them, and the inclusion of nine of them was particularly striking to Jonson's contemporaries. The publication of the *Workes* and a grant in February of the same year for an annual royal pension consolidated Jonson's position and, although not in name, Jonson became Poet Laureate.

The Flemish artist Abraham van Blyenberch, about whom little is otherwise known, worked in England for a brief period between 1617 and 1621. His style was broad, sophisticated and distinctive, and the small group of pictures that he is known to have painted during his time in England indicates that he was working in the highest circles of court patronage.[1] Although the portrait of Jonson is not signed, it is by far the best of the surviving versions of this portrait, and is stylistically very close to the signed works by the artist. It is known that Blyenberch painted Jonson, apparently for the court favourite George Villiers, 1st Duke of Buckingham (1592–1628), in whose young son's collection a portrait of Jonson by Blyenberch was recorded in 1635.[2]

This is the only known portrait of Jonson with a good claim to have been painted from life. It is exactly the kind of relatively modest, straightforward presentation, without elaborate accessories, that would be expected in a portrait of a successful literary man at this time. It is exceptional, however, among such portraits for the skill and sophistication with which it is executed, conveying a real sense of Jonson's individuality and character. Jonson was described in 1617 as having a 'Mountaine belly' and 'rockye face', which can well be imagined from this portrait.[3] That a painter of Blyenberch's stature should have been involved in such a commission is a testament to Jonson's very high standing among his peers, but probably also to the status and connections of his patrons. William Herbert, 3rd Earl of Pembroke (1580–1630), whose portrait by Blyenberch is signed and dated 1617, was one of Jonson's most important patrons and may perhaps have been involved in arranging the commission; Buckingham, who apparently owned the painting during Jonson's lifetime, and is therefore likely to have commissioned it, was one of the most prominent men at court and a notable patron of art. CM

1 He painted Charles, Prince of Wales, later Charles I (1600–49), William Herbert, 3rd Earl of Pembroke, and the connoisseur Robert Ker, 1st Earl of Ancrum (1578–1654).
2 Randall Davies, 'An Inventory of the Duke of Buckingham's Pictures, etc., at York House in 1635', *Burlington Magazine*, X, 1907, p.380.
3 *Conversations with William Drummond of Hawthornden*, in C.H. Herford, Percy Simpson and Evelyn Simpson (eds), *Ben Jonson*, 11 vols (Clarendon Press, Oxford, 1925–52), vol.1, p.677.

84. John Fletcher (1579–1625), *c.*1620

Unknown artist

Oil on panel
920 × 710mm (36¼ × 28 in)
Inscribed on paper on table: 'The pensell and the penn have strivd/together To shew thy face and witt/Flecher) and whether Have donn/Ther best, I know not, but confess/Non but thy owne penn could/Thy witt express'; upper left in background: 'POET FLETCHER'.
Private collection

Provenance Apparently purchased by Edward Hyde, 1st Earl of Clarendon, and in his collection by about 1683–5; by descent in the Clarendon collection

Literature Bodleian MS Clarendon 92 ff.253–4, no.54; Guy de la Bédoyère (ed.), *Particular Friends: The Correspondence of Samuel Pepys and John Evelyn* (Boydell Press, Woodbridge, 1997), pp.194–5; Strong 1969, vol.1, p.123, and pl.244 in vol.2; Robin Gibson, *Catalogue of Portraits in the Collection of the Earl of Clarendon* (Paul Mellon Centre for Studies in British Art, London, 1977), no.65, pp.59–60;

John Fletcher was one of the most successful and prolific playwrights of the Jacobean period. Known primarily for his collaborations with Francis Beaumont (1584/5–1616), he also wrote a substantial number of plays on his own, and worked with other authors, including Shakespeare. *Cardenio* (now lost), *The Famous History of the Life of King Henry VIII* (known at the time as *All is True*) and *The Two Noble Kinsmen* were all jointly written by Shakespeare and Fletcher. Other plays show the cross-fertilization of ideas in the two men's works: Fletcher's *The Woman's Prize* is written as a sequel to Shakespeare's *The Taming of the Shrew*; and his *The Woman Hater*, *Philaster* and *Bonduca* were influenced by Shakespeare's *Measure for Measure*, *Hamlet* and *Cymbeline* respectively. Conversely, Shakespeare's *The Tempest* draws on Fletcher's *The Faithful Shepherdess*. In 1613 Fletcher appears to have taken over Shakespeare's role as chief playwright for the King's Men.

Fletcher came from a higher social background than many of his playwright contemporaries: his father became Bishop of London; and his uncle, Giles Fletcher the Elder, was a diplomat and writer. Both, however, were ultimately disgraced and Fletcher had to make his own way in the world from a relatively young age. His earliest play, *The Woman Hater*, written in 1607, was also the first of many written in collaboration with Francis Beaumont. At this time he and Beaumont appear to have been part of Ben Jonson's circle at the Mermaid Tavern. Beaumont and Fletcher's first real success was their third play, *Philaster* or *Love Lyes a-Bleeding*, in 1610. This play seems to have initiated the fashion for romantic tragicomedy, the genre in which Fletcher mainly worked from that time on, and which was to be one of the most important literary genres of the period.

Alongside his collaborations with Beaumont, among which the best-known are *The Maid's Tragedy* and *A King and No King*, Fletcher also wrote his own plays. After Beaumont's death in 1616 Fletcher continued to write on his own, but he evidently preferred working with others. He collaborated with Nathan Field (cat.52) on five plays and then very extensively with Philip Massinger (1583–1640). Although Fletcher's work was hugely popular during his lifetime and in the later seventeenth and eighteenth centuries, its characteristic combination of high emotion, exploration of difficult sexual and political themes, ironic tone and lack of poetic metaphor did not find favour with nineteenth- and twentieth-century audiences.

The only known portrait of Fletcher to have been produced during his lifetime, this painting shows him as a prosperous and well-dressed man with the tools of his trade – paper and pens – alongside him. The relative ostentation with which he is dressed, with his elaborate belt and expensive doublet with precious-metal decorations, known as aglets, contrasts strikingly with the simpler presentation of Ben Jonson (cat.83) and Shakespeare (cat.3), playwrights from more humble origins. The verse written on the paper beside him pays a compliment to Fletcher's wit and expresses conventional sentiments about the inability of a painting to convey the mind of the sitter. Nothing is known about the circumstances of the commission, but it is difficult to imagine that Fletcher himself would have specified this rather feeble verse, and it seems more likely that the painter added it under the instructions of a friend or patron of the playwright. CM

85. Edward de Vere, 17th Earl of Oxford (1550–1604), 17th century after a portrait of 1575

Unknown artist

Oil on canvas
743 × 635 mm (29¼ × 25 in)
Inscribed in a later hand (eighteenth century?) top right: 'Edward vere 17th earle of Oxford/Lord high Chamberlaine of England/Married 1st Anne Daught to/Wm Cecil Lord Burghley 2dly/Eliz Daughter to Tho. Trenthem of Rochester in Com. Stafford /and died 24th of June 1604'
Private collection; on loan to the National Portrait Gallery, London (NPG L111)

Provenance Seen by George Vertue in the collection of Edward Harley, 2nd Earl of Oxford, 1747?; inherited by the 2nd Duke of Portland; thereafter by descent to the current owner

Literature Charlton Ogburn, *The Mysterious William Shakespeare* (Dodd, Mead & Co., New York, 1984)

Edward de Vere, Earl of Oxford, was esteemed within his own lifetime as a talented courtier-poet and was a patron of players from 1580 to 1602. He was also considered by Francis Meres (1565/6–1647; cat.59) to be a comic dramatist, although none of his plays survive. His poems were published in compilations, including *Paradise of Dainty Devices* (1576), *Art of Poesy* (1589) and *England's Parnassus* (1600). He was educated at Queens' College, Cambridge, and later in the household of the humanist Sir Thomas Smith (1513–77). Following his father's death, he became a ward of the Crown and, under the guardianship of William Cecil, Lord Burghley (1520/1–98), he joined Elizabeth I's retinue. Between 1575 and 1576 he travelled to Paris, Strasburg and Venice and returned to England having developed a taste for continental fashions and perfumed luxuries; like the Earl of Southampton (cats 46, 47), he became notorious for his extravagance and feminized dress. It is possible that Lord Burghley was thinking of him, when he advised his own son not to suffer 'thy sons to pass the Alps, for they shall learn nothing there but pride, blasphemy and atheism'.[1]

Accounts from the period suggest that Oxford was a man of flamboyant habits and he openly flirted with Catholicism and homosexuality, discarding his wife Anne Cecil (1556–88), the daughter of Lord Burghley, for the company of a Venetian choirboy. Yet, despite provoking dislike among courtiers such as Sir Philip Sidney and the Earl of Leicester, he was protected from mishap by his high rank at court and his link with Lord Burghley. In 1581 he was briefly imprisoned in the Tower when his mistress Anne Vavasour (active 1580–1621), one of the Queen's maids of honour, gave birth to a son. He was later reconciled with his wife, and became a commissioner at the trial of Mary, Queen of Scots, but, despite his high rank, he never received the prestigious Order of the Garter.

From the 1920s Oxford's name was championed, like Francis Bacon's and Christopher Marlowe's, as a possible author of Shakespeare's plays. Despite continued interest in this theory, few established scholars now consider him as a likely candidate. This portrait is a seventeenth-century version of an earlier painting of 1575, which was probably painted while he was travelling in Europe. TC

1 Joel Hurstfield, *The Queen's Wards: Wardship and Marriage Under Elizabeth I* (Longman, Green and Co., London, 1958), p.257.

Ætatis Suæ 25
1575
Edward Vere 17th Earle of Oxford
Lord high Chamberlaine of England
Married 1st Ann Daughter to
Wm Cecil Lord Burghley 2dly
Eliz Daughter to Thos Trentham
of Roucester in Com: Stafford
and died 24th of June 1604

86. Mary Sidney, Countess of Pembroke? (1561–1621), *c.*1590

Nicholas Hilliard (*c.*1547–1619)

Watercolour and bodycolour on vellum laid onto a playing card (two spades visible on reverse)
Diameter 54mm (2 ⅛ in)
Inscribed on verso of card mount: 'The Lady Mary/Sydney Countess/of Pembroke'
National Portrait Gallery, London (NPG 5994)

Provenance Possibly Robert Sidney, 1st Earl of Leicester (1563–1626); possibly by descent in the collection of the Earls of Leicester; Anne Howard, wife of Sir William Yonge (*c.*1693–1755), Bt.; her niece, The Hon. Mrs Mary Anson; given by her to George Simon, 2nd Earl of Harcourt (1736–1809); by descent in the Harcourt family to Viscount Harcourt; accepted by HM Treasury in lieu of capital transfer tax after the death of Viscount Harcourt in 1979; allocated to the National Portrait Gallery, London, in 1988

Literature Roy Strong, 'The Leicester House Miniatures: Robert Sidney, 1st Earl of Leicester and his Circle', *Burlington Magazine*, CXXVII, October 1985, pp.694–701

Mary Sidney was one of the first significant female writers in English, and an important patron of poets. The daughter of Sir Henry Sidney (1529–86), she was, like Elizabeth I and a small number of other aristocratic women, highly educated in the humanist tradition. She married Henry Herbert, 2nd Earl of Pembroke (*c.*1538–1601), and was the mother of William (cat.87) and Philip (1584–1650), the 3rd and 4th Earls. At Wilton, the Pembrokes' house in Wiltshire (see fig.57, p.172), she created an important and extensive literary circle; among her admirers and protégés were John Donne (cat.80) and Samuel Daniel (cat.91).

After the death of her brother, the poet Sir Philip Sidney (1554–86), Mary Sidney took on his role as a supporter and significant patron of poets. She supervised the publication of Philip Sidney's *Arcadia*, which had been written at her behest and was dedicated to her, and wrote poems, particularly celebrating his achievement. She also completed and published his metrical paraphrase of the Psalms. *Antonius*, her translation of Robert Garnier's play *Marc Antoine*, was the first dramatization of the story of Antony and Cleopatra in England. Shakespeare drew on her characterization and elements of her phrasing in his *Antony and Cleopatra*.

This miniature was painted at the time when Mary Sidney's literary patronage and writing were at their height. Although, as is so often the case with portraits of this period, the identity of the sitter is not absolutely certain, it is supported by the identifying inscription on the reverse, which appears to be from the first half of the seventeenth century, and by its shared provenance with miniatures portraying members of, or people connected with, the Sidney family. The miniature is characteristic of Hilliard's work at the peak of his career, exploiting the sitter's spectacular ruff to full decorative effect and contrasting its starched formality with the fresh flowers pinned to her dress and hair. There are no other recorded likenesses of Mary Sidney apart from an engraving of her in later life (1618) by Simon De Passe. TC and CM

87. William Herbert, 3rd Earl of Pembroke (1580–1630), dated 1611

Isaac Oliver (*c.*1565–1617)

Watercolour with body colour on vellum
Oval, 53 × 43mm (2 × 1⅝in)
Signed with a monogram and dated at left centre: 'I' with superimposed 'O'/1611
Folger Shakespeare Library, Washington, DC (FPM 10)

Provenance Mr Anderson in 1865; collection of W.E. Bools, Enderby House, Clapham; Bools sale, Sotheby's, 22 June 1903, lot 1435, for £56

Literature William L. Pressly, *A Catalogue of Paintings in the Folger Shakespeare Library: 'As Imagination Bodies Forth'* (Yale University Press, New Haven and London, 1993), cat.194

When the First Folio of Shakespeare's collected plays was published in 1623, the editors John Heminges (bap.1566, d.1630) and Henry Condell (1576?–1627) dedicated the volume to Pembroke and his brother Philip Herbert. Pembroke was the son of Henry Herbert and Mary Sidney (cat.86) and, when he succeeded to his father's title, he inherited sizeable estates in Wales and the marches, as well as a large income. A politically astute courtier and favourite of James I, he became a highly significant patron and protector of poets and writers, including George Chapman (cat.90) and Ben Jonson (cat.83). Jonson even claimed that Pembroke sent him the sizeable sum of £20 every New Year's Day to purchase books for his library.[1]

Apart from the dedication in the First Folio, it is difficult to assess what direct involvement Pembroke may have had with Shakespeare during his lifetime. Yet Heminges and Condell state that both Pembroke and his brother 'have beene pleas'd to thinke these trifles some-thing, heeretofore; and have prosequuted both them, and their Author living, with so much favour'. They also call Shakespeare, 'your servant' and explain that the volume 'ask'd' to be dedicated to them as they had liked the plays 'so much' when they were performed.[2] In 1603 the King's Men's certainly played at Wilton House, Wiltshire, Pembroke's family seat (fig.57, p.172), and the Earl of Pembroke appears to have known and patronized some of Shakespeare's close professional colleagues, such as Richard Burbage (1568–1619; cat.51). As a Jacobean courtier, Pembroke would have seen Shakespeare perform as an actor at court and have been familiar with most of the plays performed by the King's Men. Pembroke's name has also been linked with the initials 'W.H', cited as the 'begetter' of the sonnets, although most critics consider this association is unlikely.

This exquisitely painted miniature shows Pembroke as a man of thirty-one, around the time he was actively attempting to increase his power and patronage at James I's court. The earring he wears in his left ear appears to be a finger ring set with a black stone and the black ribbon modishly tied to the ring may have had personal significance. Around his neck is a wide blue ribbon, which probably supported his Garter badge, which is just out of the viewer's sight. The miniaturist Isaac Oliver had trained with the celebrated master of Elizabethan miniature painting, Nicholas Hilliard (*c.*1547–1619), but Oliver's softer style, with a greater degree of illusionism, became popular in the early Jacobean period. The costume has been meticulously rendered to depict the Earl's fashionable and sumptuous tailoring, and Oliver takes particular care to show the intricacies of the lace collar and the slashes in the doublet that reveal a sliver of pink lining alongside the white fabric beneath. TC

1 Philip Sidney, *Conversations of Ben Jonson with William Drummond of Hawthornden* (Gay and Bird, London, 1904), p.35.
2 William Shakespeare, *Comedies, Histories and Tragedies* (Isaac Jaggard and Edward Blount, London, 1623), sig. A2v-A3r.

88. Francis Bacon, later Baron Verulam and Viscount St Alban (1561–1626), 1578

Nicholas Hilliard (*c.*1547–1619)

Watercolour and bodycolour on vellum laid on card
75 × 62mm (3 × 2⅜ in)
Inscribed along the left-hand edge: 1578 SI TABULA DARETUR DIGNA; and, along the right-hand edge: ANIMUM MALLEM Æ^S S.18. ('It would be preferable if a picture deserving of his mind could be brought about. In his 18th year')
Temporarily allocated to the National Portrait Gallery, see Provenance

Provenance Said to have come from the French royal collection; James Edwards (1757–1816) in 1803; John Adair Hawkins from at least 1825 until at least 1860; . . .; D.M. Currie sale, at Christie's, lot 53, on 15 May 1903, in which the picture was called *Portrait of a Young Gentleman* and bought by Colonel H.E. Lindsay; thence by descent in the collection of the Dukes of Rutland; accepted by HM Government in lieu of inheritance tax in 2005 and awaiting permanent allocation

Literature N. Blakiston, 'Nicholas Hilliard as a Traveller', *Burlington Magazine*, XCI, no.555, 1949, p.169; Roy Strong, 'Nicholas Hilliard's Miniature of Francis Bacon Rediscovered and other Minutiae', *Burlington Magazine*, CVI, no.736, 1964, p.337

Francis Bacon was one of the great intellectual figures of late Elizabethan and Jacobean England: a philosopher, scientist, statesman and lawyer. The son of Sir Nicholas Bacon (1510–79), Lord Keeper to Elizabeth I, he made rapid progress in politics under James I, and in 1618 he was appointed Lord Chancellor. However, only three years later he was impeached for bribery and his political career came to an end. He spent the remainder of his life in retirement, dedicating himself to scholarship, in the form of natural philosophy.

Bacon's *Essays*, writings mainly on moral and political topics, were his most popular published works, both during his lifetime and subsequently. His great works of natural philosophy were *The Advancement of Learning* (1605), later translated into Latin and expanded as *De Augmentis* (1623), and *Novum Organum* (1620). The apparent presence of aspects of Bacon's philosophical interests in Shakespeare's plays and poetry, along with a reluctance to believe that literature of such power and sophistication could have been written by a man without a university education, have led some to the conclusion that Bacon was, in fact, the true author of these works, but most modern Shakespeare scholarship dismisses this view.

From the autumn of 1576 until early in 1579, the young Francis Bacon lived in France, in the household of Sir Amias Paulet (*c.*1532–88), Ambassador to the French court. Paulet reported in December 1576 that various people had joined him, including 'Mr Helyer', who, it is clear from later references, was the miniaturist Nicholas Hilliard. While he was in France, Hilliard stayed in various households, and it is likely that he came across Bacon on more than one occasion.

This miniature is one of a group that the artist produced during his time in France, and it testifies to the qualities that made Hilliard one of the few English artists of the sixteenth century to have an international reputation during his lifetime. While there is no absolute proof that the sitter is Bacon, the circumstantial evidence in favour of this identification is compelling: Bacon and Hilliard were moving in the same circles during the time the miniature was painted; Bacon's age in 1578 corresponds with that given on the miniature; and the rest of the inscription is particularly fitting for a young man who already had a reputation for his considerable intellectual abilities. CM

89. Sir Walter Ralegh (1554–1618), *c*.1585

Nicholas Hilliard (*c*.1547–1619)

Watercolour on vellum stuck onto card
Oval, 48 × 41mm (1⅞ × 1⅝ in)
National Portrait Gallery, London (NPG 4106)

Provenance Earls of Carlisle at Castle Howard; sold from collections of Viscount Morpeth, at Sotheby's, lot 116, on 14 May 1959; purchased with the aid of the National Art Collections Fund and the Pilgrim Trust in 1959

Literature Strong 1969, pp.255–6; Roy Strong with contributions from V.J. Murrell, *Artists of the Tudor Court: The Portrait Miniature Rediscovered 1520–1620* (Victoria and Albert Museum, London, 1983)

An important courtier, explorer and military and naval commander, Ralegh was also an esteemed court poet whose verses circulated in manuscript during his lifetime. In the early 1580s his charismatic personality and good looks attracted the attentions of Queen Elizabeth I and he became one of her favourites. She used to refer to him affectionately as her 'silly pugge', and nicknamed him 'water'. The intense rivalry of the Elizabethan court is at the heart of his poetic endeavours. The 'Cynthia poems', which style the Queen as a moon goddess, were written to express his despair at losing the Queen's favour after his secret marriage to the pregnant Elizabeth Throckmorton (1565–1647) and imprisonment in the Tower of London. It is difficult to date many of the poems attributed to him and the authorship of several has been questioned, but his reputation as a writer of highly charged love poems is undiminished. His dislike of James I meant that he fell dramatically from favour after 1603. From 1603 to 1616 he was imprisoned in the Tower of London on charges of treason. While there, he wrote poetry and a major work entitled *History of the World*, which was published in 1614. After an unsuccessful trip to find El Dorado in South America, he was eventually executed in 1618.

This exquisitely painted miniature shows Ralegh as an elegant man of around thirty, at the height of his influence with the Queen. His wide cartwheel ruff with expensive cutwork lace offsets his neatly groomed features, and, in common with the sitter in the Chandos portrait (cat.3), he wears an earring, which is almost hidden beneath his curly locks and the edge of the ruff. The level of intricate detail captured by Hilliard is exceptional, and even though some of the features of the face have faded, and the silver highlights have oxidized, this portrait remains a highly regarded work.
TC

90. George Chapman (1559/60–1634), published 1616

Attributed to William Hole or Holle (b. before 1600, d.1624)

Line engraving
255 × 170mm (10 × 6 5/8 in)
Inscribed around the oval: ÆTA: LVII. M.DC. XVI. GEORGIVS CHAPMANVS HOMERI METAPHRASTES.; outer rim, top left: HAC EST LAURIGERI FACIES DIUINA GEORGI; around the outer rim, top right: HIC PHOEBI DECUS EST; PHOEBINUMA DEUS; in the clouds: CONSCIVM EVASI DIEM
National Portrait Gallery, London (NPG D2941)

Provenance Acquired in 1992

Literature A.M. Hind, *Engraving in England in the Sixteenth and Seventeenth Centuries: The Reign of James I*, vol.2 (Cambridge University Press, 1952), pp.316–40; R.T. Godfrey, *Printmaking in Britain: A General History from its Beginnings to the Present Day* (Phaidon Press, London, 1979), p.17; Fredson Bowers (ed.), *Elizabethan Dramatists' Dictionary of Literary Biography*, vol.62 (Gale Research, Detroit, 1987), p.5

Chapman was a celebrated poet and a dramatist for the Lord Admiral's Men, the main company of players to rival the King's Men. He was the second son of a Herefordshire yeoman, and it is not clear whether he attended university. Continually in search of patrons, Chapman was often short of money and wrote plays for several companies, as well as numerous poems. As a writer of comedies and tragedies, he gained popular acclaim and, while some of his work is lost, around nineteen new plays were composed by him and performed between 1596 and 1611. The playful parody and occasionally biting political satire of his dramatic work resulted in several confrontations with authority. His involvement in *Eastwood Ho!*, written in collaboration with Ben Jonson (cat.83) and John Marston (1576–1634) landed both Chapman and Jonson in prison for two months because of its criticism of the Scots, the King's accent and the number of recently created knighthoods.

Towards the end of his life Chapman devoted himself to classical translations and this print was made as a frontispiece to his translation of *The Whole Works of Homer,* published in 1616. The unusual format – with Chapman's head among the clouds – may be designed to reflect his absorption in literary endeavours and the words in the clouds, CONSCIVM EVASI DIEM might be translated as 'I will escape the conscious day'. He seems to have used the inscription, which also appears on a later printed portrait of Chapman, as a personal motto.

The engraver William Hole was an established printmaker by around 1607. He worked principally for book publishers, supplying copperplate engraving for works by Jonson and Michael Drayton (cat.81), together with musical scorebooks. This print is one of Hole's most technically accomplished engravings and must have been designed to an elaborate brief provided by Chapman. There are few other portraits of Chapman from life, and this one may have derived from a drawing as it appears to be meticulously observed, showing two moles upon his nose, the individual strands of his bushy beard and even curling tufts of hair on the top of his balding head. TC

91. Samuel Daniel (1562/3–1619), published 1609

Thomas Cockson or Coxon (active 1609–36)

Line engraving
176 × 122mm (6⅞ × 4¾in)
Inscribed top centre: 'The Civile Wares. . .'; bottom centre: 'Printed at London by Simon Watersoune 1609'
National Portrait Gallery, London (NPG D2254)

Provenance Fleming collection, 1931

Literature A.M. Hind, *Engraving in England in the Sixteenth and Seventeenth Centuries: The Reign of James I*, vol.1 (Cambridge University Press, 1952), pp.244, 252

Like Michael Drayton, the poet and historian Samuel Daniel was a near contemporary of Shakespeare, but Daniel's interests were far removed from the crowd-pleasing entertainments of the public theatre. His introspective poems and verses, which drew upon humanist thought, attracted a succession of noble patrons including Charles Blount, Baron Mountjoy (1563–1606), Margaret Clifford, Countess of Cumberland (1560–1616) and Queen Anne (cat.76). He studied at Magdalen Hall (now College), Oxford in the early 1580s, but did not take a degree, and soon after he travelled to Paris and later Italy. By the early 1590s he had established a reputation as a supremely talented poet, his work acclaimed by Spenser and borrowed by Shakespeare. At this time he may have lived at Wilton House, Wiltshire among a circle of writers who formed around the patroness Mary Herbert, Countess of Pembroke (cat.86), to whom he dedicated his 'Delia' sonnets in 1592. In 1599, perhaps his most important poem *Musophilus* was published – a complex work with many questioning voices that drew upon the work of Michel de Montaigne (cat.64).

With his links to important patrons, he was one of the first poets to congratulate the new King on his accession in 1603, and Queen Anne commissioned him to write several masques including *The Vision of Twelve Goddesses* performed at Hampton Court by the Queen and her ladies in 1604. Daniel was disdainful of plays and masques, however, viewing them as little more than light-hearted ephemera. This set him in conflict with Ben Jonson (cat.83), who also wrote masques for the Queen. By 1607 he had become a groom of the Queen's privy chamber, which gave him financial stability. In the last years of his life he wrote a highly successful history of medieval England dedicated to the Queen, and in time the success and acclaim of his histories eclipsed his reputation as a poet.

Few other lifetime portraits of Daniel exist and this engraving served to accompany one of his greatest literary achievements, *The Civile Wares* published in 1609. It shows him dressed as a gentleman positioned in an oval frame with personifications of Neptune (Greek god of the sea) and Ceres (Greek goddess of agriculture) on either side. The first part of this poem was first published in 1595 and achieved considerable acclaim; it is probable that Shakespeare drew on it in writing *Richard II*. TC

DEATH AND LEGACY

The will and the plays

Wee Wondred (Shakespeare) that thou
went'st so soone
From the World=Stage to the Graves
Tyring-Room

(From a commendatory poem in
the First Folio by James Mabbe)

Around 1614, when Shakespeare was fifty, he stopped writing and began to spend more time in Stratford-upon-Avon where, in 1616, he dictated his will. He was now a wealthy man with considerable assets and he left most of his estate to his eldest daughter Susanna. Several of his friends from London were remembered with bequests of money to buy rings of remembrance. At the age of fifty-two Shakespeare died, and on 25 April 1616 he was buried in Holy Trinity Church, Stratford-upon-Avon.

His fellow actors and writers paid tribute to his achievements some years later in the introduction to the First Folio edition of his collected plays, published in 1623. He was heralded by his friend Ben Jonson as the 'soule of the Age' and 'wonder of our stage' and as a man who was 'not of an age, but for all time'.

92a, b, c. The last will and testament of William Shakespeare, 25 March 1616

Manuscript, ink on paper
410 × 310mm (16⅛ × 12¼in)
The National Archives, UK, PCC Prob 1/4

Provenance Prerogative Court of Canterbury

Literature Chambers 1930, vol.2, pp.169–80; Schoenbaum 1975, pp.242–50; David Thomas and Jane Cox, *Shakespeare in the Public Records* (Her Majesty's Stationery Office, London, 1985), pp.24–5

William Shakespeare drafted his will in January 1616, and then redrafted it on 25 March, not least because of the marriage of his daughter Judith (1585–1662) to Thomas Quiney (1589–*c*.1662) on 10 February. No final copy was ever made – hence the deletions and interlineations – and Shakespeare simply signed each of the three sheets.

Shakespeare left his entire freehold estate to his elder daughter, Susanna (1583–1649), the wife of John Hall (1574/5–1635). This does not necessarily indicate favouritism: such a bequest was essential if the family was to maintain its newly acquired gentry status. The bequest to his other daughter, Judith, was in the form of a generous marriage settlement: she was to receive £100 immediately and another £50 if she surrendered her interest in a copyhold property to her sister, Susanna. She was also to receive the interest on a further £150, the capital to be settled on her after three years. If she died without heirs, this could pass to 'such husband' as she might be married to, provided he had previously settled on her land to that value. This rather churlish description of Quiney can probably be explained by the fact that he had recently fathered an illegitimate child by another woman, both of whom had died a few days before.

Shakespeare left to his sole surviving sibling, his sister Joan Hart, £20, all his wearing apparel and the life tenancy of the house where she lived. Her three sons received £5 apiece. Various local friends were given personal gifts: his sword went to Thomas Combe (1589–1657), Thomas Russell (1570–1634) received £5 and his lawyer, Francis Collins £13 6*s*. 8*d*. His godson, William Walker (b.1608), aged seven, was left 20*s*. 'in gold' and his Stratford friends, Hamlet Sadler (d.1624), William Reynolds (1575–1633), Anthony Nash (d.1622) and Thomas Nash (1593–1647) were each given 26*s*. 8*d*. to buy rings. His business partners in London, John Heminges (bap.1566?, d.1630), Richard Burbage (cat.51) and Henry Condell (1576?–1627) were remembered in the same way. It is notable that his wife Anne, whose Christian name is omitted, received only his second-best bed and this bequest was inserted only after the will was redrafted. By the standards of the time, such cursory treatment was unusual.

The will was drawn up while Shakespeare was resident in Stratford and he lived for nearly another month, dying on 23 April 1616. If he was ill when he made his will, he does not say so: 'sick in body' was the usual phrase, whereas he declared himself, but again formulaically, as 'in perfect heath [health]'. RB

cat.92a **The last will and testament of William Shakespeare**

cat.92b **The last will and testament of William Shakespeare**

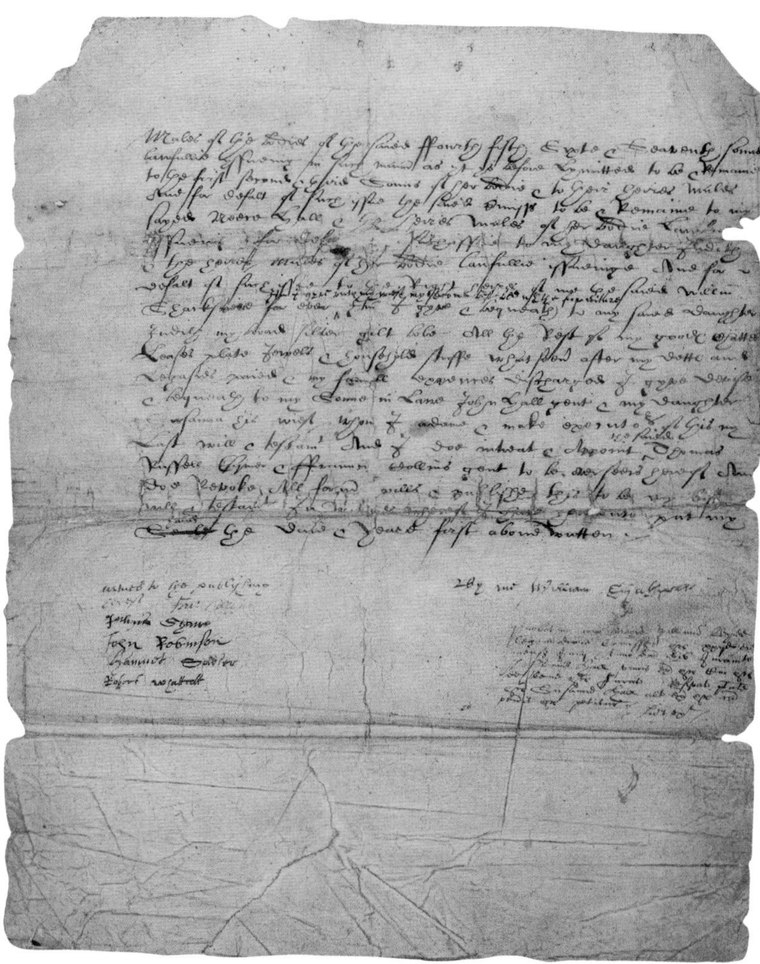

cat.92c **The last will and testament of William Shakespeare with signature** (mid right of page)

93. Signet ring with death's head, merchant's mark, *c*.1600

English?

Gold, white enamel
23 × 24mm (7/8 × 7/8in)
Inscribed: NOSSE TE IPSVM ('Know thyself [and thou shalt know God]')
Victoria and Albert Museum, London, M.18–1929

Provenance Harman-Oates Collection

Literature C.C. Oman, *Catalogue of Rings* (Victoria and Albert Museum, London, 1930), nos.566 and 739; Charles Oman, *British Rings 800–1914* (Batsford, London, 1974), p.124, no.85 F; Shirley Bury, *Jewellery Gallery Summary Catalogue* (Victoria and Albert Museum, London, 1982), p.199, 33 I 14, p.202, 33 J 34

The will and testament of William Shakespeare, dated 1616, follows a long-standing tradition of bequeathing a personal memento such as a ring to friends and family (cat.92).

In the sixteenth and seventeenth centuries the bequest of an existing ring as a token of love or friendship was increasingly replaced by the testator bequeathing money for the purchase of a ring, or an executor being given names for whom he should acquire rings in commemoration of the deceased. Later in the seventeenth century rings were frequently given as commemorative tokens to be worn by the mourners during the funeral service.

With changing religious sentiments and high mortality rates, jewellery with *memento mori* devices and inscriptions became fashionable during the time of Shakespeare, reminding their wearers 'thou shalt die' and impressing on them the futility of earthly possessions. *Memento mori* rings – mainly in gold – were particularly popular, and showed emblems of mortality, such as death's heads, crossbones, miniature skeletons and hourglasses, which, together with inscriptions in English or Latin, alluded to the transience of life. As so often described in wills of the period, they formed personal keepsakes of the deceased in commemoration or as a sign of mourning. BCS

94. Death's-head ring, *c*.1600–40

English?

Silver-gilt, with diamonds and black and white enamel
24 × 19mm (7/8 × 3/4in)
Museum of London, 62.120/96

Provenance Acquired by Sir John Evans in the 1850s; thereafter by descent; given to the Museum of London in 1962 from the collection of Dame Joan Evans

Literature Tessa Murdoch, *Treasures and Trinkets: Jewellery in London from Pre-Roman Times to the 1930s* (exh. cat., Museum of London, 1991), pp.42–3 and 75–6; J. Walgrave (ed.), *Een Eeuw van Schittering diamantjuwelen uit de 17de eeuw* (Antwerp, 1993), cat.21, p.111, cat.34

Although the type of ring that Shakespeare bequeathed to his friends is unspecified in his will, the rings displayed here are representative of contemporary types. Memorial rings were not only given or bequeathed as a lasting token of remembrance, gratitude and affection at death, but were also exchanged in betrothal and marriage.[1]

Death's-head rings seem to have been particularly fashionable in England, although examples also survive in the Musée de la Renaissance, Ecouen, in the Museum für Angewandte Kunst, Vienna, and the National Museum of Budapest. Death's heads appear frequently in jewellery and many other decorative devices at this period as the line 'Do not speak like a death's-head; do not bid me remember mine end' in Shakespeare's *Henry IV* makes clear.[2]

The death's-head ring in the Museum of London's collection is particularly interesting because it contains rose diamonds in the eye sockets, a table-cut diamond on one shoulder and a round rough stone on the other. There is some evidence to suggest that memorial rings were refashioned and recycled, and the presence of the rough stone in an otherwise perfect jewel could indicate secondary use. HF

1 London Metropolitan Archives, Diocese of London Consistory Court Records, MS DL/C/216/251v/525.
2 *The Second Part of King Henry IV* (Act II, Scene iv, line 255).

95. Posy ring, *c*.1600

English

Gold
Diameter 20mm (3/4in)
Inscribed: BEHOWLD THY END
Museum of London, 62.120/112

Provenance Acquired by Sir John Evans in the 1850s; thereafter by descent; given to the Museum of London in 1962 from the collection of Dame Joan Evans

96. Signet ring with death's head and initials 'AB', *c*.1600

English?

Gold
20 × 22mm (3/4 × 7/8in)
Victoria and Albert Museum, London, 921–1871

Provenance Waterton Collection

cat.93

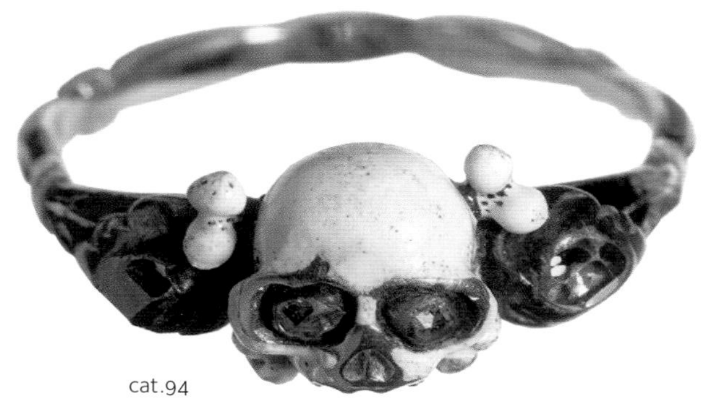
cat.94

cat.95

cat.96

97. Rosewater basin, 1597–8

London

Silver, parcel-gilt
Diameter 463mm (18¼in); depth 65mm (2½in)
Inscribed: Goldsmith's mark RB above a mullet (five-pointed wheel of a spur); the Company arms engraved in the well of the bowl were added in the nineteenth century
Merchant Taylors' Company, London

Provenance Traditionally said to have been bequeathed to the Company by Richard Maye (elected Master in 1583, died 1587), whose arms are engraved on the central boss, yet the Company's Court Minutes from June 1588, describing the original gift, indicate this piece of 1597–8 was a later replacement[1]

Literature Hubert Dynes Ellis, *A Short Description of the Ancient Silver Plate belonging to the Worshipful Company of Merchant Taylors* (Waterlow & Sons Ltd, London, 1892), p.10; F.M. Fry and R.S. Tewson, *Illustrated Catalogue of Silver Plate of the Worshipful Company of Merchant Taylors* (private publication, London, 1929), pp.27–8

On his death in 1616, Shakespeare left his youngest daughter Judith a 'broad silver gilt bole [bowl]', the only piece of household plate to be specifically identified in his will and most likely describing a large shallow drinking vessel on a raised foot. Contemporary paintings of civic or domestic dining depict gilt standing bowls filled with wine, as well as plain silver versions piled high with fruits and sweetmeats.[2] The fact that Shakespeare possessed such a costly piece, much more expensive than pewter, brass and earthenware vessels, demonstrates that silver was more readily available for men of his class from the mid sixteenth century than ever before.[3] A decline in the price of precious metals combined with rising prosperity meant that large silver drinking vessels, ewers and basins (this one weighs a hefty 2 kilograms/71 ounces approximately), enjoyed a prominent position on the sideboard or 'buffet' in non-aristocratic homes and civic and guild halls. Contemporaries commented on this widespread use of silver, which was largely an English phenomenon. The historian and topographer William Harrison (1535–93) noted in *A Description of England* (first published as part of Raphael Holinshed's *Chronicles* in 1577; cat.62) how 'in the houses of knights, gentlemen, merchantmen, and some other wealthy citizens, it is not geson [uncommon] to behold generally their great provision of tapestry, Turkey work [carpets], pewter, brass, fine linen, and thereto costly cupboards of plate, worth five or six hundred or a thousand pounds … .'[4]

Although impressive as a status symbol, a basin of this type was primarily a functional object. In *The Taming of the Shrew* Gremio alludes to an important dining ritual of an affluent household 'richly furnished with plate and gold/ Basins and ewers to lave [wash] her dainty hands' (Act II, Scene i, lines 339–40). Lacking forks until well into the seventeenth century, the English maintained the medieval custom of washing greasy hands after a meal from a basin filled with warm, flower-scented water. As basins were brought to each guest at the table and appreciated at close range, they were often elaborately decorated. Marine imagery was highly fashionable at this time, alluding to the vessels' watery function. Here the goldsmith has hammered into relief rippling waves, dolphins and sea monsters. SL

1 The minutes read: 'There was delivered into the handes of [?our] M[aster] by M[istress] Marie Maye… a Basson and Ewer of silver parcell guilte…'
2 See, for example, drinking vessels at the 'Banquet of the Bruges Magistrates' by Anthony Claeissens 1574, Groeninge Museum, Bruges, reproduced in Philippa Glanville, *Silver in Tudor and Early Stuart England* (V&A Publications, London, 1990), p.242.
3 I would like to thank the silver historian Philippa Glanville, whose advice and extensive research on the social context of domestic silver during this period has proved invaluable (see note 2 above).
4 William Harrison, *Harrison's Description of England in Shakespeare's Youth*, ed. F.J. Furnivall from the first two editions of Holinshed's *Chronicles* (1577 and 1587) (The New Shakspere Society, London, 1877 and 1878).

98. Rapier, *c.*1600

English

Steel, the hilt damascened with gold and overlaid with silver
945 × 140 × 115mm (37¼ × 5½ × 4½ in)
Victoria and Albert Museum, London, M.2974-1931

Provenance Bequeathed by G.H. Ramsbottom through the National Art Collections Fund, London

Literature J.F. Hayward, *Swords and Daggers* (Her Majesty's Stationery Office, London, 1963), 18a

In 1601, Shakespeare had inherited the coat of arms of his father and the right to style himself a gentleman (cats 54, 55). An important symbolic and decorative element of a gentleman's costume was his sword. This sword is not among the most elaborate examples that survive and would have been suitable for a gentleman or man of moderate means. Shakespeare owned his own example to wear on formal occasions and at court. He left it in his will to Thomas Combe (1589–1657). Worn in a scabbard and suspended from a slung belt, a sword boasted of the status and honour of its owner. In England, permissible lengths of blades and degrees of decoration were controlled according to rank by sumptuary laws.

The rapier developed as a fencing sword, but by the 1570s rapiers were generally intended for civilian use. They were usually made in sets with daggers, and had two-sided blades for slashing and thrusting, while daggers were used for parrying. The blade of this sword is one-sided and is not the original.

It was common for civilian sword hilts to be decorated in as rich a way as possible without impairing their function. This rapier has the classic 'swept' hilt fashionable in Europe from about 1570 to 1630. The bar protecting the hand rises in an elegant double curve from the knuckle guard to the ten-sided pommel. The hilt is engraved and inlaid with gold wire, an Islamic technique known as 'damascening', and is also overlaid with silver. Damascening was probably introduced into Europe via great trading cities such as Venice. Many English swords of the period were decorated in this way and 'damaskers' mentioned in contemporary accounts were specialist craftsmen. AP

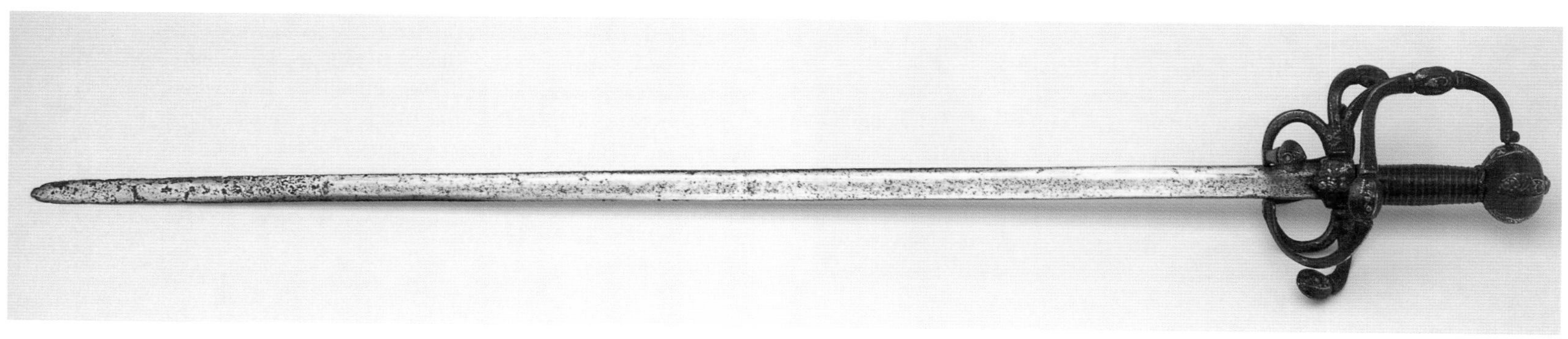

Detail of cat.85

THE PLAYS

About half of Shakespeare's plays were published in his lifetime. They appeared in a small format known as a 'Quarto', which is a book made up of a sheet of paper folded to form four leaves (eight pages). Some Quartos were reprinted several times. Several different versions of some of the plays were in circulation at one time, deriving, for example, from theatrical manuscripts or the author's own papers. As printers often used different sources to compile the Quartos (known as Q1, Q2, Q3, etc.), the texts of some plays varied, sometimes considerably, from version to version. From 1598 the author's name 'William Shake-speare' or 'W. Shakespeare' began to appear on the title page. The following pages show a selection of the quartos, which were first published in his lifetime. The spelling and wording in the titles is as they appear in the original quartos with the modernized spellings in brackets.

Seven years after Shakespeare's death, in 1623, a collected edition of his plays known as the First Folio was published, compiled by his friends and fellow actors John Heminges (bap.1566, d.1630) and Henry Condell (1576–1627). The First Folio included many plays that had never been published before.

99.

THE True Tragedie of Richarde Duke of Yorke (*True Tragedy of Richard Duke of York*), later known as *Henry VI, Part 3*, 1600 (first published 1595)

William Shakespeare (1564–1616)

Printed book, 'Printed at London by W.W. [William White] for T.M. [Thomas Millington], and are to be sold at his shoppe under Saint Peters Church in Cornewall [Cornhill]' (known as Q2)
Quarto
The British Library, London, C.12.h.9, open at title page

Provenance From the Library of George III, presented in 1823

100.

THE Whole Contention betweene the two Famous Houses, LANCASTER and YORKE (*The Whole Contention of . . . York and Lancaster*), 1619

William Shakespeare

Printed book, 'Printed at London, for T.P. [Thomas Pavier]' (known as Q3)
Quarto
The British Library, London, c.12 g.13, open at title page

Provenance From the Library of George III, presented in 1823

Illustrated on p.204

Cat.99 is a copy of the *True Tragedy of Richard Duke of York*, the second edition of a play written probably in 1591, before the foundation of the Lord Chamberlain's Men in 1594, the company with which Shakespeare was to be most closely associated. The play, first printed in 1595, is a short version, probably reconstructed from memory by actors who had taken part in it, of the third instalment of Shakespeare's four-part series of plays depicting the history of England during the reigns of Henry VI and Richard III. The second and third of these plays appear to have been written before the first. They were originally printed, and probably acted, as the first and second parts of *The Contention of the Two Famovs Houses of Yorke and Lancaster*. When fuller and more authoritative texts were printed in the First Folio, they were retitled as *Henry VI, Parts Two and Three,* and were known by these titles until the Oxford *Complete Works*, of 1986, restored the original titles. This play includes the line 'Oh Tygers hart, wrapt in a womans hide!', which was parodied in *Greene's Groatsworth of Witte* of 1592, where the author accused Shakespeare of being 'an vpstart Crow, beautified with our feathers, that with his *Tygers hart wrapt in a Players hyde*, supposes he is as well able to bombast out a blanke verse as the best of you'.

THE Whole Contention betweene the two Famous Houses, LANCASTER and YORKE is an edition that reprinted both parts of *The Contention*. It was printed by William Jaggard for the publisher Thomas Pavier in 1619, falsely dated 1600, as part of a failed attempt to bring out a collection of Shakespeare's plays. SW

101.

The most lamentable tragedie of Titus Andronicus (*Titus Andronicus*), 1611 (first published 1594)

William Shakespeare

Printed book, 'Printed [by Edward Allde] for Eedward [*sic*] White, and are to be solde at his shoppe, nere the little north dore of Pauls, at the signe of the Gun' (known as Q3)
Quarto
The British Library, London, C.34 k.60, open at fol. F3vF4r

Provenance David Garrick (1717–79), bequeathed in 1779

Illustrated on p.204

Shakespeare's first tragedy was so popular in its own time that the first edition, of 1594, was read almost to pieces: it survives in only one copy, which turned up in Sweden in 1904 when it was bought by the American collector Henry Clay Folger for £2,000. It is now in the Folger Shakespeare Library, Washington, DC. The copy illustrated is of the third edition, of 1611. When this was reprinted in the First Folio, of 1623, a new scene was added, presumably from a theatrical manuscript.

Titus Andronicus tells a horrifying story of bloodshed, mutilation and revenge. After being raped, Titus's daughter, Lavinia, makes one of the most appalling entries in all drama, with her hands cut off and her tongue cut out. In the pages shown here she attempts to reveal to her father, Titus, and her uncle, Marcus, what happened to her. The play is partly based on an episode in Ovid's long poem *Metamorphoses*. Shakespeare has Lavinia bring on stage a copy of the book, which she opens at the tragic tale of Philomel, raped by Tereus. Then, taking her uncle's staff in her mouth and guiding it with the stumps of her arms, she traces the names of her attackers in the sand. This copy of the play belonged to the eighteenth-century actor David Garrick, who did not, however, perform in it. SW

102.
THE TRAGEDY OF King Richard the third (*Richard III*), 1598 (first published 1597)
William Shakespeare

Printed book,'Printed by Thomas Creede for Andrew Wise, dwelling in Paules Church-yard at the signe of the Angell' (known as Q2)
Quarto
The British Library, London, C.34. K.46, open at fol. A2r

Provenance Halliwell-Phillipps, 1858

Illustrated on p.204

This is a copy of the second edition of *Richard III*, printed in 1598. The play had first appeared in print in the previous year. For its subject matter it makes use of the 1587 edition of Holinshed's *Chronicles* (cat.62), and was probably written between 1592 and 1593. It was exceptionally popular in print as well as in performance, being reprinted in quarto in 1602, 1605, 1612, 1622, 1629 and 1634. The title page of the First Quarto leaves readers no doubt as to either the centrality or the villainy of the title character: '*The Tragedy of King Richard the Third*. Containing, His treacherous Plots against his brother Clarence: the pittiefull murther of his innocent nephewes: his tyrannicall vsurpation: with the whole course of his detested life, and most deserued death.'

Unlike the first edition, this one names the author – '*By* William Shake-speare' – indicating his increasing fame. The text of the play as printed in the First Folio of 1623 differs in many respects from this, showing that it was set up in part from an independent manuscript.

Following on closely from *Henry VI, Parts One, Two and Three*, *Richard III* brings to a triumphant conclusion Shakespeare's first sequence of history plays. The page illustrated shows the opening speech, beginning 'Now is the winter of our discontent,/Made glorious summer by this sonne of Yorke', which has become one of Shakespeare's most famous soliloquies. Even in his own time, a Cambridge student play of around 1600 showed it being used as an audition speech. SW

103.
Loues labours loft (*Love's Labour's Lost*), 1631 (first published 1598)
William Shakespeare

Printed book, 'Printed by W.S. [William Stansby] for John Smethwicke, and are to be sold at his Shop in Saint Dunstones Churchyard under the Diall' (known as Q2)
Quarto
The British Library, London, C.34.k21 open at title page

Provenance David Garrick (1717–79), bequeathed in 1779

Illustrated on p.205

This is the second surviving edition of the play printed in 1598 as '*A* PLEASANT Conceited Comedie CALLED, Loues labors lost'. The title page of that edition names 'W. Shakspere' as the play's author and boasts that it had been 'presented before her Highnes [Queen Elizabeth I] this last Christmas'. It may be a reprint of an earlier edition, now lost. It is badly printed, with many obvious errors. Like the first edition of *Much Ado About Nothing* (cat.109), it gives every sign of having been printed directly from Shakespeare's own manuscript. This is evident above all from the fact that it incorporates both unrevised and revised versions of at least two passages, one of them in Biron's great speech on love, which must derive from the author's papers. The second edition, illustrated, is a reprint of the earlier one, but its title page calls the play 'A WITTIE AND PLEASANT COMEDIE' and states that it has been 'Acted by his Maiesties Seruants at *the* Blacke-Friers *and the* Globe'.

Love's Labour's Lost is one of the few Shakespeare plays that do not tell a pre-existing story. Shakespeare invented its slender plot of the King of Navarre and his three courtier friends whose vow to abstain from female company and to devote themselves to study for three years is challenged, with predictable results, by the arrival of the Princess of France with three of her ladies. SW

104.

A Midsommer nights Dreame (*A Midsummer Night's Dream*), 1619 (first published 1600)

William Shakespeare

Printed book, 'Printed by James Roberts' (known as Q2)
Quarto
The British Library, London, C.34.k.30, open at fol. B2vB3r

Provenance David Garrick, bequeathed in 1779

Illustrated on p.205

This is the second edition of what has become one of Shakespeare's most popular plays. It had first been printed in 1600 from his own manuscript. The title page of both editions states that it had 'beene sundry times pub-*lickely acted, by the Right honoura*-ble the Lord Chamberlaine his *seruants*', and declares firmly that the play was '*Written by William Shakespeare*'. The play was reprinted with only minor differences in 1619, but with the false date of 1600, and then again, from a copy of the Second Quarto, in the First Folio of 1623, with corrections along with other changes apparently representing alterations made in rehearsal and performance.

The left-hand page of the opening illustrated shows part of the scene in which Bottom the weaver and his companions (often called the mechanicals, i.e. labourers, or artisans) prepare for the play they hope to perform for the wedding of Duke Theseus and Hippolyta. Bottom tries unsuccessfully to persuade his companions to let him play the Lion's part as well as the hero, Pyramus, and enjoys thinking about what sort of beard he will wear. In modern editions this scene ends the first act, but for much of Shakespeare's time plays were both printed and acted continuously, so the next scene follows straight on, with the direction for the entry of a fairy and Robin Goodfellow, now more commonly known as Puck.

This copy belonged to the great eighteenth-century actor David Garrick (1717–79), who may be the author of one of the numerous adaptations of the play, a musical version of 1755 called *The Fairies*. SW

105.

THE MOST EX-cellent and lamentable Tragedie, of Romeo and Iuliet (*Romeo and Juliet*), 1599 (first published 1597)

William Shakespeare

Printed book, 'Printed by Thomas Creede, for Cuthbert Burby, and are to be sold at his shop neare the Exchange' (known as Q2)
Quarto
The British Library, London, C.12 g.18, open at title page

Provenance From the Library of George III, presented in 1823

Illustrated on p.205

This is the second and more authoritative early edition of Shakespeare's popular tragedy. Probably written between 1593 and 1595, it had been printed anonymously in 1597 as '*AN* EXCELLENT conceited [witty] Tragedie *OF* Romeo and Iuliet as it hath been often (with great applause) plaid publiquely, by the right Ho-nourable the L. of *Hunsdon* his Seruants', that is by Shakespeare's company as it was known between July 1596 and March 1597. That was what is known as a pirated text, probably deriving from early performances rather than directly from Shakespeare's manuscript. The title page of this second, longer edition repeats the same information (while not describing the tragedy as 'conceited'), but claims to be 'Newly corrected, augmented, and amended', and is clearly printed from Shakespeare's own papers in an attempt to replace a corrupt text with a more accurate one. It still does not name the author, and is badly printed.

The story of Romeo and Juliet was well known before Shakespeare wrote his play, which is based fairly closely on a long poem printed in 1562, *The Tragicall Historye of Romeus and Juliet written first in Italian by Bandell* [Bandello], *and nowe in Englishe by Ar*[thur] *Br*[ooke]. SW

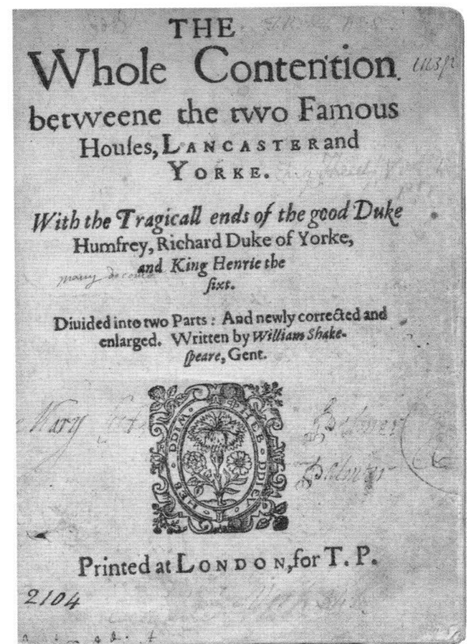

THE
Whole Contention
betweene the two Famous
Houses, LANCASTER and
YORKE.

With the Tragicall ends of the good Duke
Humfrey, Richard Duke of Yorke,
and King Henrie the
sixt.

Diuided into two Parts: And newly corrected and
enlarged. Written by *William Shake-*
speare, Gent.

Printed at LONDON, for T. P.

cat.100

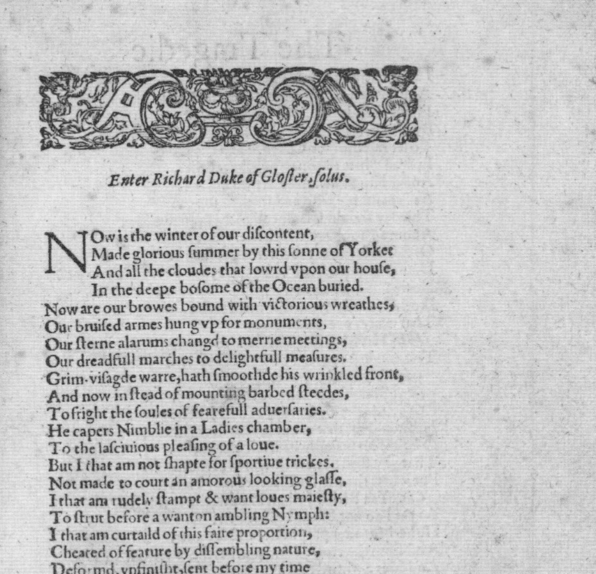

Enter Richard Duke of Gloster, solus.

NOw is the winter of our discontent,
Made glorious summer by this sonne of Yorke:
And all the cloudes that lowrd vpon our house,
In the deepe bosome of the Ocean buried.
Now are our browes bound with victorious wreathes,
Our bruised armes hung vp for monuments,
Our sterne alarums changd to merrie meetings,
Our dreadfull marches to delightfull measures.
Grim-visagde warre, hath smoothde his wrinkled front,
And now in stead of mounting barbed steedes,
To fright the soules of fearefull aduersaries.
He capers Nimblie in a Ladies chamber,
To the lasciuious pleasing of a loue.
But I that am not shapte for sportiue trickes,
Not made to court an amorous looking glasse,
I that am rudely stampt & want loues maiesty,
To strut before a wanton ambling Nymph:
I that am curtaild of this faire proportion,
Cheated of feature by dissembling nature,
Deformd, vnfinisht, sent before my time
Into this breathing world scarce half made vp.
And that so lamely and vnfashionable,
That dogs barke at me as I halt by them:
Why I in this weake piping time of peace
Haue no delight to passe away the time,
Vnlesse to spie my shadow in the sunne,
And descant on mine owne deformitie:
And therefore since I cannot prooue a louer
To entertaine these faire well spoken daies,

A 2 I am

cat.102

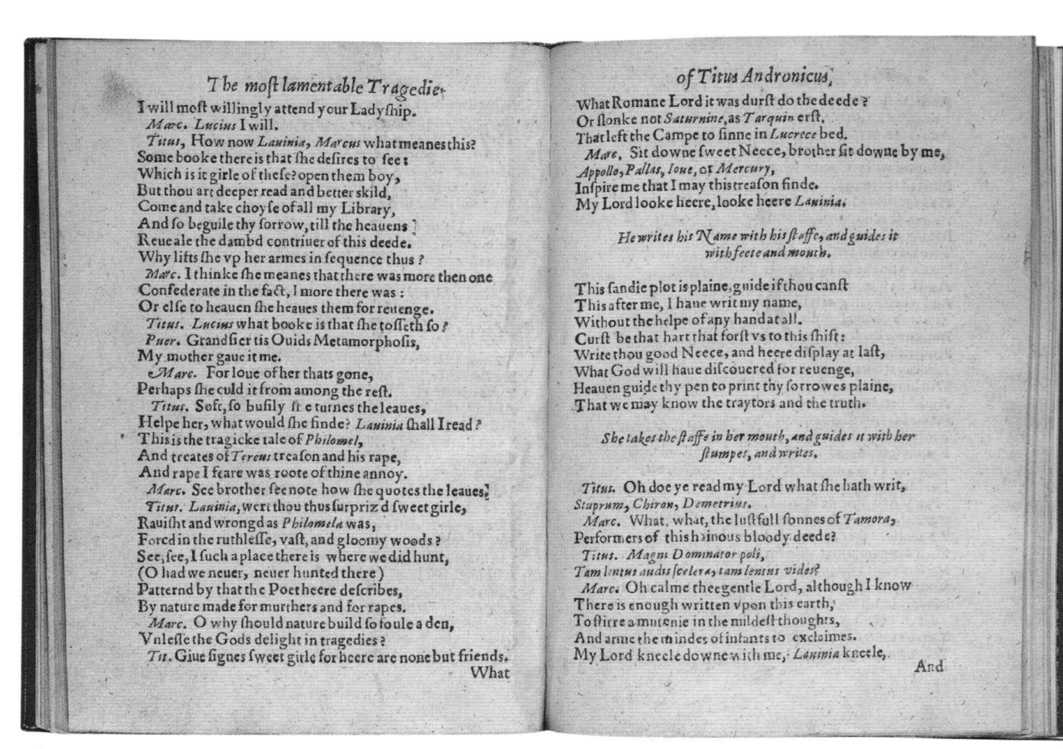

The most lamentable Tragedie

I will most willingly attend your Ladyship.
Marc. Lucius I will.
Titus, How now *Lauinia*, *Marcus* what meanes this?
Some booke there is that she desires to see:
Which is it girle of these? open them boy,
But thou art deeper read and better skild,
Come and take choyse of all my Library,
And so beguile thy sorrow, till the heauens
Reueale the dambd contriuer of this deede.
Why lifts she vp her armes in sequence thus?
Marc. I thinke she meanes that there was more then one
Confederate in the fact, I more there was:
Or else to heauen she heaues them for reuenge.
Titus. Lucius what booke is that she tosseth so?
Puer. Grandsier tis Ouids Metamorphosis,
My mother gaue it me.
Marc. For loue of her thats gone,
Perhaps she culd it from among the rest.
Titus. Soft, so busily she turnes the leaues,
Helpe her, what would she finde? *Lauinia* shall I read?
This is the tragicke tale of *Philomel*,
And treates of *Tereus* treason and his rape,
And rape I feare was roote of thine annoy.
Marc. See brother see note how she quotes the leaues.
Titus. Lauinia, wert thou thus surpriz d sweet girle,
Rauisht and wrongd as *Philomela* was,
Forced in the ruthlesse, vast, and gloomy woods?
See, see, I such a place there is where we did hunt,
(O had we neuer, neuer hunted there)
Patternd by that the Poet heere describes,
By nature made for murthers and for rapes.
Marc. O why should nature build so foule a den,
Vnlesse the Gods delight in tragedies?
Tit. Giue signes sweet girle for heere are none but friends.
What

of Titus Andronicus,

What Romane Lord it was durst do the deede?
Or slonke not *Saturnine*, as *Tarquin* erst,
That left the Campe to sinne in *Lucrece* bed.
Marc. Sit downe sweet Neece, brother sit downe by me,
Appollo, Pallas, Ioue, or *Mercury*,
Inspire me that I may this treason finde.
My Lord looke heere, looke heere *Lauinia*.

He writes his Name with his staffe, and guides it
with feete and mouth.

This sandie plot is plaine, guide if thou canst
This after me, I haue writ my name,
Without the helpe of any hand at all.
Curst be that hart that forst vs to this shift:
Write thou good Neece, and heere display at last,
What God will haue discouered for reuenge,
Heauen guide thy pen to print thy sorrowes plaine,
That we may know the traytors and the truth.

She takes the staffe in her mouth, and guides it with her
stumpes, and writes.

Titus. Oh doe ye read my Lord what she hath writ,
Stuprum, Chiron, Demetrius.
Marc. What, what, the lustfull sonnes of *Tamora*,
Performers of this hainous bloody deede?
Titus. Magni Dominator poli,
Tam lentus audis scelera, tam lentus vides?
Marc. Oh calme thee gentle Lord, although I know
There is enough written vpon this earth,
To stirre a mutenie in the mildest thoughts,
And arme the mindes of infants to exclaimes.
My Lord kneele downe with me, *Lauinia* kneele,
And

cat.101

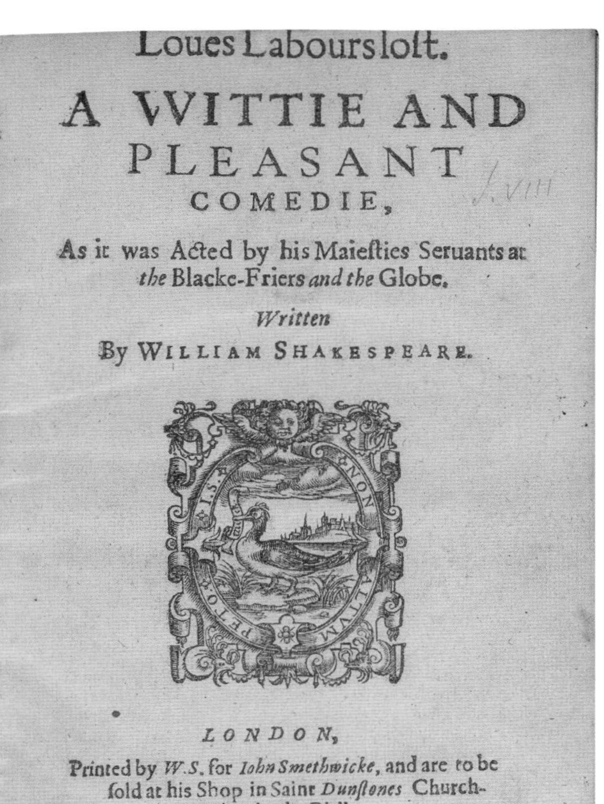

Loues Labours lost.

A WITTIE AND PLEASANT COMEDIE,

As it was Acted by his Maiesties Seruants at the Blacke-Friers and the Globe.

Written By WILLIAM SHAKESPEARE.

LONDON,

Printed by *W.S.* for *Iohn Smethwicke*, and are to be sold at his Shop in Saint *Dunstones* Church-yard vnder the Diall.

1631.

cat.103

THE MOST EXcellent and lamentable Tragedie, of Romeo and *Iuliet.*

Newly corrected, augmented, and amended:

As it hath bene sundry times publiquely acted, by the right Honourable the Lord Chamberlaine his Seruants.

LONDON

Printed by Thomas Creede, for Cuthbert Burby, and are to be sold at his shop neare the Exchange.

1599.

cat.105

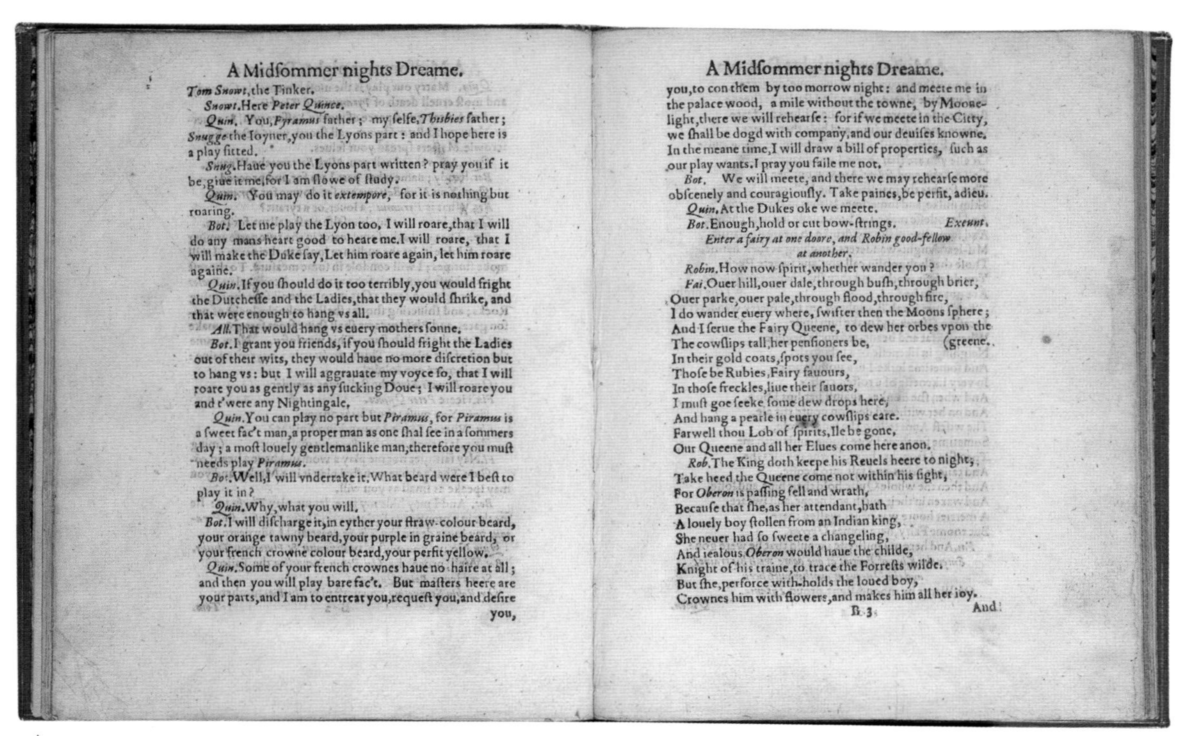

A Midsommer nights Dreame.

Tom Snowt, the Tinker.

Snowt. Here *Peter Quince*.

Quin. You, *Pyramus* father; my selfe, *Thisbies* father; *Snugge* the Ioyner, you the Lyons part: and I hope here is a play fitted.

Snug. Haue you the Lyons part written? pray you if it be, giue it me, for I am slowe of study.

Quin. You may do it *extempore*, for it is nothing but roaring.

Bot. Let me play the Lyon too, I will roare, that I will do any mans heart good to heare me. I will roare, that I will make the Duke say, Let him roare again, let him roare againe.

Quin. If you should do it too terribly, you would fright the Dutchesse and the Ladies, that they would shrike, and that were enough to hang vs all.

All. That would hang vs euery mothers sonne.

Bot. I grant you friends, if you should fright the Ladies out of their wits, they would haue no more discretion but to hang vs: but I will aggrauate my voyce so, that I will roare you as gently as any sucking Doue; I will roare you and t'were any Nightingale.

Quin. You can play no part but *Piramus*, for *Piramus* is a sweet fac't man, a proper man as one shal see in a sommers day; a most louely gentlemanlike man, therefore you must needs play *Piramus*.

Bot. Well, I will vndertake it. What beard were I best to play it in?

Quin. Why, what you will.

Bot. I will discharge it, in eyther your straw-colour beard, your orange tawny beard, your purple in graine beard, or your french crowne colour beard, your perfit yellow.

Quin. Some of your french crownes haue no haire at all; and then you will play bare fac't. But masters heere are your parts, and I am to entreat you, request you, and desire you,

A Midsommer nights Dreame.

you, to con them by too morrow night: and meete me in the palace wood, a mile without the towne, by Moonelight, there we will rehearse: for if we meete in the Citty, we shall be dogd with company, and our deuises knowne. In the meane time, I will draw a bill of properties, such as our play wants. I pray you faile me not.

Bot. We will meete, and there we may rehearse more obscenely and couragiously. Take paines, be perfit, adieu.

Quin. At the Dukes oke we meete.

Bot. Enough, hold or cut bow-strings. *Exeunt.*

Enter a fairy at one doore, and Robin good-fellow at another.

Robin. How now spirit, whether wander you?

Fai. Ouer hill, ouer dale, through bush, through brier,
Ouer parke, ouer pale, through flood, through fire,
I do wander euery where, swifter then the Moons sphere;
And I serue the Fairy Queene, to dew her orbes vpon the (greene.
The cowslips tall, her pensioners be,
In their gold coats, spots you see,
Those be Rubies, Fairy fauours,
In those freckles, liue their sauors,
I must goe seeke some dew drops here,
And hang a pearle in euery cowslips eare.
Farwell thou Lob of spirits, Ile be gone,
Our Queene and all her Elues come here anon.

Rob. The King doth keepe his Reuels heere to night,
Take heed the Queene come not within his sight,
For *Oberon* is passing fell and wrath,
Because that she, as her attendant, hath
A louely boy stollen from an Indian king,
She neuer had so sweete a changeling,
And iealous *Oberon* would haue the childe,
Knight of his traine, to trace the Forrests wilde.
But she, perforce with-holds the loued boy,
Crownes him with flowers, and makes him all her ioy.

B 3 And

cat.104

106.

THE Tragedie of King Richard the Second (*The Tragedy of King Richard II*), 1598 (first published 1597)

William Shakespeare

Printed book, 'Printed by Valentine Simmes for Andrew Wise, and are to be sold at his shop in Paules churchyard at the signe of the Angel' (known as Q2)
Quarto
The British Library, London, 1598, C.34 k.42, open at fol. H1vH2r

Provenance David Garrick, bequeathed in 1779

Richard II, written by 1595, first appeared in print in 1597 in an edition which, while saying that the play had 'beene publikely acted' by Shakespeare's company, the Lord Chamberlain's Men, did not name its author. The second edition, of 1598, does name Shakespeare and was reprinted in the same year. The play was popular partly because it was topical. It portrays the usurpation of Richard II by Harry Bolingbroke, Duke of Hereford, who during the course of the play becomes Henry IV. Elizabeth I, born in 1533, was clearly coming to the end of her reign, and had no obvious successor; she was often compared to Richard II, and feared, with justice, that she might suffer the same fate. In 1601 the Earl of Essex (cat.68) rebelled unsuccessfully against her rule, and was executed. The play was performed on the eve of the rebellion in an attempt to raise support for it. It was printed for the fourth time in 1608 in an edition of which the title page says that it has 'new additions of the Parliament sceane, and the deposing of King Richard'. The likelihood is that the added material had been written at the same time as the rest of the play but omitted when it was printed. The First Folio (1623) includes a better version of this scene, probably taken from a theatre manuscript.

Richard II is the first of Shakespeare's second-written series of English history plays which goes on to dramatize the reigns of Henry IV and Henry V. The pages on display show the meeting of the deposed King with his Queen as he is led to the Tower of London, where he is to be murdered. SW

107.

The moſt excellent Hiſtorie of the Merchant of Venice (*The Merchant of Venice*), 1600

William Shakespeare

Printed book, 'Printed by I. R. [James Roberts] for Thomas Heyes, and are to be sold in Paules Church-yard at the signe of the Greene Dragon' (known as Q1)
Quarto
The British Library, London, C.12 g.32, open at title page

Provenance From the Library of George III, presented in 1823

Illustrated on p.210

This is the first edition of *The Merchant of Venice*, probably written in 1596 or 1597, registered for publication in July 1598, when it was given the subtitle of *The Jew of Venice,* and eventually printed in 1600 in an exceptionally accurate text. Nineteen copies are known, one of which came to light only during the 1970s. This edition was reprinted in 1619, when it was falsely dated 1600, and also forms the basis for the text in the First Folio (cats 1, 117), for which a theatre manuscript was also consulted. The title page notes that the play had been performed by the Lord Chamberlain's Men, the company with which Shakespeare had worked since its foundation in 1594. Shakespeare is clearly identified as the author. We know of two performances before King James I at Whitehall in 1605. The subtitle ('With the extreame crueltie ...') emphasizes the villainy of Shylock, no doubt reflecting his prominence in performance, while incorrectly implying that he cuts off a pound of Antonio's flesh. In fact, his intention to do so is thwarted by Portia's skill.

The stories on which Shakespeare based his play, one of the pound of flesh, the other of a wooing by the choice of one among three caskets, were well known; Shakespeare used an Italian version of the former, told by Ser Giovanni Fiorentino in his collection of tales called *Il Pecorone* ('The Dunce') of 1558. SW

108.

THE HISTORY OF HENRIE THE FOVRTH (*Henry IV, Part 1*), 1599 (first published 1598)

William Shakespeare

Printed book, 'Printed by S. S. [Simon Stafford] for Andrew Wise, dwelling in Paules Churchyard, at the signe of the Angell' (version known as Q2)
Quarto
The British Library, London, C.34 k.6, open at title page

Provenance David Garrick, bequeathed in 1779

Illustrated on p.210

The First Quarto edition of the first of Shakespeare's Falstaff plays survives in only a single sheet, now in the Folger Shakespeare Library, Washington, DC. This copy is the third edition to be printed. The play caused a furore because in its earliest performances the character now known as Sir John Falstaff bore the name of Sir John Oldcastle. This historical character from the reign of Henry IV was the ancestor of William Brooke, Lord Cobham (d.1597), Lord Chamberlain and thus patron of Shakespeare's company at the time the play was first performed. It seems that the Cobham family objected so strongly to the portrayal of their ancestor as the old reprobate Falstaff that the company felt obliged to change the character's name. The play was registered for publication on 25 February 1598 with a reference to 'Sir Iohn Falstoff'. The existence of three editions within less than two years is no doubt a reflection of the play's early notoriety, as well of the instant popularity, which has continued over the centuries, of its principal comic character. His original name was restored in 1986 in the Oxford edition of *The Complete Works*, causing a furore even greater than its first use.

The History of Henrie the Fovrth, as it was originally called, is now known as Part One because it was soon followed by a sequel. It is the second play in Shakespeare's second-written sequence of plays on English history, taking off where *The Tragedy of King Richard II* ends. SW

109.

Much adoe about Nothing (*Much Ado about Nothing*), 1600 (first published 1600)

William Shakespeare

Printed book, 'Printed by V. S. [Valentine Simms] for Andrew Wise and William Aspley' (known as Q1)
Quarto
The British Library, London, C.34 k. 31, open at fol. G3vG4r

Provenance David Garrick, whose coat of arms is displayed in gold on both, bequeathed 1779

This is the First Quarto edition of Shakespeare's *Much Ado about Nothing*, printed in 1600; it was not reprinted until the First Folio of 1623 (cats 1, 117). The title page of the Quarto describes it as having been '*sundrie times publikely* acted by the right honourable, the Lord Chamberlaine his seruants. Written by William Shakespeare'. The play, written probably in or soon after 1598, was popular in its own time, and has become one of Shakespeare's best-loved comedies. This Quarto edition is of special interest in having very obviously been printed from Shakespeare's own papers, which had not been thoroughly revised. The clearest indication of this is the presence in the pages of the names of actors instead of the characters whom they would have played, showing that Shakespeare had particular individuals in mind for these roles. The actors Kemp and Couley (Cowley) here take the place of Dogberry and Verges, the play's two principal comic characters. Will Kemp (active 1585–1602) was for several years the Lord Chamberlain's Men's leading comic actor. He left the company in 1599, and, in the following year, famously morris-danced from London to Norwich, commemorating the feat in a book called *Kemps nine daies wonder* (fig.6, p.24). Richard Cowley, probably born in 1568, appears to have joined the company when it was formed, in 1584, and to have stayed with it until he died. SW

110.

THE Chronicle Hiftory of Henry the fift (*The Life of King Henry V*), 1619 (first published 1600)

William Shakespeare

Printed book, 'Printed [by William Jaggard] for T.P. [Thomas Pavier]', falsely dated 1608
(known as Q3 or 'the Pavier quarto')
Quarto
The British Library, London, C.34 k.14, open at title page

Provenance David Garrick, bequeathed in 1779

Illustrated on p.211

Henry V has a complicated textual history. It first appeared in print in 1600 in a short version, which, for instance, lacks the Choruses that form a substantial and greatly admired part of the text we know today. It was probably reconstructed from a full text by actors who had taken part in an early performance given, perhaps on tour, in an abbreviated version. The 1600 version was reprinted in 1602 and again in 1619, when it was falsely dated 1608; this is the edition illustrated here. It is one of a group of ten Shakespearian and pseudo-Shakespearian editions known as the Pavier quartos because they were printed without authority and in some cases with false dates by Thomas Pavier (active 1600–25), along with William Jaggard (1569–1623), who, with his son Isaac (active 1613–27), printed the First Folio (1623). The version of *Henry V* in the First Folio is much longer and clearly derives from Shakespeare's own papers.

This is the last written of Shakespeare's two sequences of plays dealing with English history from the reign of Richard II to Richard III. It is based on the *Chronicles* (1577, enlarged 1587) compiled by Raphael Holinshed (cat.62). This is one of the few Shakespeare plays to which we can assign a firm date of composition. The Chorus to Act V refers to the Earl of Essex's expedition to Ireland, indicating that it was written between 27 March and 28 September 1599. SW

111.

The Tragedie of HAMLET Prince of Denmarke (*Hamlet*), 1611 (first published 1603)

William Shakespeare

Printed book, 'Printed [by George Eld] for John Smethwicke, and are to be sold at his shoppe in Saint Dunstons Church yeard in Fleetstreet. Under the Diall' (known as Q3)
Quarto
The British Library, London, C. 34. k.4, open at title page

Provenance David Garrick, bequeathed 1779

Illustrated on p.211

The most influential play ever written, probably in 1600, made its first appearance in print in the modest form of a Quarto edition of 1603, in a short and particularly corrupt text ascribed to Shakespeare but apparently put together by actors who had performed in it. In what looks like an attempt to redeem Shakespeare's reputation, it was soon followed by the Quarto of 1604, which proclaims itself to be 'Newly imprinted and enlarged to almost as much againe as it was, according to the true and perfect coppie', and which appears to have been printed from Shakespeare's manuscript. The copy illustrated is of the first, 1611 reprint of that Quarto. A third, considerably revised text appeared in the First Folio of 1623. For centuries, as with *King Lear*, editors have attempted to create a single text by drawing eclectically on the early witnesses, but in recent years their independent status has been recognized.

The copy shown here is among the many play texts bequeathed to the British Library by the great actor David Garrick, who played the title role with enormous success from 1742, when he was twenty-five, until he retired, at the age of fifty-nine, in 1776. SW

112.

THE Historie of Troylus and Cresseida (*Troilus and Cressida*), 1609

William Shakespeare

Printed book, 'Imprinted by G. Eld for R. Bonian and H. Walley, and are to be sold at the spred Eagle in Paules Church-yeard, over against the great north doore' (known as Q1a)
Quarto
The British Library, London, 163.i.12, open at title page

Provenance George Steevens, c.1800; John Ker, 3rd Duke of Roxburgh; from the Library of George III, presented in 1823

This is a copy of the second issue of the first edition of *Troilus and Cressida*. The play has a complicated textual history. It was registered for publication on 7 February 1603, when it was said to be in the repertoire of the Lord Chamberlain's Men. Publication did not follow until 1609, when it was newly registered and was said again, on its title page, to have been 'acted by the Kings Maiesties seruants [formerly the Lord Chamberlain's Men] at the Globe'.

During the printing, however, this title page was replaced by a different one (known as a 'cancel'), omitting the reference to performance and adding an anonymous, cryptic, but cleverly written, epistle which represents the most substantial early piece of Shakespeare criticism. Addressed by 'A neuer writer, to an euer reader', it states that this is 'a new play, neuer stal'd with the Stage [never made common by being performed on the public stage], neuer clapper-clawd [praised with clapping] with the palmes of the vulger, and yet passing full of the palme commicall [graced with the laurels – palm branches – of comedy]'.

When the play came to be included in the First Folio of 1623 it was to have been printed from the Quarto, but was apparently withdrawn because the copyright was not available, and was replaced by *Timon of Athens*. At the last minute, however – too late for the play to be listed in the table of contents – a substantially different, theatrical text became available and the play was printed from a copy of the Quarto annotated with reference to it. The existence of a theatre manuscript apparently revised by Shakespeare indicates that the play had indeed been acted, though not necessarily by 1603.

Troilus and Cressida, based on events of the Trojan War, is the most philosophical of all Shakespeare's plays, a bitter tragicomedy of war and sex. SW

113.

THE Tragedy of Othello, The Moore of Venice (*Othello*), 1622

William Shakespeare

Printed book; 'Printed by N.O. [Nicholas Okes] for Thomas Walkley, and are to be sold at his shop, at the Eagle and Child, in Brittans Bursse' (known as Q1)
Quarto
The British Library, London, 34 k.33, open at fol. D2vD3r

Provenance Marmaduke Ffarrels; David Garrick, bequeathed in 1779

This is the first edition of *Othello*, one of Shakespeare's greatest tragedies, written around 1603 and performed at court, before King James I, in 1604. It was not printed until 1622, in the only early Quarto edition of any of Shakespeare's plays to be divided into acts (with the exception of Act III). The title page reads: 'The Tragœdy of Othello, The Moore of Venice. *As it hath beene diuerse times acted at the* Globe, and at the Black-Friers, by *his Maiesties Seruants*. Written by William Shakespeare.' In 1623 it reappeared in a different, longer version in the First Folio.

Shakespeare based the play on a story by the Italian, Giovanni Battista Giraldi Cinthio (1504–73), published in his *Hecatommithi* (1565), a collection of short tales, which Shakespeare appears to have read in the original. In Act I, Iago devises his plot to convince Othello that his wife, Desdemona, has committed adultery with Cassio. Then at the start of Act II, the action moves from Venice to Cyprus, where the Governor, Montano, awaits the arrival through a storm at sea of Othello and Desdemona. This copy was bequeathed to the British Library by David Garrick, the great eighteenth-century actor, who played both Othello and Iago. The final pages of the printed text are missing and have been supplied in manuscript by an early owner. SW

The most excellent
Historie of the *Merchant of Venice.*

VVith the extreame crueltie of *Shylocke* the Iewe towards the sayd Merchant, in cutting a iust pound of his flesh: and the obtayning of *Portia* by the choyse of three chests.

As it hath beene diuers times acted by the Lord Chamberlaine his Seruants.

Written by William Shakespeare.

AT LONDON,
Printed by *I. R.* for Thomas Heyes, and are to be sold in Paules Church-yard, at the signe of the Greene Dragon.
1600.

cat.107

THE
HISTORY OF
HENRIE THE
FOVRTH;

With the battell at Shrewsburie, *betweene the King and Lord* Henry Percy, *surnamed* Henry Hotspur of the North.

VVith the humorous conceits of Sir Iohn Falstalffe.

Newly corrected by *W. Shake-speare.*

AT LONDON,
Printed by *S. S.* for *Andrew VVise*, dwelling in Paules Churchyard, at the signe of the Angell. 1599.

cat.108

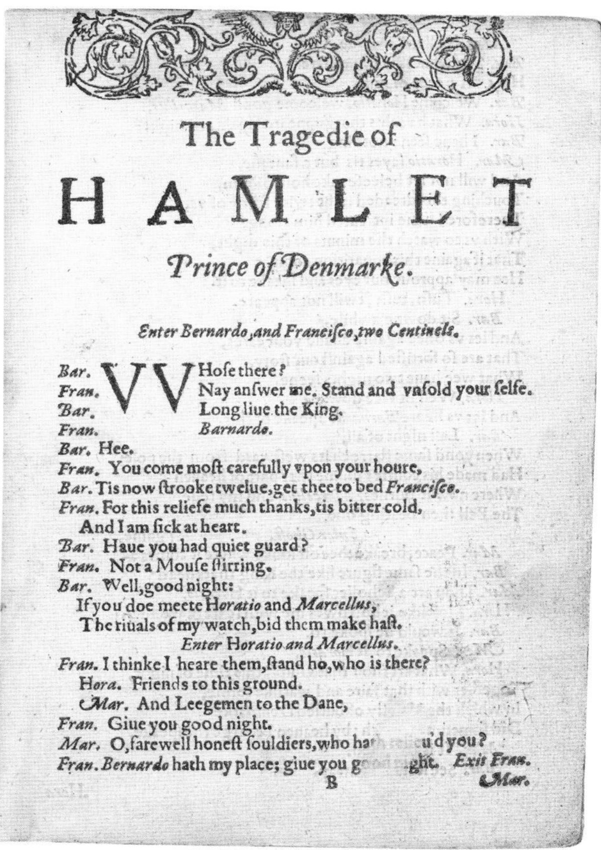

The Tragedie of

HAMLET

Prince of Denmarke.

Enter Bernardo, and Francisco, two Centinels.

Bar. VVHose there?
Fran. Nay anſwer me. Stand and vnfold your ſelfe.
Bar. Long liue the King.
Fran. *Barnardo.*
Bar. Hee.
Fran. You come moſt carefully vpon your houre,
Bar. Tis now ſtrooke twelue, get thee to bed *Franciſco.*
Fran. For this reliefe much thanks, tis bitter cold,
And I am ſick at heart.
Bar. Haue you had quiet guard?
Fran. Not a Mouſe ſtirring.
Bar. Well, good night:
If you doe meete *Horatio* and *Marcellus*,
The riuals of my watch, bid them make haſt.
Enter Horatio and Marcellus.
Fran. I thinke I heare them, ſtand ho, who is there?
Hora. Friends to this ground.
Mar. And Leegemen to the Dane,
Fran. Giue you good night.
Mar. O, farewell honeſt ſouldiers, who ha[illegible]u'd you?
Fran. *Bernardo* hath my place; giue you g[illegible]ght. *Exit Fran.*
B *Mar.*

cat.111

THE
Chronicle Hiſtory
of Henry the fift, with his
battell fought at *Agin Court* in
France. Together with an-
cient Piſtoll.

*As it hath bene ſundry times playd by the Right Honou-
rable the Lord Chamberlaine his
Seruants.*

Printed for *T. P.* 1608.

cat.110

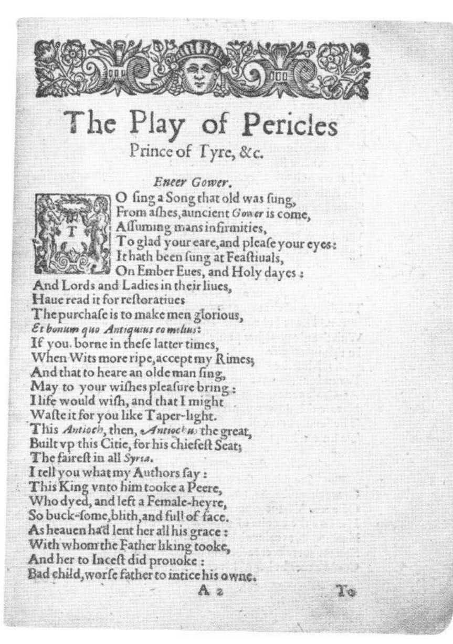

The Play of Pericles
Prince of Tyre, &c.

Eneer Gower.

TO ſing a Song that old was ſung,
From aſhes, auncient *Gower* is come,
Aſſuming mans infirmities,
To glad your eare, and pleaſe your eyes:
It hath been ſung at Feaſtiuals,
On Ember Eues, and Holy dayes:
And Lords and Ladies in their liues,
Haue read it for reſtoratiues
The purchaſe is to make men glorious,
Et bonum quo Antiquius eo melius:
If you. borne in theſe latter times,
When Wits more ripe, accept my Rimes;
And that to heare an olde man ſing,
May to your wiſhes pleaſure bring:
I life would wiſh, and that I might
Waſte it for you like Taper-light.
This *Antioch*, then, *Antiochus* the great,
Built vp this Citie, for his chiefeſt Seat;
The faireſt in all *Syria.*
I tell you what my Authors ſay:
This King vnto him tooke a Peere,
Who dyed, and left a Female-heyre,
So buck-ſome, blith, and full of face.
As heauen had lent her all his grace:
With whom the Father liking tooke,
And her to Inceſt did prouoke:
Bad child, worſe father to intice his owne.
A 2 To

cat.115

114.
M. William Shak-speare: HIS True Chronicle Historie of the life and death of King LEAR and his three Daughters (*King Lear*), 1608

William Shakespeare

Printed book, 'Printed [by Nicholas Okes] for Nathaniel Butter, and are to be sold at his shop in Pauls Church-yard at the signe of the Pide Bull neere St. Austins Gate' (known as Q1)
Quarto
The British Library, London, C.34 k.17, fol. G3v–G4r

Provenance Thomas Middleton; John Cooper; Halliwell-Phillipps, 1858

This is the first edition of what many consider to be Shakespeare's greatest play, written around 1605–6. The title page, which gives unusual prominence to Shakespeare's name, claims that the tragedy '*was played before the Kings Maiestie at Whitehall vpon S.* Stephans *night in Christmas Hollidayes*'. The text is very poorly printed, with numerous obvious errors, resulting at times in unintelligibility. It was long suspected to have been put together from actors' memories, but now seems more likely to have been printed from Shakespeare's own papers. It was reprinted in 1619, and again in 1655, with a number of intelligent but unauthoritative corrections.

The text printed in the First Folio is radically different. It adds about 100 lines and omits around 300, including a whole scene in which the mad Lear stages a mock trial of his evil daughters, Goneril (Gonorill or Gonoril) and Regan. It has innumerable differences of wording and phrasing, allocates speeches to different characters, and varies the action. For centuries editors, assuming that both texts derive from a single lost original, conflated them, but in 1986 the Oxford editors, acting on the belief that the later text represents a revised version of the earlier, printed them as two separate plays. SW

115.
The Play of Pericles (*Pericles*), 1609

William Shakespeare and George Wilkins (active 1603–8)

Printed book, 'Imprinted at London: [by William White and Thomas Creede] for Henry Gosson, and are to be sold at the signe of the Sunne in Pater-noster row, &c.' (known as Q1)
Quarto
The British Library, London, C.34 k.36, open at sig. A2r

Provenance David Garrick, bequeathed in 1779

Illustrated on p.211

This is a copy of the first edition of a play which recent scholarship – in spite of the title-page ascription to Shakespeare – regards as the result of a collaboration between him and George Wilkins. A domestic tragedy by Wilkins, *The Miseries of Inforst Mariage*, based on a horrifying real-life story of murders that took place in Yorkshire in 1605, was performed by the King's Men soon after the events it depicts. It appeared in four separate editions from 1607 to 1637. Wilkins also wrote a prose version of the story of Pericles, *The Painfull Aduentures of Pericles Prince of Tyre, Being* The true History of the Play of *Pericles,* as it was lately presented by the worthy and ancient Poet *John Gower,* published in 1608, a year before the play, but nevertheless incorporating passages from it. The play text is so badly printed that editors are led to draw on the novel to patch it up. Nevertheless, *Pericles*, which tells of the wanderings over a period of many years of its hero, of the apparent death of his wife, Thaisa, and of the birth, loss and recovery of his daughter, Marina (born at sea), has passages of great power and beauty, most of all in the climactic scene in which Pericles, who has fallen into a coma, is restored to life by his long-lost daughter. It is based in part on the story of Apollonius of Tyre as told in the poem *Confessio Amantis* by John Gower (*c*.1330–1408), who is the play's narrator. Doubts about whether Shakespeare wrote the whole play are reinforced by the fact that it was not included in the First Folio of 1623. It was added to the second issue of the Third Folio in 1664. SW

116.

THE RAIGNE OF KING EDVVARD the third (*Edward III*), 1596

William Shakespeare?

Printed book; 'Printed for Cuthbert Burby' (known as Q1)
Quarto
The British Library, London, C.21.c.50, open at title page

Provenance Purchased by the British Museum Library before 1787–1812

Printed anonymously in 1596 with the statement that it had been '*sundrie times plaied about the Citie of London*', and registered for publication in the previous December, this history play was not included in the First Folio, as we should expect if it had been known to be entirely by Shakespeare. It was, however, attributed to him in an unreliable catalogue of 1656, and again by the scholar Edward Capell (1713–81) in 1760. Since then it has hovered uneasily on the fringes of the Shakespeare canon, with many scholars supposing that Shakespeare might have written at least the scenes involving the Countess of Shrewsbury. In recent years the development of increasingly sophisticated tests for authorship, along with growing evidence that Shakespeare collaborated with other writers, especially in the early and later parts of his career, has strengthened the case for supposing that he was at least partly responsible for the play. Although in 1986 it was not included in the Oxford edition of *The Complete Works*, it was added as a collaborative play to the revised second edition of 2005.

Like Shakespeare plays of the same period, such as *The Tragedy of King Richard II* and *The Life and Death of King John*, it is written entirely in verse. Its treatment of historical events, deriving from the 1535 translation by Lord Berners of Froissart's *Chronicles*, is loose. Like *The Life of King Henry V*, it is concerned with wars between England and France; Edward's son the Black Prince is a principal character. In the main scenes ascribed to Shakespeare, Edward attempts in vain to seduce the Countess of Salisbury, expressing his passion in lyrical verse that would be at home in one of Shakespeare's early plays such as *The Two Gentlemen of Verona*. SW

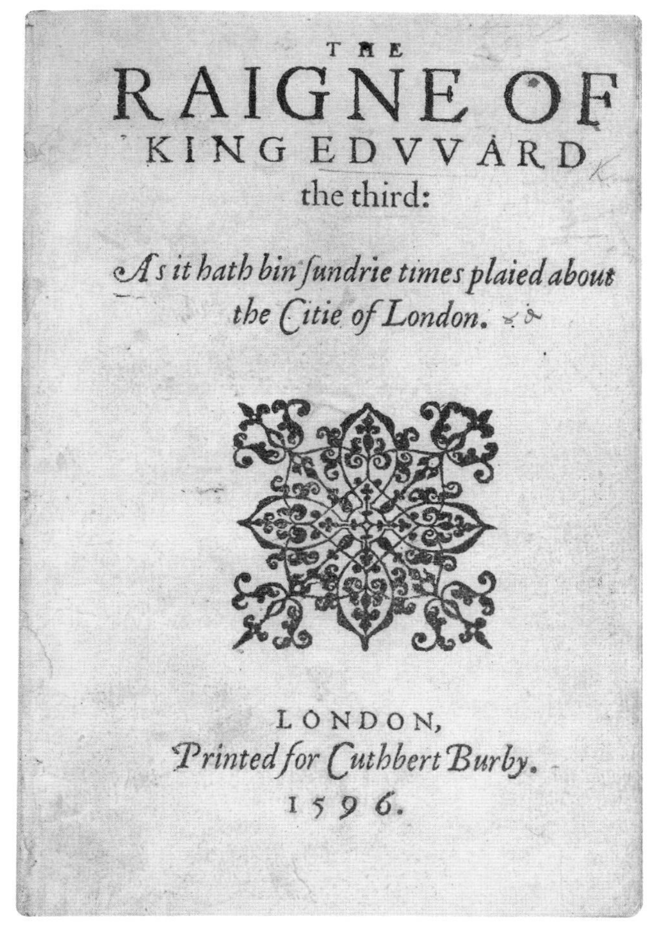
THE
RAIGNE OF
KING EDVVARD
the third:
As it hath bin sundrie times plaied about the Citie of London.

LONDON,
Printed for Cuthbert Burby.
1596.

117. *MR. WILLIAM SHAKESPEARES COMEDIES, HISTORIES, & TRAGEDIES. Publifhed according to the True Originall Copies* (First Folio), 1623

William Shakespeare

Printed book, 'Printed by Isaac Jaggard, and Ed. Blount'
Folio
The Bodleian Library, University of Oxford, Arch G c. 8, open at the list of plays

Provenance Edmond Malone (1741–1812); Richard, Lord Sunderlin (1738–1816), who in 1815 presented it to the University of Oxford

Literature W.W. Greg, *The Shakespeare First Folio* (Clarendon Press, Oxford, 1956); Charlton Hinman, *The Printing and Proof-Reading of the First Folio of Shakespeare*, 2 vols (Clarendon Press, Oxford, 1963); Anthony James West, *The Shakespeare First Folio: The History of the Book, An Account of the First Folio Based on its Sales and Prices, 1623–2000*, vol.1 (Oxford University Press, Oxford, 2001); *A New Worldwide Census of First Folios*, vol.2 (Oxford University Press, Oxford, 2003)

The First Folio edition of 'MR WILLIAM SHAKESPEARES COMEDIES, HISTORIES, AND TRAGEDIES', published in 1623, seven years after he died, is one of the world's most important books. Without it we should almost certainly have no texts of sixteen of his most important plays, including *Macbeth*, *Antony and Cleopatra*, *Twelfth Night*, *As You Like It* and *The Tempest*, which were published here for the first time, along with variant texts of many other plays. The engraved frontispiece is the exceptionally rare first state of the portrait of Shakespeare by Martin Droeshout, one of the very few likenesses with any claim to authenticity (cat.1). The volume also contains important tributes to Shakespeare, such as Ben Jonson's long poem 'To the memory of my beloued, The AVTHOR MR. WILLIAM SHAKESPEARE: AND what he hath left vs', in which he addresses Shakespeare as '*Sweet Swan of* Auon!' and says '*He was not of an age, but for all time*!'

The book was compiled by Shakespeare's fellow actors John Heminges and Henry Condell and dedicated to the brothers William (1580–1630) and Philip (1584–1650) Herbert, Earls of Pembroke and Montgomery, who are described as Shakespeare's admirers and patrons (see cat.87). It was reprinted in 1632, 1663 and 1685.

Probably about 1,000 copies of the first edition were printed, selling for between 15*s* (unbound) and £1. Because of its size, far more copies of the Folio survive than of Quarto editions of single plays. Worldwide, around 250 are known, in various states of preservation; some eighty are in the Folger Shakespeare Library, Washington, DC.

The copy illustrated belonged to the great Shakespeare scholar and editor, Edmond Malone (1741–1812). To it he has added nineteen additional manuscripts and later engravings, some of them representing Shakespeare, which are pasted on new leaves and bound among the opening pages. Among them is an early letter concerning the shortage of dogs for bear-baiting. The page shown lists the plays, which are separated into Comedies, Histories and Tragedies, and Malone has added by hand the title of 'Troylus & Cressida'. This play was omitted from the original list and added to the volume at a late stage in its printing (cat.111). SW

A CATALOGVE of the seuerall Comedies, Histories, and Tragedies contained in this Volume.

COMEDIES.

HISTORIES.

TRAGEDIES.

†. This play seems to have been inadvertently omitted by the first Editors & afterwards printed & inserted between the Histories & Tragedies.— This appears by its not being mentioned in this table (which could not have been printed till the whole work was finished) & also by its being unpaged — except only on one leaf — E.M.

MR. WILLIAM SHAKESPEARES

COMEDIES, HISTORIES, & TRAGEDIES.

Publiſhed according to the True Originall Copies.

LONDON

Printed by Iſaac Iaggard, and Ed. Blount. 1623.

NATIONAL IDENTITY AND THE AFTERLIFE OF SHAKESPEARE'S PORTRAITS

MARCIA POINTON

Anyone travelling in the British Isles can be left in no doubt that Shakespeare is alive and well. In Stratford-upon-Avon's Henley Street, tourists gather to photograph the Bard's birthplace or to visit 'the world of Shakespeare'. The represented facial features that have become as familiar as those of Alexander the Great, Socrates or the Emperor Augustus, accost us from pub signs, switch cards,[1] book spines and advertisements for everything from auctions of car number plates to whisky. Shakespeare's head is now an accepted emblem – something to be readily appropriated for diverse purposes.

From the seventeenth century onwards there has been intense interest in Shakespeare's portrait, in his actual appearance, as a way of reaching a greater understanding of the man himself. This essay is about the *life* of the Bard in the sense of the 'afterlife', or the mythologization of an historic and literary personality through pictorial imagery. When we speak of historic characters what we refer to as 'portraits' are often only remotely connected with the subjects whose names these images or sculptures bear.

There are no eyewitness accounts of Shakespeare's likeness. It is impossible to authenticate beyond doubt the image of Shakespeare against any known reality. Even if documentation of this kind had survived, we should still need to regard it as a form of interpretation. Portraits – and I include photographic portraits – are fictions that work with the idea of the real, arranging a series of motifs that are associated with the corporeal and physiological presence of a sitter into a synthetic image. Depicted 'likeness' and 'truth to life' are pictorial effects produced by artists translating a multitude of sightings and other sense impressions, as well as bodies of knowledge derived from third parties about character and appearance, onto a two-dimensional surface. Our longing to know something about the appearance of great and famous individuals, as well as about those we love and hate, provides room for the imagination to roam, space for fantasy. The very absence of an uncontested portrait from Shakespeare's own lifetime – his elusive identity – merely sharpens this process, makes the quest more urgent, and the prize more unattainable.

The cultural vacuum ensured by the absence of an undisputed portrait has, it seems, licensed the displacement of the fascination with the historical individual, Shakespeare, onto his surroundings. We have Goethe's Weimar, Mozart's Vienna, and Wordsworth's Grasmere, as well as a host of other locations defined by their

William Shakespeare, title page of First Folio, 1623 (cat.117)

literary associations. In the case of Shakespeare, we can perhaps see at work in a particularly acute way the process of reification whereby the material remnants come to stand in for a past that is understood to be subliminal. Visiting Stratford for the first time in 1898, this writer epitomizes this process:

> To stand beneath the roof that first sheltered Shakespeare and to let one's fancy flit about the rooms, is to experience a delight ... one can then understand and appreciate the feeling which brings men and women from far lands ... to this little Midland town, that they may stand in the small, mean-looking apartment where Shakespeare was born. For Americans, especially, it is easy to see wherein the fascination lies – coming ... to this quiet, old-world place ... they are deeply moved when they contemplate the unpretentious nature of the home into which 'the most imperial intellect of all time' was born.[2]

Shakespeare – as imaged through the topography of his birthplace – offers an opportunity for the materialization of particular personal acts of imagination. When Sir Walter Scott visited Stratford in April 1828, he wrote in his journal: 'We visited the tomb of the mighty wizard. It is in the bad taste of James I's reign but what a magic does the locality possess. There are stately monuments of forgotten families but when you have seen Shakespeare what care we for all the rest?'[3]

In this essay I shall suggest that images deriving from portraits of Shakespeare, and in particular from the Chandos portrait (cat.3), offer an exceptionally well-documented example of portraiture functioning in the creation of narratives of national identity. In our imagination, our desire for a lost past, for national greatness, for what is real and authentic – as opposed to ephemeral – can be played out. Such fantasies all depend ultimately upon the conviction that Shakespeare, the historical subject, can be grasped and known. Shakespeare portraiture is a story of the triumph of art over life, and of desire over knowledge. Over time this dynamic has been strongly sustained by national institutions, such as the National Portrait Gallery, London, whose re-opening to its current building in 1896 was celebrated in *Punch* with a cartoon in which portraits of Shakespeare and his founding companions in the national pantheon have literally come alive and are led smiling by Britannia into their new home.[4]

Within the traditions of portrait iconography the customary way of representing individuals is to give them attributes through which they may be identified. In the case of a writer like Shakespeare, his attributes are his plays. There is, therefore, a strong tendency to portray him with his characters; in an explicit analogy with the Old Testament act of creation he appears as their creator. It is thus, flanked by Falstaff, Hal and other characters, that Shakespeare appears in the statue by Lord Ronald Gower erected in Stratford in 1908, in William Blake's portrait bust of 1800 for William Hayley's library at Felpham, now in Manchester City Art Gallery, and in nineteenth-century frontispieces to popular editions of the works, such as that by the Dalziel Brothers to *Knight's Pictorial Shakespeare*.[5]

The difficulty of producing a posthumous likeness of a writer, a likeness that must be an imaginative projection however successfully it draws on earlier effigies, engravings and other representations, is a consequence of the contested history of

'Shakespeare'; the name Shakespeare can never merely signify an individual in history, its meanings are forever changing, and forever challenging classification. The paradox of an image that will always be overwhelmed by the subject's words is already recognized, of course, in Ben Jonson's famous lines to accompany the frontispiece to the First Folio: 'O, could he but have drawne his wit/As well in brasse, as he hath hit/His face, the Print would then surpasse/All, that was ever writ in brasse./But since he cannot, Reader, looke/Not on his Picture, but his Booke.' These lines constitute an instruction to ignore the image because the poet's words are his portrait.

When I refer to 'Shakespeare', I intend the name to be understood as a signifier of Jacobean culture, English greatness, dramatic excellence. One consequence of the compelling range of 'Shakespeare' is that his figure is incorporated into dramatic tableaux shaped by popular contemporary literary notions and performance practice as for example, with Shakespeare seated, Hamlet-like, in his study surrounded by volumes of Plutarch and Holinshed, in an engraving of *c.*1860 (by Albert Payne after G.E. Hicks, after a no longer extant late eighteenth-century painting by Benjamin Wilson), and the German lithograph after J.F.A. Schrader in which Shakespeare, arrested for poaching in the Charlecote estate, is brought before Sir Thomas Lucy (fig.59).[6]

There are just a few serious historical contenders as portraits of Shakespeare; some of them have served as effigies and types on which artists and sculptors have based their work. There are other images that have functioned as portraits for owners, viewers and consumers and which are, therefore, also portraits of Shakespeare in the sociological sense. The Droeshout type – from the engraving by Martin Droeshout the Younger

fig.62 **Shakespeare arrested for poaching on the Charlecote estate**, 19th century
Lithograph after J.F.A. Schrader
Shakespeare Birthplace Trust

(1601–after 1639) that appeared in the First Folio in 1623 (cat.1) – is that used by Blake and by Picasso, who subverted the revered head of Shakespeare in a drawing that became a household image through the Cambridge University Press cover of *The New Shakespeare* (fig.60).[7] It often reappears, sometimes half length, as in the original, but more often simply head and shoulders. The Droeshout type is also that most frequently reproduced by publishers for dust-jackets of the works.

The Chandos portrait has a long history as the matrix for a vast number of popular replicas; it was used by the publisher Jacob Tonson the Elder (1655–1736) as his shop sign and trademark (see, for example the title page of *The Spectator*). The basic Tonson bust was elaborated by an unknown engraver into a full-length figure in a graceful Apollo Belvedere derived posture standing before an Anne Hathaway type cottage.[8] Gerard Van der Gucht 'Frenchified' Chandos with allegorical figures as early as 1709, George Vertue reversed the image in 1719 for the folio series of heads published by Houbraken, and by the mid eighteenth century it was widely known as a head and shoulders with, or without, rococo frame and ornament.[9] It provided the portrait image for De Rapin's *History of England* of 1725 (fig.61), and was meticulously copied by Ozias Humphrey in 1783 for the Shakespeare editor, Malone, who carefully recorded the provenance of both the original and his drawing on 29 June 1784.[10] The Chandos portrait also provided the inspiration for many busts, as in the garden scene by John Hamilton Mortimer representing the Powell family in 1768 (Garrick Club, London) and in John Flaxman's monument to George Steevens of 1800.[11] It remained immensely popular throughout the nineteenth century[12] and its appeal remains undiminished today, as the souvenir shops of Stratford-upon-Avon testify.

What, then, does this vast array of imagery contribute to what Benedict Anderson in 1983 called the creation of 'imagined communities'? Born before the Act of Union of 1707 that brought together England, Wales and Scotland under one legislature, Shakespeare was undoubtedly English and, despite a slight tendency to associate him with a unified British identity, he has remained quintessentially a signifier of Englishness – hence the poignancy of Sir Walter Scott's encounter with his effigy, the Scottish bard moved at contemplating the site of the mortal remains of his great English predecessor.

For the eighteenth century, Shakespeare represented what was English and what was modern. Thus in Hogarth's virulent attack upon the Italophile Lord Burlington, *Masquerades and Operas* (1724),[13] the works of Shakespeare, Pope and Swift are being carted away before William Kent's Palladian gateway crowned by busts of Raphael and Michelangelo. Shakespeare was thus a key player in the battle of the ancients versus the moderns. Here imagery could more accurately strike its target than words, since by merely setting Shakespeare's bust alongside those of Tasso or Cervantes the point could be made that these moderns were a match for Homer and Virgil. Nor was there any need in imagery to account for the vagaries of Shakespeare's style when judged by the canon of Racine or Corneille. In the grounds of Stowe House in Buckinghamshire, where William Kent designed for Lord Cobham a Temple of British Worthies in the 1730s, Shakespeare heads a pantheon of British literati. Moreover, the medium of the portrait bust with its associations with imperial Rome is inescapably nationalistic.

fig.60 **Cover of The New Shakespeare edition of *As You Like It*,** 1971
Line drawing of Shakespeare by Pablo Picasso, 1968
Cambridge University Press, Cambridge

fig.61 **Shakespeare portrait from De Rapin's *History of England***, 1785
John Goldar, John Taylor
Line engraving, 290mm × 199mm (11 3/8 × 7 7/8 in)
National Portrait Gallery, London (NPG D20572)

That Shakespeare is representative of national identity can be demonstrated most clearly when we observe that in times of war or of threatened hostilities to the nation, his image is constructed and reproduced with particular intensity. Indeed, the most famous image of Shakespeare after the Chandos portrait, his memorial in Westminster Abbey, was erected at a moment of great national anxiety. It is an entirely synthetic production, by the sculptor Peter Scheemakers, after a design by William Kent. It combines the pointed beard and domed head of the effigy in Holy Trinity Church, Stratford-upon-Avon, dating from *c.*1623 (cat.2), with the déshabillé relaxation of the Chandos portrait. The figure was given the 'scissor leg' pose fashionable in eighteenth-century portraiture, but with a slight stiffness, alluding perhaps to Nicholas Hilliard's famous miniature *Young Man among Roses* (1585–95). The effigy wears the eighteenth-century version of Van Dyck costume that was fashionable among the sitters of Reynolds and Gainsborough and is accompanied by busts of Elizabeth I, Henry V and Richard III. The monument is a profoundly nationalistic gesture: it was erected as a result of a campaign in 1739 when England was preparing for war with France.[14] From 1740 to 1741 it was installed in Poet's Corner in the south-west transept of Westminster Abbey. The portrait heads carved on the base emphasize the nationalist narrative. Elizabeth was the monarch of Shakespeare's youth and stood for invincibility before the Spanish Armada, and Henry V was Shakespeare's most charismatic warlord. It is surely significant that this, rather than the Stratford effigy or the Chandos portrait, was used in the early years of Margaret Thatcher's government for the £20 note in the first Bank of England series to carry historic portraits (fig.62).

Boydell's Shakespeare Gallery, which opened in 1789, may be understood at one level as a direct response to the threat of Napoleon.[15] It is therefore ironic that the engraver and publisher John Boydell (active 1720–1804) was ruined by the fact that the war stopped the French market for English prints. A major work of sculpture to serve both as grand entrance to the Gallery in Pall Mall and, in an engraving by Benjamin Smith of 1796, as the frontispiece (the metaphorical entrance) to the collection of engravings that he commissioned after the paintings displayed in the Gallery, was commissioned by Boydell from Thomas Banks R.A. The engraving also appeared, with a valuable record of the façade of this now demolished edifice, in the *European Magazine*. The alto-relievo shows Shakespeare poised elegantly on a rocky summit (the pinnacle of Parnassus, no doubt), accompanied by the muse of Painting on the right and Drama on the left. It eventually found a resting place in a quiet corner of New Place Gardens in Stratford-upon-Avon.[16]

fig.62 **£20 banknote** (detail), 1980s
The Bank of England, London

Shakespeare served also as a national icon during the First and the Second World Wars.[17] Wartime seems to have provoked bouts of discovery; while claims are made periodically for unknown portraits of Shakespeare from the late seventeenth century to our own day, it is the case that they occur more frequently in wartime and that such claims at those times are framed within a particular nationalist rhetoric. The publication in 1917 of a Chandos-derived portrait of Shakespeare surrounded by rousing passages from Shakespeare's works pertaining to England, and intended for use in schools, invoked intense nationalist nostalgia (cat.63).[18] The mood of the Great War invocations of Shakespeare is summed up by Arthur St John Adcock in 1914 in an article headed 'The Poetry of War' published in a journal called *The Reader*. Adcock self-righteously defends the nation of shopkeepers, the greatest of whom he claims was Shakespeare, against the Prussians who cultivate fierce moustaches and wear spiked helmets. This article is accompanied by a bust of Shakespeare and a quotation from *The Second Part of Henry VI* (Act III, Scene ii, line 233): 'Thrice is he armed that hath his quarrel just'.[19]

If a Shakespeare is needed, one will certainly be found. The significance of discourses and representations of historic cultural materials for political and ideological ends is vividly demonstrated at the end of Second World War, when, in August 1948, in the British sector of Berlin, the population was entertained to a concert of Tudor music by the Cambridge madrigal society, performances of *Measure for Measure* (with its appropriately pacific themes) and (less explicably) John Webster's *The White Devil* by the Marlowe Society, along with lectures on Shakespeare by such luminaries as Allardyce Nicoll and Henry Charlton. The concert took place in a spacious mansion in the Grunewald district; in an exaggerated imperialist flourish, the house was decorated for the occasion with the flags of St George and St Andrew, while British soldiers dressed up as beefeaters stood guard.

Shakespeare portraits were eminently open to appropriation and adaptation. In 1762, David Garrick (1717–79), the distinguished Shakespearean actor, built a Shakespeare Temple in his garden beside the Thames at Twickenham. The statue by Louis-François Roubiliac now in the British Museum was the centrepiece; Garrick was

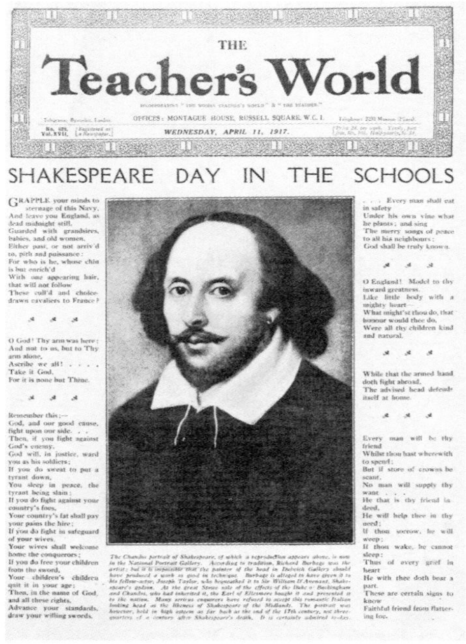

THE
Teacher's World

OFFICES: MONTAGUE HOUSE, RUSSELL SQUARE, W.C. 1.

WEDNESDAY, APRIL 11, 1917.

SHAKESPEARE DAY IN THE SCHOOLS

GRAPPLE your minds to sternage of this Navy,
And leave you England, as dead midnight still,
Guarded with grandsires, babies, and old women,
Either past, or not arriv'd to, pith and puissance:
For who is he, whose chin is but enrich'd
With one appearing hair, that will not follow
These cull'd and choice-drawn cavaliers to France?

O God! Thy arm was here;
And not to us, but to Thy arm alone,
Ascribe we all! . . . .
Take it God,
For it is none but Thine.

Remember this;—
God, and our good cause, fight upon our side. . .
Then, if you fight against God's enemy,
God will, in justice, ward you as his soldiers;
If you do sweat to put a tyrant down,
You sleep in peace, the tyrant being slain;
If you do fight against your country's foes,
Your country's fat shall pay your pains the hire;
If you do fight in safeguard of your wives,
Your wives shall welcome home the conquerors;
If you do free your children from the sword,
Your children's children quit it in your age;
Then, in the name of God, and all these rights,
Advance your standards, draw your willing swords.

The Chandos portrait of Shakespeare, of which a reproduction appears above, is now in the National Portrait Gallery. According to tradition, Richard Burbage was the artist; but it is impossible that the painter of the head in Dulwich Gallery should have produced a work so good in technique. Burbage is alleged to have given it to his fellow-actor, Joseph Taylor, who bequeathed it to Sir William D'Avenant, Shakespeare's godson. At the great Stowe sale of the effects of the Duke of Buckingham and Chandos, who had inherited it, the Earl of Ellesmere bought it and presented it to the nation. Many serious enquirers have refused to accept this romantic Italian looking head as the likeness of Shakespeare of the Midlands. The portrait was however, held in high esteem as far back as the end of the 17th century, not three-quarters of a century after Shakespeare's death. It is certainly admired to-day.

. . . . Every man shall eat in safety
Under his own vine what he plants; and sing
The merry songs of peace to all his neighbours:
God shall be truly known.

O England! Model to thy inward greatness,
Like little body with a mighty heart—
What might'st thou do, that honour would thee do,
Were all thy children kind and natural.

While that the armed hand doth fight abroad,
The advised head defends itself at home.

Every man will be thy friend
Whilst thou hast wherewith to spend;
But if store of crowns be scant,
No man will supply thy want . . .
He that is thy friend in deed,
He will help thee in thy need;
If thou sorrow, he will weep;
If thou wake, he cannot sleep;
Thus of every grief in heart
He with thee doth bear a part.
These are certain signs to know
Faithful friend from flattering foe.

fig.63 ***The Teacher's World: Shakespeare Day in the Schools***, 11 April 1917
Heinz Archive, National Portrait Gallery, London

portrayed with his family, master of this domain, by Johan Zoffany (1733–1810). He was also depicted by Thomas Gainsborough from *c.*1766 to 1769 in a pose that draws on Scheemakers's monument to Shakespeare in Westminster Abbey, beside a pediment bearing a Rysbrack bust of Shakespeare. This painting was destroyed in 1946. The theme was taken up by the popular press: the *London Magazine* of 1769, for example, placed a bare-headed Garrick in classical profile alongside a bust of Shakespeare projected from the Chandos portrait which is, of course, full face (fig.64). The great Stratford Jubilee, a gigantic festival conceived and organized by Garrick – the culmination of which was Garrick saluting Shakespeare in an ode on the occasion – took place in 1769. Those attending acquired Shakespeare favours[20] and those unable to attend could see Garrick's oration as engraved by J. Saunders after Van der Gucht in 1773,[21] or enjoy the sensational image of Garrick delivering his ode surrounded by Shakespearean characters by Caroline Watson after Robert Edge Pine.[22] For the late eighteenth century, therefore, Shakespeare was understood to have been preserved by Garrick, who thereby possessed a special claim to knowledge.

In the early years of the last century, another person of theatrical disposition laid claim to a personal link with Shakespeare, using the medium of portraiture to demonstrate that connection in his search for public recognition. Shakespeare Hirst (a name he gave himself), according to the *Yorkshire Weekly Post* of 1 March 1902, was a small-time antique dealer in Yorkshire who owned, and exhibited for a fee, paintings attributed to Raphael, Cimabue, Leonardo, Rubens and other acknowledged masters.[23] Chief among his exhibits was a supposed portrait of Shakespeare painted by Adam Elsheimer in Rome in 1608. On Shakespeare's birthday (supposedly St George's Day, 23 April) in 1906, Hirst addressed all fine art critics in support of his own portrait of Shakespeare. The Chandos portrait, Hirst claimed, was largely the work of Sir Joshua Reynolds and the Stratford effigy a 'scarecrow bust'.[24]

fig.64 **Garrick and Shakespeare**, 1769
J. Miller
Stipple engraving
122 × 195mm (4¾ × 7⅝in)
National Portrait Gallery, London
(NPG D20571)

Shakespeare portraits can never have had, either before or since, such an impassioned spokesman as Shakespeare Hirst, nor such a distinguished activist as David Garrick. Yet hundreds of individuals have invested in Shakespeare imagery emotively, if not also financially. The word 'souvenir' means 'memory' and reminders, or memories of Shakespeare have been a staple of the national economy and, particularly, of Stratford-upon-Avon and Westminster Abbey since the early eighteenth century. The Heinz Archive at the National Portrait Gallery, London, contains many files of letters from hopeful collectors around the world begging for authentication of images found, purchased and inherited. Few now possess libraries adorned with busts, as was customary in eighteenth-century England, but mantelpieces, pianos, bookshelves, desks and other domestic surfaces, as well as scrapbooks and photo albums, testify to the national significance of the Shakespeare image and to the possibilities for personal appropriation and customization.

For many years a quasi-scientific discourse of authenticity has centred on a death mask found in Darmstadt and associated with Shakespeare (fig.65).[25] Enquiries into the identity of the mask have been going on since the 1820s,[26] and techniques of superimposition have been around since the eighteenth century.[27] There is, moreover, an issue of national pride in debates over the death mask. Germany in the nineteenth century led the world in Shakespeare scholarship, something undoubtedly problematic for the English-speaking nations.[28] The cultural context for the early twentieth-century fascination with the idea of an authentic portrait of Shakespeare is embedded in the history of the Darmstadt death mask. It is perhaps most vividly exemplified by the impassioned endeavours of the American artist William Page, who had been commissioned in the 1870s to produce lifesize pictures of the head of Christ and the head of Shakespeare. Unable, for obvious reasons, to locate a satisfactorily authentic portrait of Christ, Page became obsessed by the idea of Shakespeare's death mask, went to Germany in search of it and subsequently published his account, an extraordinarily mystical and reverential piece.[29] The recent interest in the Darmstadt death mask is, therefore, less a new discovery than part of a longstanding preoccupation with authenticating one image by reference to another.

fig.65 **Darmstadt death mask**
Gypsum, 246 × 165mm (9⅝ × 6½in); depth at nose 105mm (4⅛in)
Universtäts- und Landesbibliothek Darmstadt

A death mask is not a portrait, nor is it in any sense 'true' to a living subject; it is a work of art, albeit a fairly literal one. All a death mask can show is the face after death; it is not a portrait, it is a representation of a face after the physiological changes associated with death have taken place. It is, moreover, extremely unlikely that anyone would have made a death mask of Shakespeare. Only royalty or nobility were accorded this honour at this period; the popularization of death masks of poets and artists is part of the romantic nineteenth-century interest in artistic physiognomy.

We will never know what Shakespeare looked like. What is important for us is to recognize the extent and diversity of reproductive portraiture of the Bard and to acknowledge what lies behind the continuing desire for the authentic image, the Shakespeare grail.[30] Whether in popular culture or at the level of high art, the Chandos portrait of Shakespeare has been, for over three centuries, a matrix that has generated a vast progeny so pervasive that the portrait of Shakespeare – even when reduced to a cipher – is instantly recognizable. As an emblem of national identity and cultural pride it is without rival.

Notes

This is a revised version of my essay published in *Shakespeare Jahrbuch*, vol.133, 1997, pp.29–53. Most of the material upon which this essay is based is to be found either in the Heinz Archive at the National Portrait Gallery, London, or in the Shakespeare Birthplace Trust, Stratford-upon-Avon. I am extremely grateful to the staff of both institutions for the courteous and constructive way in which they helped me in my research.

1 The National Westminster Bank used a holograph portrait of Shakespeare on its bank card from 1994.

2 J.A. Hammerton, 'A First Visit to Stratford-upon-Avon', *The Birmingham Weekly Post*, 16 April 1898.

3 W.E.K. Anderson (ed.), *The Journal of Sir Walter Scott* (Oxford University Press, Oxford, 1972), p.454.

4 *Punch*, 11 April 1896. For an illustration of this cartoon in the context of the foundation of the National Portrait Gallery, London, see Epilogue in Pointon 1993.

5 *Knight's Pictorial Shakespeare. New Edition, with Additional Illustrations* (Virtue & Co., London and New York, *c*.1838).

6 Shakespeare Birthplace Trust, Stratford-upon-Avon, P 26. IV. C and P 26. IV, e.

7 The drawing is in a private collection. National Portrait Gallery, London, negative 12040.

8 Undated engraving, signed I. Fougeron (an engraver active in London in the eighteenth century), Shakespeare Birthplace Trust, P.26 IV (b).

9 See Piper 1964, pp.16–17, for a discussion of these interpretations. For full details see F. O'Donoghue, FSA, *Catalogue of Engraved British Portraits* 4 (British Museum, London, 1914).

10 See photograph in Heinz Archive, National Portrait Gallery, London.

11 St Matthias, Poplar. See Piper 1964, p.34. G. Steeven's own collection of Shakespeare imagery can be found in his fully illustrated Shakespeare in the John Rylands Library, University of Manchester (18 volumes at 22347).

12 See, for example, Le Goux after S. Harding with a view of the Globe beneath (undated, *c*.1840) and an anonymous engraved bust in an oval surrounded by four portraits of nineteenth-century actors and actresses, the Stratford effigy and a view of Stratford (unsigned and undated), both Stratford Birthplace Trust.

13 First state, February 1723–4. See R. Paulson, *Hogarth*, vol.I: *The Modern Moral Subject 1697–1732* (Rutgers UP, New Brunswick, and London, 1991), pl.20.

14 See Ingrid Roscoe, 'The Monument to the Memory of Shakespeare', *Church Monuments* (Church Monument Society, England, 1994, IX) and M. Dobson, *The Making of a National Poet: Shakespeare, Adaptation and Authorship 1660–1769* (Blackwell Publishers, Oxford, 1992).

15 Walter Pape and Frederick Burwick (eds), *Boydell's Shakespeare Gallery* (Verlag Peter Pomp, Bottrop, 1996).

16 See Elinor S. Schaffer, p.76, in Walter Pape and Frederick Burwick, op. cit.

17 For a very interesting comparison of the tercentenary celebrations of 1916 in England and Germany see Balz Engler, 'Shakespeare in the Trenches', *Shakespeare Survey* (Cambridge University Press, Cambridge, 1991), vol.44.

18 *The Teacher's World* (Montagu House, Russell Square, London), 11 April 1917, copy in Heinz Archive, National Portrait Gallery, London.

19 A. St John Adcock, 'The Poetry of War', *The Reader* (London: n.p., October 1914), copy in the Heinz Archive, National Portrait Gallery, London.

20 For details of portraiture in this medium, see Ogden 1910.

21 Reproduced and discussed in Piper 1964, pp.30–1.

22 Dated 1784, used as a frontispiece in M. Dobson, op. cit., where it is wrongly attributed to Charles Watson. The painting by Pine, who died in 1788, is now lost. Nor is the date known. See W.L. Pressly, *A Catalogue of Paintings in the Folger Shakespeare Library* (Yale University Press, London and New Haven, 1993), no.120.

23 Keighley Snowden, 'A Despised Collector' (*Yorkshire Weekly Post*, Saturday, 1 March 1902), cutting, Heinz Archive, National Portrait Gallery, London.

24 Broadsheet 'Shakespeareana. Another Birthday Gift, April 23rd 1906', Heinz Archive, National Portrait Gallery, London.

25 Interest in this death mask, the origins of which are exhaustively discussed in Wislicenus 1913, and which was popularized in the magazine section of the *New York Sunday American* (27 February 1916), has recently been revived by the forensically related work of Prof. Dr Hildegard Hammerschmidt-Hummel. Her findings were reported widely in the English press – see, for example, the *Daily Mail* (19 October 1995) and *The Times* (24 April 1996) – and published in full as 'What did Shakespeare Look Like? Authentic Portraits and the Death Mask. Methods and Results of the Tests of Authenticity' in *Symbolism*, vol.1, 1999. I am grateful to Prof. Dr Hammerschmidt-Hummel for communicating with me personally. I regret that I remain as an historian unconvinced by her findings.

26 See Boaden 1824; Wivell 1827; Scharf 1864; Robinson 1887 and Wall 1890.

27 An attempt to superimpose the Chandos onto the Droeshout portrait was engraved by T. Trotter and published by W. Richardson, 1 November 1794. A specimen of this engraving is in the Heinz Archive, National Portrait Gallery, London, where a more recent unpublished thesis using similar techniques (L. Gurney, 'Droeshout's Dilemma and the Authenticity of the Grafton Portrait', ms, 1966) can also be found.

28 See B. Engler, op. cit.

29 William Page first published his account in *Scribner's Magazine*, May 1876; it was reprinted in Page 1876.

30 An example of the continuing interest is the article 'Is This the Real Shakespeare?' by Graham Dark ('New Discovery Shows Him as Young Man of Good Looks'), published in the *Daily Express* (4 June 1958); an example of the scepticism could be the cartoon in the arts section of the *Independent* (24 March 1994), in which a search for Shakespeare produces an alias for Cervantes and, ultimately for Elvis ('All shaked up!').

THE LOST YEARS 1585–92

William Shakespeare probably left Stratford-upon-Avon sometime after 1585. He is not mentioned again until 1592 when he appears to have settled in London. It is not clear where he may have been during the intervening years and there are many theories concerning his whereabouts. This was a turbulent period in British history: Mary, Queen of Scots (b.1542) was executed in 1587 and the following year saw the invasion by Spain and defeat of the Spanish Armada. Yet these troubles did not diminish the public appetite for entertainment. One strong possibility is that Shakespeare joined one of the many travelling theatre companies.

The main companies of players wore the livery of their powerful patrons and occasionally performed at court. The lists below provide details of the places visited by some of these companies during Shakespeare's 'lost years'.

NOTE

The following lists are not complete and rely upon published interpretations of provincial records. Unless a month is stated the order of visits to particular towns may not be chronological.

The Lord Admiral's (Howard's) Men (*c.*1576–1603)

The patronage of this company changed with the office of Lord Admiral. After 1594 the company become the chief rival of the Lord Chamberlain's Men, Shakespeare's own company. The Admiral's Men were the first to perform Marlowe's highly popular two-part play on the history of Tamburlaine (cat.23).

1585 June: Dover, Kent;
27 December: Greenwich, Kent
1586 5 January: Greenwich, Kent;
February and May: Ipswich, Suffolk;
July: Rye, Sussex
Also in 1585–6: Leicester; Coventry, Warwickshire; Folkestone, Kent
1587 May: Aldeburgh, Suffolk
Also in 1586–7: Norwich, Norfolk; Coventry, Warwickshire; Leicester; York; Southampton, Hampshire; Bath, Somerset; Exeter, Devon; Plymouth, Devon
1588 29 December: Richmond, Surrey
1589 11 February: Windsor, Surrey
1588–90 Cambridge
1590 3 March: Greenwich, Kent;
June: Rye, Sussex; New Romney, Kent;
September: Gloucester;
October: Faversham, Kent;
27 December: Richmond, Surrey
Also in 1587–90: Coventry, Warwickshire; Ipswich, Suffolk; Maidstone, Kent; Canterbury, Kent; Folkstone, Kent; Marlborough, Wiltshire; Winchester, Hampshire; Bristol; Oxford
1591 16 February: Greenwich, Kent;
October: Faversham, Kent
1590–1 Oxford; Southampton, Hampshire; Winchester, Hampshire; Gloucester
1592 August: Ipswich, Suffolk;
September: Rye, Sussex;
December: Leicester
Also in 1591–2: Aldeburgh, Suffolk; Folkestone, Kent; Oxford; Bath, Somerset

Leicester's Men (1559–88)

Robert Dudley, Earl of Leicester (1532–88) had a strong interest in the theatre and his players performed at court soon after Queen Elizabeth's accession. Under the probable stewardship of James Burbage (*c.*1531–97), father of Richard Burbage (cat.51), they toured the provinces and they were in Stratford-upon-Avon in 1586–7.

1585 summer: Norwich, Norfolk; Leicester; *June*: Sudbury, Ipswich, Suffolk; *July*: Kirtling, Cambridgeshire; *August*: Bath, Somerset;
December: The Hague, Low Countries
Also in 1584–5: Gloucester; Coventry, Warwickshire
1586 January: Low Countries; *March*: Exeter, Devon; *c.March*: Abingdon, Berkshire; *April*: Utrecht, Low Countries; *May–June*: Low Countries; *June–September*: Denmark;
27 December: Greenwich, Kent
Also in 1585–6: Abingdon, Berkshire
1587 January: Maidstone, Kent; *March*: Rye, Sussex; *March*: Dover, Kent; *March*: Southampton, Hampshire; *March–April*: New Romney, Kent; *c. March–April*: Marlborough, Wiltshire; *April*: Lyme Regis, Dorset; Bristol; *April–June*: Bath, Somerset; *c.April–June*: Exeter, Devon; Gloucester; *April–June*: Leicester; *June–July*: Nottingham; *July*: Lathom, Lancashire; *July–August*: Coventry, Warwickshire; *December*: Oxford
Also in 1586–7: Saxony; Norwich, Norfolk; Canterbury, Fordwich, Kent; Exeter, Devon; Gloucester; Stratford-upon-Avon, Warwickshire
1588 January–February: New Romney, Kent; *February*: Dover, Kent; *February*: Rye, Sussex; *April*: Reading, Berkshire; Lyme Regis, Dorset; *April–July*: Nottingham; *May*: Plymouth, Devon; *c.May*: Exeter, Devon; *May–June*: Bath, Somerset; *June*: Bristol; Gloucester; *July*: York; *September*: Norwich, Norfolk; Aldeburgh, Suffolk; Ipswich, Suffolk; Exeter, Devon [*Robert Dudley, Earl of Leicester died 4 September 1588*]

Lord Strange's Men (late 1580s–1594?)

Ferdinando Stanley, Lord Strange and later 5th Earl of Derby (cat.44) apparently maintained two troupes of players. Strange's Men performed at Court on several occasions and from the early 1590s they performed at the Rose Theatre in London. It is very probable that Shakespeare was one of Strange's Men although he may have left the company with Richard Burbage in about 1591. They were the first company to perform *Titus Andronicus*.

1584–5 Beverley, Yorkshire
1587–8 Coventry, Warwickshire
1589 November: Cross Keys, London
1590 27 December: Richmond, Surrey; Greenwich, Kent
Also in 1590–91: Theatre, London
1591 16 February: Greenwich, Kent;
27, 28 December: Whitehall, London
1592 6, 8 February: Whitehall, London;
February–June: Rye, Sussex; *July*: Canterbury, Kent; *August*: Bristol;
October: Oxford
Also in this year: Bristol; Bath, Somerset; Maidstone, Faversham, Folkestone, Kent; Cambridge; Gloucester; Coventry, Warwickshire
1592 27, 31 December: Hampton Court

The Queen's Men (1583–1603)

The Queen's Men was established as a new company in 1583 and had rights to play inside the city of London. It drew some of the most talented and successful actors from existing troupes. On occasion, the company would temporarily divide in order to tour the widest range of locations in a given year and thus the list provided here does not refer to a single company.

1584–5 January–February: Greenwich, Kent; *spring*: Cambridge; *May*: Greenwich, Kent; *Christmas*: Greenwich, Kent
Also in 1585–6: Norwich Cathedral, Norfolk; Exeter, Devon; Bristol; Coventry, Warwickshire; Lydd, Kent; Bridgwater, Somerset
1586 c.May–June: Norwich, Norfolk;

c.June–July: Bath, Somerset; *c.July*: Abingdon, Berkshire; Oxford; *August*: Nottingham; *c.August*: Leicester; Lynn, Norfolk; *September*: Lydd, Canterbury, Maidstone, Kent; Rye, Sussex; *September–October*: Dover, Kent; *October*: Ipswich, Suffolk; Kirtling, Cambridgeshire; *Christmas*: Greenwich, Kent
Also in 1586–7: Norwich Cathedral, Norfolk; Stratford-upon-Avon, Warwickshire; Worcester; Canterbury, Kent
1587 *June*: Thame, Oxford; Trinity College, Cambridgeshire; *c.June*: Abingdon, Berkshire; Saffron Walden, Essex; *July*: Ipswich, Suffolk; Gloucester; Bath, Somerset; Aldeburgh, Suffolk; Bristol; Southampton, Hampshire; *August*: Lynn, Norfolk; Rye, Sussex; New Romney, Kent; Nottingham; *c.August*: Dover, Kent: *August–September*: Leicester; Faversham, Kent; *September*: Beverley, Yorkshire; York; Coventry, Warwickshire; *October–December*: Maidstone, Kent; *c.November*: Saffron Walden, Essex; *December*: Aldeburgh, Suffolk; *Christmas*: Greenwich, Kent
Also in 1587–8: Coventry, Warwickshire
1588 *March* Canterbury, Kent; *March–April*: New Romney, Kent; Lydd, Kent; *April*: Dover, Kent; Rye, Sussex; *June*: Lyme Regis, Dorset; *c.June*: Exeter, Devon; *June*: Plymouth, Devon; *July*: Gloucester; Bath, Somerset; Bristol; *August*: Bath, Somerset; Bristol; *c.August*: Worcester; *October*: New Park, Lancashire; *October–November*: Nottingham; *November*: Leicester; *December*: Norwich, Norfolk; Ipswich, Suffolk; *c.December*: Oxford; Lynn, Norfolk; *Christmas*: Dover, Kent
Also in 1588–9: Hythe, Folkestone, Kent; Lyme Regis, Dorset; Coventry, Warwickshire
1589 *January*: Faversham, Kent; *February*: Canterbury, New Romney, Lydd, Kent; Rye, Sussex; *February–March*: Maidstone, Kent; *March*: Winchester, Hampshire; *spring*: Nottingham; *April*: Gloucester; *May*: Leicester; Ipswich, Aldeburgh, Suffolk; *June*: Norwich, Norfolk; *summer*: Canterbury, Kent; *July*: Lathom, Lancashire; *August*: Maidstone, Dover, Kent; Rye, Sussex; *c.August*: Folkestone, New Romney, Kent; *September*: Reading, Berkshire; Winchester, Hampshire; Knowsley, Lancashire; Carlisle, Cumberland; *c.September*: Dublin, Ireland; *October*: Bristol; Edinburgh, Scotland; *c.October*: Exeter, Devon; *November*: Bath, Somerset; Chester Cathedral, Cheshire; *Christmas*: Richmond, Surrey
Also in 1589–90: Folkestone, Lydd, Kent; Marlborough, Wiltshire; Coventry, Warwickshire
1590 *January*: Faversham, Kent; *March*: Greenwich, Kent; *April*: Norwich, Norfolk; *June*: Knowsley, Lancashire; *July*: Shrewsbury, Ludlow, Shropshire; *c.July*: Bridgnorth, Shropshire; Oxford; *August*: Canterbury, Kent; Bristol; New Romney, Kent; Rye, Sussex; *August–September*: Gloucester; Nottingham; *September–October*: Chester Cathedral, Cheshire; *October*: Leicester; *c.October*: Shrewsbury, Shropshire; Christmas: Richmond, Surrey
Also in 1590–91: Folkestone, Fordwich, Lydd, Kent; Oxford; Stratford-upon-Avon, Warwickshire
1591 *January*: Maidstone, Canterbury, Dover, Kent; *February*: Greenwich, Kent; Winchester, Hampshire; Southampton, Hampshire; *February–March*: Bristol; *c.March*: Gloucester; *March*: Coventry, Warwickshire; *May*: Ipswich, Suffolk; Maidstone, Kent; *c.May*: Canterbury, Kent; *June*: Faversham, New Romney Kent; Aldeburgh, Suffolk; Winchester, Hampshire; Lynn, Norwich, Norfolk; *c.June*: Cambridge; Saffron Walden, Essex; *June*: Southampton, Hampshire; *July*: Poole, Dorset; *c.July*: Weymouth, Dorset; *c.August*: Bath, Somerset; Bristol; Leicester; Newark, Nottinghamshire; *August*: Newcastle, Northumberland; Winkburn, Nottinghamshire; Coventry, Warwickshire; *September*: Aldeburgh, Suffolk; *c.October*: Chester Cathedral, Cheshire; Worcester; *October*: Coventry, Warwickshire
Also in 1591–2: Maidstone, Fordwich, Folkestone, Lydd, Kent; Bath, Somerset; Stratford-upon-Avon, Coventry, Warwickshire
1592 Rochester, Faversham, Kent; *March*: Canterbury, Kent; *May*: Ipswich, Suffolk; Norwich, Norfolk; *c.May*: Aldeburgh, Suffolk; Saffron Walden, Essex; *June*: Cambridge University; *c.June–July*: Gloucester; *July*: Bristol; York; *c.July*: Leicester; Nottingham; *August*: Bath, Somerset; Southampton, Hampshire; *c.August*: Winchester, Hampshire; *August–September*: Cambridge; *October*: Aldeburgh, Suffolk; *c.October*: Ipswich, Suffolk; *c.November*: Faversham, Kent; *November*: Canterbury, Kent
Also in 1592–3: New Romney, Maidstone, Fordwich, New Romney, Kent; Coventry, Stratford-upon-Avon, Warwickshire

Pembroke's Men (*c.*1592–93)

The playing company of Henry Herbert, 2nd Earl of Pembroke (born in or after 1538–1601), performed at court on several occasions. The company members probably included William Shakespeare and Richard Burbage and several others who joined the Lord Chamberlain's Men in 1594. The company performed several of Shakespeare's plays including *The Taming of the Shrew*, *Henry VI* (*Parts 2 and 3*) and *Richard III*.

1592 *October–December*: Leicester
1592–3 Ludlow, Shrewsbury, Shropshire; Coventry, Warwickshire; Bath, Somerset; Ipswich, Suffolk

Sussex's Men (1584–93/4)

Henry Radcliffe, 4th Earl of Sussex (1533–93) was one of the patrons of a group who enjoyed a high reputation in the provinces, mainly due to the fame of their comic actor Richard Tarlton (d.1588), who later defected to the Queen's Men. Some of the members of Pembroke's Men probably joined Sussex's Men for a short period in 1593–4.

1585 *May*: Dover, Kent; *July*: Bath, Somerset
Also in 1585–6: Coventry, Warwickshire
1586 *May*: Bath, Somerset
Also in 1586–7: Ipswich, Suffolk
1587 York; autumn: Leicester; *September*: Coventry, Warwickshire
Also in 1587–8: Coventry, Warwickshire; Bath, Somerset
1588 *April*: Ipswich, Suffolk
Also in 1588–9: Aldeburgh, Suffolk
1589 *February*: Leicester; *March*: Ipswich, Suffolk; *November*: Leicester
Also in this year: Faversham, Kent
1590 *February*: Ipswich, Suffolk
Also in 1590–91: Gloucester
1591 *February*: Southampton, Hampshire; *March*: Coventry, Warwickshire; *August*: Leicester
1592–3 Ipswich, Suffolk; Newcastle, Northumberland; York

For more information see:

Chambers 1930; Gurr 1996; Siobhan Keenan, *Travelling Players in Shakespeare's England* (Palgrave Macmillan, Basingstoke, 2002); Scott McMillin and Sally-Beth MacLean, *The Queen's Men and their Plays* (Cambridge University Press, 1998)

SELECT BIBLIOGRAPHY

ASTINGTON 1999
John Astington, *English Court Theatre 1558–1642* (Cambridge University Press, 1999)

BECKERMAN 1962
Bernard Beckerman, *Shakespeare at the Globe 1599–1609* (Macmillan, New York, 1962)

BEDNARZ 2001
James P. Bednarz, *Shakespeare & the Poets' War* (Columbia University Press, New York, 2001)

BENTLEY 1941–68
G.E. Bentley, *The Jacobean and Caroline Stage*, 7 vols (Clarendon Press, Oxford, 1941–68)

BERRY 1987
Herbert Berry, *Shakespeare's Playhouses* (AMS, New York, 1987)

BLUNT 1940
Anthony Blunt, *Artistic Theory in Italy 1450–1600* (Clarendon Press, Oxford, 1940)

BOADEN 1824
James Boaden, *An Inquiry into the … Portraits of Shakespeare* (printed for Robert Triphook, London, 1824)

BROOKS 2000
Douglas A. Brooks, *From Playhouse to Printing House: Drama and Authorship in Early Modern England* (Cambridge University Press, 2000)

BURNS 1990
Edward Burns, *Character: Acting and Being on the Pre-Modern Stage* (Macmillan, Basingstoke, 1990)

BUTLER 1984
Martin Butler, *Theatre and Crisis 1632–1642* (Cambridge University Press, 1984)

CHAMBERS 1923
E.K. Chambers, *The Elizabethan Stage*, 4 vols (Clarendon Press, Oxford, 1923)

CHAMBERS 1930
E.K. Chambers, *William Shakespeare: A Study of Facts and Problems*, 2 vols (Clarendon Press, Oxford, 1930)

CHAMBERS 1971
D. Chambers, '"A Speaking Picture": Some Ways of Proceeding in Literature and the Fine Arts in the late Sixteenth and Early Seventeenth Centuries', in Hunt 1971, pp.28–57

COBBE AND WELLS 2006
Alec Cobbe and Stanley Wells (eds), *Shakespeare's Lovely Boy: A Poet and his Patron* (The Cobbe Foundation in association with the Shakespeare Birthplace Trust, Stratford-upon-Avon, 2006)

COOK 1981
Ann Jennalie Cook, *The Privileged Playgoers of Shakespeare's London 1576–1642* (Princeton University Press, Princeton, 1981)

COOPER 1992
Pat Astley Cooper, 'The Portrait of William Brodrick', *The Wandsworth Historian, Journal of the Wandsworth Historical Society*, no.64, 1992, pp.5–7

COOPER 2002
Tarnya Cooper, *Memento Mori Portraiture: Painting, Protestant Culture and the Patronage of Middle Elites in England and Wales 1540–1630*, 2 vols, University of Sussex, 2002 (unpublished D.Phil thesis)

COX AND KASTAN 1997
John D. Cox and David Scott Kastan (eds), *A New History of Early English Drama* (Columbia University Press, New York, 1997)

DOBSON AND WELLS 2001
Michael Dobson and Stanley Wells (eds), *The Oxford Companion to Shakespeare* (Oxford University Press, Oxford, 2001)

DRIVER 1964
Olive Wagner Driver, *The Shakespearean Portraits and Other Addenda* (Metcalf printing and publishing, Northampton, Mass., 1964)

DRIVER 1966
O.W. Driver, *The Shakespearean Portraits and Other Addenda* (rev. ed., Metcalf Printing Co., Northampton, Mass., 1966)

ECCLES 1991–3
Mark Eccles, 'Elizabethan Actors', *Notes and Queries*, vol.236, 1991, pp.38–49, pp.454–461; vol.237, 1992, pp.293–303; vol.238, 1993, pp.165–176

EDMOND 1982
M. Edmond, 'The Chandos Portrait: A Suggested Painter', *Burlington Magazine*, vol. 124, March 1982, pp.146–9

EDMOND 1991
M. Edmond, 'It was for Gentle Shakespeare Cut', *Shakespeare Quarterly*, vol. 43, no.3, autumn 1991, pp.339–44

EDMONDSON AND WELLS 2004
Paul Edmondson and Stanley Wells, *Shakespeare's Sonnets* (Oxford University Press, Oxford, 2004)

ENSING 1991
Rita J. Ensing, 'William Brodrick, the King's Embroiderer', *The Wandsworth Historian, Journal of the Wandsworth Historical Society*, no.63, 1991, pp.1–5

ERNE 2003
Lukas Erne, *Shakespeare as Literary Dramatist* (Cambridge University Press, 2003)

FAIRCHILD 1937
Arthur H.R. Fairchild, 'Shakespeare and the Arts of Design', *The University of Missouri Studies*, vol. 7, January 1937, pp.1–198

FOAKES 1985
R.A. Foakes, *Illustrations of the English Stage, 1580–1642* (Scolar Press, London, 1985)

FOAKES 2002
R.A. Foakes, *Henslowe's Diary* (Cambridge University Press, 2002)

FOAKES AND RICKERT 1961
R.A. Foakes and R.T. Rickert (eds), *Henslowe's Diary* (Cambridge University Press, 1961)

FOISTER 1981
Susan Foister, 'Paintings and other Works of Art in Sixteenth-century English Inventories', *Burlington Magazine*, vol. 123, May 1981, pp.273–282

FOISTER 1995
Susan Foister, 'Sixteenth-century English Portraiture and the Idea of the Classical', *Albion's Classicism: The Visual Arts in Britain, 1550–1660*, ed. Lucy Gent (Yale University Press, London, and New Haven, 1995), pp.163–180

FORSTER 1849
H.R. Forster, *A Few Remarks on the Chandos Portrait of Shakespeare Recently Purchased at Stowe* (fifty copies for private distribution, London, 1849)

FRISWELL 1864
J.H. Friswell, *Life Portraits of William Shakespeare* (Sampson Low, Son & Marston, London, 1864)

GAIR 1982
Reavley Gair, *The Children of Paul's: The Story of a Theatre Company, 1553–1608* (Cambridge University Press, 1982)

GREENBLATT 2004
Stephen Greenblatt, *Will in the World: How Shakespeare Became Shakespeare* (Jonathan Cape, London, 2004)

GREENWOOD 1925
Sir Granville George Greenwood, *The Stratford Bust and the Droeshout Engraving* (Cecil Palmer, London, 1925)

GURNEY 1966?
Lawrence Gurney, *Droeshout's Dilemma and the authenticity of the Grafton Portrait* (privately printed, n.d., 1966?)

GURR 1970
Andrew Gurr, *The Shakespearean Stage 1574–1642* (1st ed., Cambridge University Press, 1970)

GURR 1987A
Andrew Gurr, *Playgoing in Shakespeare's London* (Cambridge University Press, 1987; 2nd ed., 1996)

GURR 1987B
Andrew Gurr, *The Shakespearean Stage 1574–1642* (2nd ed., Cambridge University Press, 1987)

GURR 1992
Andrew Gurr, *The Shakespearean Stage 1574–1642* (3rd ed., Cambridge University Press, 1992)

GURR 1996
Andrew Gurr, *The Shakespearian Playing Companies* (Clarendon Press, Oxford, 1996)

GURR 2001
Andrew Gurr, *The Culture of Playgoing in Shakespeare's England: A Collaborative Debate* (Cambridge University Press, Cambridge and New York, 2001)

GURR 2004
Andrew Gurr, *The Shakespeare Company, 1594–1642* (Cambridge University Press, 2004)

HARBAGE, SCHOENBAUM AND WAGONHEIM 1989
Alfred Harbage, Samuel Schoenbaum and Sylvia Stoler Wagonheim (eds), *Annals of English Drama, 975–1700* (3rd ed., Routledge, New York, 1989)

HARRISON 1966
G.B. Harrison (ed.), *Henrie Chettle, Kind-Heartes Dreame (1592) and William Kemp, Nine Daies Wonder (1600)* (rpt, Barnes and Noble, New York, 1966)

HEARN 1995
Karen Hearn (ed.), *Dynasties: Painting in Tudor and Jacobean England 1530–1630* (Tate Publishing, London, 1995)

HODGES, SCHOENBAUM AND LEONE 1981
C. Walter Hodges, Samuel Schoenbaum and Leonard Leone, *The Third Globe: Symposium for the Reconstruction of the Globe Playhouse, Wayne State University, 1979* (Wayne State University Press, Detroit, 1981)

HONAN 1998
Park Honan, *Shakespeare: A Life* (Oxford University Press, Oxford, 1998)

HOTSON 1931
Leslie Hotson, 'The Adventure of the Single Rapier', *Atlantic Monthly*, vol. 148, July–December 1931, pp.26–31

HOTSON 1977
Leslie Hotson, *Shakespeare by Hilliard* (Chatto & Windus, London, 1977)

HUNT 1971
John Dixon Hunt (ed.), *Encounters: Essays on Literature and the Visual Arts* (Studio Vista, London, 1971)

HUNT 1985
John Dixon Hunt, 'The Visual Arts in Shakespeare's Work' in *Shakespeare in Context*, 1985, pp.425–31

JOURNAL OF THE RUTGERS UNIVERSITY LIBRARIES 1979
Author, 'What Shakespeare looked like . . .', *The Journal of the Rutgers University Libraries*, vol. 61, no.1, June 1979, pp.1–19

KASTAN 1999
David Scott Kastan (ed.), *A Companion to Shakespeare* (Blackwell, Oxford, 1999)

KASTAN 2001
David Scott Kastan, *Shakespeare and the Book* (Cambridge University Press, 2001)

KING 1992
T.J. King, *Casting Shakespeare's Plays: London Actors and Their Roles, 1590–1642* (Cambridge University Press, 1992)

KNUTSON 1991
Roslyn Lander Knutson, *The Repertory of Shakespeare's Company, 1594–1613* (University of Arkansas Press, Fayuetteville, 1991)

KNUTSON 2001
Roslyn Lander Knutson, *Playing Companies and Commerce in Shakespeare's Time* (Cambridge University Press, Cambridge and New York, 2001)

LOWENTHAL 1985
D. Lowenthal, *The Past is a Foreign Country* (Cambridge University Press, 1985)

MERES 1598
Francis Meres, *Palladis Tamia, Wits Treasury, being the second part of the Wits Common wealth* (P. Short for Cuthbert Burbie, London, 1598)

MURPHY 2003
Andrew Murphy, *Shakespeare in Print: A History and Chronology of Shakespeare Publishing* (Cambridge University Press, 2003)

NUNGEZER 1929
Edwin Nungezer, *A Dictionary of Actors* (Yale University Press, New Haven, 1929)

OGDEN 1910; 1912
W.S. Ogden, 'Shakespeare's Portraiture: Painted, Graven and Medallic', *The British Numismatic Journal*, vol. 7, 1910, pp.143–198 (reprinted; Bernard Quaritch, London, 1912)

ORLIN 2000
Lena Cowen Orlin, *Material London, ca. 1600* (University of Pennsylvania Press, Philadelphia, 2000)

ODNB 2004
Brian Harrison (ed.), *Oxford Dictionary of National Biography*, 60 vols (Oxford University Press, Oxford, 2004)

PAGE 1876
William Page, 'A Study of Shakespeare's Portraits', *Scribner's Magazine*, May 1876 (published as a book, Chiswick Press, London, 1876)

PIPER 1964
David Piper, *O Sweet Mr Shakespeare I'll have his Picture* (National Portrait Gallery, London, 1964)

POINTON 1993
Marcia Pointon, *Hanging the Head: Portraiture and Social Formation in Eighteenth-century England* (Yale University Press, London, and New Haven, 1993)

ROBINSON 1887
Stanley Robinson, *The Portraits and Likenesses of Shakespeare. An Authentic Account* (n.p., London, 1887)

RUTTER 1984
Carol Chillington Rutter (ed.), *Documents of the Rose Playhouse* (Manchester University Press, Manchester, 1984)

SANFORD 2002
Rhonda Lemke Sanford, *Maps and Memory in Early Modern England* (Palgrave, New York and Basingstoke, 2002)

SCHARF 1864
George Scharf, 'On the Principal Portraits of Shakespeare', *Notes and Queries* (Oxford University Press, Oxford, 23 April 1864; reprinted as a book, Spottiswoode & Co., London, 1864)

SCHOENBAUM 1975
Samuel Schoenbaum, *William Shakespeare: A Documentary Life* (Clarendon Press in association with The Scholar Press, Oxford, 1975)

SCHOENBAUM 1981
Samuel Schoenbaum, *William Shakespeare: Records and Images* (rev. ed., The Scholar Press, Oxford, 1981)

SCHOENBAUM 1987
Samuel Schoenbaum, *Shakespeare: A Compact Documentary Life* (rev. ed., Oxford University Press, Oxford, 1987)

SCHOENBAUM 1991
Samuel Schoenbaum, *Shakespeare's Lives,* (Clarendon Press, Oxford, 1991)

SHAPIRO 2005
James Shapiro, *1599: A Year in the Life of William Shakespeare* (Faber and Faber, London, 2005)

SHAPIRO 1977
Michael Shapiro, *Children of the Revels: The Boys' Companies of Shakespeare's Time and Their Plays* (Columbia University Press, New York, 1977)

SPIELMANN 1907
M.H. Spielmann, 'The Portraits of Shakespeare', *The Works of William Shakespeare*, vol. 10, A.H. Bullen (The Shakespeare Head Press, Stratford-upon-Avon, 1907; 25 copies printed for separate circulation; National Portrait Gallery copy presented to Lionel Cust by the author)

SPIELMANN 1924
M.H. Spielmann, *The Title Page of the First Folio of Shakespeare's Plays, A comparative study of the Stratford Monument* (Humphrey Milford, Oxford University Press, Oxford, 1924)

STRONG 1969
Roy Strong, *National Portrait Gallery Tudor and Jacobean Portraits* (HMSO, London, 1969)

TIPPING 1925
Avray Tipping, 'Peper Harow', *Country Life*, vol. 26, December 1925

TITTLER 2004
Robert Tittler, 'Portraiture, Politics and Society', *A Companion to Tudor Britain* (Blackwell, Oxford, 2004)

VICKERS 2002
Brian Vickers, *Shakespeare, Co-author: A Historical Study of Five Collaborative Plays* (Oxford University Press, Oxford, 2002)

VINCENT 2003
Susan Vincent, *Dressing the Elite: Clothes in Early Modern England* (Berg, Oxford, 2003)

WAGONHEIM 1989
Sylvia Stoler Wagonheim, *Annals of English Drama 975–1700* (Routledge, London, 1989)

WALL 1890
A.H. Wall, *Shakespeare's Face. A Monologue* (Herald Printing Office, 1890)

WELLS 2002
Stanley Wells, *Shakespeare: For All Time* (Macmillan, London, 2002)

WELLS AND TAYLOR 2005
Stanley Wells and Gary Taylor (eds), *The Oxford Shakespeare – The Complete Works* (Oxford University Press, Oxford, 2005)

WHITHORNE 1962
Thomas Whithorne, *The Autobiography of Thomas Whythorne*, ed. James M. Osborn (Clarendon Press, Oxford, 1962)

WICKHAM, BERRY AND INGRAM 2000
Glynne Wickham, Herbert Berry and William Ingram (eds), *English Professional Theatre, 1530–1660* (Cambridge University Press, 2000)

WILES 1987
David Wiles, *Shakespeare's Clown: Actor and Text in the Elizabethan Playhouse* (Cambridge University Press, 1987)

WISLICENUS 1913
P. Wislicenus, *Nachweise zu Shakespeare's Totenmaske: Die Echtheit der Maske* (Eugen Diedrichs Verlag, Jenna; H. Hohman, Darmstadt, 1913; the National Portrait Gallery copy contains MS letters from the author)

WIVELL 1827
A. Wivell, *An Inquiry into … the Shakespeare Portraits* (published by the author, London, 1827)

WOOD 2003
Michael Wood, *In Search of Shakespeare* (BBC Worldwide, London, 2003)

WOODALL 1997
Joanna Woodall, *Portraiture: Facing the Subject (Critical Introductions to Art)* (Manchester University Press, Manchester, 1997)

YOUNG 1987
Alan Young, *Tudor and Jacobean Tournaments* (George Philip & Son, London, 1987)

WEBSITES

http://absoluteshakespeare.com
www.folger.edu/ (Folger Shakespeare Library, Washington, DC)
www.rsc.org.uk (Royal Shakespeare Company)
www.shakespeare.com
www.shakespeare-online.com
www.shakespeare.org.uk (Shakespeare Birthplace Trust)
www.shakespeares-globe.org (Shakespeare's Globe Theatre)
www.stratford-upon-avon.co.uk

INDEX

INDEX

ACKNOWLEDGEMENTS

The idea of staging an exhibition on Shakespeare and the Chandos portrait for our anniversary year in 2006 was first raised by Sandy Nairne, soon after his arrival as Director of the Gallery in 2002. I am particularly grateful to him for his enthusiastic support throughout the course of this project.

As with any project of this scale there are many people who have helped to bring both the exhibition and the book to fruition. First and foremost I am delighted to be able to thank the many lenders who have generously agreed to part with object of huge cultural importance for this exhibition. Without their generosity and willingness to discuss the possibility of lending years in advance, the exhibition would simply not have been staged. I would like to thank the following at various institutions for their patient advice regarding loans and their help at the initial stages of research: Bruce Barker Benfield, Robert Bearman, Jamie Beveridge, Erin Blake, Stella Butler, Grey Colley, Barrie Cook, Barbara O'Connor, Ian Dejardin, Ann Donnelly, Richard Edgcumbe, Edwina Ehrman, Hazel Forsyth, Moira Goff, Stella Halkyard, Kate Harris, Hugo Hocknell, K. Van der Hoek, David Howells, Nicola Kalinsky, Arthur Macgregor, Giles Mandelbrote, Susan North, Gail Kern Paster, Jan Piggott, Robin Whittaker and Robert Yorke.

Numerous people have helped with the research for this exhibition. As an art historian, rather than a literary scholar I knew from the outset that the success of this project would depend upon bringing together a group of advisers and literary specialists. In this respect I am particularly indebted to Professor Stanley Wells from the Shakespeare Birthplace Trust. His immense knowledge and meticulous approach over the course of this project has helped to make this a greater book. All the exhibition associates listed on p.8 have also given guidance and provide support for the project in many different ways. I am particularly grateful to Sally-Beth MacLean who provided advice on touring theatre companies and to Mark Rylance for his advice, enthusiasm and thoughtful approach to this subject. Jennifer Tiramani was kind enough to spend several hours talking with me about costume of this period, and the sample material on p.50 has been made by Jordan Colls, Christine Prentis, Karl Robinson and Jenny Tiramani. My thanks to Nick de Somogyi for providing help at various stages of this project, including researching the information on travelling theatre companies on pp.226–7 as well as supplying the transcript on p.113. I would also like to thank Jane Cunningham and the staff of the Witt Library at the Courtauld Institute.

I also owe a debt of gratitude to my colleague at the National Portrait Gallery Catharine MacLeod, Seventeenth Century Curator, who kindly read my text in draft form. Her support and advice and insight into the period has greatly enriched this project. I am also indebted to Ruth Kenny, Jane Eade and Rab MacGibbon, and Robin Francis and the staff in the Heinz Archive at the National Portrait Gallery, who have helped with the research process in many different ways. In addition, I have been aided by a succession of talented and highly dedicated voluntary curatorial interns: Megan Fontenella, Hannah Lake, Renee Callaghan and Sarah Lindsey, without whose help I would not have found the time to research or write this book. In addition Rene Weis, Andrew Gurr, Robert Tittler and Paul Dove have also provided guidance in the research process. Of course, I am also very grateful to all my fellow authors, particularly Stanley Wells, James Shapiro and Marcia Pointon whose contributions have helped to provide a rich and diverse context for the material evidence presented in this book.

A critical part of this exhibition involved undertaking technical analysis on several portraits in this exhibition. I am grateful to Libby Sheldon, Ian Tyers, Kate Stoner and Clare Richardson who helped to compile a vital body of technical data to allow us to reinterpret some of these images. I am also very grateful to Sophie Plender for her help and advice in mapping the condition and material history of the Chandos portrait, to Andie Gall for her painstaking conservation work on several of the portraits in this exhibition and also to Helen White and Richard Hallas.

The elegant design of the exhibition was produced by Charles Marsden Smedley with both enthusiasm and attention to detail and the catalogue has been similarly designed by the indefatigable Philip Lewis. The energy and enthusiasm of Amy Meyers and Elisabeth Fairman at the Yale Center for British Art resulted in the decision that the exhibition should tour to Yale and I am grateful to them for their collaboration and support. The conference that accompanies the exhibition has been generously supported by the Paul Mellon Centre for British Art. It has been organized with the help of Lena Orlin, from the University of Maryland and with support from staff at Kings College, London.

Finally, I have been ably supported by an exceptional team of dedicated staff at the National Portrait Gallery, whose enthusiasm for the project has been invaluable. Two key people have worked tirelessly to bring the exhibition and catalogue to a successful conclusion: the exhibitions manager Claire Evertitt co-ordinated the exhibition loans, design and installation of the exhibition with dedication and admirable efficiency, and Caroline Brooke Johnson co-ordinated the production of this book with great skill and energy. Thanks also to Ruth Müller-Wirth, the production manager, for her exacting standards. Many others have helped in different ways, both Kathleen Soriano and Jacob Simon have provided consistent support throughout the course of this project. In addition, Rosie Wilson compiled the many images used for this book, David Saywell produced innovative IT programmes, and David McNeff and Tim Moreton have helped to co-ordinate works from our own collections. Joanna Banham, Stephen Allen and their team worked to develop an inspiring and informative programme of educational events. Penny Dearsley has helped with administration, and Pim Baxter, Neil Evans, Hazel Sutherland, John Haywood, Jonathan Rowbotham and Naomi Conway have organised press, marketing, publicity and fundraising.

Tarnya Cooper

SIXTEENTH CENTURY CURATOR, NATIONAL PORTRAIT GALLERY

PICTURE CREDITS

The Ashmolean Museum, Oxford: fig.9, cat.43; The Bank of England: fig.62; The Most Hon. Marquess of Bath, Longleat House, Warminster, Wiltshire: cat.60; James Marshall and Marie-Louise Osborn Collection, Beinecke Rare Book and Manuscript Library, Yale University fig.15; Berkeley Will Trust: cat.45; © The Bodleian Library, University of Oxford: fig.6, cats 15, 16, 23, 48, 61, 75, 117; By permission of the British Library, London: figs 17, 20, 21, cats 1, 24–6, 34, 49, 50, 59, 62–6, 99–116; © The Trustees of the British Museum cats 73, 78; Universitäts- und Landesbibliothek, Darmstadt fig.65; The Duke of Buccleuch & Queensbury, KT: cat.47; The Chancellor, Masters and Scholars of The University of Cambridge: cat.71; Cambridge University Press: fig.60; © All rights reserved. Canadian Conservation Institute. Reproduced with the permission of the Minister, Public Works and Government Services, 2005: cat.5; Private collection: cat.84; The College of Arms, London: cat.54a, b; The Master and Fellows of Corpus Christi College, Cambridge: cat.22; Photograph: Photographic Survey, The Courtauld Institute of Art, London: figs 12, 33; The Governors of Dulwich College, London/Photo: John Hammond: fig.7, cats 19, 28, 30, 35, 53; By permission of the Trustees of Dulwich Picture Gallery, London: figs 8, 24, 53, 54, cats 51, 52; © Fitzwilliam Museum, University of Cambridge: cat.46; By permission of the Folger Shakespeare Library, Washington, DC: figs 10, 23, 42; cats 6, 55, 87; © This item is reproduced by permission of The Huntington Library, San Marino, Califonia: fig.2; © Museum of London: fig.4, cats 13, 14, 18, 29, 33, 36, 42, 94, 95; Executors of the late Lord Lothian: cat.80; Merchant Taylors' Company: cat.97; The National Archives, UK: cats 12, 70, 72, 74, 79, 92a, b, c; National Portrait Gallery, London: figs 11, 16, 18, 19, 25, 27, 29–32, 40, 41, 56, 61, 63, 64, cats 2, 3, 67–9, 76, 77, 81–3, 86, 89–91; © Norwich Castle Museum and Art Gallery: cat.31; Reproduced by kind permission of the Worshipful Company of Painter-Stainers', London: fig.28; © By permission of the Earl of Pembroke and the Trustees of the Wilton House Trust, Wiltshire: fig.60; Royal Albert Memorial Museum and Art Gallery, Exeter: fig.13; © Royal Shakespeare Company, Stratford-upon-Avon: figs 43, 44, 47, 48, cat.8; Reproduced by courtesy of the Director and the University Librarian, The John Rylands University Library, The University of Manchester: figs 35–40, cat.4; © Shakespeare Birthplace Trust, Stratford-upon-Avon: figs 1, 3, 5, cats 7, 9–11, 56–9; Trustees of Olive Countess Fitzwilliam's Chattels Settlement by permission of Lady Juliet Tadgell: fig.34; Libby Sheldon, University College, London: figs 26, 45, 46; UCL Art Collections, University College, London: cat.20; University Library, Utrecht: cat.27; V&A Images/Victoria and Albert Museum: cats 32, 37–41, 93, 96, 98; Wandsworth Museum, London: fig.14; Diocesan Archives (Worcestershire Record Office): cat.17; Yale Center for British Art, Paul Mellon Collection: cat.21

The following objects will not be exhibited at the Yale Center of British Art, New Haven:

Cats 1, 15, 16, 22–5, 34, 37, 39, 40, 47–50, 52, 57, 59, 60–6, 73, 75, 80, 97, 99–117. At the time of going to press, it was not confirmed whether the following objects would be exhibited: cats 10, 11, 17, 45, 56, 58, 82.